KEEP YOUR HANDS OFF EIZOUKEN!

02

STORY AND ART BY

大童澄瞳
SUMITO OOWARA

CONTENTS

KEEP YOUR HANDS OFF EIZOUKEN! VOL. 2
TRANSLATED BY KUMAR SIVASUBRAMANIAN
SPECIAL THANKS FOR TRANSLATION ASSISTANCE: CHITOKU TESHIMA
LETTERING AND RETOUCH BY SUSIE LEE AND STUDIO CUTIE
EDITED BY CARL GUSTAV HORN

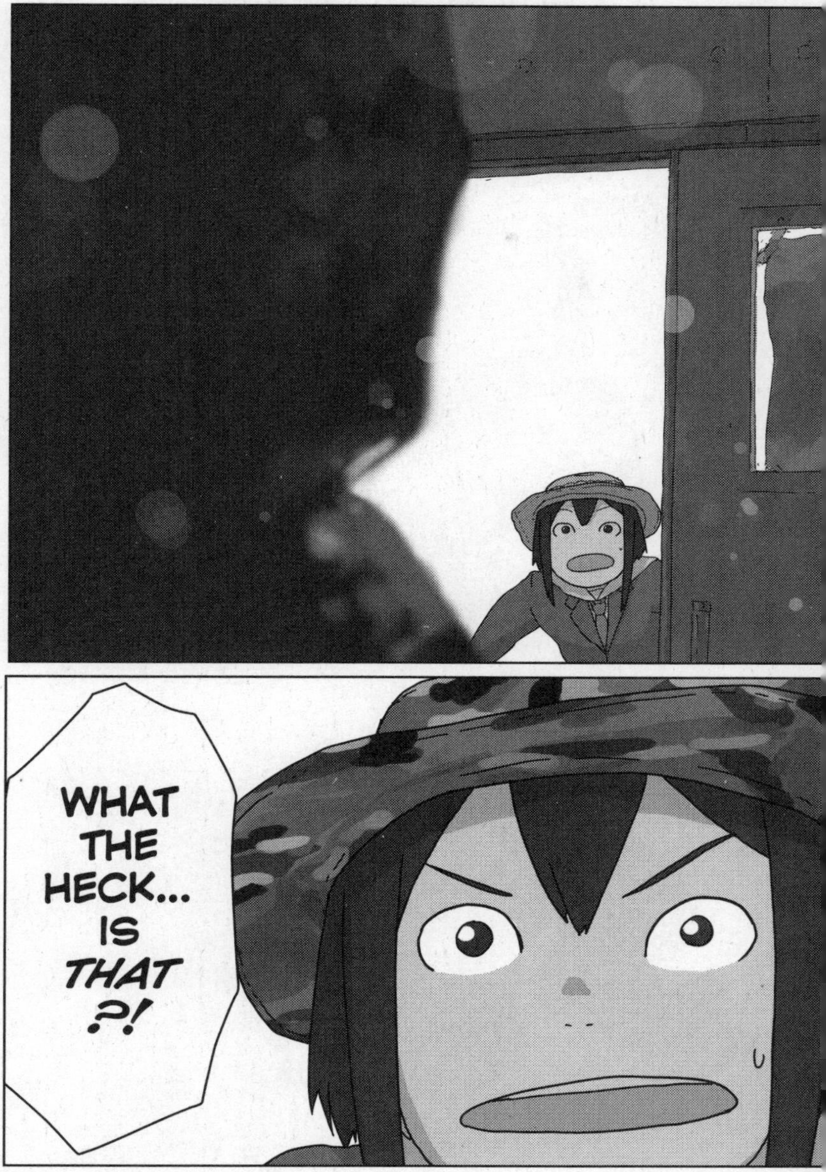
WHAT THE HECK... IS *THAT* ?!

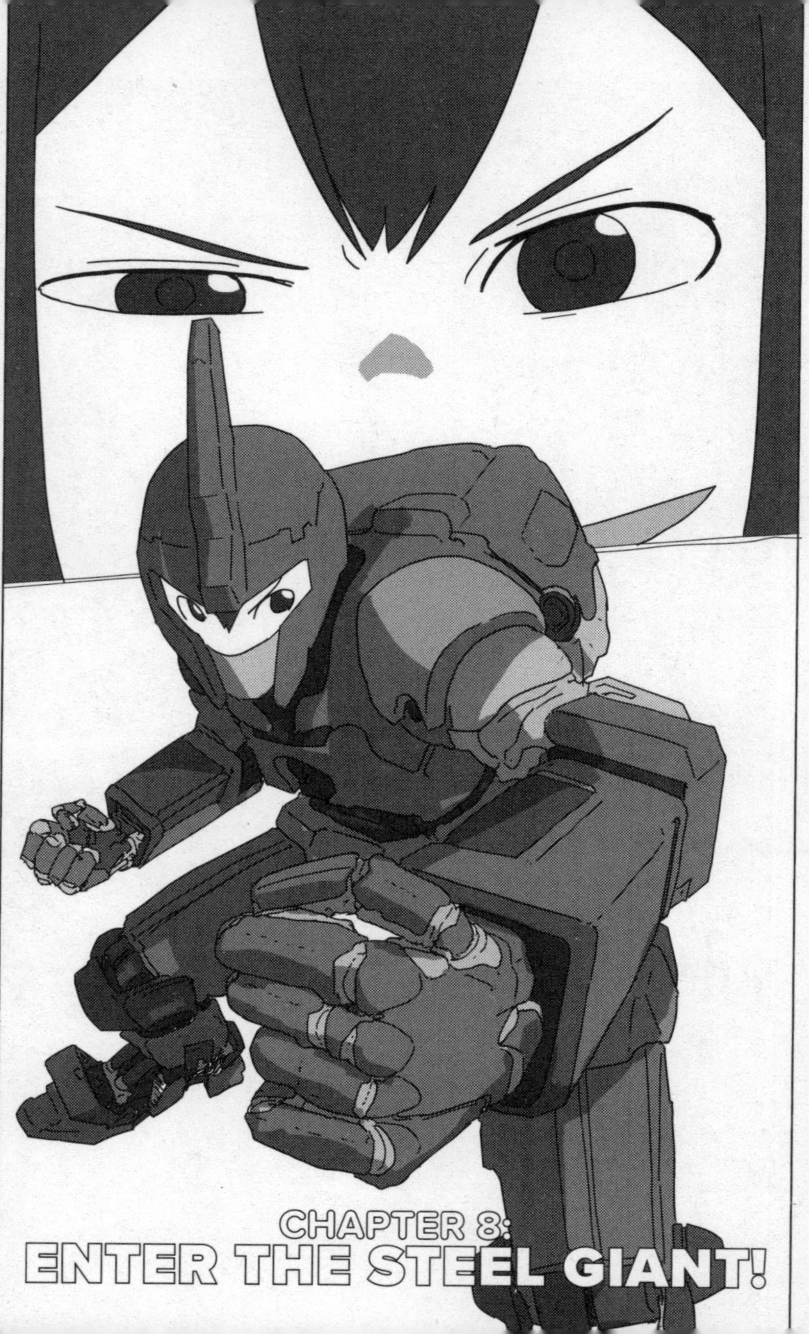

CHAPTER 8: ENTER THE STEEL GIANT!

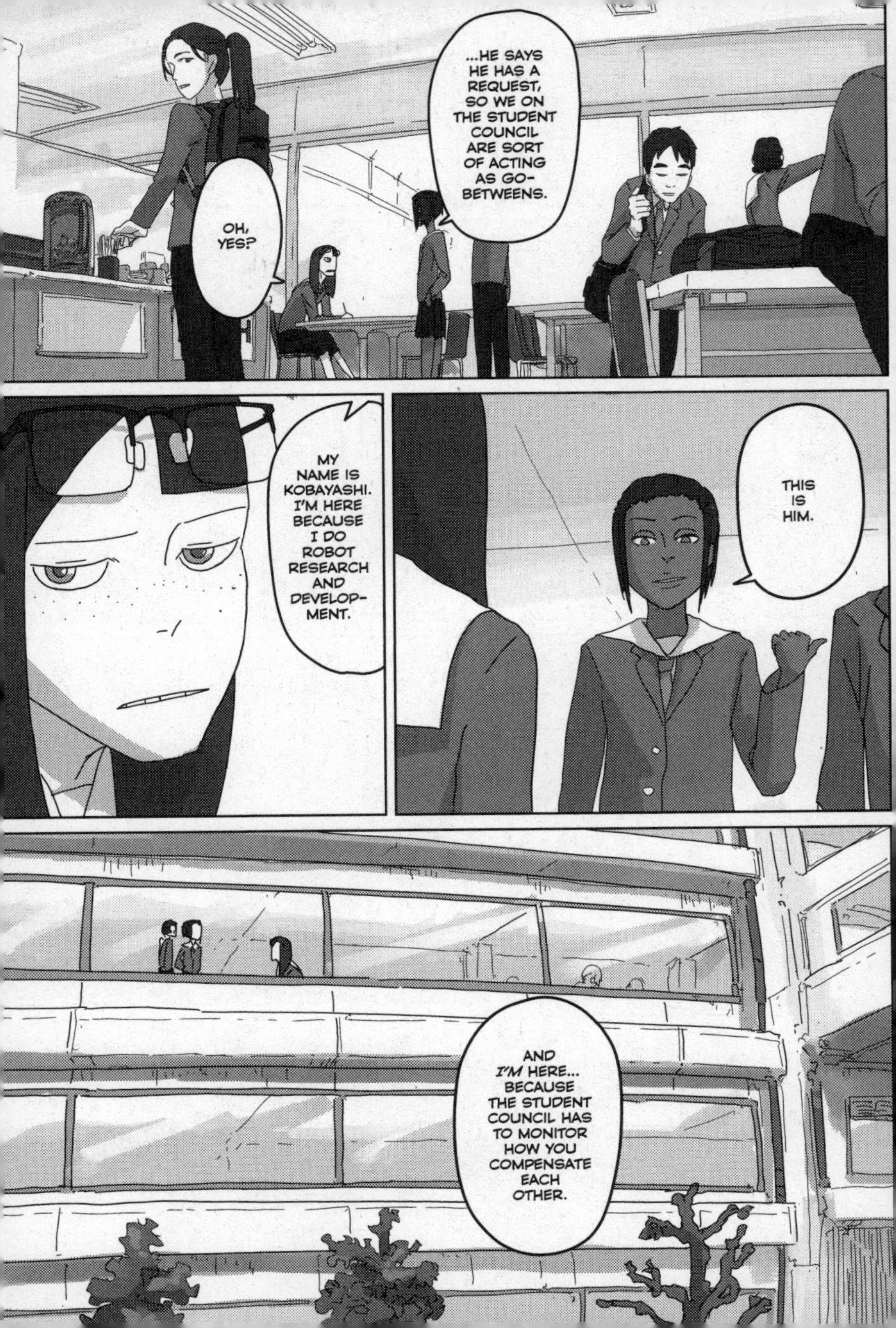
...HE SAYS HE HAS A REQUEST, SO WE ON THE STUDENT COUNCIL ARE SORT OF ACTING AS GO-BETWEENS.
OH, YES?
THIS IS HIM.
MY NAME IS KOBAYASHI. I'M HERE BECAUSE I DO ROBOT RESEARCH AND DEVELOPMENT.
AND *I'M* HERE... BECAUSE THE STUDENT COUNCIL HAS TO MONITOR HOW YOU COMPENSATE EACH OTHER.

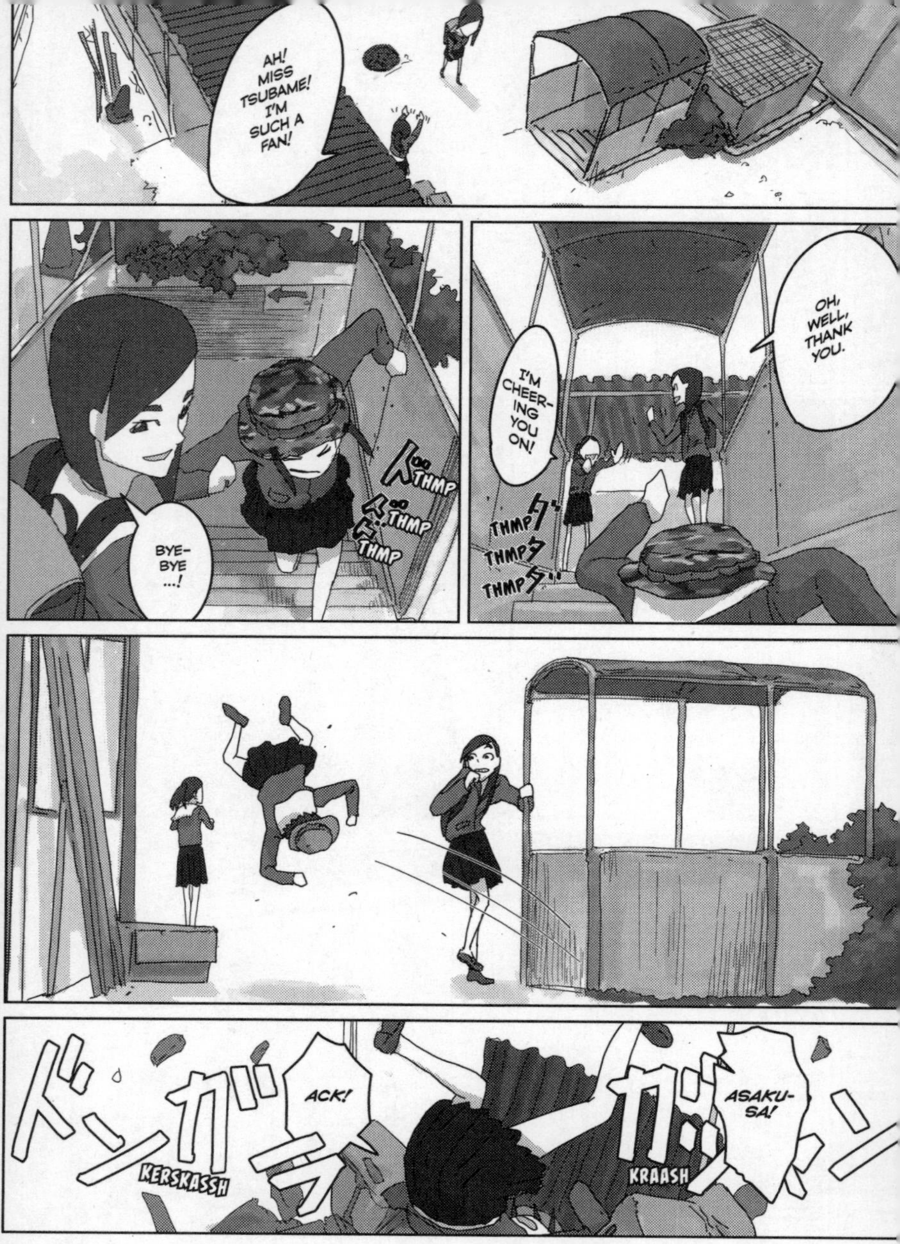
AH! MISS TSUBAME! I'M SUCH A FAN!
OH, WELL, THANK YOU.
I'M CHEER-ING YOU ON!
THMP
THMP
THMP
THMP
THMP
THMP
BYE-BYE ...!
ASAKUSA!
KRAASH
ACK!
KERSKASSH

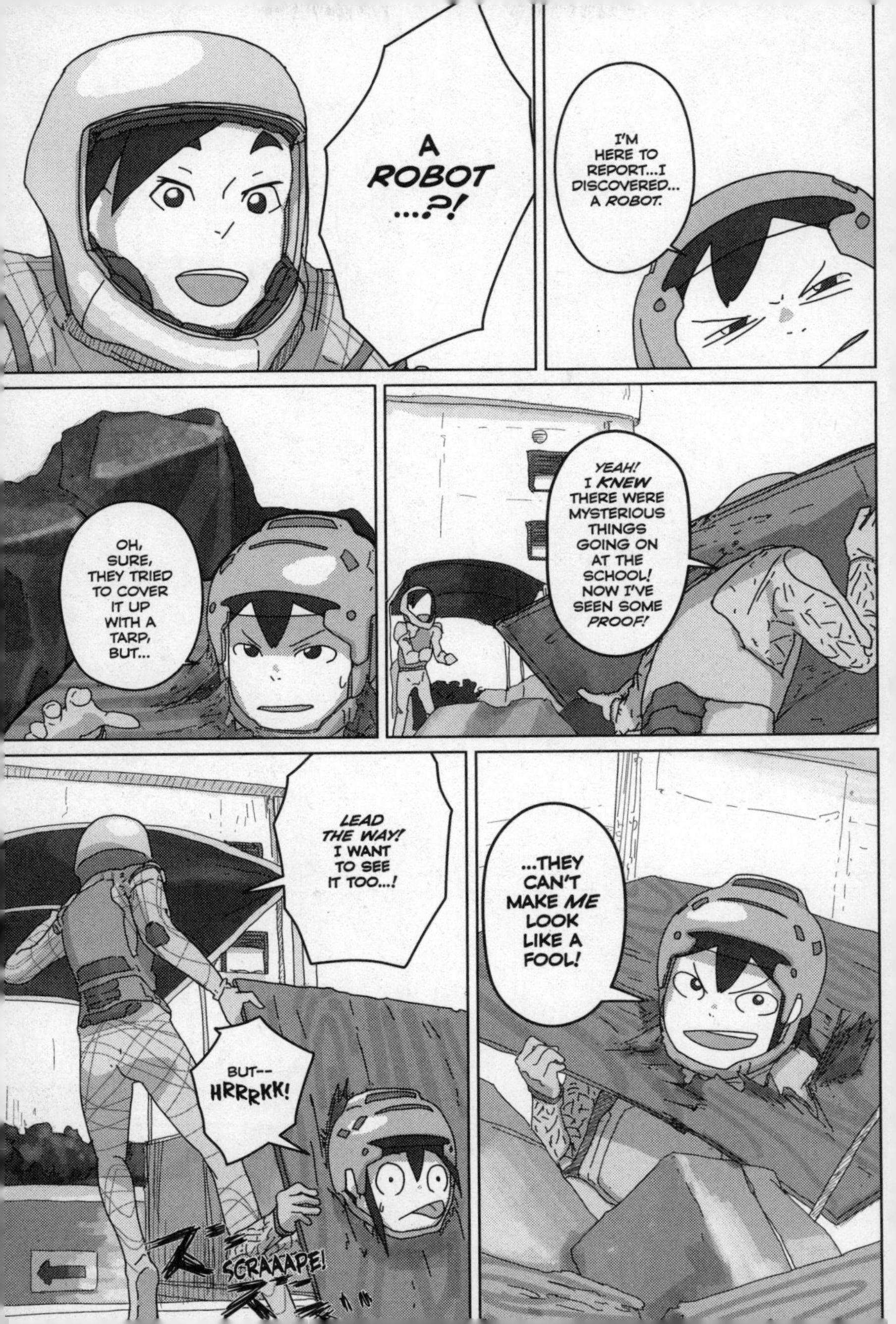
I'M HERE TO REPORT...I DISCOVERED... A ROBOT.
A ROBOT ...?!
YEAH! I KNEW THERE WERE MYSTERIOUS THINGS GOING ON AT THE SCHOOL! NOW I'VE SEEN SOME PROOF!
OH, SURE, THEY TRIED TO COVER IT UP WITH A TARP, BUT...
...THEY CAN'T MAKE ME LOOK LIKE A FOOL!
LEAD THE WAY! I WANT TO SEE IT TOO...!
BUT-- HRRRKK!
SCRAAAPE!

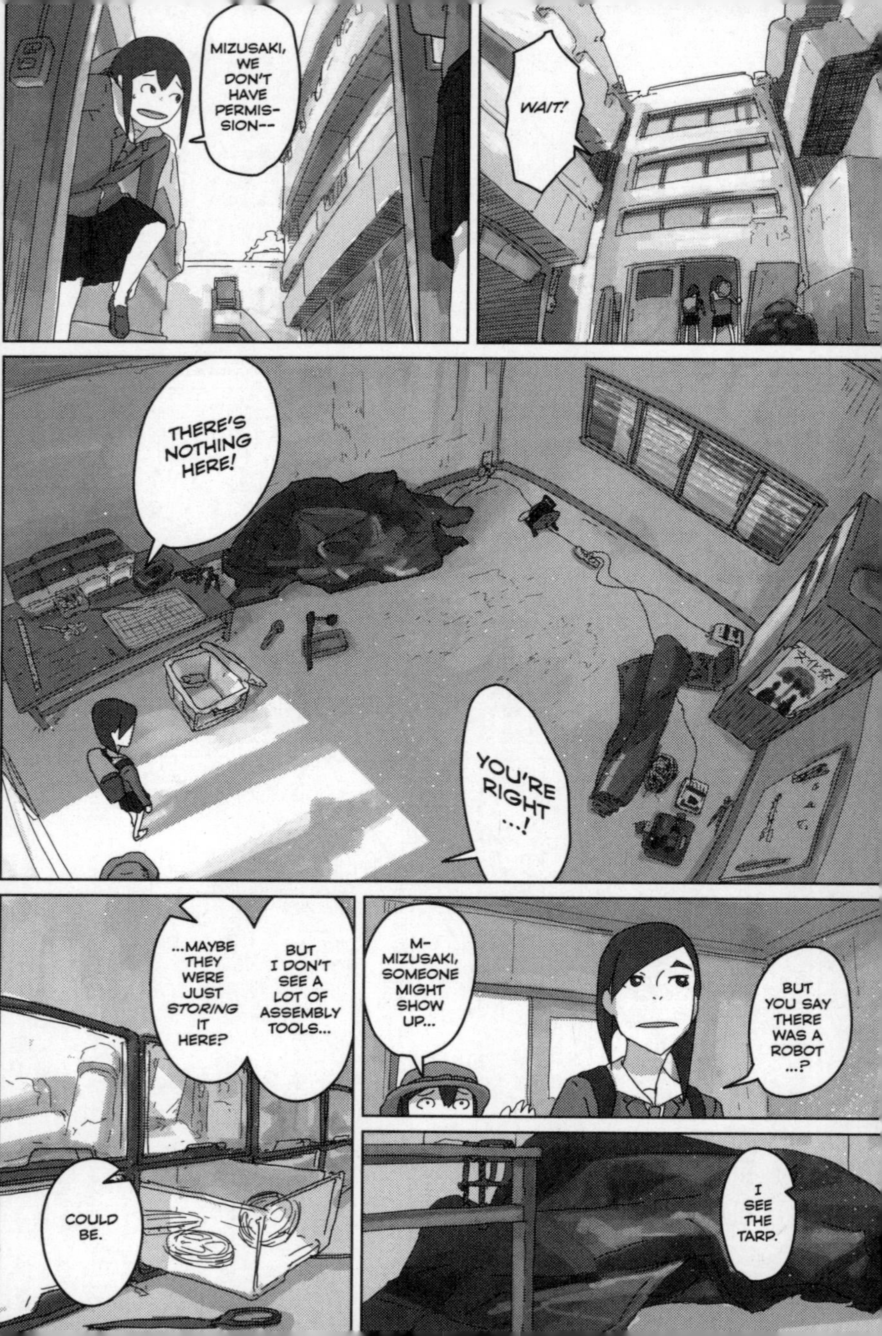
WAIT!
MIZUSAKI, WE DON'T HAVE PERMISSION--
THERE'S NOTHING HERE!
YOU'RE RIGHT ...!
BUT YOU SAY THERE WAS A ROBOT ...?
M-MIZUSAKI, SOMEONE MIGHT SHOW UP...
I SEE THE TARP.
BUT I DON'T SEE A LOT OF ASSEMBLY TOOLS...
...MAYBE THEY WERE JUST *STORING* IT HERE?
COULD BE.

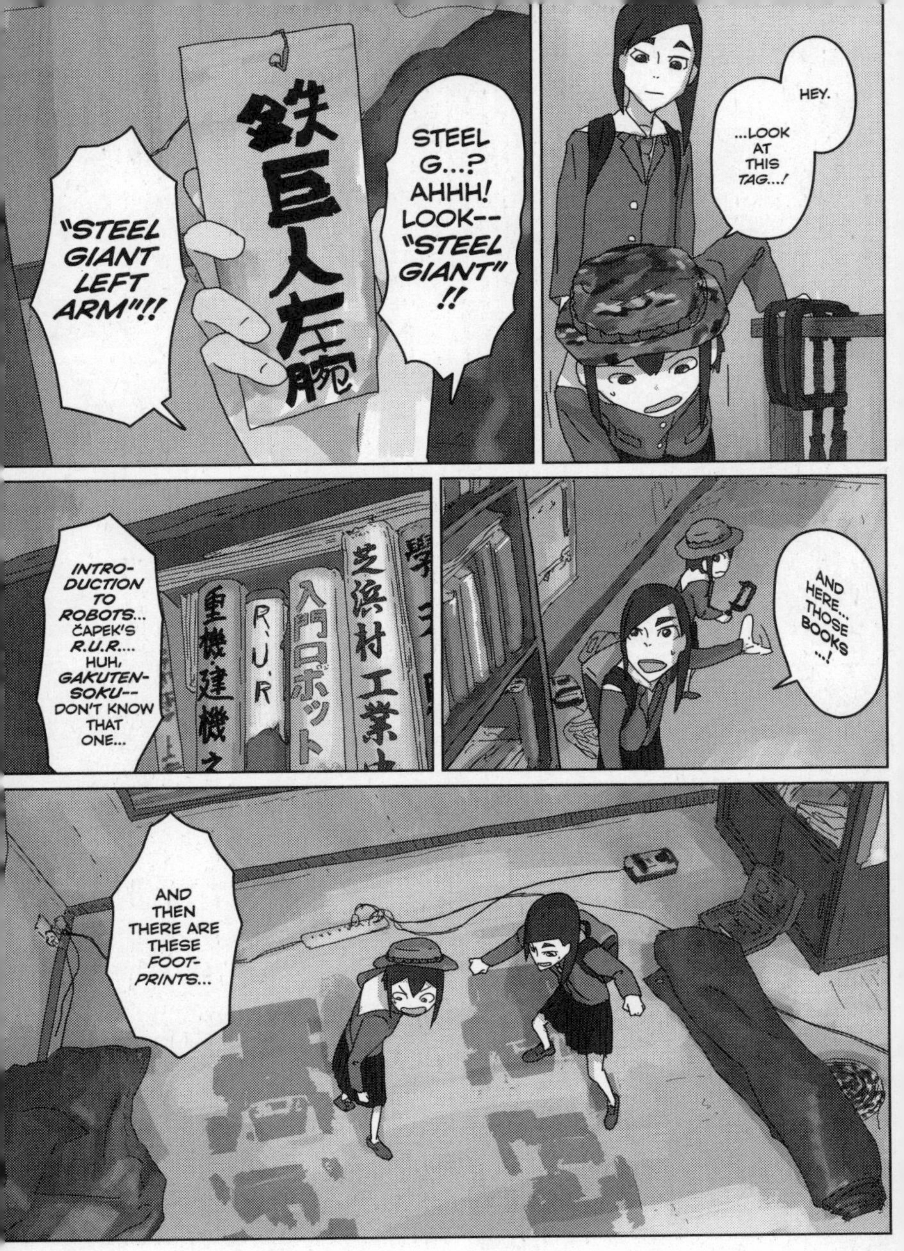
HEY.
...LOOK AT THIS TAG...!
鉄巨人左腕
STEEL G...? AHHH! LOOK-- "STEEL GIANT"!!
"STEEL GIANT LEFT ARM"!!
AND HERE... THOSE BOOKS...!
R.U.R
入門ロボット
INTRODUCTION TO ROBOTS... ČAPEK'S R.U.R.... HUH, GAKUTENSOKU-- DON'T KNOW THAT ONE...
AND THEN THERE ARE THESE FOOTPRINTS...

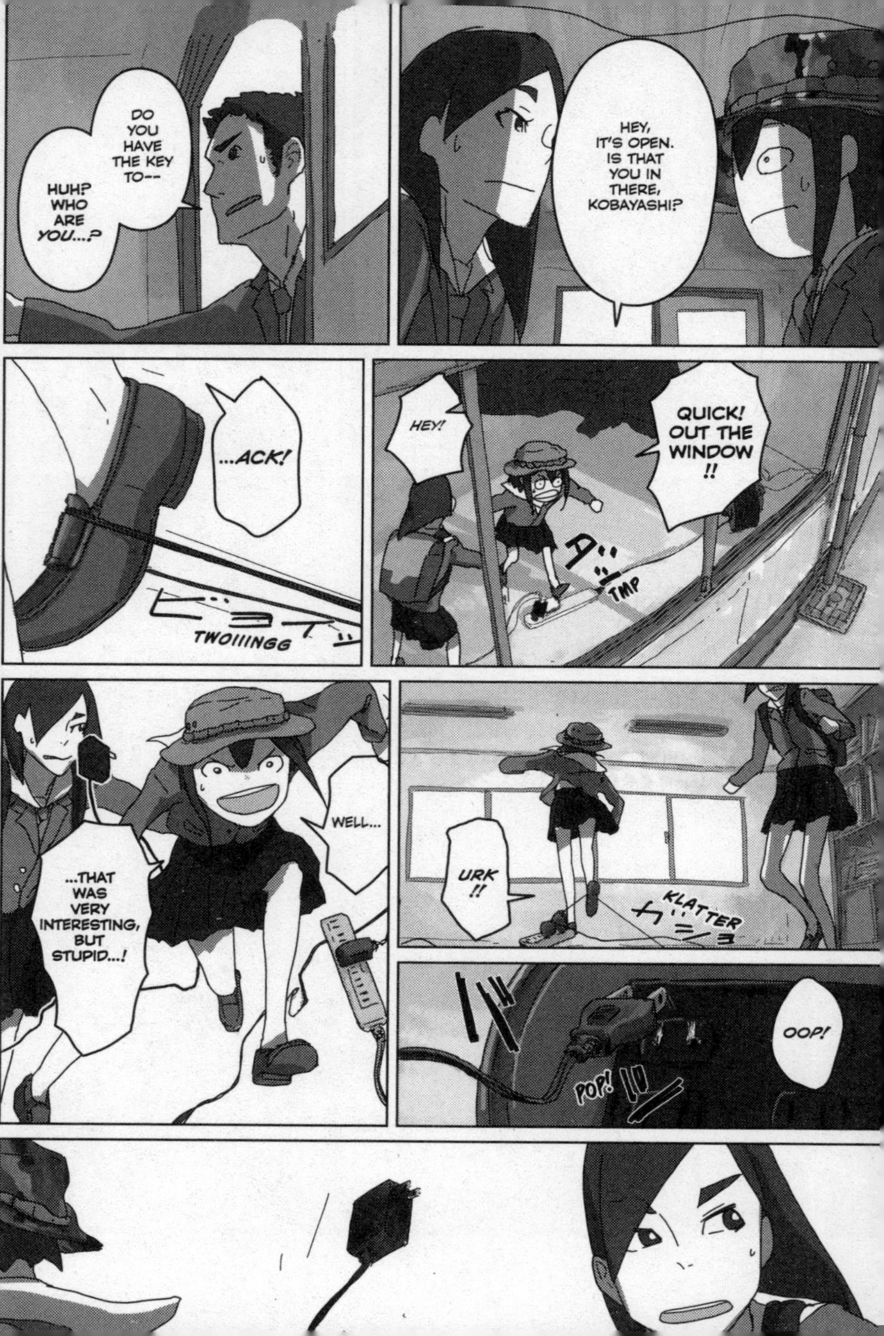

HEY, IT'S OPEN. IS THAT YOU IN THERE, KOBAYASHI?
DO YOU HAVE THE KEY TO--
HUH? WHO ARE YOU...?
QUICK! OUT THE WINDOW !!
HEY!
TMP
...ACK!
TWOIIIINGG
URK !!
KLATTER
OOP!
POP!
WELL...
...THAT WAS VERY INTERESTING, BUT STUPID...!

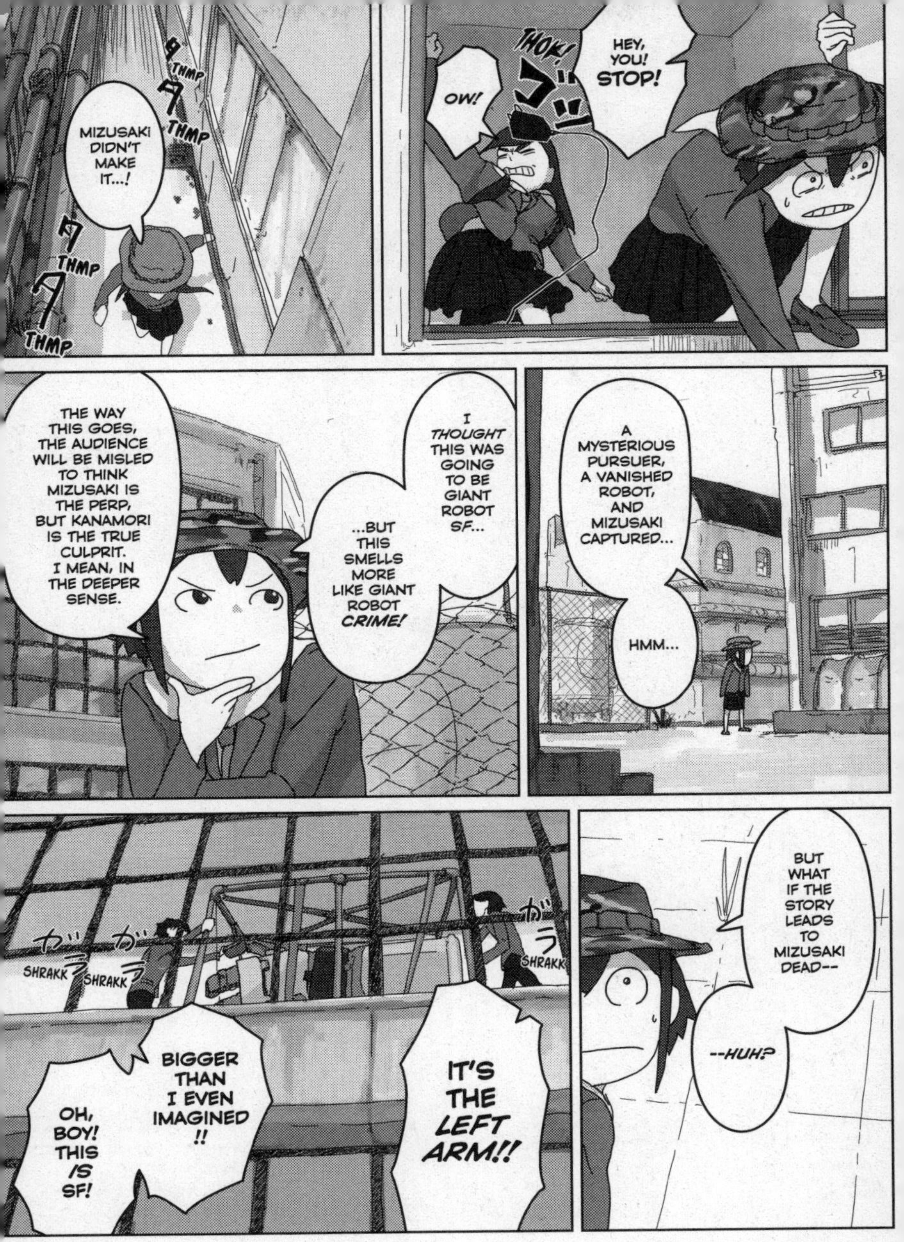
HEY, YOU! STOP!
THOK!
OW!
MIZUSAKI DIDN'T MAKE IT...!
THMP
THMP
THMP
THMP
A MYSTERIOUS PURSUER, A VANISHED ROBOT, AND MIZUSAKI CAPTURED...
HMM...
I *THOUGHT* THIS WAS GOING TO BE GIANT ROBOT SF...
...BUT THIS SMELLS MORE LIKE GIANT ROBOT *CRIME!*
THE WAY THIS GOES, THE AUDIENCE WILL BE MISLED TO THINK MIZUSAKI IS THE PERP, BUT KANAMORI IS THE TRUE CULPRIT. I MEAN, IN THE DEEPER SENSE.
BUT WHAT IF THE STORY LEADS TO MIZUSAKI DEAD--
--*HUH?*
SHRAKK
IT'S THE *LEFT* ARM!!
BIGGER THAN I EVEN IMAGINED!!
SHRAKK
SHRAKK
OH, BOY! THIS *IS* SF!

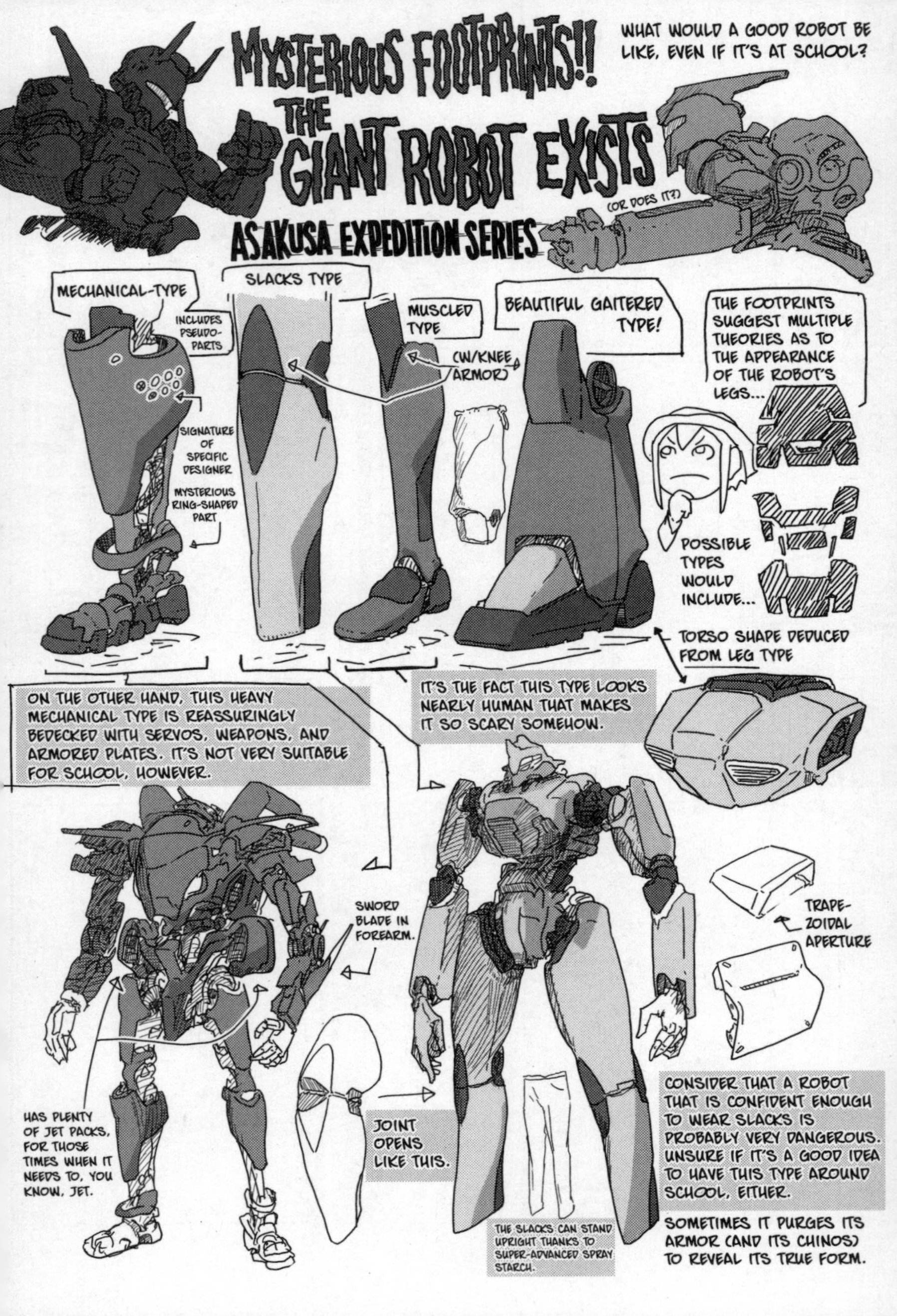
MYSTERIOUS FOOTPRINTS!! THE GIANT ROBOT EXISTS
(OR DOES IT?)
ASAKUSA EXPEDITION SERIES
WHAT WOULD A GOOD ROBOT BE LIKE, EVEN IF IT'S AT SCHOOL?
MECHANICAL-TYPE
INCLUDES PSEUDO-PARTS
SIGNATURE OF SPECIFIC DESIGNER
MYSTERIOUS RING-SHAPED PART
SLACKS TYPE
MUSCLED TYPE
(W/KNEE ARMOR)
BEAUTIFUL GAITERED TYPE!
THE FOOTPRINTS SUGGEST MULTIPLE THEORIES AS TO THE APPEARANCE OF THE ROBOT'S LEGS...
POSSIBLE TYPES WOULD INCLUDE...
TORSO SHAPE DEDUCED FROM LEG TYPE
ON THE OTHER HAND, THIS HEAVY MECHANICAL TYPE IS REASSURINGLY BEDECKED WITH SERVOS, WEAPONS, AND ARMORED PLATES. IT'S NOT VERY SUITABLE FOR SCHOOL, HOWEVER.
IT'S THE FACT THIS TYPE LOOKS NEARLY HUMAN THAT MAKES IT SO SCARY SOMEHOW.
SWORD BLADE IN FOREARM.
TRAPE-ZOIDAL APERTURE
HAS PLENTY OF JET PACKS, FOR THOSE TIMES WHEN IT NEEDS TO, YOU KNOW, JET.
JOINT OPENS LIKE THIS.
THE SLACKS CAN STAND UPRIGHT THANKS TO SUPER-ADVANCED SPRAY STARCH.
CONSIDER THAT A ROBOT THAT IS CONFIDENT ENOUGH TO WEAR SLACKS IS PROBABLY VERY DANGEROUS. UNSURE IF IT'S A GOOD IDEA TO HAVE THIS TYPE AROUND SCHOOL, EITHER.
SOMETIMES IT PURGES ITS ARMOR (AND ITS CHINOS) TO REVEAL ITS TRUE FORM.

"ANCIENT SHIBAHAMA" CIVILIZATION

A TWISTED SCIENTIFIC CULTURE REACHED THROUGH THE POWER OF SHAMANISM

(IS MAYBE WHAT THEY HAD)

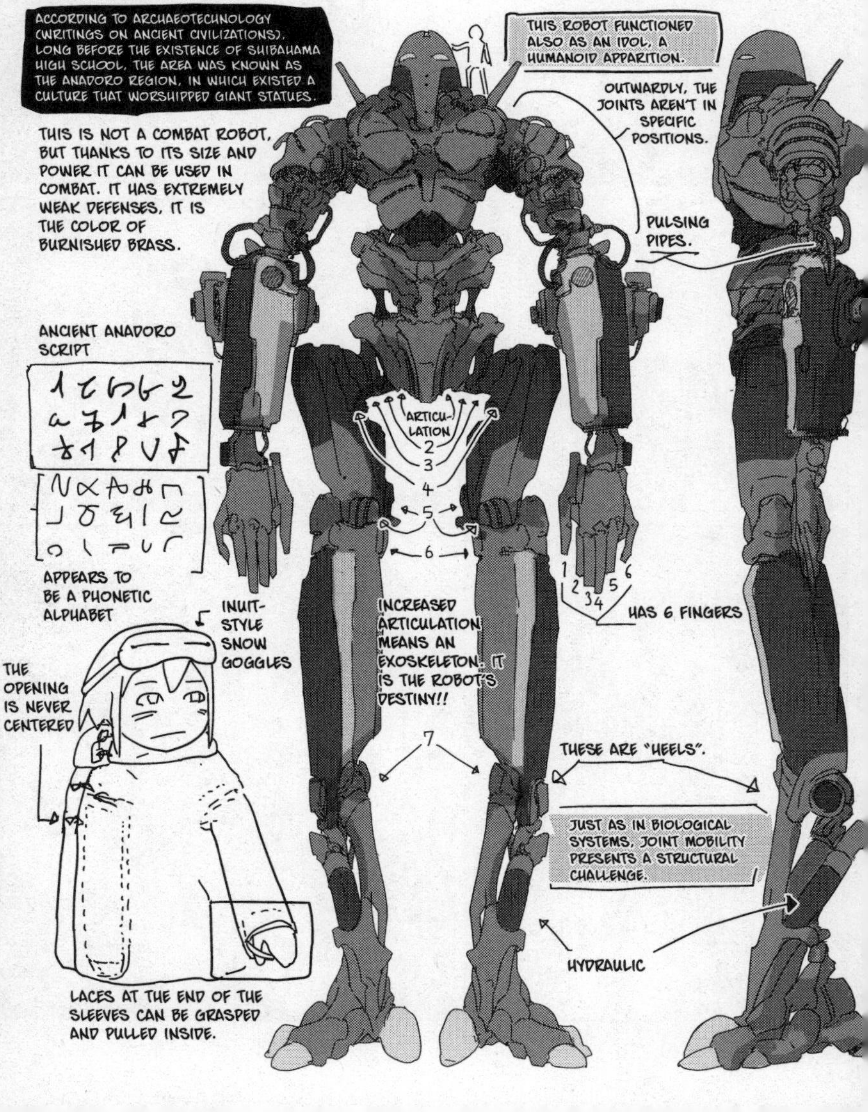
ACCORDING TO ARCHAEOTECHNOLOGY (WRITINGS ON ANCIENT CIVILIZATIONS), LONG BEFORE THE EXISTENCE OF SHIBAHAMA HIGH SCHOOL, THE AREA WAS KNOWN AS THE ANADORO REGION, IN WHICH EXISTED A CULTURE THAT WORSHIPPED GIANT STATUES.
THIS ROBOT FUNCTIONED ALSO AS AN IDOL, A HUMANOID APPARITION.
OUTWARDLY, THE JOINTS AREN'T IN SPECIFIC POSITIONS.
THIS IS NOT A COMBAT ROBOT, BUT THANKS TO ITS SIZE AND POWER IT CAN BE USED IN COMBAT. IT HAS EXTREMELY WEAK DEFENSES, IT IS THE COLOR OF BURNISHED BRASS.
PULSING PIPES.
ANCIENT ANADORO SCRIPT
ARTICU-LATION
2
3
4
5
6
APPEARS TO BE A PHONETIC ALPHABET
1 2 3 4 5 6
HAS 6 FINGERS
INUIT-STYLE SNOW GOGGLES
INCREASED ARTICULATION MEANS AN EXOSKELETON. IT IS THE ROBOT'S DESTINY!!
THE OPENING IS NEVER CENTERED
7
THESE ARE "HEELS".
JUST AS IN BIOLOGICAL SYSTEMS, JOINT MOBILITY PRESENTS A STRUCTURAL CHALLENGE.
HYDRAULIC
LACES AT THE END OF THE SLEEVES CAN BE GRASPED AND PULLED INSIDE.

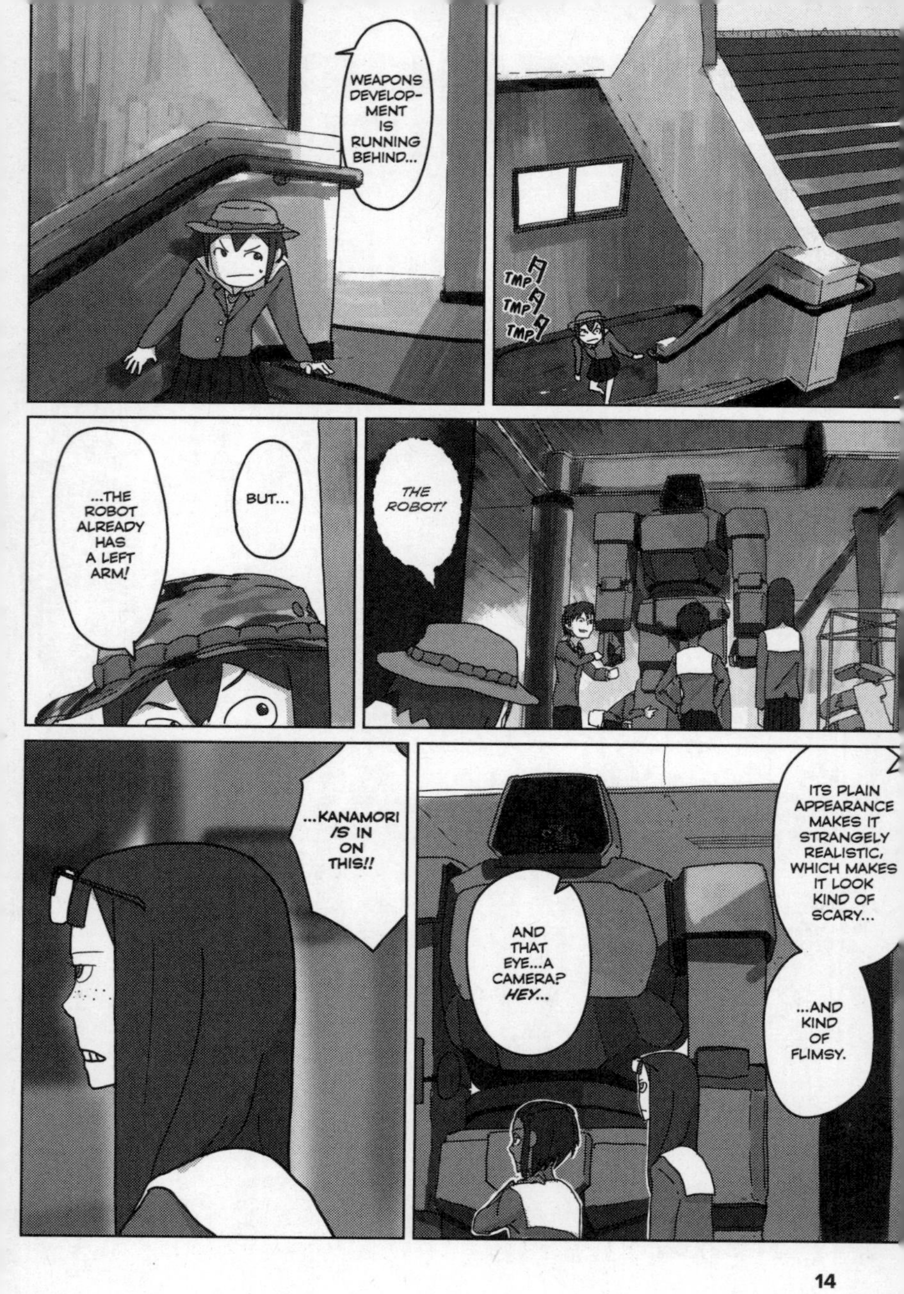
TMP TMP TMP
WEAPONS DEVELOPMENT IS RUNNING BEHIND...
THE ROBOT!
BUT...
...THE ROBOT ALREADY HAS A LEFT ARM!
ITS PLAIN APPEARANCE MAKES IT STRANGELY REALISTIC, WHICH MAKES IT LOOK KIND OF SCARY...
...AND KIND OF FLIMSY.
AND THAT EYE...A CAMERA? HEY...
...KANAMORI IS IN ON THIS!!

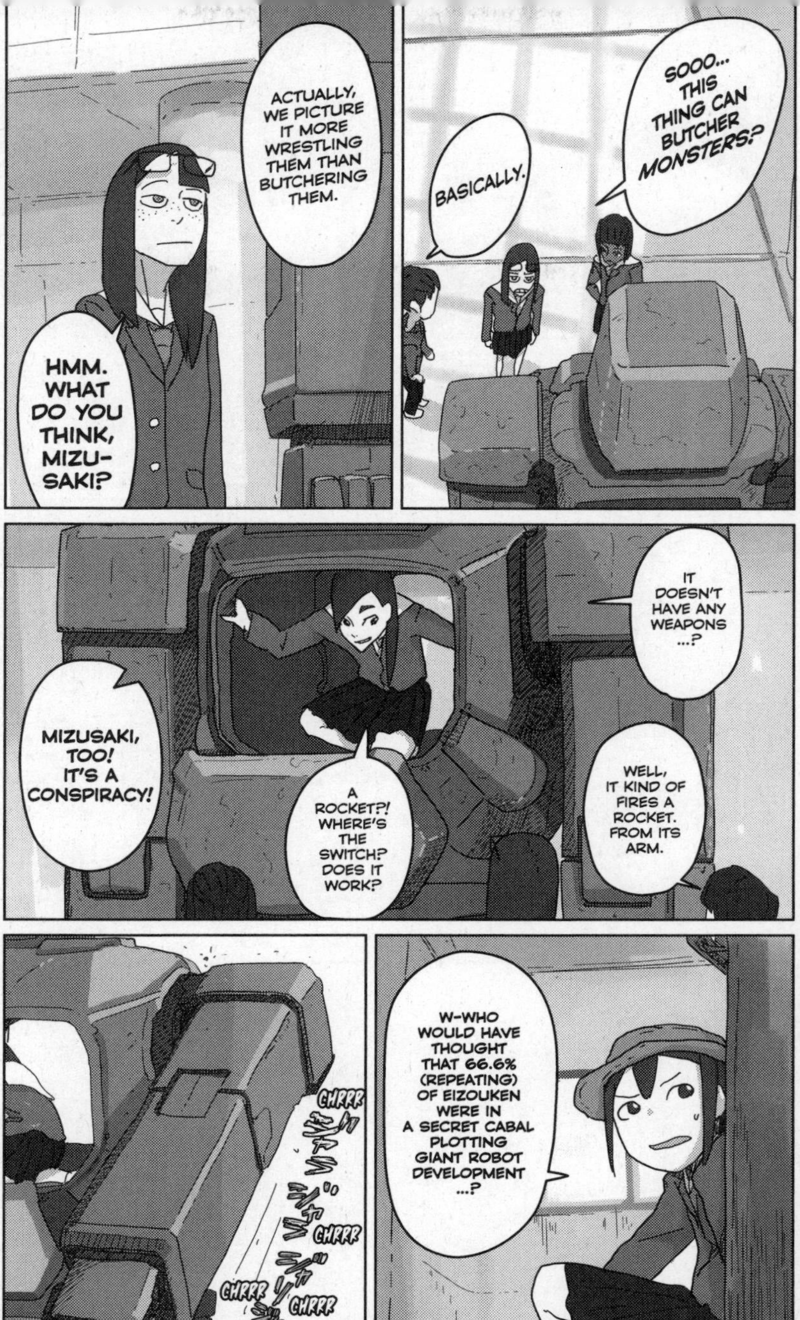
SOOO... THIS THING CAN BUTCHER MONSTERS?
BASICALLY.
ACTUALLY, WE PICTURE IT MORE WRESTLING THEM THAN BUTCHERING THEM.
HMM. WHAT DO YOU THINK, MIZU-SAKI?
IT DOESN'T HAVE ANY WEAPONS ...?
WELL, IT KIND OF FIRES A ROCKET. FROM ITS ARM.
A ROCKET?! WHERE'S THE SWITCH? DOES IT WORK?
MIZUSAKI, TOO! IT'S A CONSPIRACY!
W-WHO WOULD HAVE THOUGHT THAT 66.6% (REPEATING) OF EIZOUKEN WERE IN A SECRET CABAL PLOTTING GIANT ROBOT DEVELOPMENT ...?
GHRRR
GHRRR
GHRRR
GHRRR

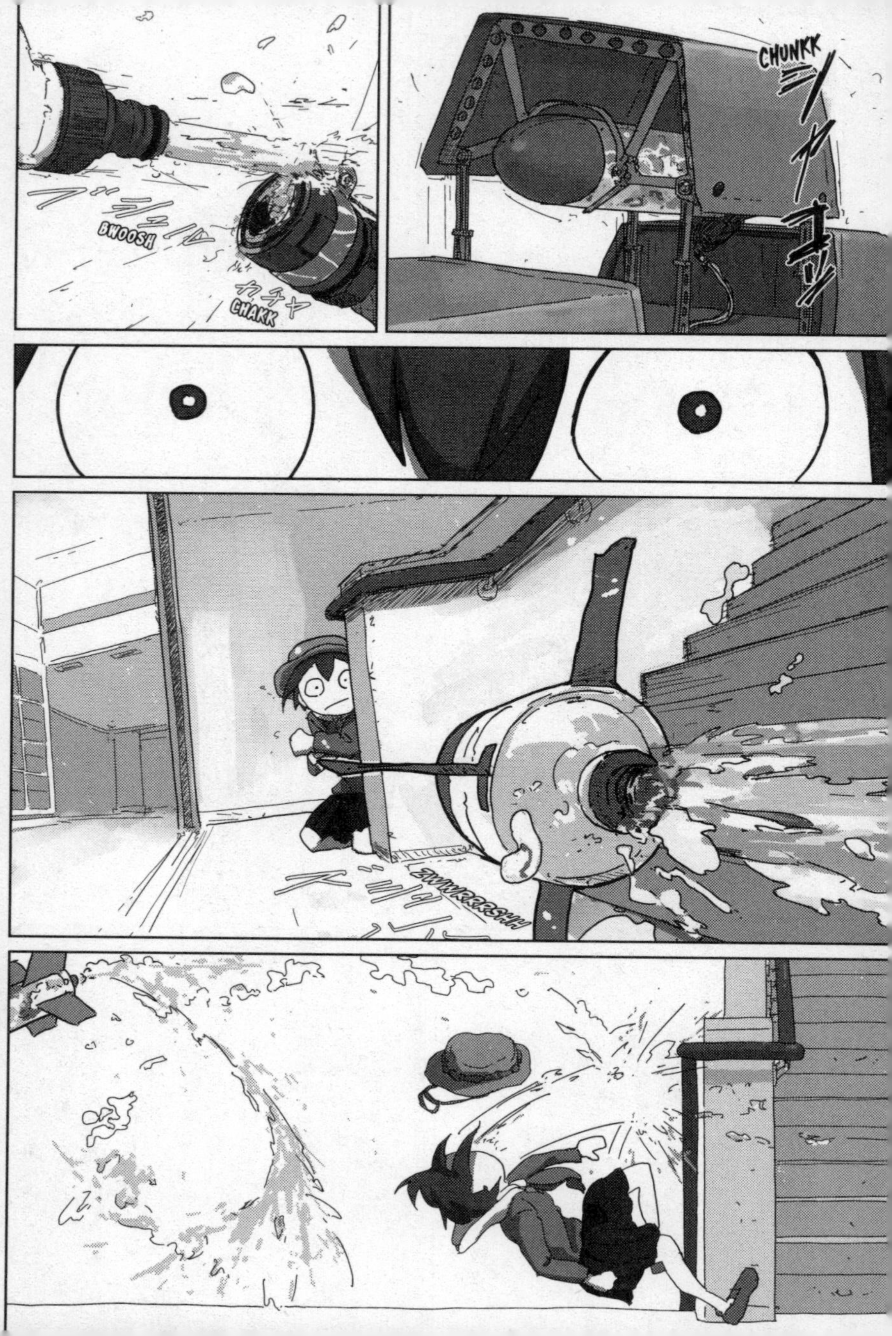
CHUNKK
BWOOSH
CHAKK
ZWWRRRSHH

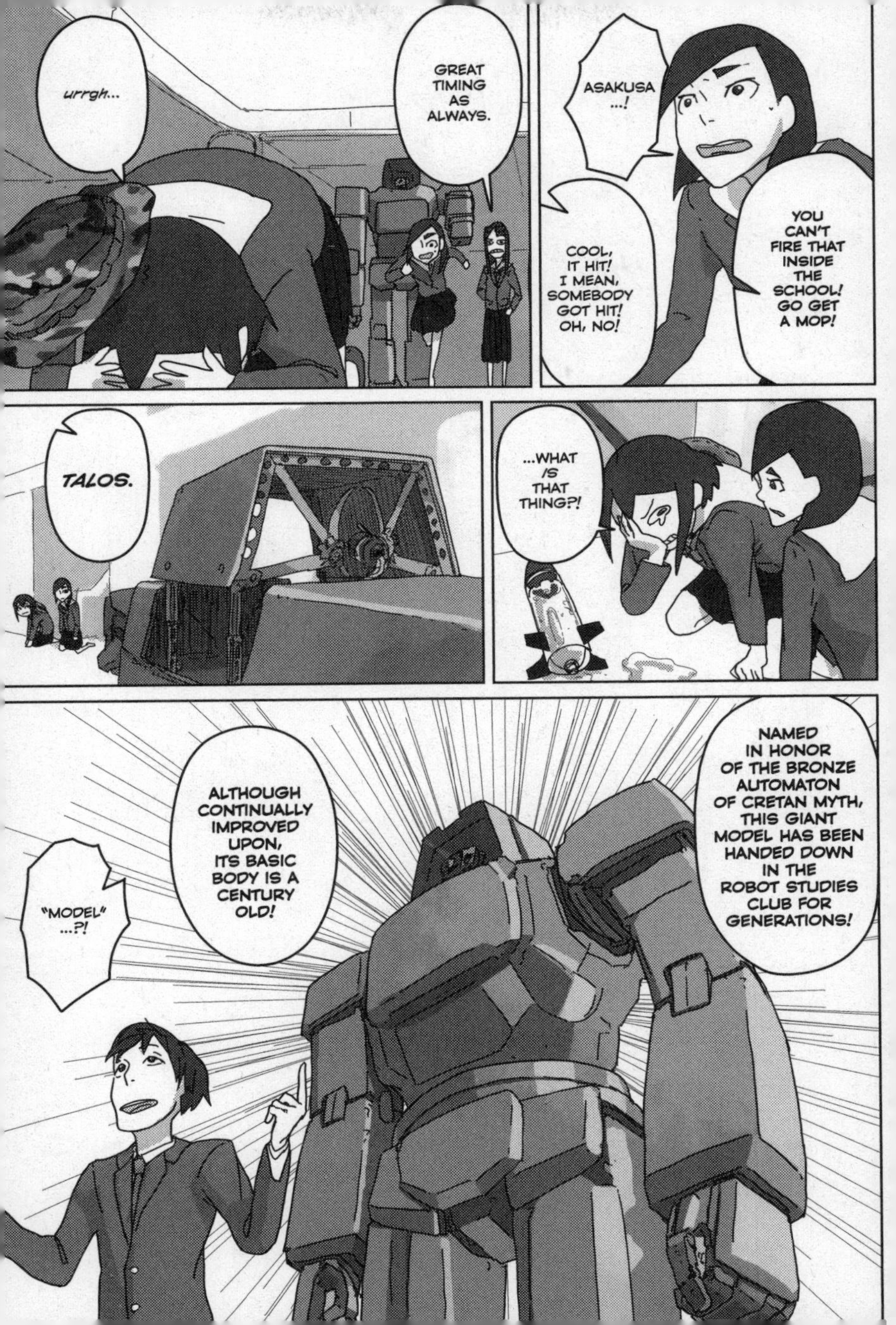
ASAKUSA ...!
YOU CAN'T FIRE THAT INSIDE THE SCHOOL! GO GET A MOP!
COOL, IT HIT! I MEAN, SOMEBODY GOT HIT! OH, NO!
GREAT TIMING AS ALWAYS.
urrgh...
...WHAT *IS* THAT THING?!
TALOS.
NAMED IN HONOR OF THE BRONZE AUTOMATON OF CRETAN MYTH, THIS GIANT MODEL HAS BEEN HANDED DOWN IN THE ROBOT STUDIES CLUB FOR GENERATIONS!
ALTHOUGH CONTINUALLY IMPROVED UPON, ITS BASIC BODY IS A CENTURY OLD!
"MODEL" ...?!

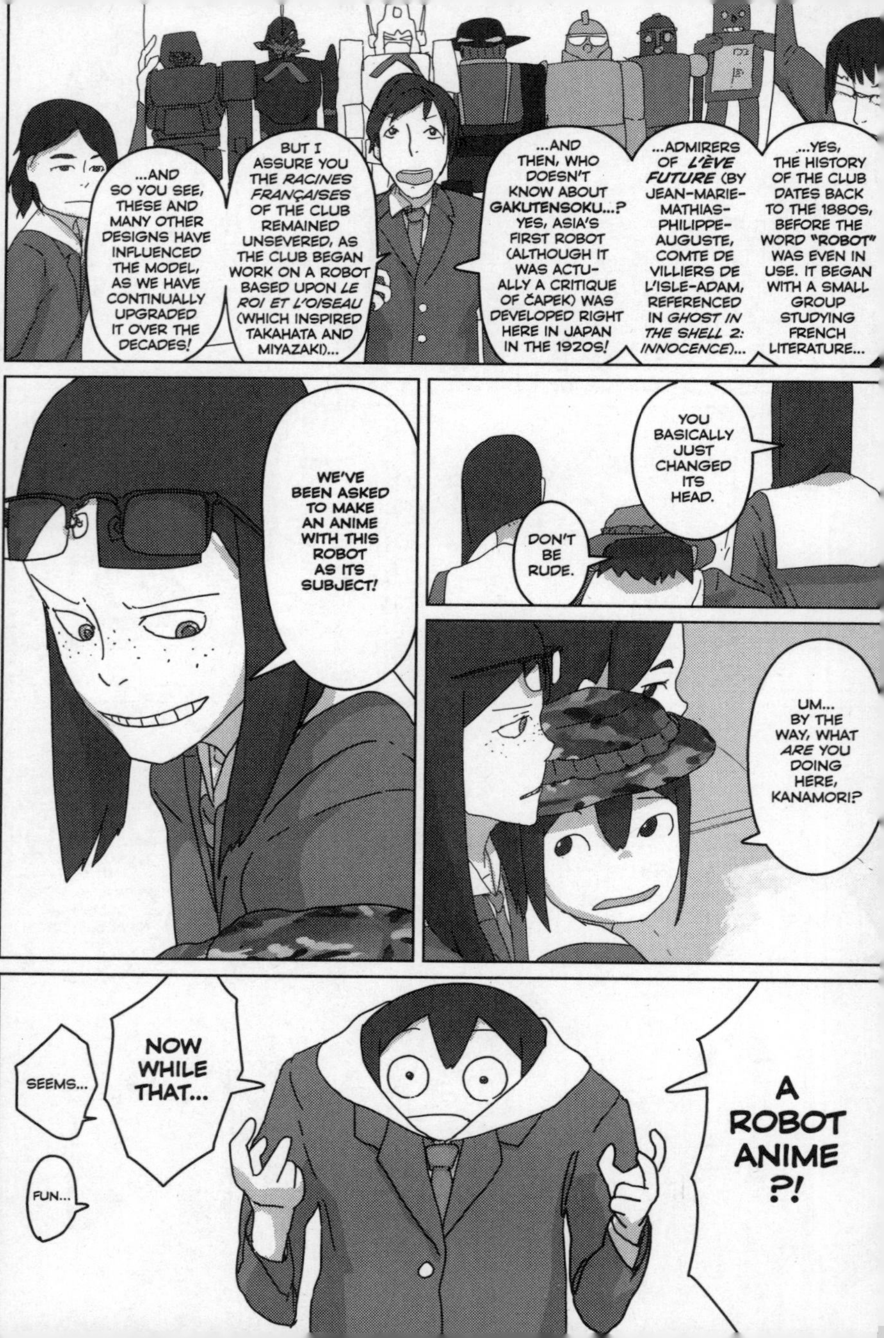
...YES, THE HISTORY OF THE CLUB DATES BACK TO THE 1880S, BEFORE THE WORD "ROBOT" WAS EVEN IN USE. IT BEGAN WITH A SMALL GROUP STUDYING FRENCH LITERATURE...
...ADMIRERS OF *L'ÈVE FUTURE* (BY JEAN-MARIE-MATHIAS-PHILIPPE-AUGUSTE, COMTE DE VILLIERS DE L'ISLE-ADAM, REFERENCED IN *GHOST IN THE SHELL 2: INNOCENCE*)...
...AND THEN, WHO DOESN'T KNOW ABOUT GAKUTENSOKU...? YES, ASIA'S FIRST ROBOT (ALTHOUGH IT WAS ACTUALLY A CRITIQUE OF ČAPEK) WAS DEVELOPED RIGHT HERE IN JAPAN IN THE 1920S!
BUT I ASSURE YOU THE *RACINES FRANÇAISES* OF THE CLUB REMAINED UNSEVERED, AS THE CLUB BEGAN WORK ON A ROBOT BASED UPON *LE ROI ET L'OISEAU* (WHICH INSPIRED TAKAHATA AND MIYAZAKI)...
...AND SO YOU SEE, THESE AND MANY OTHER DESIGNS HAVE INFLUENCED THE MODEL, AS WE HAVE CONTINUALLY UPGRADED IT OVER THE DECADES!
YOU BASICALLY JUST CHANGED ITS HEAD.
DON'T BE RUDE.
UM... BY THE WAY, WHAT *ARE* YOU DOING HERE, KANAMORI?
WE'VE BEEN ASKED TO MAKE AN ANIME WITH THIS ROBOT AS ITS SUBJECT!
A ROBOT ANIME ?!
NOW WHILE THAT...
SEEMS...
FUN...

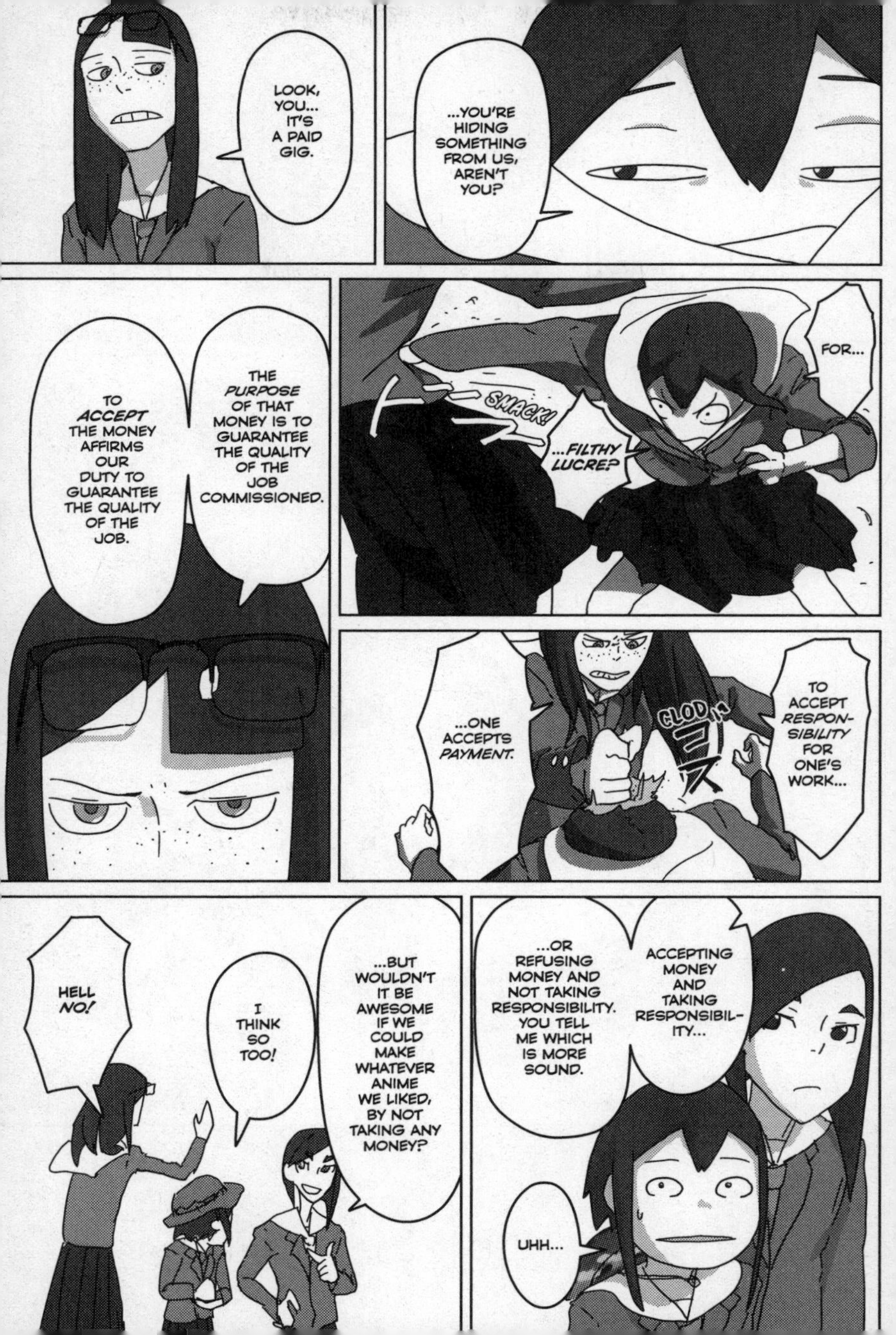
...YOU'RE HIDING SOMETHING FROM US, AREN'T YOU?
LOOK, YOU... IT'S A PAID GIG.
FOR...
SMACK!
...FILTHY LUCRE?
TO ACCEPT RESPONSIBILITY FOR ONE'S WORK...
CLOD
...ONE ACCEPTS PAYMENT.
THE PURPOSE OF THAT MONEY IS TO GUARANTEE THE QUALITY OF THE JOB COMMISSIONED.
TO ACCEPT THE MONEY AFFIRMS OUR DUTY TO GUARANTEE THE QUALITY OF THE JOB.
ACCEPTING MONEY AND TAKING RESPONSIBILITY...
...OR REFUSING MONEY AND NOT TAKING RESPONSIBILITY. YOU TELL ME WHICH IS MORE SOUND.
UHH...
...BUT WOULDN'T IT BE AWESOME IF WE COULD MAKE WHATEVER ANIME WE LIKED, BY NOT TAKING ANY MONEY?
I THINK SO TOO!
HELL NO!

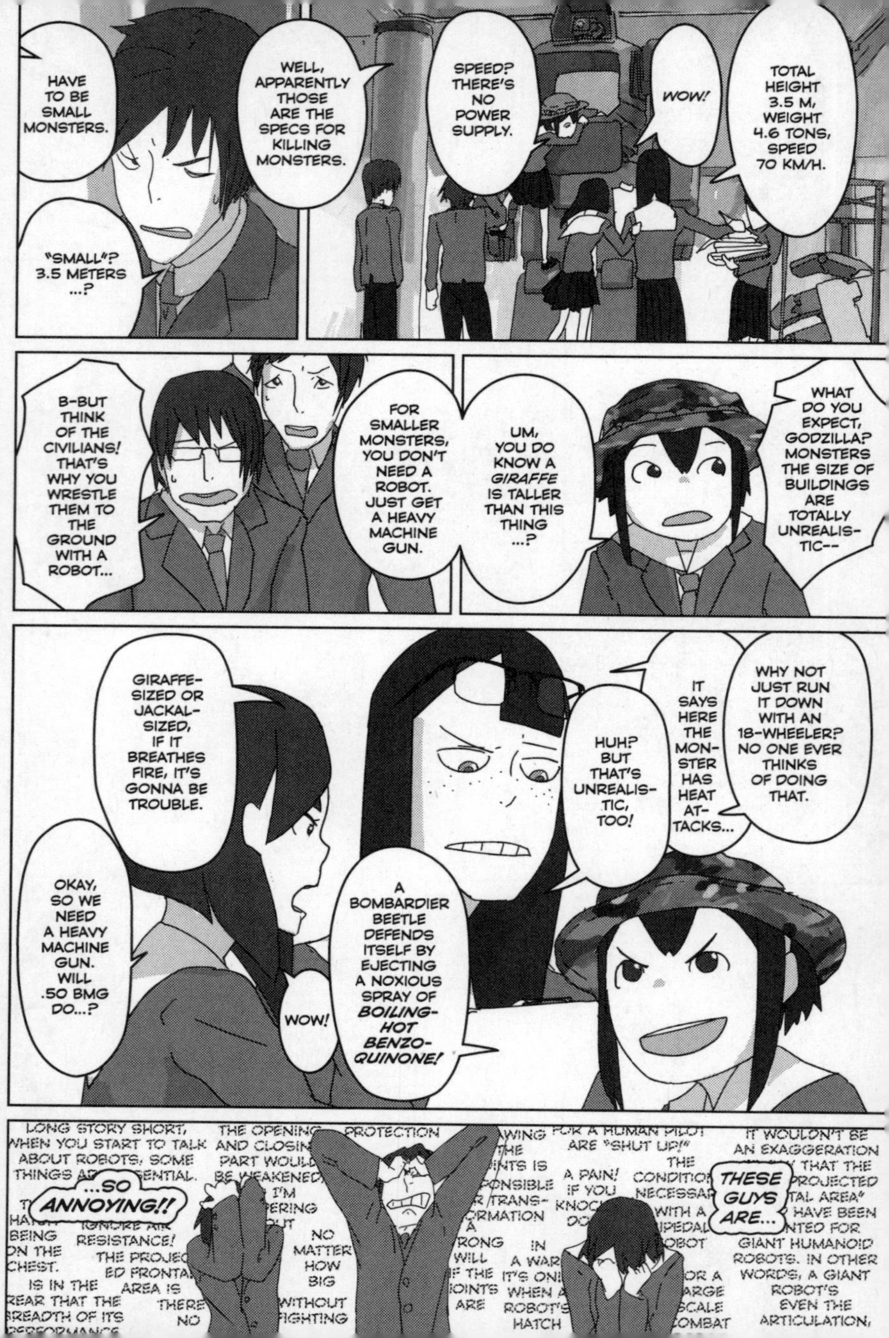
TOTAL HEIGHT 3.5 M, WEIGHT 4.6 TONS, SPEED 70 KM/H.
WOW!
SPEED? THERE'S NO POWER SUPPLY.
WELL, APPARENTLY THOSE ARE THE SPECS FOR KILLING MONSTERS.
HAVE TO BE SMALL MONSTERS.
"SMALL"? 3.5 METERS ...?
WHAT DO YOU EXPECT, GODZILLA? MONSTERS THE SIZE OF BUILDINGS ARE TOTALLY UNREALISTIC--
UM, YOU DO KNOW A *GIRAFFE* IS TALLER THAN THIS THING ...?
FOR SMALLER MONSTERS, YOU DON'T NEED A ROBOT. JUST GET A HEAVY MACHINE GUN.
B-BUT THINK OF THE CIVILIANS! THAT'S WHY YOU WRESTLE THEM TO THE GROUND WITH A ROBOT...
WHY NOT JUST RUN IT DOWN WITH AN 18-WHEELER? NO ONE EVER THINKS OF DOING THAT.
IT SAYS HERE THE MONSTER HAS HEAT ATTACKS...
HUH? BUT THAT'S UNREALISTIC, TOO!
GIRAFFE-SIZED OR JACKAL-SIZED, IF IT BREATHES FIRE, IT'S GONNA BE TROUBLE.
A BOMBARDIER BEETLE DEFENDS ITSELF BY EJECTING A NOXIOUS SPRAY OF ***BOILING-HOT BENZOQUINONE!***
WOW!
OKAY, SO WE NEED A HEAVY MACHINE GUN. WILL .50 BMG DO...?
THESE GUYS ARE...
...SO ANNOYING!!

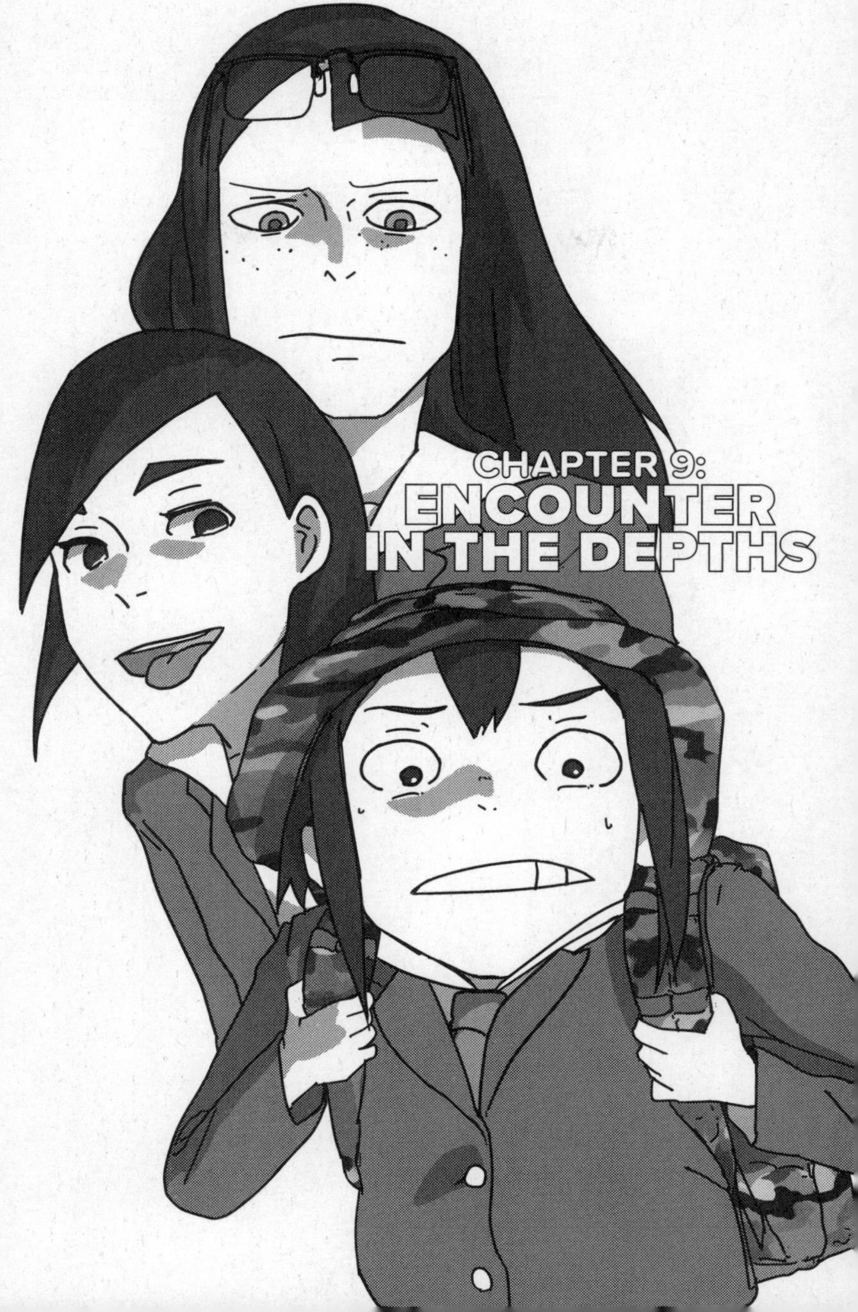
CHAPTER 9:
ENCOUNTER
IN THE DEPTHS

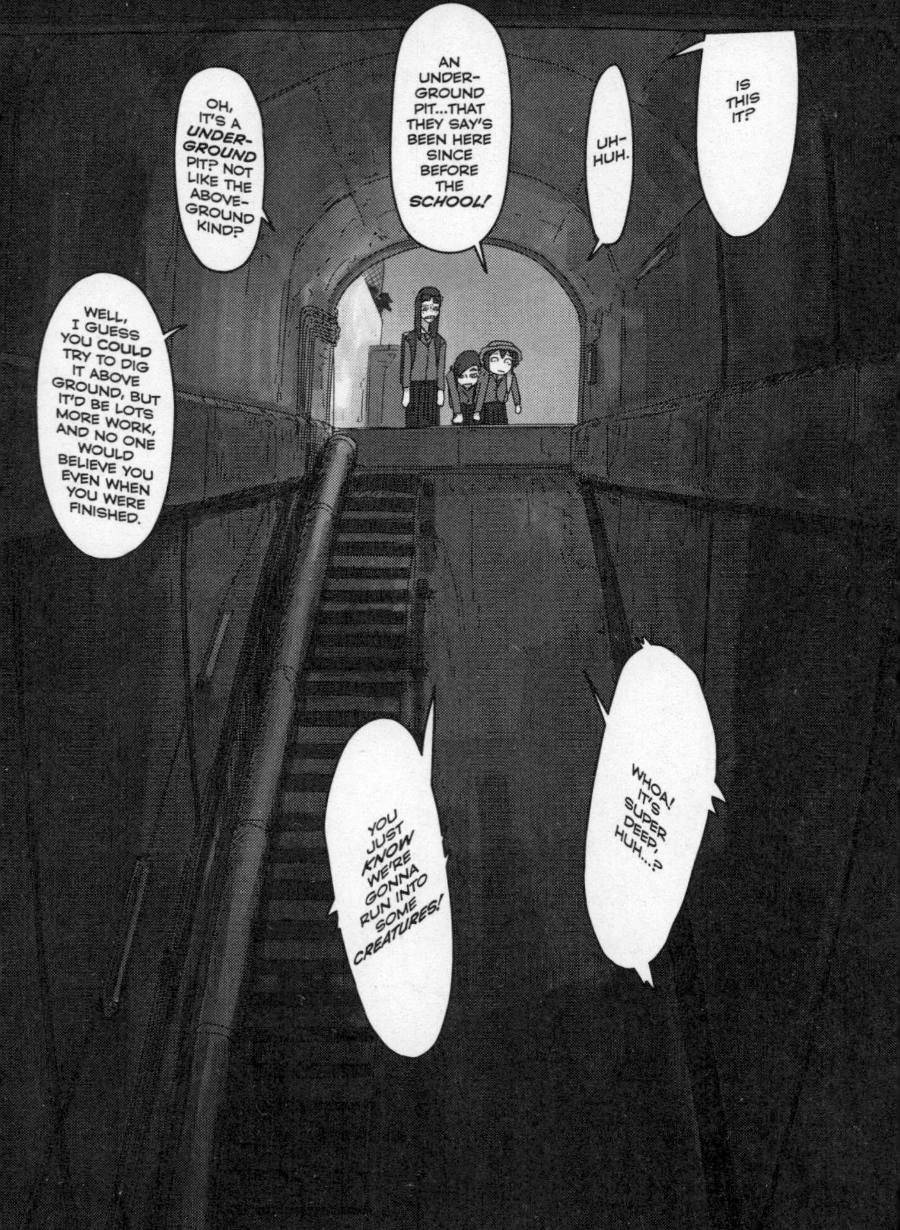
IS THIS IT?
UH-HUH.
AN UNDERGROUND PIT...THAT THEY SAY'S BEEN HERE SINCE BEFORE THE *SCHOOL!*
OH, IT'S A *UNDERGROUND* PIT? NOT LIKE THE ABOVE-GROUND KIND?
WELL, I GUESS YOU COULD TRY TO DIG IT ABOVE GROUND, BUT IT'D BE LOTS MORE WORK, AND NO ONE WOULD BELIEVE YOU EVEN WHEN YOU WERE FINISHED.
WHOA! IT'S SUPER DEEP, HUH...?
YOU JUST *KNOW* WE'RE GONNA RUN INTO SOME *CREATURES!*

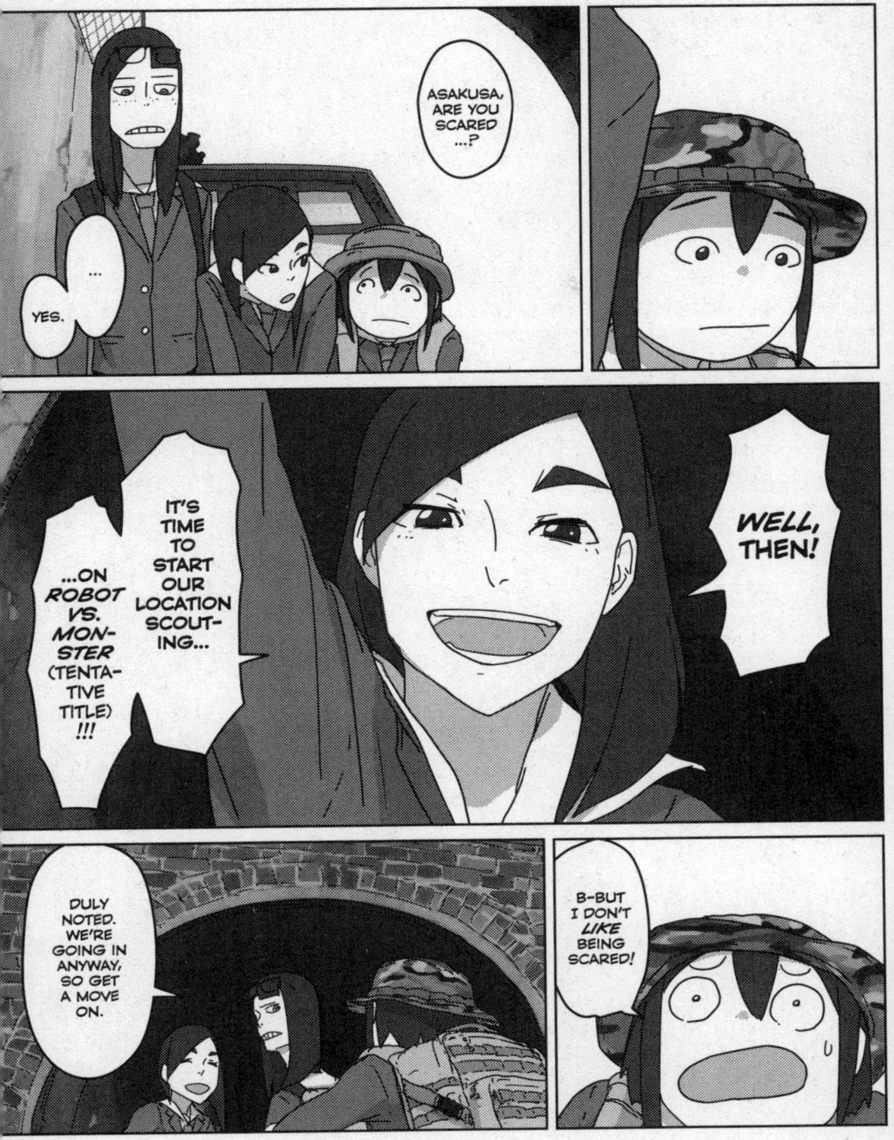
ASAKUSA, ARE YOU SCARED ...?
... YES.
WELL, THEN!
IT'S TIME TO START OUR LOCATION SCOUTING...
...ON *ROBOT VS. MONSTER* (TENTATIVE TITLE) !!!
B-BUT I DON'T *LIKE* BEING SCARED!
DULY NOTED. WE'RE GOING IN ANYWAY, SO GET A MOVE ON.

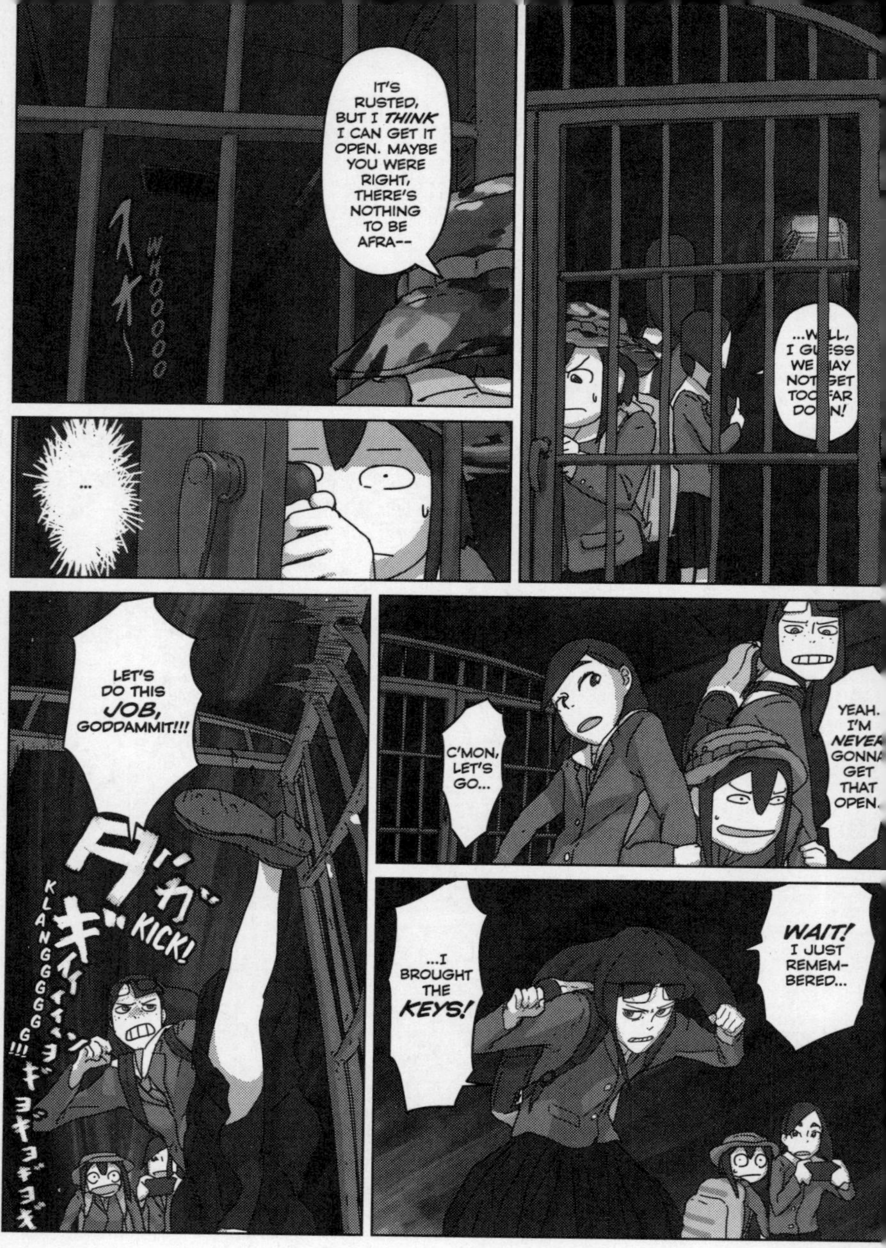

...WELL, I GUESS WE MAY NOT GET TOO FAR DOWN!
IT'S RUSTED, BUT I *THINK* I CAN GET IT OPEN. MAYBE YOU WERE RIGHT, THERE'S NOTHING TO BE AFRA--
WHOOOOOO
...
YEAH. I'M *NEVER* GONNA GET THAT OPEN.
C'MON, LET'S GO...
WAIT! I JUST REMEMBERED...
...I BROUGHT THE *KEYS!*
LET'S DO THIS *JOB,* GODDAMMIT!!!
KICK!
KLANGGGGGGG!!!

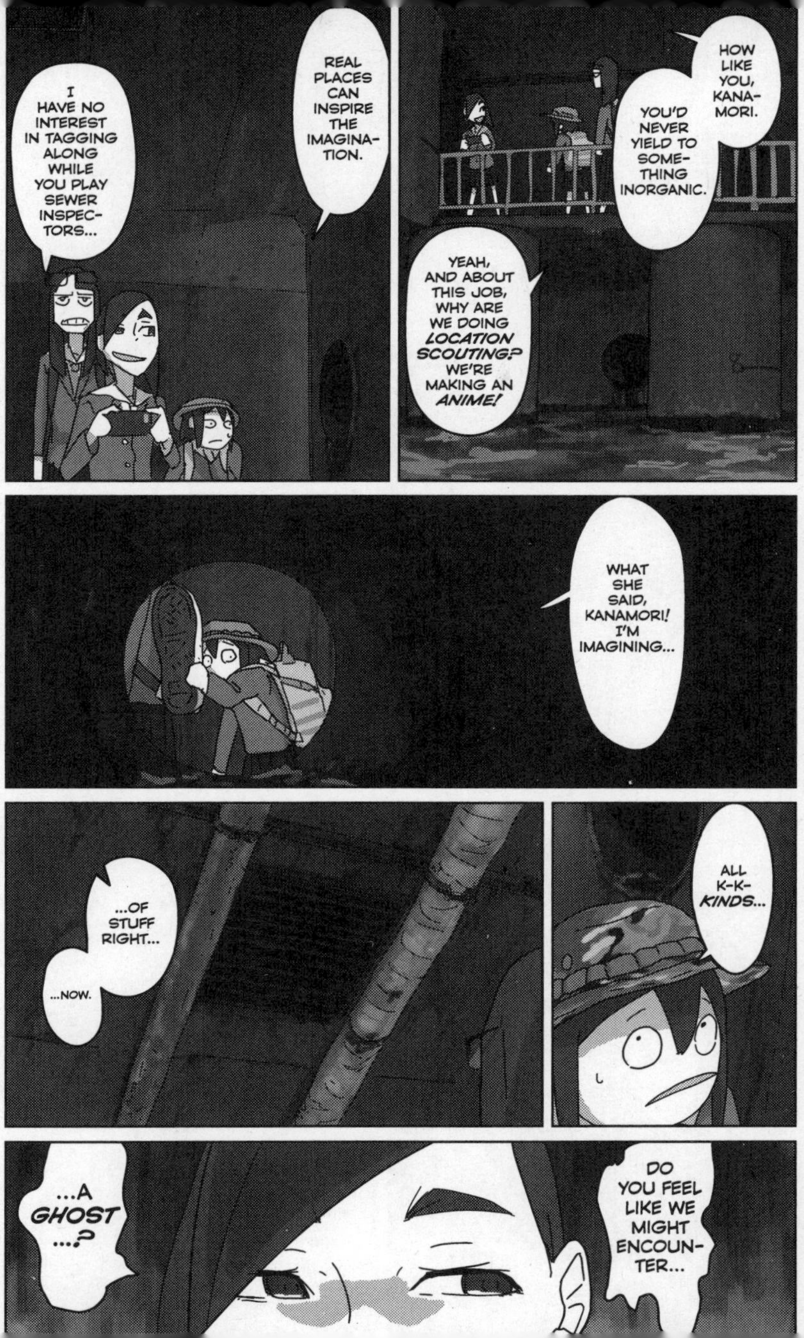
HOW LIKE YOU, KANAMORI.
YOU'D NEVER YIELD TO SOMETHING INORGANIC.
YEAH, AND ABOUT THIS JOB, WHY ARE WE DOING *LOCATION SCOUTING?* WE'RE MAKING AN *ANIME!*
REAL PLACES CAN INSPIRE THE IMAGINATION.
I HAVE NO INTEREST IN TAGGING ALONG WHILE YOU PLAY SEWER INSPECTORS...
WHAT SHE SAID, KANAMORI! I'M IMAGINING...
ALL K-K-*KINDS*...
...OF STUFF RIGHT...
...NOW.
DO YOU FEEL LIKE WE MIGHT ENCOUNTER...
...A *GHOST* ...?

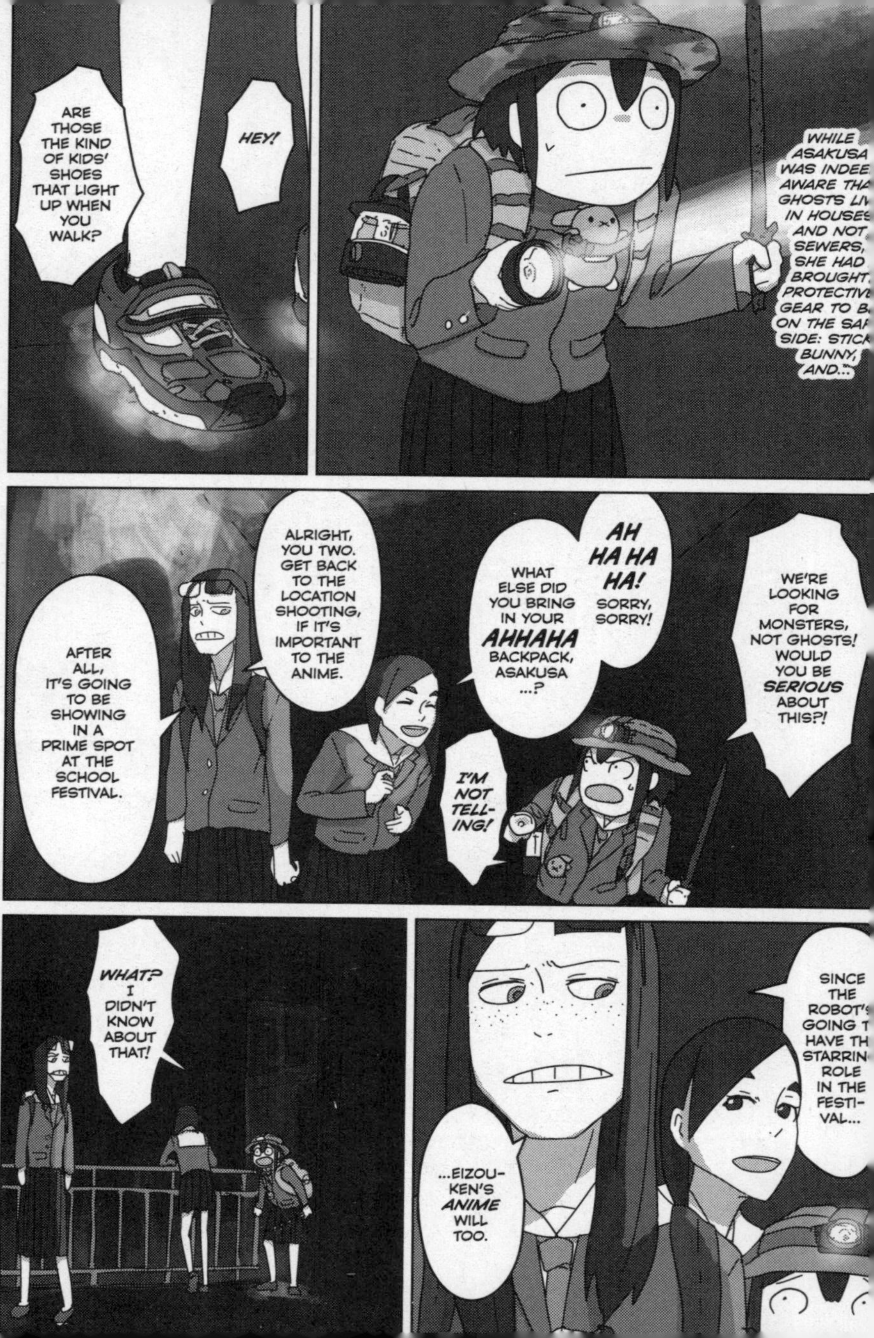
WHILE ASAKUSA WAS INDEE AWARE THA GHOSTS LIV IN HOUSES AND NOT SEWERS, SHE HAD BROUGHT PROTECTIVE GEAR TO B ON THE SA SIDE: STICK BUNNY, AND...
HEY!
ARE THOSE THE KIND OF KIDS' SHOES THAT LIGHT UP WHEN YOU WALK?
WE'RE LOOKING FOR MONSTERS, NOT GHOSTS! WOULD YOU BE SERIOUS ABOUT THIS?!
AH HA HA HA! SORRY, SORRY!
WHAT ELSE DID YOU BRING IN YOUR AHHAHA BACKPACK, ASAKUSA ...?
I'M NOT TELL-ING!
ALRIGHT, YOU TWO. GET BACK TO THE LOCATION SHOOTING, IF IT'S IMPORTANT TO THE ANIME.
AFTER ALL, IT'S GOING TO BE SHOWING IN A PRIME SPOT AT THE SCHOOL FESTIVAL.
SINCE THE ROBOT'S GOING T HAVE TH STARRIN ROLE IN THE FESTI-VAL...
...EIZOU-KEN'S ANIME WILL TOO.
WHAT? I DIDN'T KNOW ABOUT THAT!

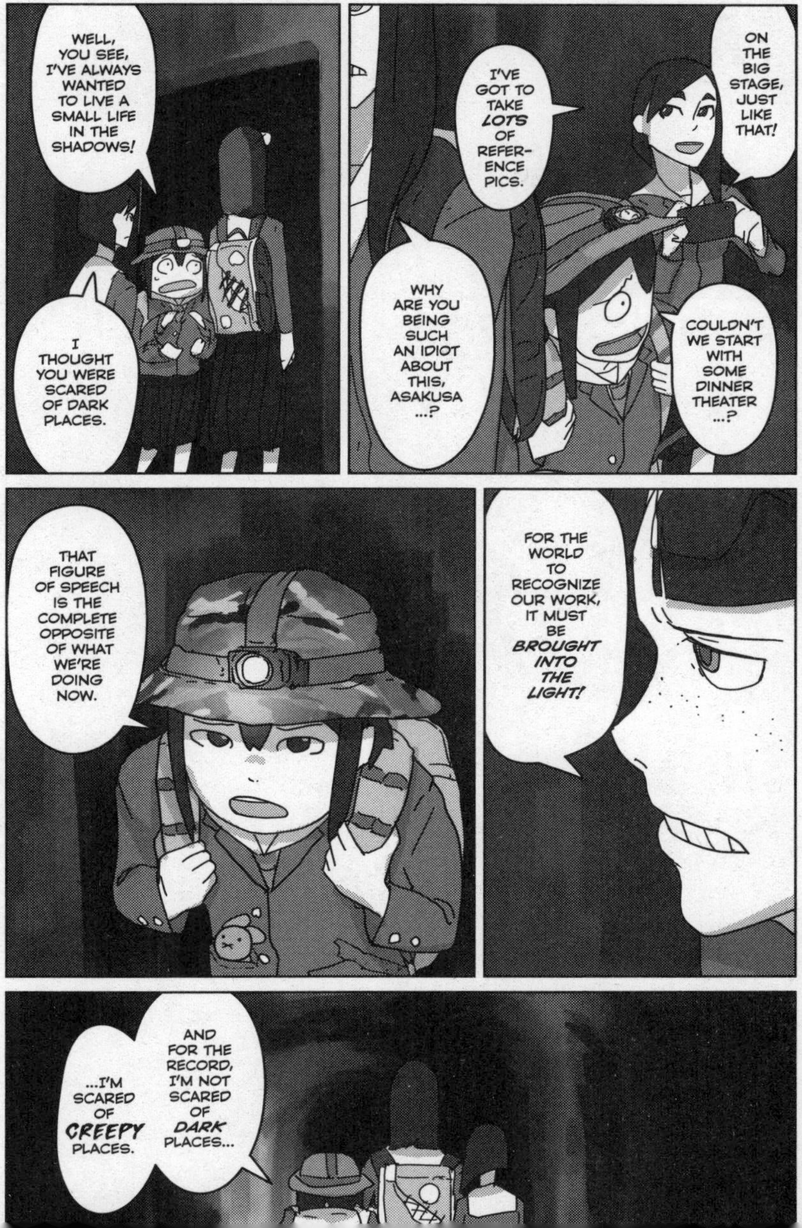
ON THE BIG STAGE, JUST LIKE THAT!
I'VE GOT TO TAKE LOTS OF REFERENCE PICS.
COULDN'T WE START WITH SOME DINNER THEATER ...?
WHY ARE YOU BEING SUCH AN IDIOT ABOUT THIS, ASAKUSA ...?
WELL, YOU SEE, I'VE ALWAYS WANTED TO LIVE A SMALL LIFE IN THE SHADOWS!
I THOUGHT YOU WERE SCARED OF DARK PLACES.
FOR THE WORLD TO RECOGNIZE OUR WORK, IT MUST BE BROUGHT INTO THE LIGHT!
THAT FIGURE OF SPEECH IS THE COMPLETE OPPOSITE OF WHAT WE'RE DOING NOW.
AND FOR THE RECORD, I'M NOT SCARED OF DARK PLACES...
...I'M SCARED OF CREEPY PLACES.

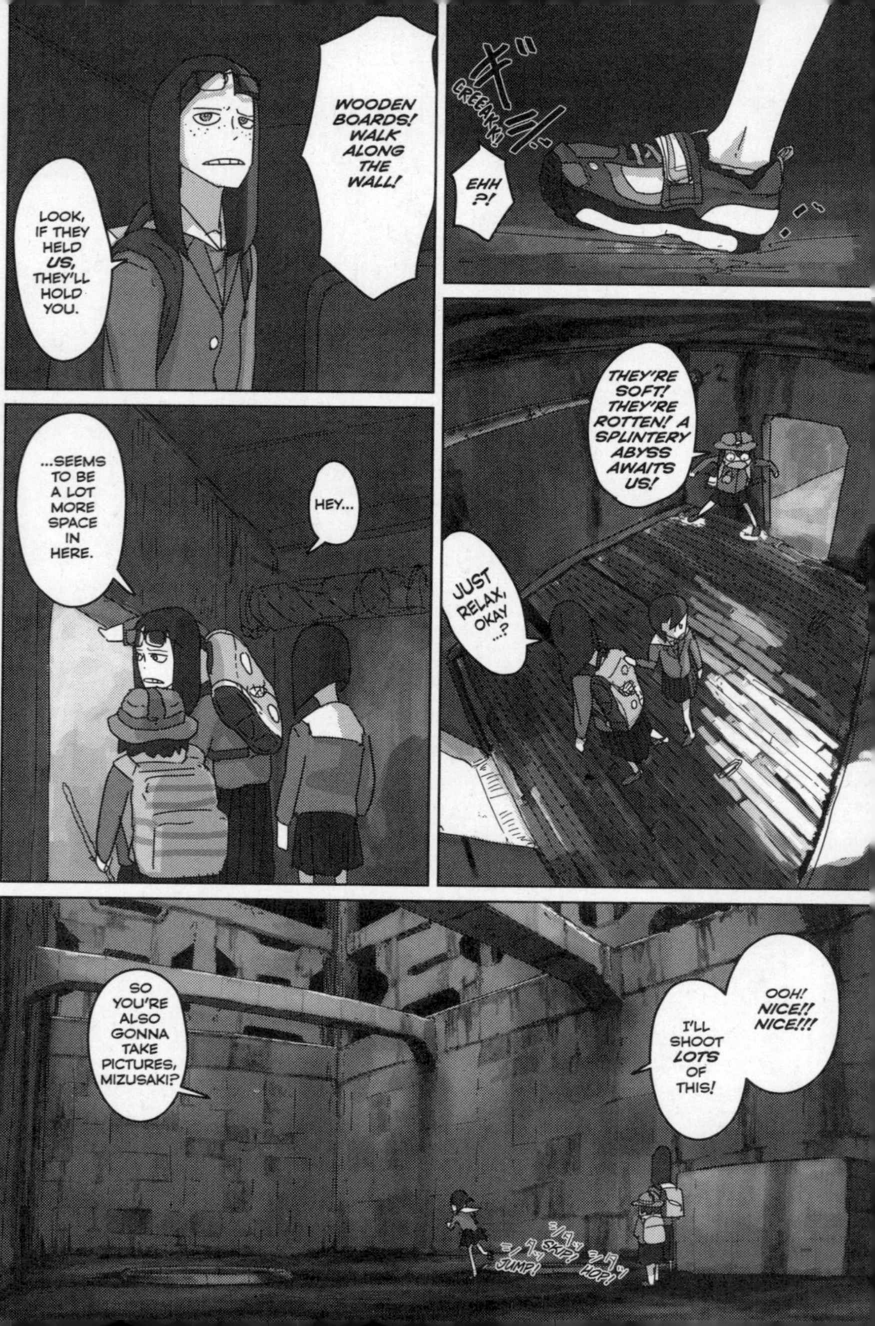
CREEEAK!
EHH?!
WOODEN BOARDS! WALK ALONG THE WALL!
LOOK, IF THEY HELD US, THEY'LL HOLD YOU.
THEY'RE SOFT! THEY'RE ROTTEN! A SPLINTERY ABYSS AWAITS US!
JUST RELAX, OKAY ...?
HEY...
...SEEMS TO BE A LOT MORE SPACE IN HERE.
OOH! NICE!! NICE!!!
I'LL SHOOT LOTS OF THIS!
SO YOU'RE ALSO GONNA TAKE PICTURES, MIZUSAKI?
HOP!
SKIP!
JUMP!

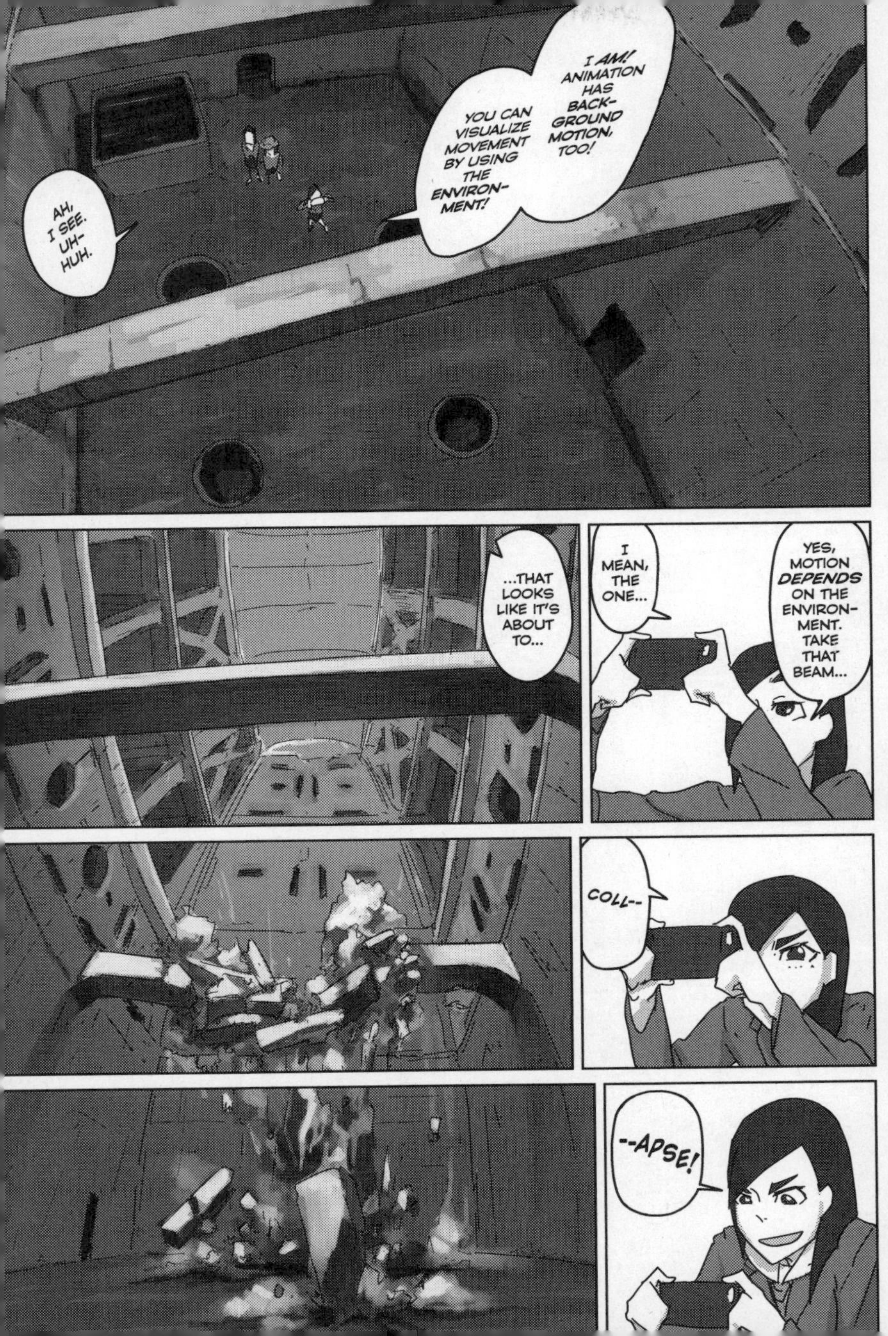
I AM! ANIMATION HAS BACK-GROUND MOTION, TOO!
YOU CAN VISUALIZE MOVEMENT BY USING THE ENVIRON-MENT!
AH, I SEE. UH-HUH.
YES, MOTION DEPENDS ON THE ENVIRON-MENT. TAKE THAT BEAM...
I MEAN, THE ONE...
...THAT LOOKS LIKE IT'S ABOUT TO...
COLL--
--APSE!

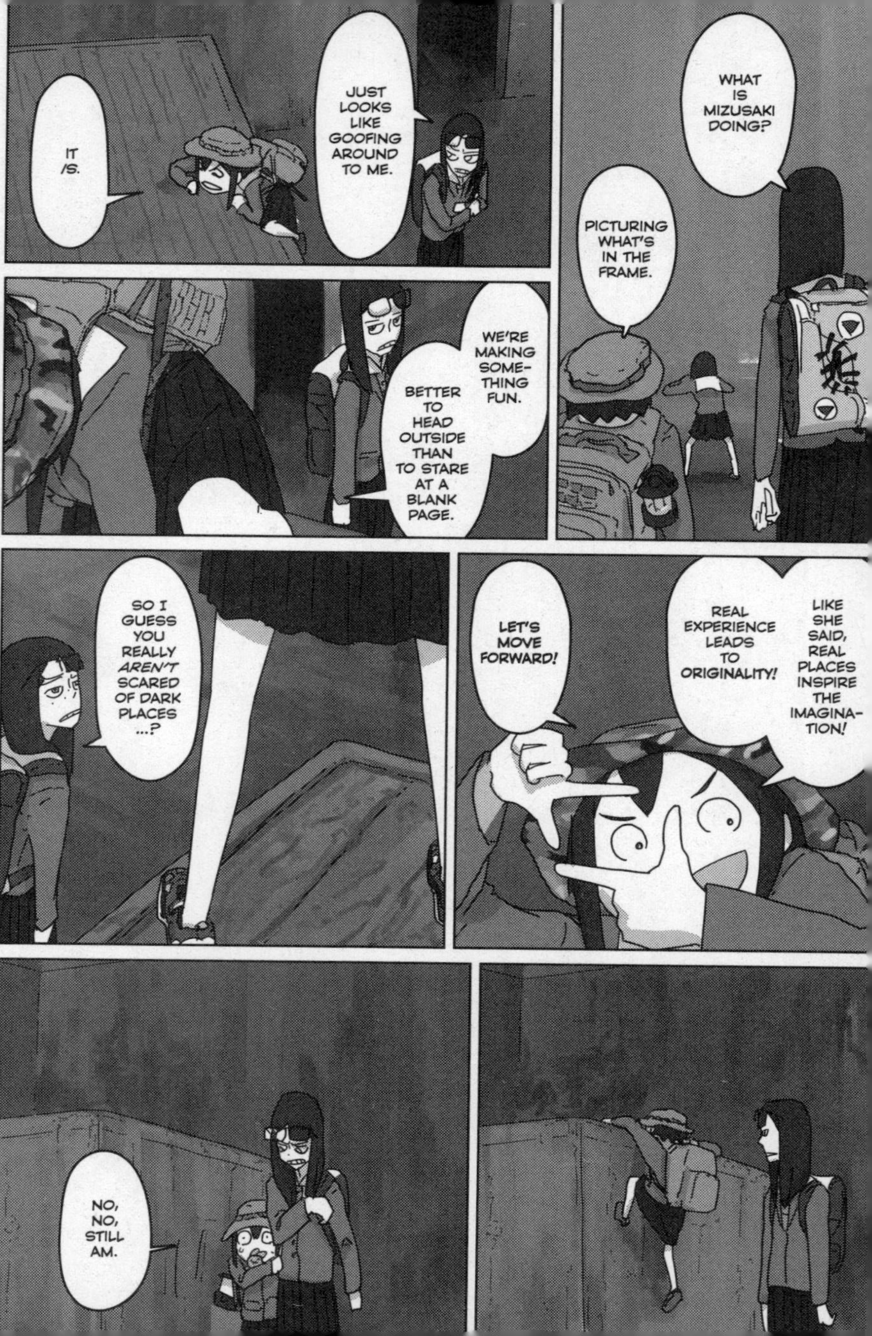
WHAT IS MIZUSAKI DOING?
PICTURING WHAT'S IN THE FRAME.
JUST LOOKS LIKE GOOFING AROUND TO ME.
IT *IS*.
WE'RE MAKING SOME-THING FUN.
BETTER TO HEAD OUTSIDE THAN TO STARE AT A BLANK PAGE.
LIKE SHE SAID, REAL PLACES INSPIRE THE IMAGINA-TION!
REAL EXPERIENCE LEADS TO ORIGINALITY!
LET'S MOVE FORWARD!
SO I GUESS YOU REALLY *AREN'T* SCARED OF DARK PLACES ...?
NO, NO, STILL AM.

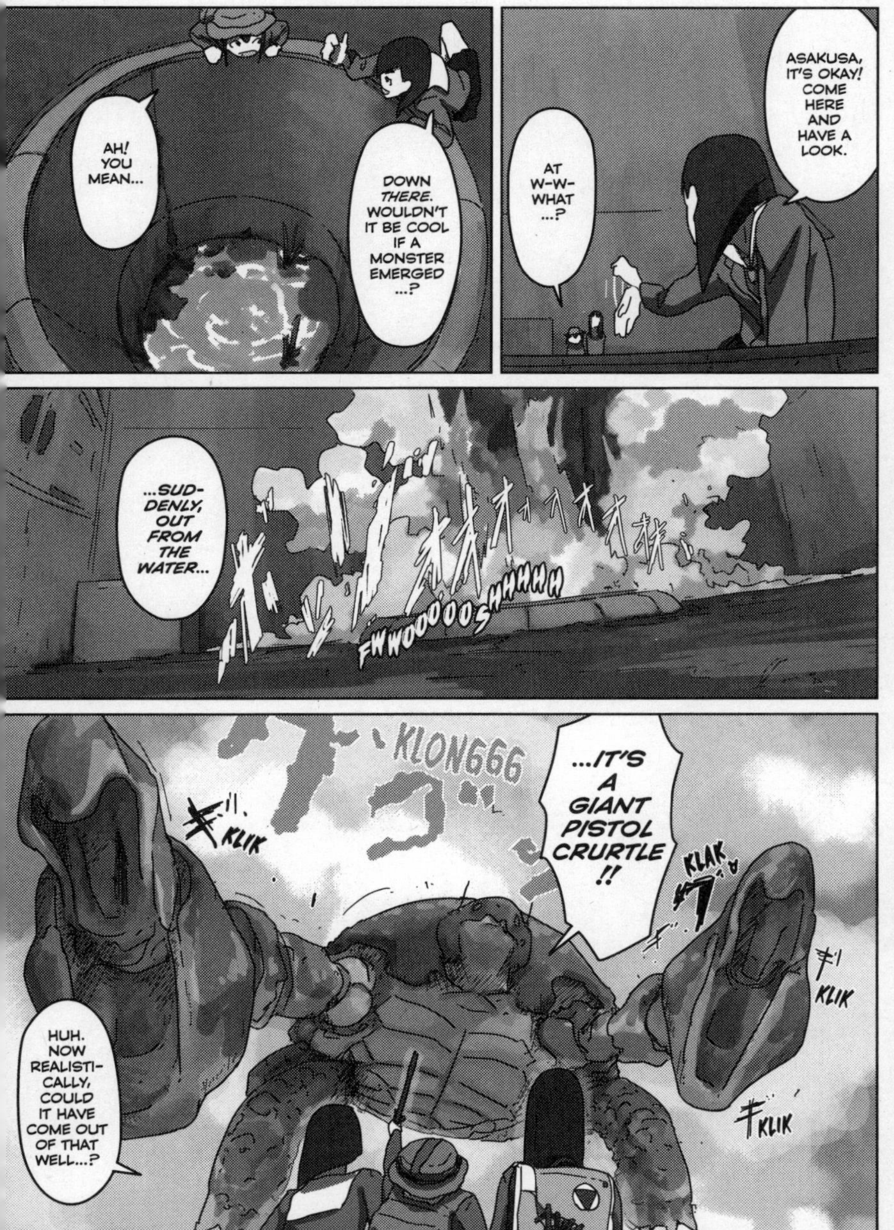
ASAKUSA, IT'S OKAY! COME HERE AND HAVE A LOOK.
AT W-W-WHAT ...?
DOWN THERE. WOULDN'T IT BE COOL IF A MONSTER EMERGED ...?
AH! YOU MEAN...
...SUDDENLY, OUT FROM THE WATER...
FWOOOOOOSHHHHH
KLIK
KLAK
...IT'S A GIANT PISTOL CRURTLE!!
KLONGGG
KLIK
KLIK
KLIK
HUH. NOW REALISTICALLY, COULD IT HAVE COME OUT OF THAT WELL...?

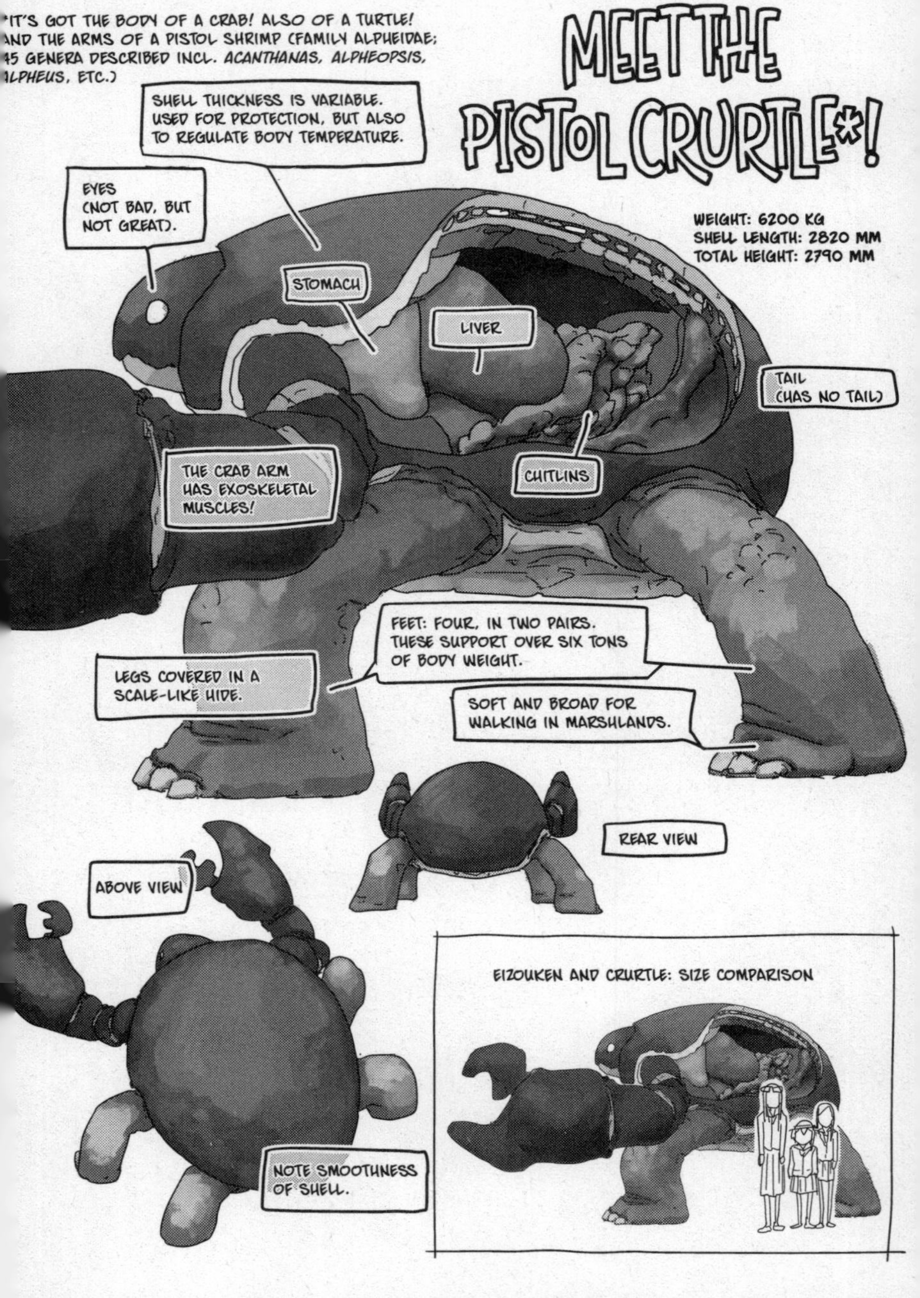
MEET THE PISTOL CRURTLE*!
*IT'S GOT THE BODY OF A CRAB! ALSO OF A TURTLE! AND THE ARMS OF A PISTOL SHRIMP (FAMILY ALPHEIDAE; 45 GENERA DESCRIBED INCL. ACANTHANAS, ALPHEOPSIS, ALPHEUS, ETC.)
SHELL THICKNESS IS VARIABLE. USED FOR PROTECTION, BUT ALSO TO REGULATE BODY TEMPERATURE.
EYES (NOT BAD, BUT NOT GREAT).
WEIGHT: 6200 KG
SHELL LENGTH: 2820 MM
TOTAL HEIGHT: 2790 MM
STOMACH
LIVER
TAIL (HAS NO TAIL)
THE CRAB ARM HAS EXOSKELETAL MUSCLES!
CHITLINS
FEET: FOUR, IN TWO PAIRS. THESE SUPPORT OVER SIX TONS OF BODY WEIGHT.
LEGS COVERED IN A SCALE-LIKE HIDE.
SOFT AND BROAD FOR WALKING IN MARSHLANDS.
REAR VIEW
ABOVE VIEW
NOTE SMOOTHNESS OF SHELL.
EIZOUKEN AND CRURTLE: SIZE COMPARISON

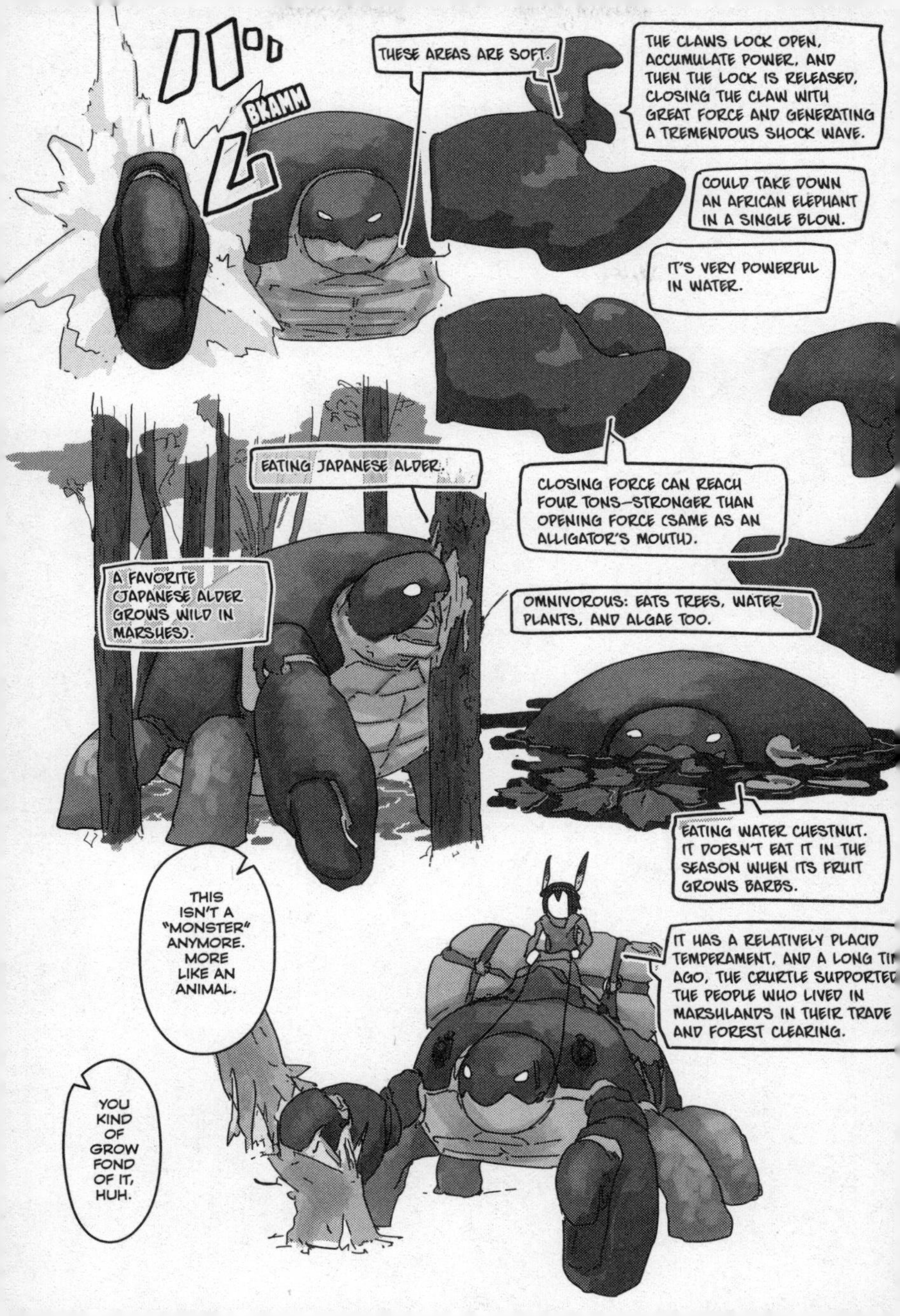
THE CLAWS LOCK OPEN, ACCUMULATE POWER, AND THEN THE LOCK IS RELEASED, CLOSING THE CLAW WITH GREAT FORCE AND GENERATING A TREMENDOUS SHOCK WAVE.
COULD TAKE DOWN AN AFRICAN ELEPHANT IN A SINGLE BLOW.
THESE AREAS ARE SOFT.
BKAMM
IT'S VERY POWERFUL IN WATER.
CLOSING FORCE CAN REACH FOUR TONS—STRONGER THAN OPENING FORCE (SAME AS AN ALLIGATOR'S MOUTH).
OMNIVOROUS: EATS TREES, WATER PLANTS, AND ALGAE TOO.
EATING WATER CHESTNUT. IT DOESN'T EAT IT IN THE SEASON WHEN ITS FRUIT GROWS BARBS.
EATING JAPANESE ALDER.
A FAVORITE (JAPANESE ALDER GROWS WILD IN MARSHES).
IT HAS A RELATIVELY PLACID TEMPERAMENT, AND A LONG TI
AGO, THE CRURTLE SUPPORTE
THE PEOPLE WHO LIVED IN MARSHLANDS IN THEIR TRADE AND FOREST CLEARING.
THIS ISN'T A "MONSTER" ANYMORE. MORE LIKE AN ANIMAL.
YOU KIND OF GROW FOND OF IT, HUH.

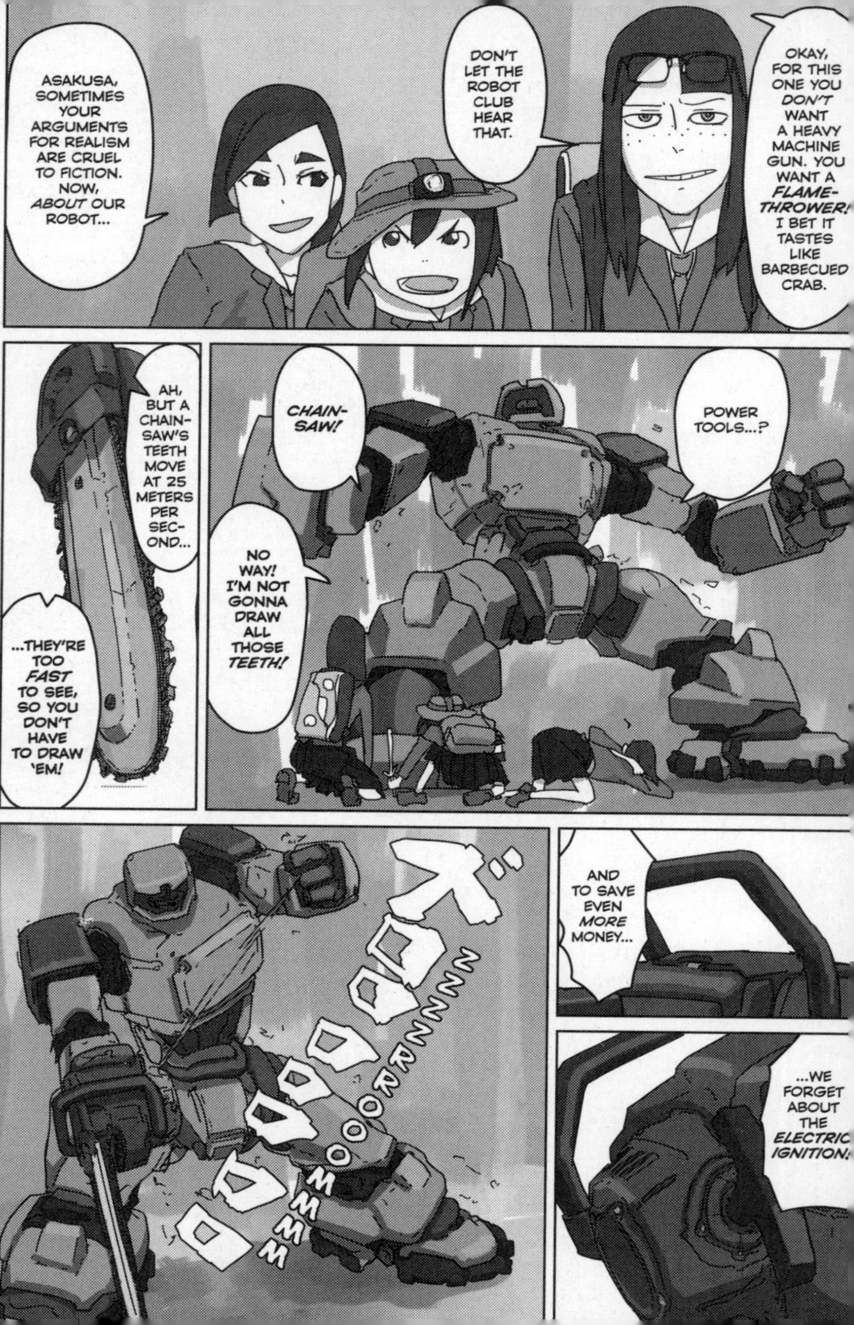
OKAY, FOR THIS ONE YOU *DON'T* WANT A HEAVY MACHINE GUN. YOU WANT A ***FLAME-THROWER!*** I BET IT TASTES LIKE BARBECUED CRAB.
DON'T LET THE ROBOT CLUB HEAR THAT.
ASAKUSA, SOMETIMES YOUR ARGUMENTS FOR REALISM ARE CRUEL TO FICTION. NOW, *ABOUT* OUR ROBOT...
POWER TOOLS...?
CHAIN-SAW!
NO WAY! I'M NOT GONNA DRAW ALL THOSE *TEETH!*
AH, BUT A CHAIN-SAW'S TEETH MOVE AT 25 METERS PER SEC-OND...
...THEY'RE TOO *FAST* TO SEE, SO YOU DON'T HAVE TO DRAW 'EM!
AND TO SAVE EVEN *MORE* MONEY...
...WE FORGET ABOUT THE ***ELECTRIC IGNITION!***
NNNNNRROOOOMMMMM

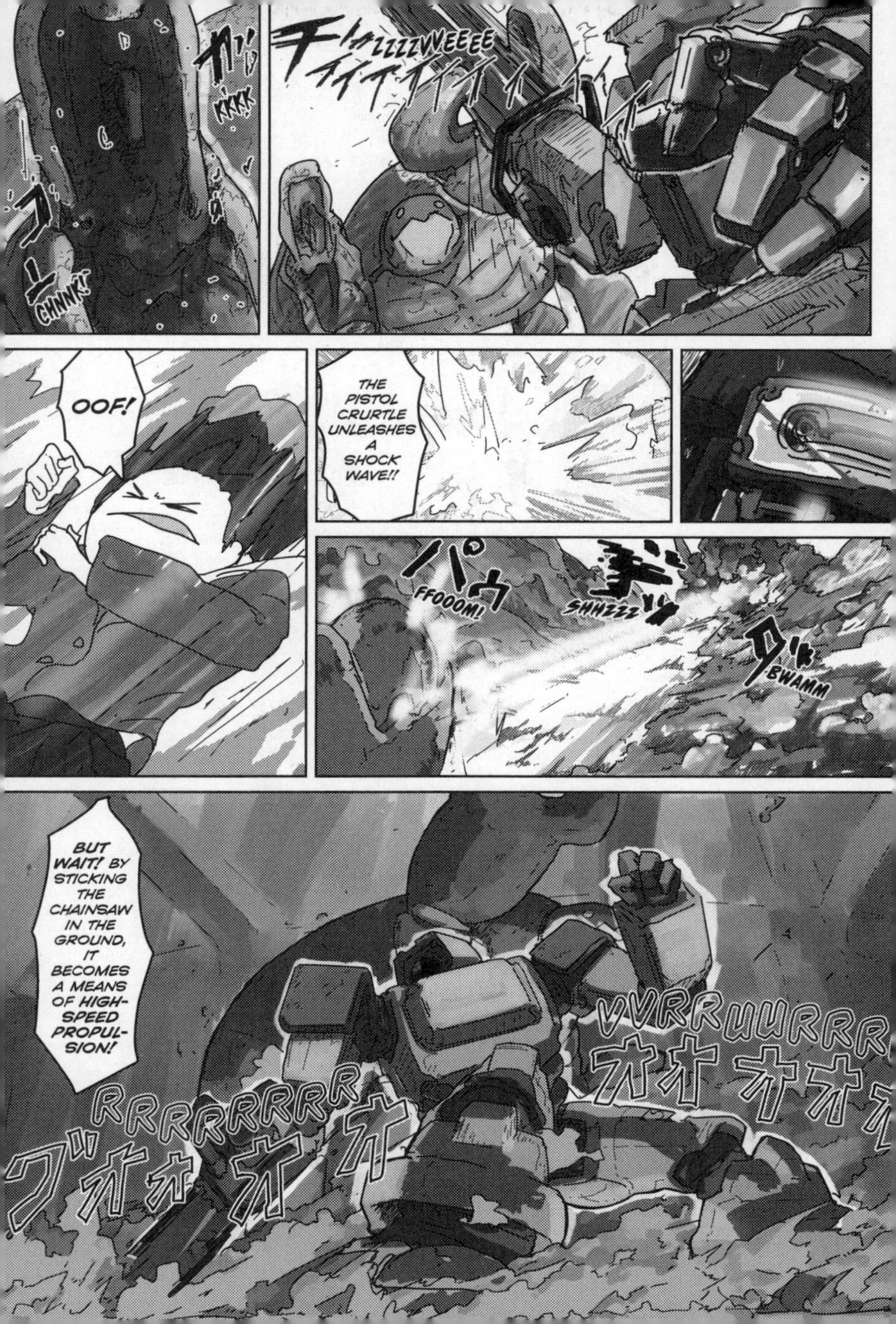
ZZZZVVEEEE
KKKK
CHNNK!
THE PISTOL CRURTLE UNLEASHES A SHOCK WAVE!!
パウ
FFOOOM!
SHHZZZ
BWAMM
OOF!
BUT WAIT! BY STICKING THE CHAINSAW IN THE GROUND, IT BECOMES A MEANS OF HIGH-SPEED PROPULSION!
VVRRRUUURRRR
RRRRRRRRR

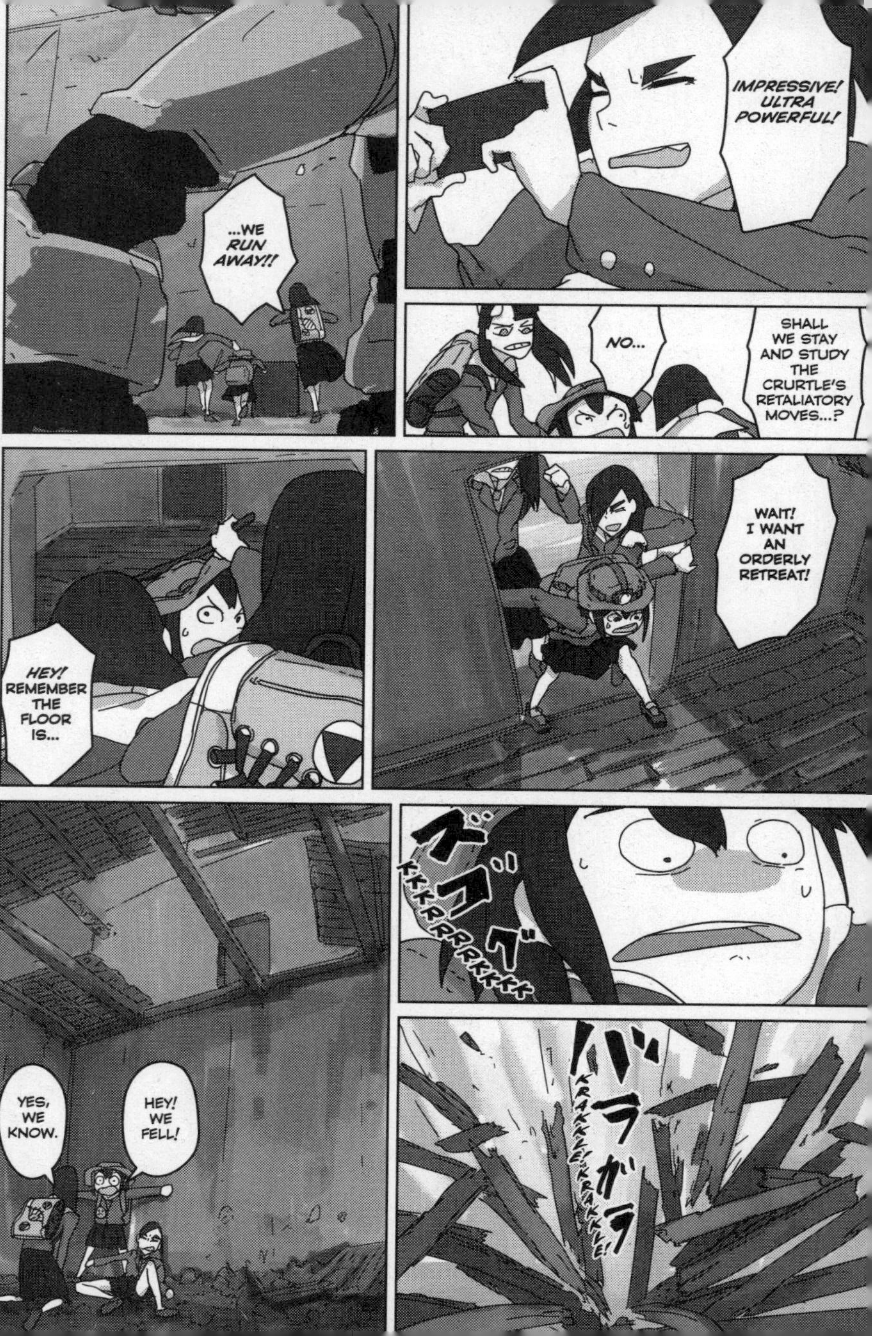
IMPRESSIVE! ULTRA POWERFUL!
SHALL WE STAY AND STUDY THE CRURTLE'S RETALIATORY MOVES...?
NO...
...WE RUN AWAY!!
WAIT! I WANT AN ORDERLY RETREAT!
HEY! REMEMBER THE FLOOR IS...
KRAKKLE KRAKKLE KRAKKLE!
HEY! WE FELL!
YES, WE KNOW.

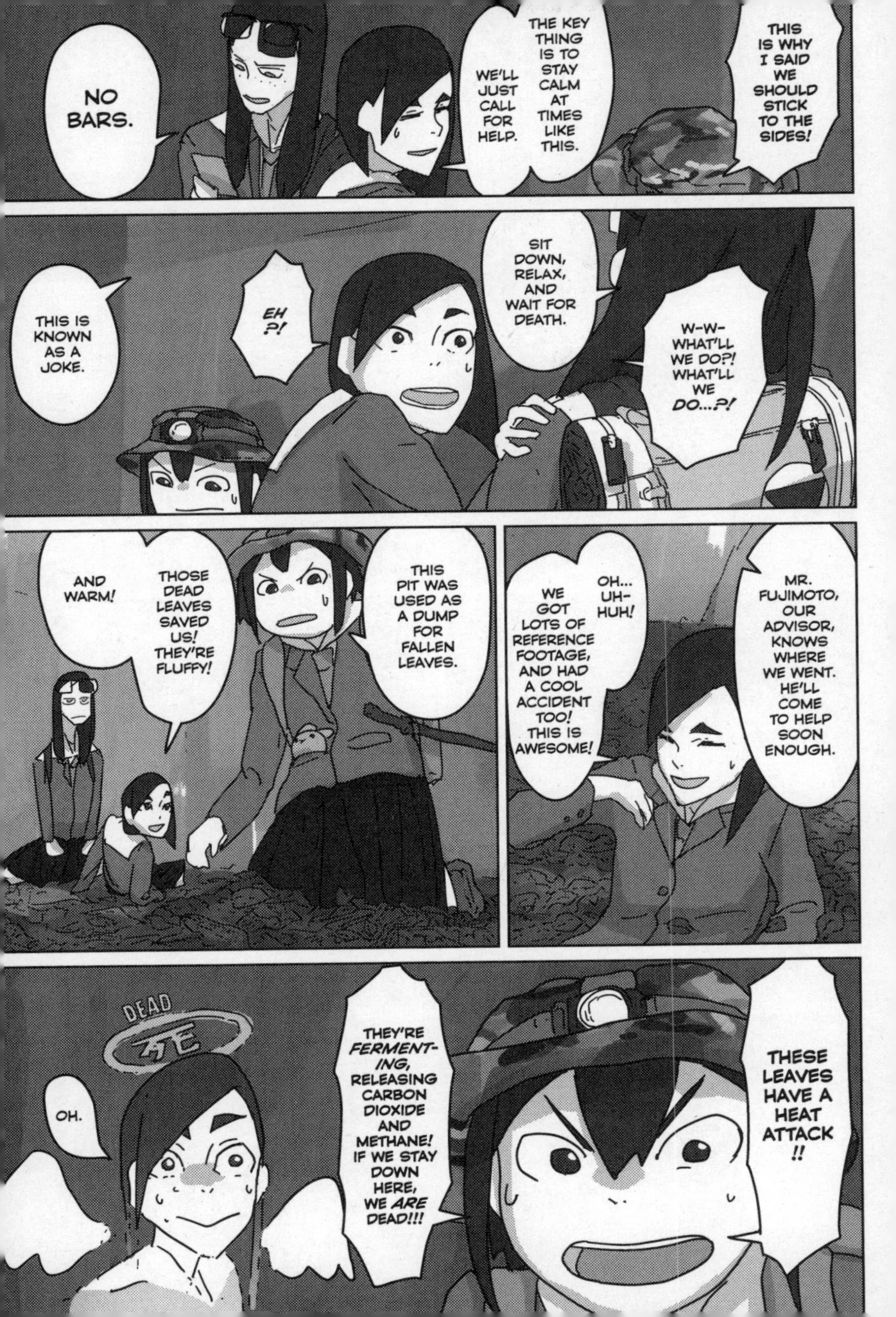
THIS IS WHY I SAID WE SHOULD STICK TO THE SIDES!
THE KEY THING IS TO STAY CALM AT TIMES LIKE THIS.
WE'LL JUST CALL FOR HELP.
NO BARS.
W-W-WHAT'LL WE DO?! WHAT'LL WE DO...?!
SIT DOWN, RELAX, AND WAIT FOR DEATH.
EH?!
THIS IS KNOWN AS A JOKE.
MR. FUJIMOTO, OUR ADVISOR, KNOWS WHERE WE WENT. HE'LL COME TO HELP SOON ENOUGH.
OH... UH-HUH!
WE GOT LOTS OF REFERENCE FOOTAGE, AND HAD A COOL ACCIDENT TOO! THIS IS AWESOME!
THIS PIT WAS USED AS A DUMP FOR FALLEN LEAVES.
THOSE DEAD LEAVES SAVED US! THEY'RE FLUFFY!
AND WARM!
THESE LEAVES HAVE A HEAT ATTACK!!
THEY'RE FERMENTING, RELEASING CARBON DIOXIDE AND METHANE! IF WE STAY DOWN HERE, WE ARE DEAD!!!
DEAD
OH.

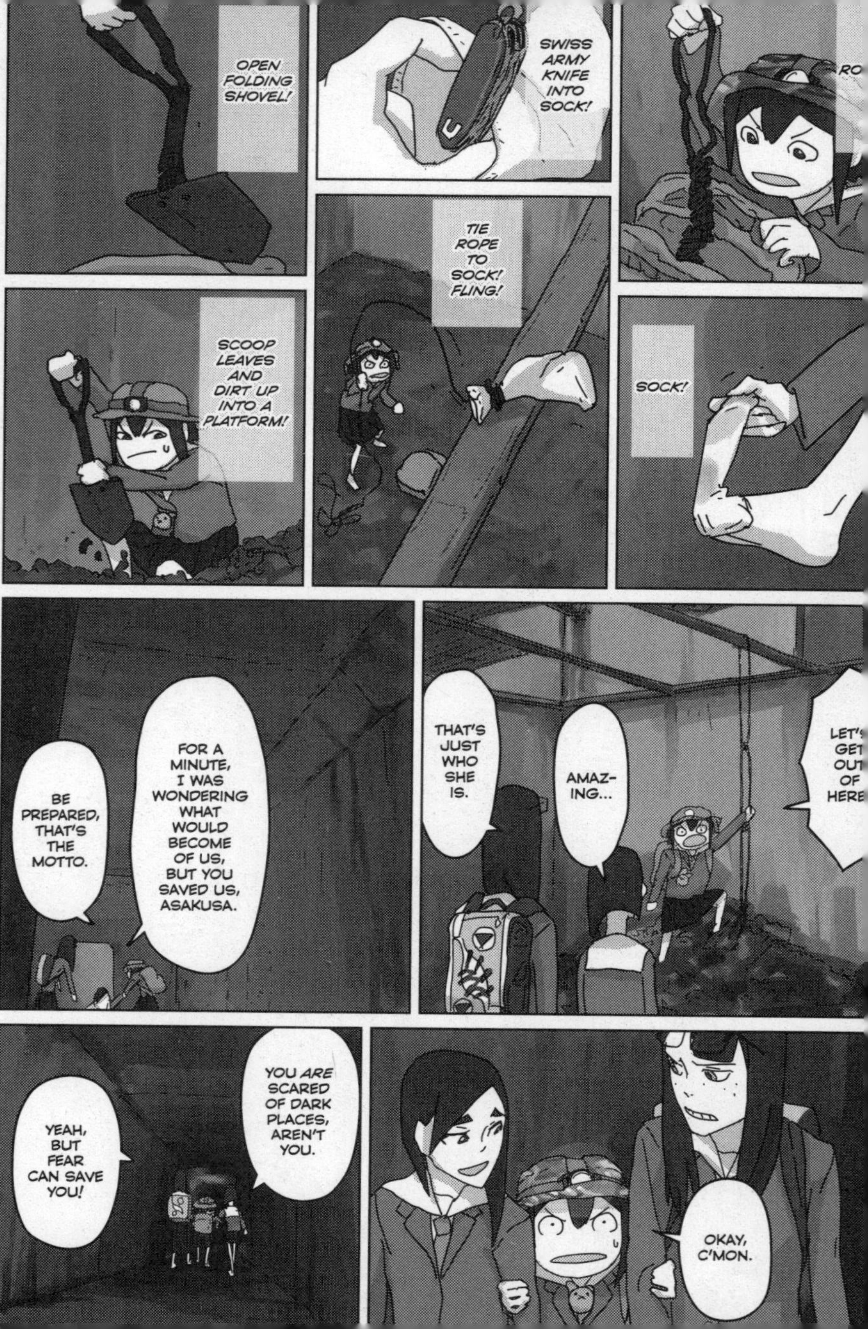
SWISS ARMY KNIFE INTO SOCK!
OPEN FOLDING SHOVEL!
SOCK!
TIE ROPE TO SOCK! FLING!
SCOOP LEAVES AND DIRT UP INTO A PLATFORM!
LET'S GET OUT OF HERE
AMAZ-ING...
THAT'S JUST WHO SHE IS.
FOR A MINUTE, I WAS WONDERING WHAT WOULD BECOME OF US, BUT YOU SAVED US, ASAKUSA.
BE PREPARED, THAT'S THE MOTTO.
OKAY, C'MON.
YOU *ARE* SCARED OF DARK PLACES, AREN'T YOU.
YEAH, BUT FEAR CAN SAVE YOU!

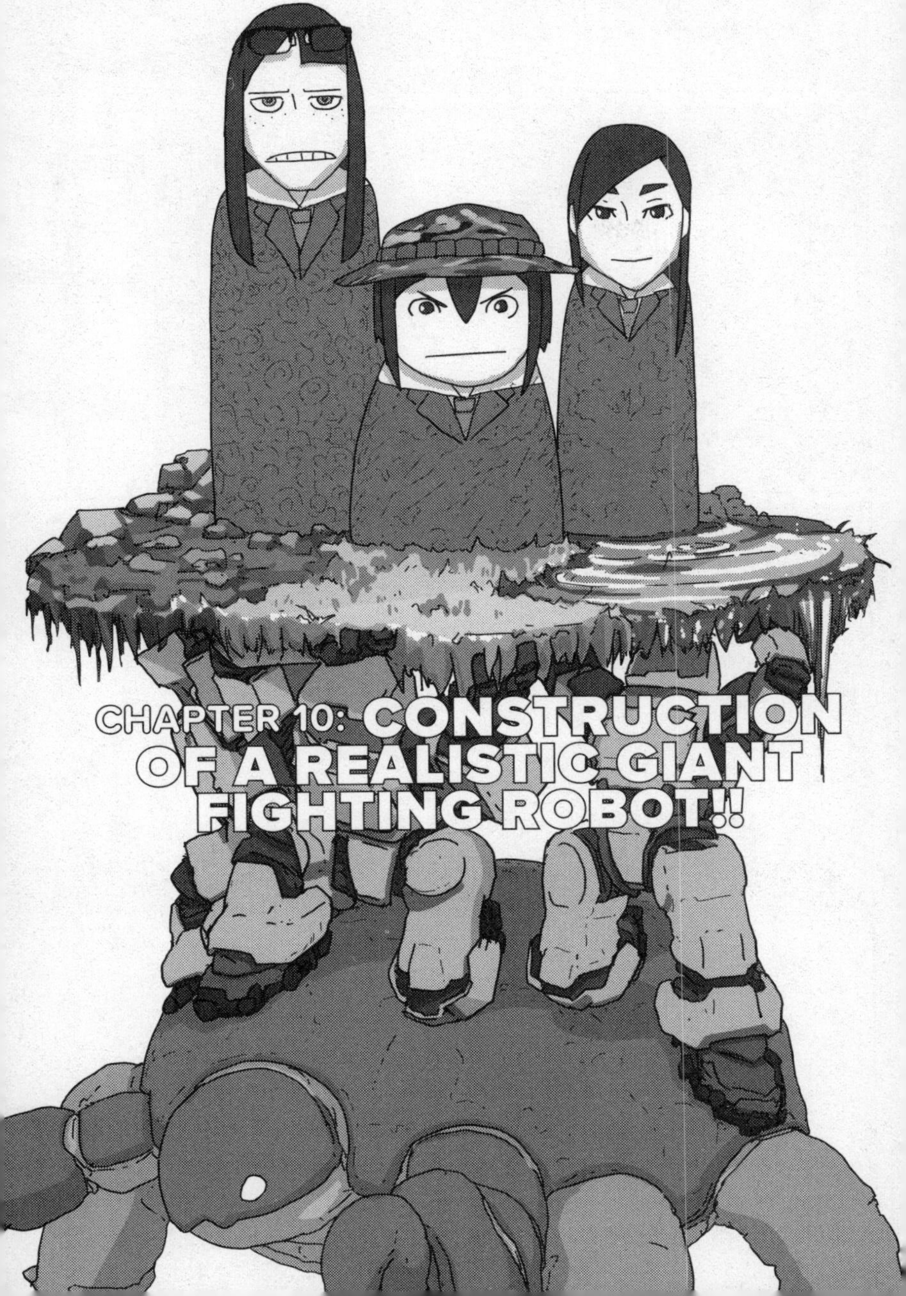
CHAPTER 10: CONSTRUCTION OF A REALISTIC GIANT FIGHTING ROBOT!!

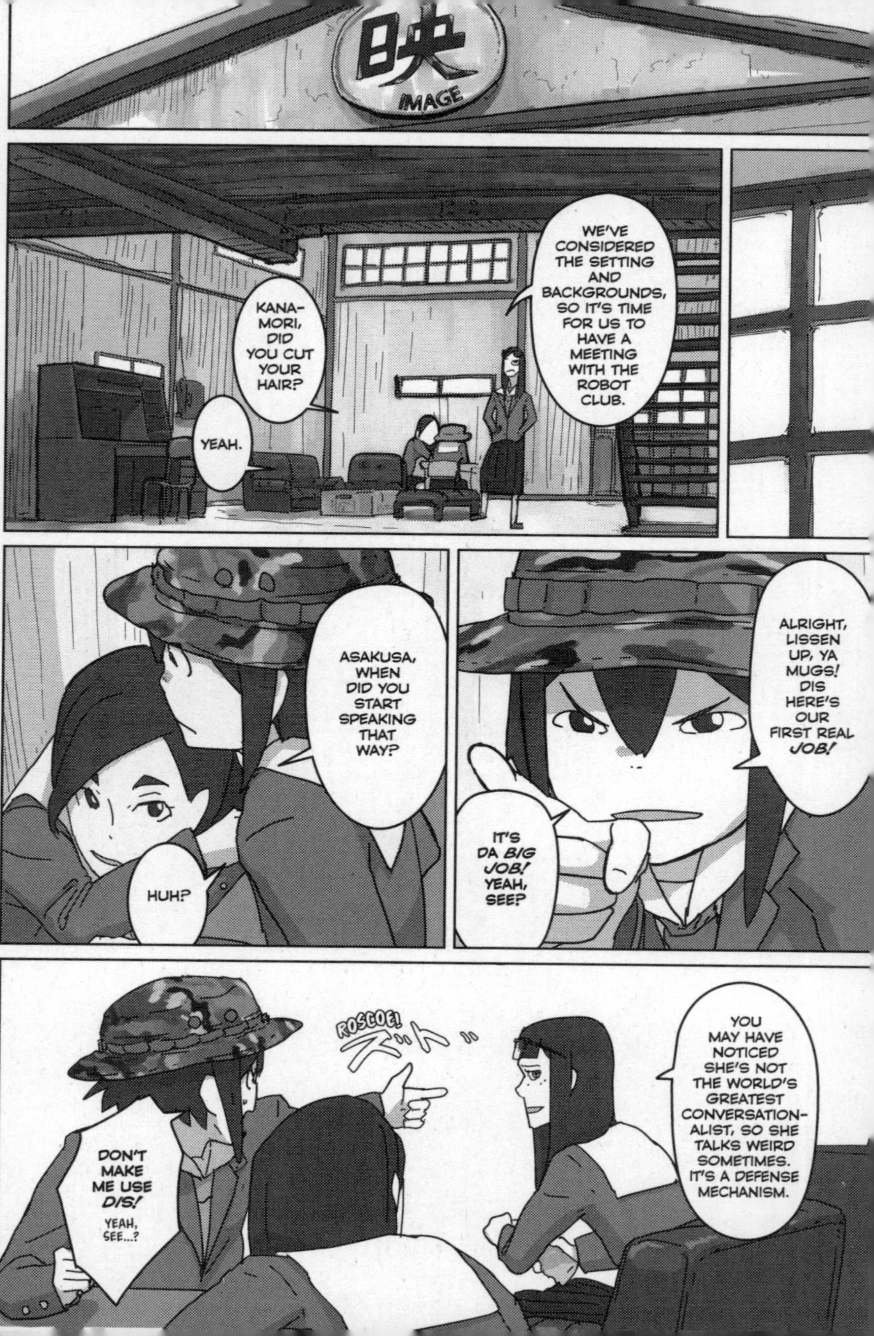
映
IMAGE
WE'VE CONSIDERED THE SETTING AND BACKGROUNDS, SO IT'S TIME FOR US TO HAVE A MEETING WITH THE ROBOT CLUB.
KANA-MORI, DID YOU CUT YOUR HAIR?
YEAH.
ALRIGHT, LISSEN UP, YA MUGS! DIS HERE'S OUR FIRST REAL *JOB!*
IT'S DA *BIG JOB!* YEAH, SEE?
ASAKUSA, WHEN DID YOU START SPEAKING THAT WAY?
HUH?
YOU MAY HAVE NOTICED SHE'S NOT THE WORLD'S GREATEST CONVERSATION-ALIST, SO SHE TALKS WEIRD SOMETIMES. IT'S A DEFENSE MECHANISM.
ROSCOE!
DON'T MAKE ME USE *DIS!*
YEAH, SEE...?

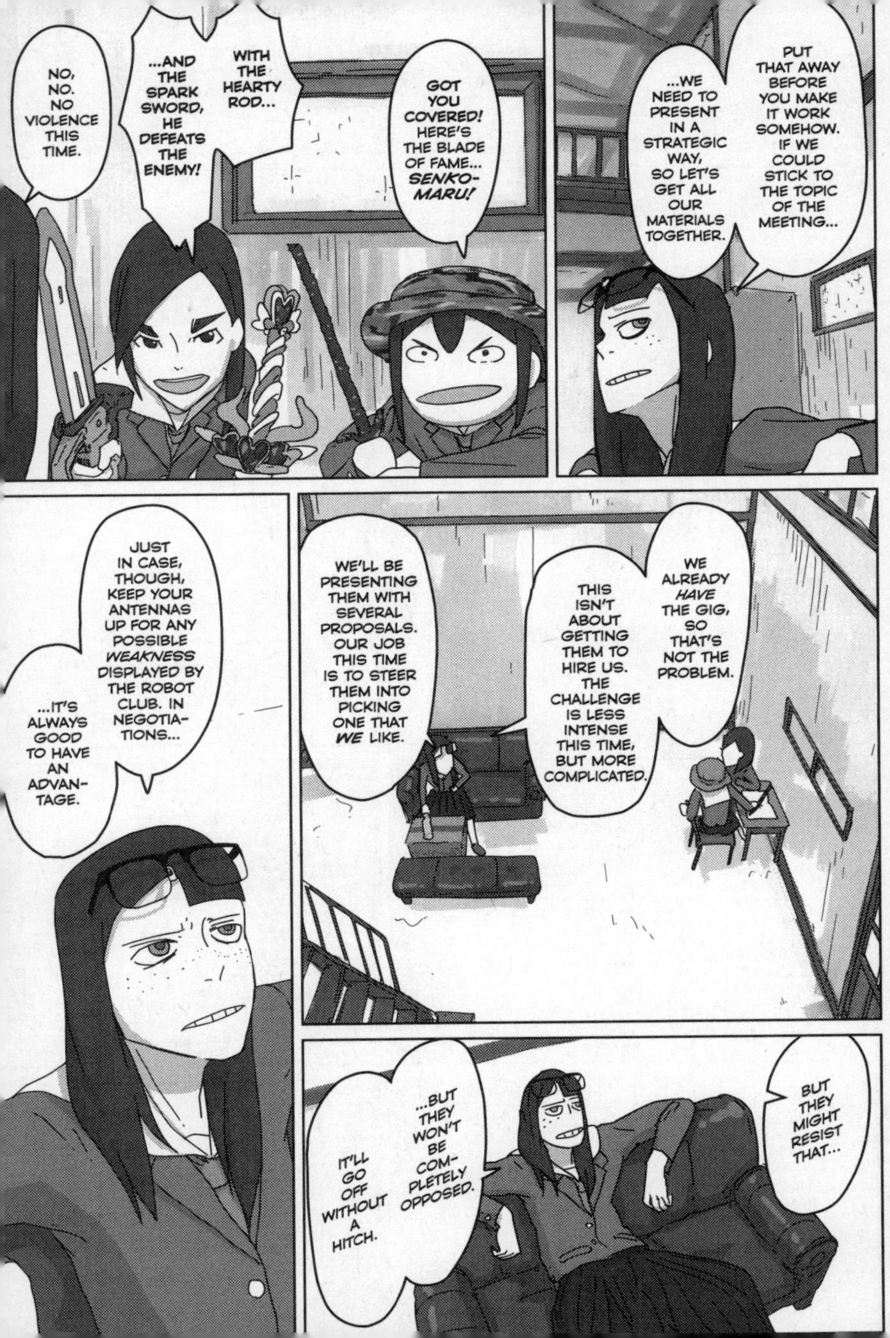
PUT THAT AWAY BEFORE YOU MAKE IT WORK SOMEHOW. IF WE COULD STICK TO THE TOPIC OF THE MEETING...
...WE NEED TO PRESENT IN A STRATEGIC WAY, SO LET'S GET ALL OUR MATERIALS TOGETHER.
GOT YOU COVERED! HERE'S THE BLADE OF FAME... *SENKO-MARU!*
WITH THE HEARTY ROD...
...AND THE SPARK SWORD, HE DEFEATS THE ENEMY!
NO, NO. NO VIOLENCE THIS TIME.
WE ALREADY *HAVE* THE GIG, SO THAT'S NOT THE PROBLEM.
THIS ISN'T ABOUT GETTING THEM TO HIRE US. THE CHALLENGE IS LESS INTENSE THIS TIME, BUT MORE COMPLICATED.
WE'LL BE PRESENTING THEM WITH SEVERAL PROPOSALS. OUR JOB THIS TIME IS TO STEER THEM INTO PICKING ONE THAT ***WE*** LIKE.
BUT THEY MIGHT RESIST THAT...
...BUT THEY WON'T BE COM-PLETELY OPPOSED.
IT'LL GO OFF WITHOUT A HITCH.
JUST IN CASE, THOUGH, KEEP YOUR ANTENNAS UP FOR ANY POSSIBLE *WEAKNESS* DISPLAYED BY THE ROBOT CLUB. IN NEGOTIA-TIONS...
...IT'S ALWAYS GOOD TO HAVE AN ADVAN-TAGE.

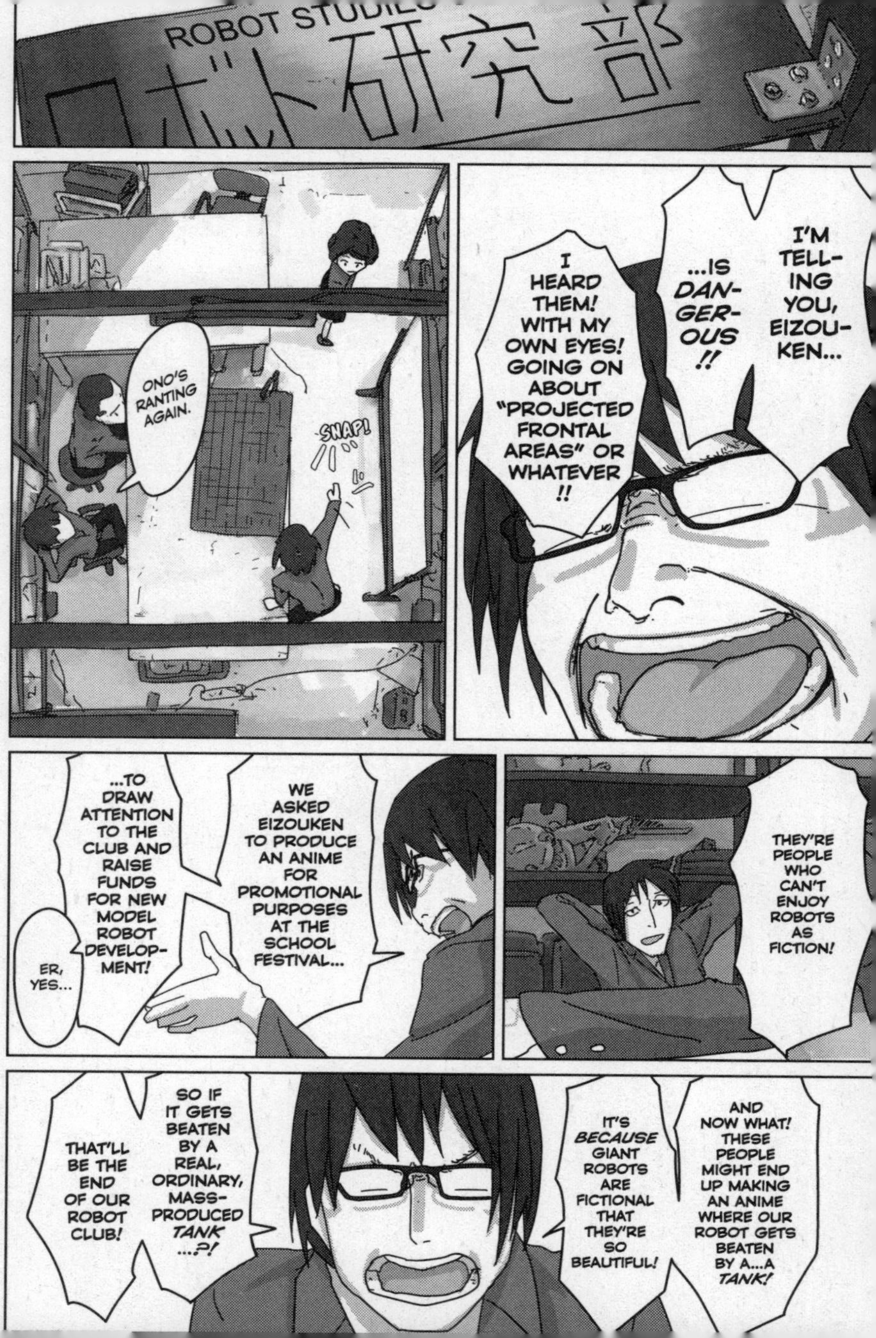
ROBOT STUDI
ロボット研究部
I'M TELLING YOU, EIZOUKEN...
...IS DANGEROUS!!
I HEARD THEM! WITH MY OWN EYES! GOING ON ABOUT "PROJECTED FRONTAL AREAS" OR WHATEVER!!
ONO'S RANTING AGAIN.
SNAP!
THEY'RE PEOPLE WHO CAN'T ENJOY ROBOTS AS FICTION!
WE ASKED EIZOUKEN TO PRODUCE AN ANIME FOR PROMOTIONAL PURPOSES AT THE SCHOOL FESTIVAL...
...TO DRAW ATTENTION TO THE CLUB AND RAISE FUNDS FOR NEW MODEL ROBOT DEVELOPMENT!
ER, YES...
AND NOW WHAT! THESE PEOPLE MIGHT END UP MAKING AN ANIME WHERE OUR ROBOT GETS BEATEN BY A...A TANK!
IT'S BECAUSE GIANT ROBOTS ARE FICTIONAL THAT THEY'RE SO BEAUTIFUL!
SO IF IT GETS BEATEN BY A REAL, ORDINARY, MASS-PRODUCED TANK...?!
THAT'LL BE THE END OF OUR ROBOT CLUB!

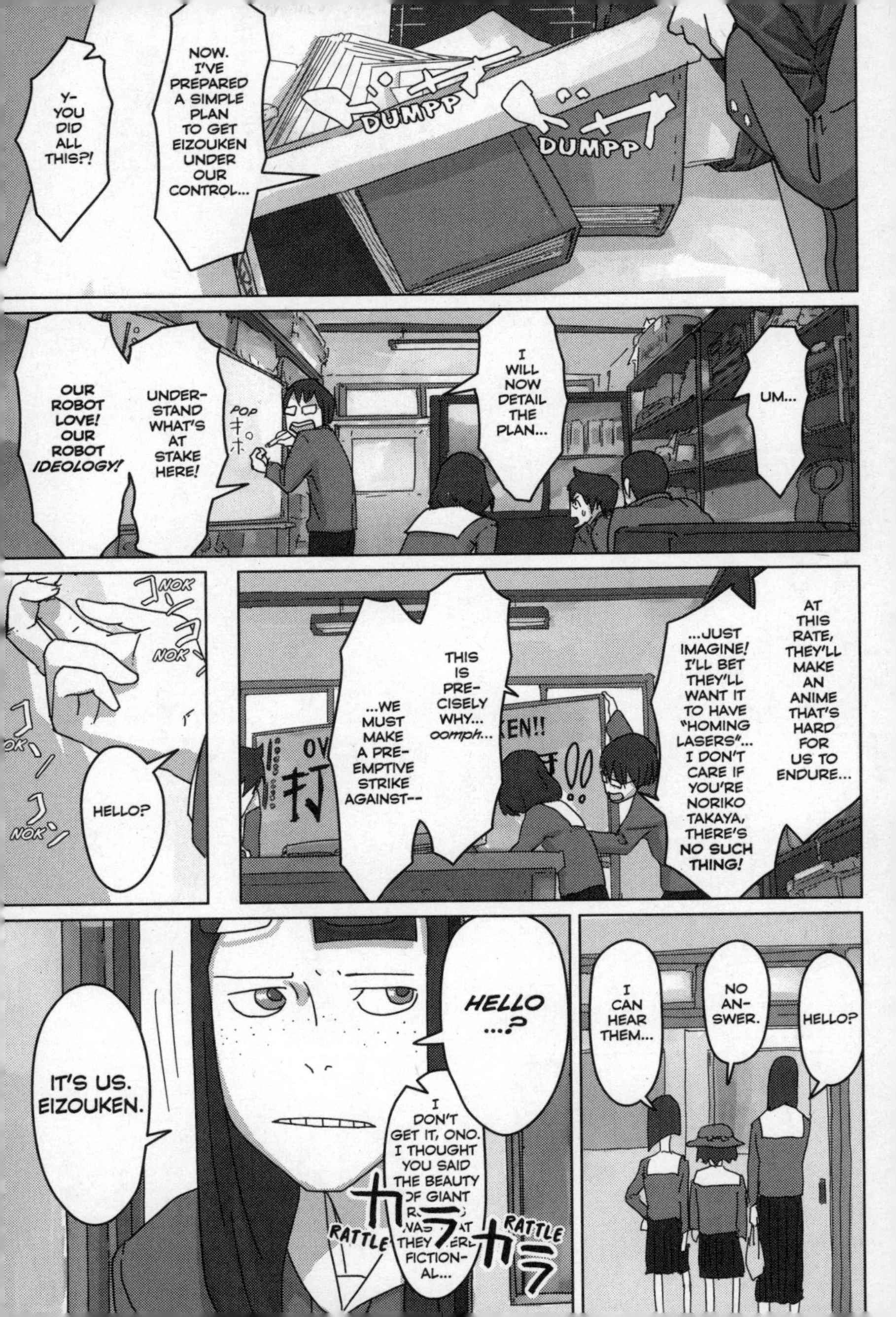
NOW. I'VE PREPARED A SIMPLE PLAN TO GET EIZOUKEN UNDER OUR CONTROL...
DUMPP
DUMPP
Y-YOU DID ALL THIS?!
UM...
I WILL NOW DETAIL THE PLAN...
POP
UNDER-STAND WHAT'S AT STAKE HERE!
OUR ROBOT LOVE! OUR ROBOT IDEOLOGY!
AT THIS RATE, THEY'LL MAKE AN ANIME THAT'S HARD FOR US TO ENDURE...
...JUST IMAGINE! I'LL BET THEY'LL WANT IT TO HAVE "HOMING LASERS"... I DON'T CARE IF YOU'RE NORIKO TAKAYA, THERE'S NO SUCH THING!
THIS IS PRE-CISELY WHY... oomph...
...WE MUST MAKE A PRE-EMPTIVE STRIKE AGAINST--
NOK
NOK
NOK
NOK
HELLO?
HELLO?
NO AN-SWER.
I CAN HEAR THEM...
HELLO ...?
I DON'T GET IT, ONO. I THOUGHT YOU SAID THE BEAUTY OF GIANT
FICTION-AL...
RATTLE
RATTLE
IT'S US. EIZOUKEN.

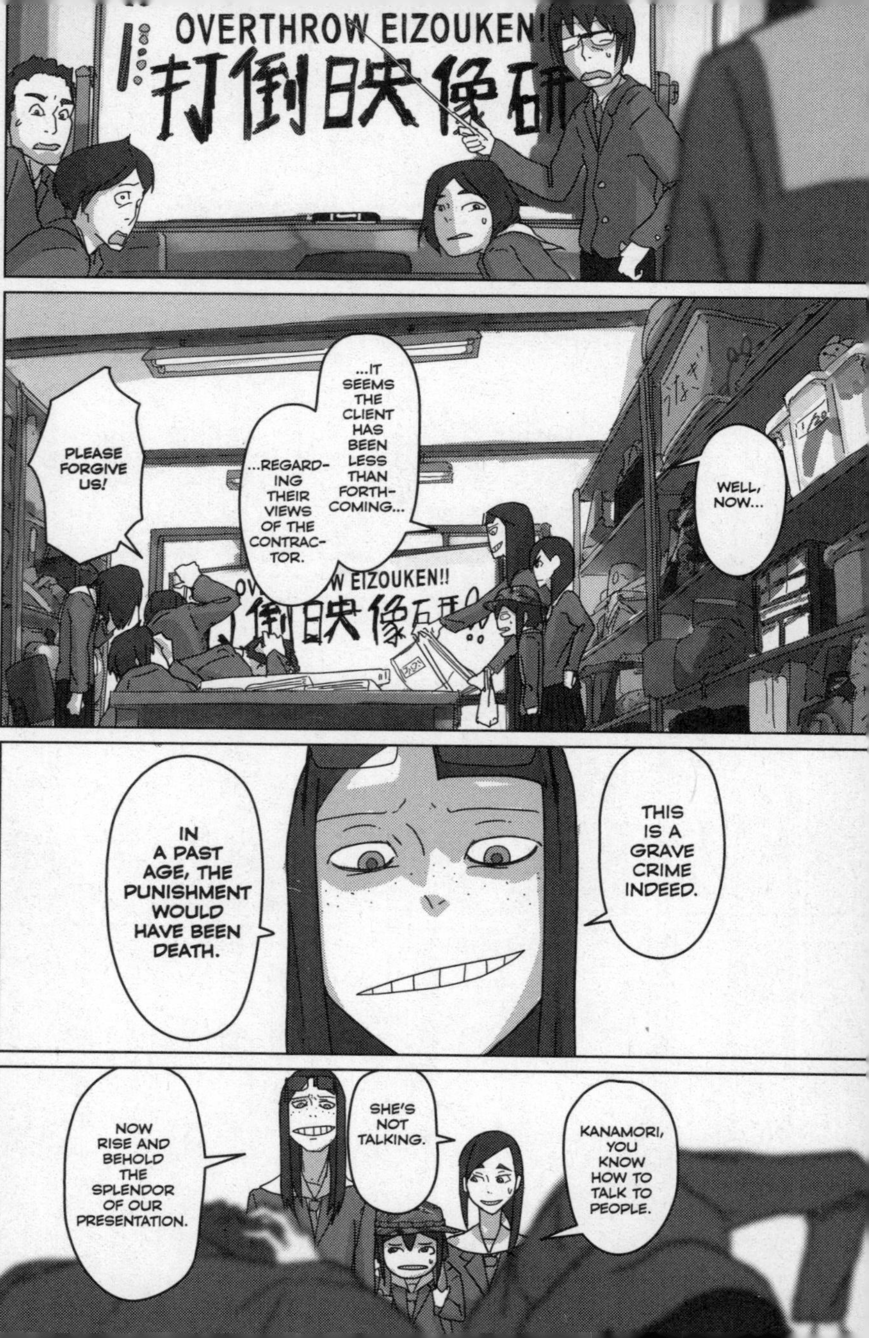
OVERTHROW EIZOUKEN!!
打倒映像研
WELL, NOW...
...IT SEEMS THE CLIENT HAS BEEN LESS THAN FORTH-COMING...
...REGARD-ING THEIR VIEWS OF THE CONTRAC-TOR.
PLEASE FORGIVE US!
THIS IS A GRAVE CRIME INDEED.
IN A PAST AGE, THE PUNISHMENT WOULD HAVE BEEN DEATH.
KANAMORI, YOU KNOW HOW TO TALK TO PEOPLE.
SHE'S NOT TALKING.
NOW RISE AND BEHOLD THE SPLENDOR OF OUR PRESENTATION.

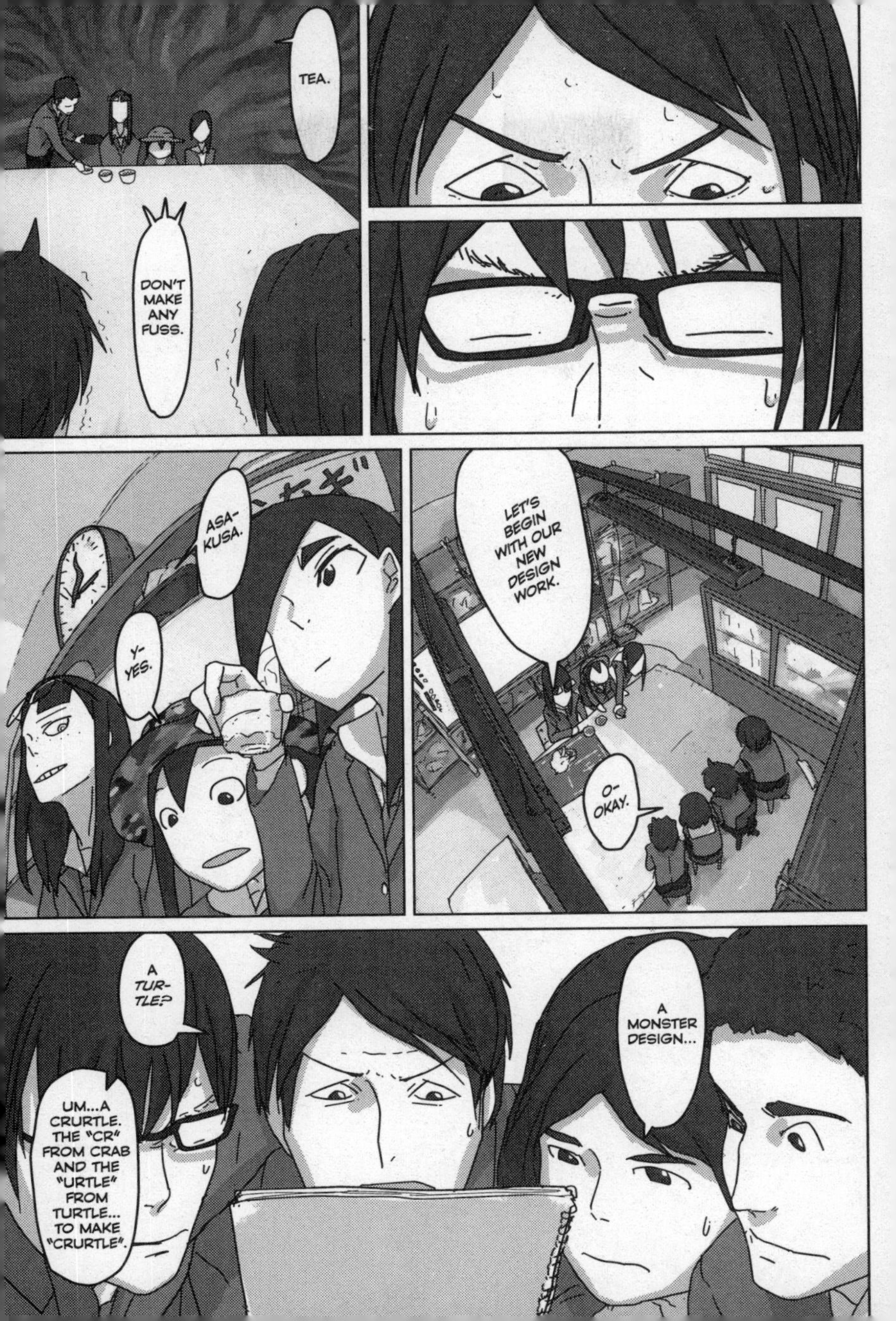
TEA.
DON'T MAKE ANY FUSS.
LET'S BEGIN WITH OUR NEW DESIGN WORK.
O-OKAY.
ASA-KUSA.
Y-YES.
A MONSTER DESIGN...
A TURTLE?
UM...A CRURTLE. THE "CR" FROM CRAB AND THE "URTLE" FROM TURTLE... TO MAKE "CRURTLE".

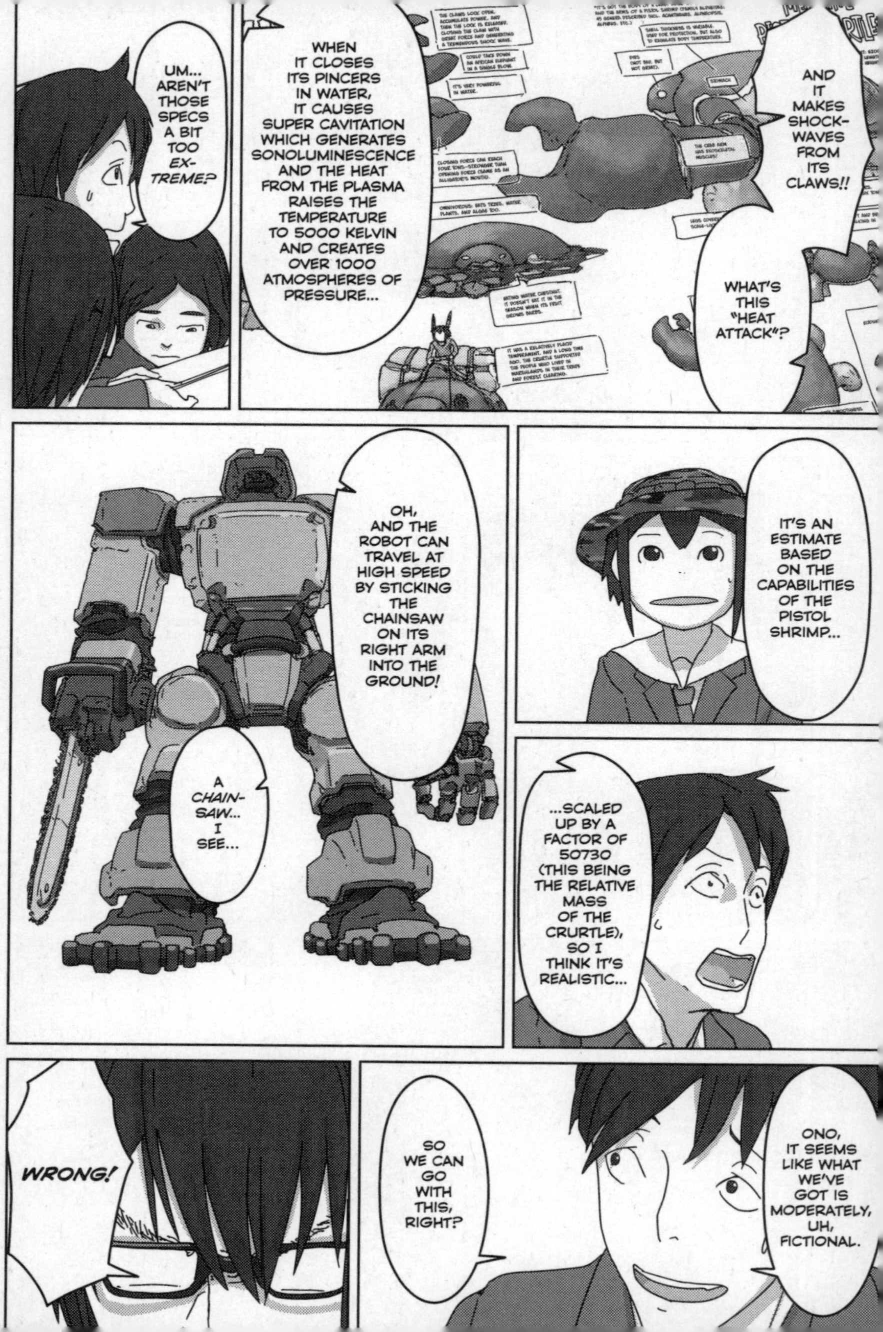
AND IT MAKES SHOCK-WAVES FROM ITS CLAWS!!
WHAT'S THIS "HEAT ATTACK"?
WHEN IT CLOSES ITS PINCERS IN WATER, IT CAUSES SUPER CAVITATION WHICH GENERATES SONOLUMINESCENCE AND THE HEAT FROM THE PLASMA RAISES THE TEMPERATURE TO 5000 KELVIN AND CREATES OVER 1000 ATMOSPHERES OF PRESSURE...
UM... AREN'T THOSE SPECS A BIT TOO *EX-TREME?*
IT'S AN ESTIMATE BASED ON THE CAPABILITIES OF THE PISTOL SHRIMP...
...SCALED UP BY A FACTOR OF 50730 (THIS BEING THE RELATIVE MASS OF THE CRURTLE), SO I THINK IT'S REALISTIC...
OH, AND THE ROBOT CAN TRAVEL AT HIGH SPEED BY STICKING THE CHAINSAW ON ITS RIGHT ARM INTO THE GROUND!
A *CHAIN-SAW*... I SEE...
ONO, IT SEEMS LIKE WHAT WE'VE GOT IS MODERATELY, UH, FICTIONAL.
SO WE CAN GO WITH THIS, RIGHT?
WRONG!

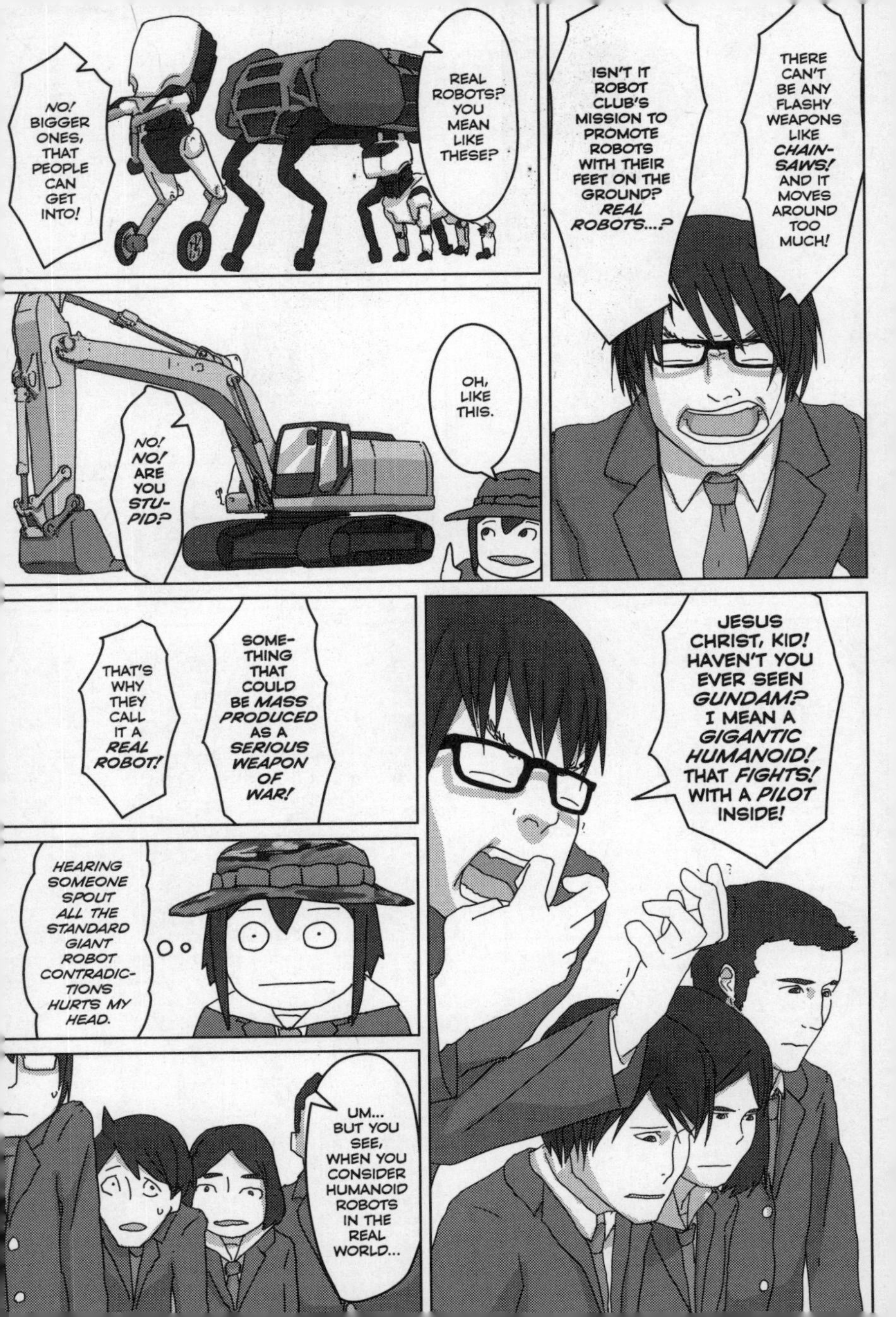
THERE CAN'T BE ANY FLASHY WEAPONS LIKE CHAIN-SAWS! AND IT MOVES AROUND TOO MUCH!
ISN'T IT ROBOT CLUB'S MISSION TO PROMOTE ROBOTS WITH THEIR FEET ON THE GROUND? REAL ROBOTS...?
REAL ROBOTS? YOU MEAN LIKE THESE?
NO! BIGGER ONES, THAT PEOPLE CAN GET INTO!
OH, LIKE THIS.
NO! NO! ARE YOU STU-PID?
JESUS CHRIST, KID! HAVEN'T YOU EVER SEEN GUNDAM? I MEAN A GIGANTIC HUMANOID! THAT FIGHTS! WITH A PILOT INSIDE!
SOME-THING THAT COULD BE MASS PRODUCED AS A SERIOUS WEAPON OF WAR!
THAT'S WHY THEY CALL IT A REAL ROBOT!
HEARING SOMEONE SPOUT ALL THE STANDARD GIANT ROBOT CONTRADIC-TIONS HURTS MY HEAD.
UM... BUT YOU SEE, WHEN YOU CONSIDER HUMANOID ROBOTS IN THE REAL WORLD...

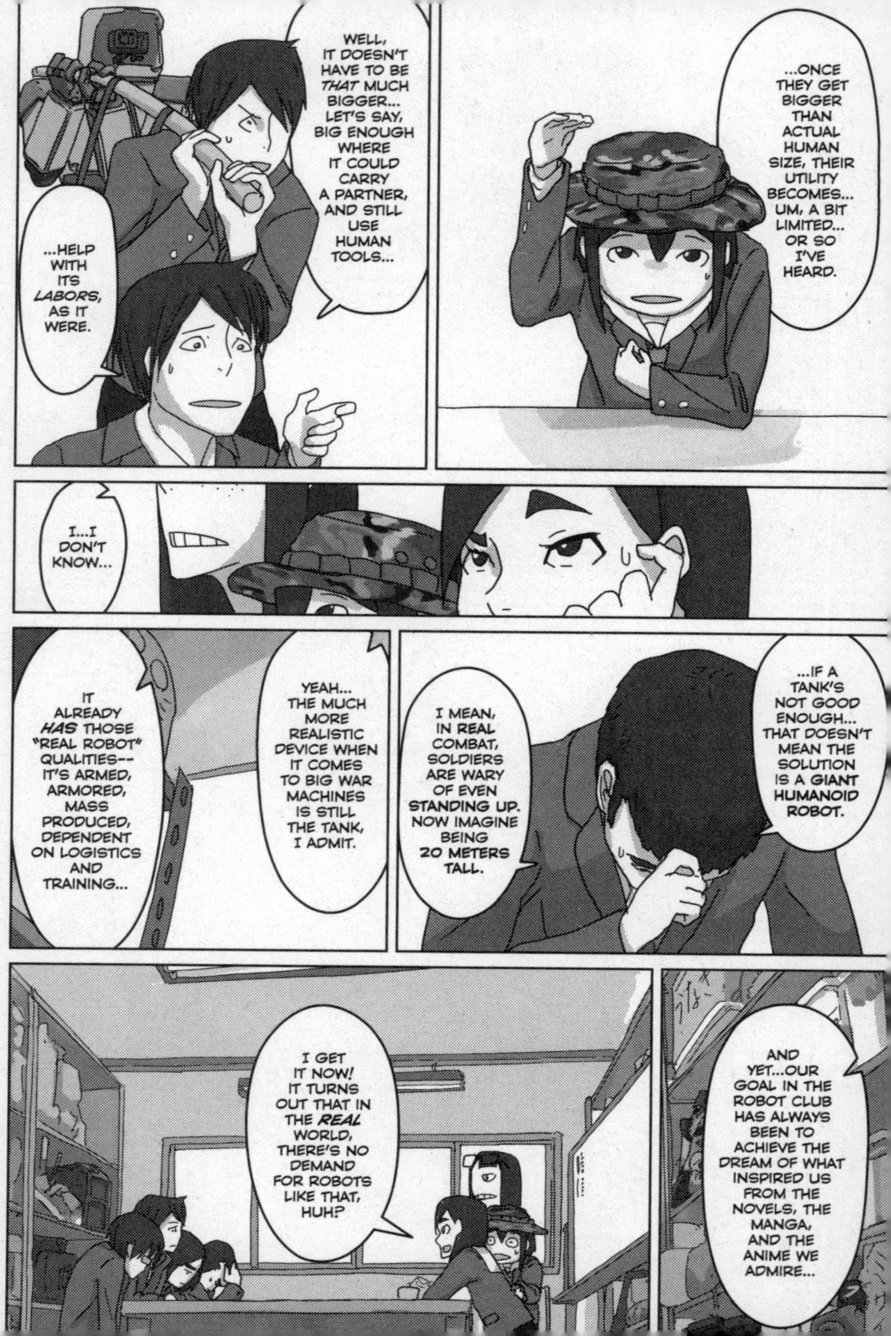
...ONCE THEY GET BIGGER THAN ACTUAL HUMAN SIZE, THEIR UTILITY BECOMES... UM, A BIT LIMITED... OR SO I'VE HEARD.
WELL, IT DOESN'T HAVE TO BE *THAT* MUCH BIGGER... LET'S SAY, BIG ENOUGH WHERE IT COULD CARRY A PARTNER, AND STILL USE HUMAN TOOLS...
...HELP WITH ITS *LABORS*, AS IT WERE.
I...I DON'T KNOW...
...IF A TANK'S NOT GOOD ENOUGH... THAT DOESN'T MEAN THE SOLUTION IS A **GIANT HUMANOID ROBOT.**
I MEAN, IN **REAL** COMBAT, SOLDIERS ARE WARY OF EVEN **STANDING UP.** NOW IMAGINE BEING **20 METERS** TALL.
YEAH... THE MUCH MORE REALISTIC DEVICE WHEN IT COMES TO BIG WAR MACHINES IS STILL THE TANK, I ADMIT.
IT ALREADY ***HAS*** THOSE "REAL ROBOT" QUALITIES-- IT'S ARMED, ARMORED, MASS PRODUCED, DEPENDENT ON LOGISTICS AND TRAINING...
AND YET...OUR GOAL IN THE ROBOT CLUB HAS ALWAYS BEEN TO ACHIEVE THE DREAM OF WHAT INSPIRED US FROM THE NOVELS, THE MANGA, AND THE ANIME WE ADMIRE...
I GET IT NOW! IT TURNS OUT THAT IN THE *REAL* WORLD, THERE'S NO DEMAND FOR ROBOTS LIKE THAT, HUH?

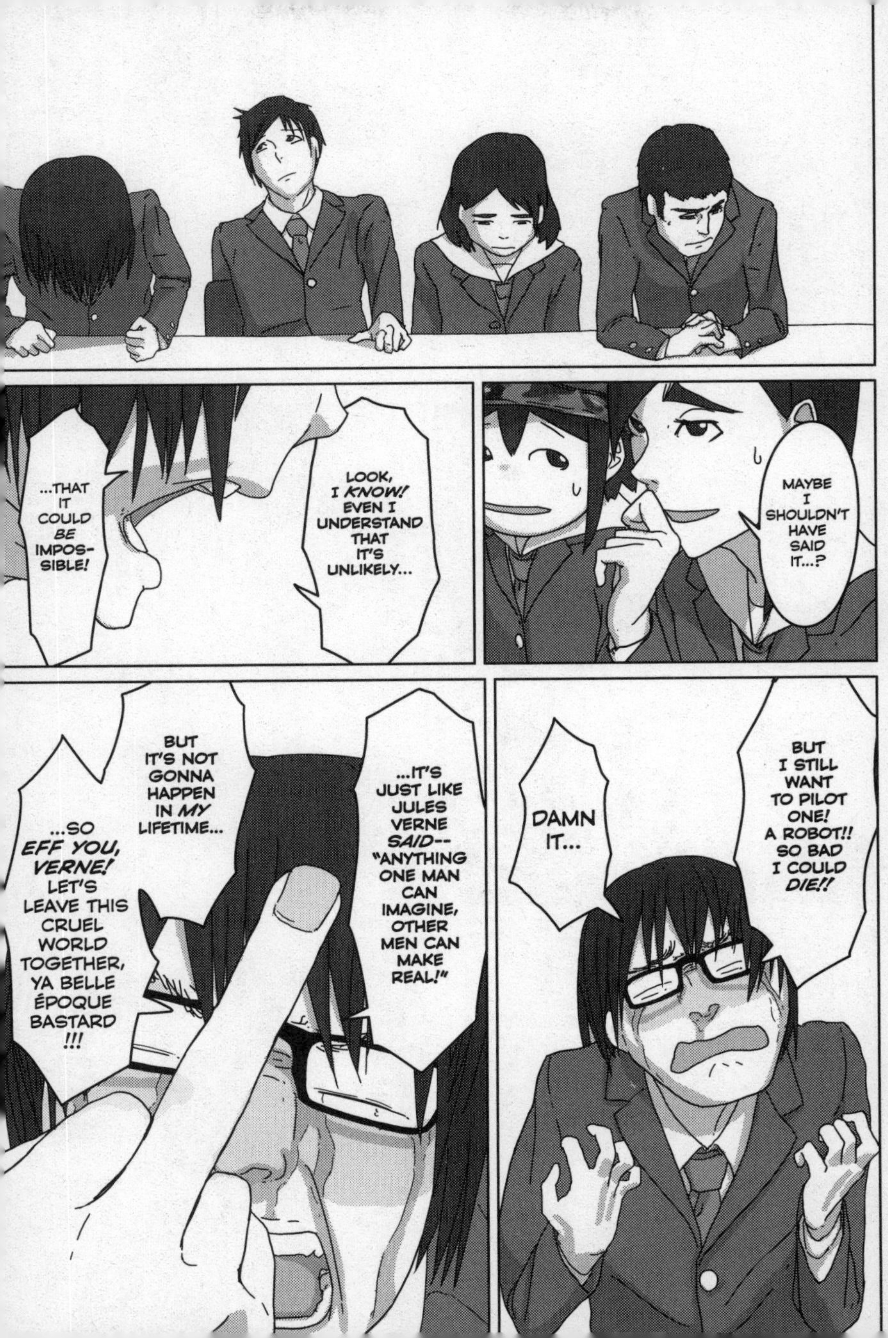
MAYBE I SHOULDN'T HAVE SAID IT...?
LOOK, I *KNOW!* EVEN I UNDERSTAND THAT IT'S UNLIKELY...
...THAT IT COULD *BE* IMPOSSIBLE!
BUT I STILL WANT TO PILOT ONE! A ROBOT!! SO BAD I COULD *DIE!!*
DAMN IT...
...IT'S JUST LIKE JULES VERNE *SAID*-- "ANYTHING ONE MAN CAN IMAGINE, OTHER MEN CAN MAKE REAL!"
BUT IT'S NOT GONNA HAPPEN IN *MY* LIFETIME...
...SO ***EFF YOU, VERNE!*** LET'S LEAVE THIS CRUEL WORLD TOGETHER, YA BELLE ÉPOQUE BASTARD !!!

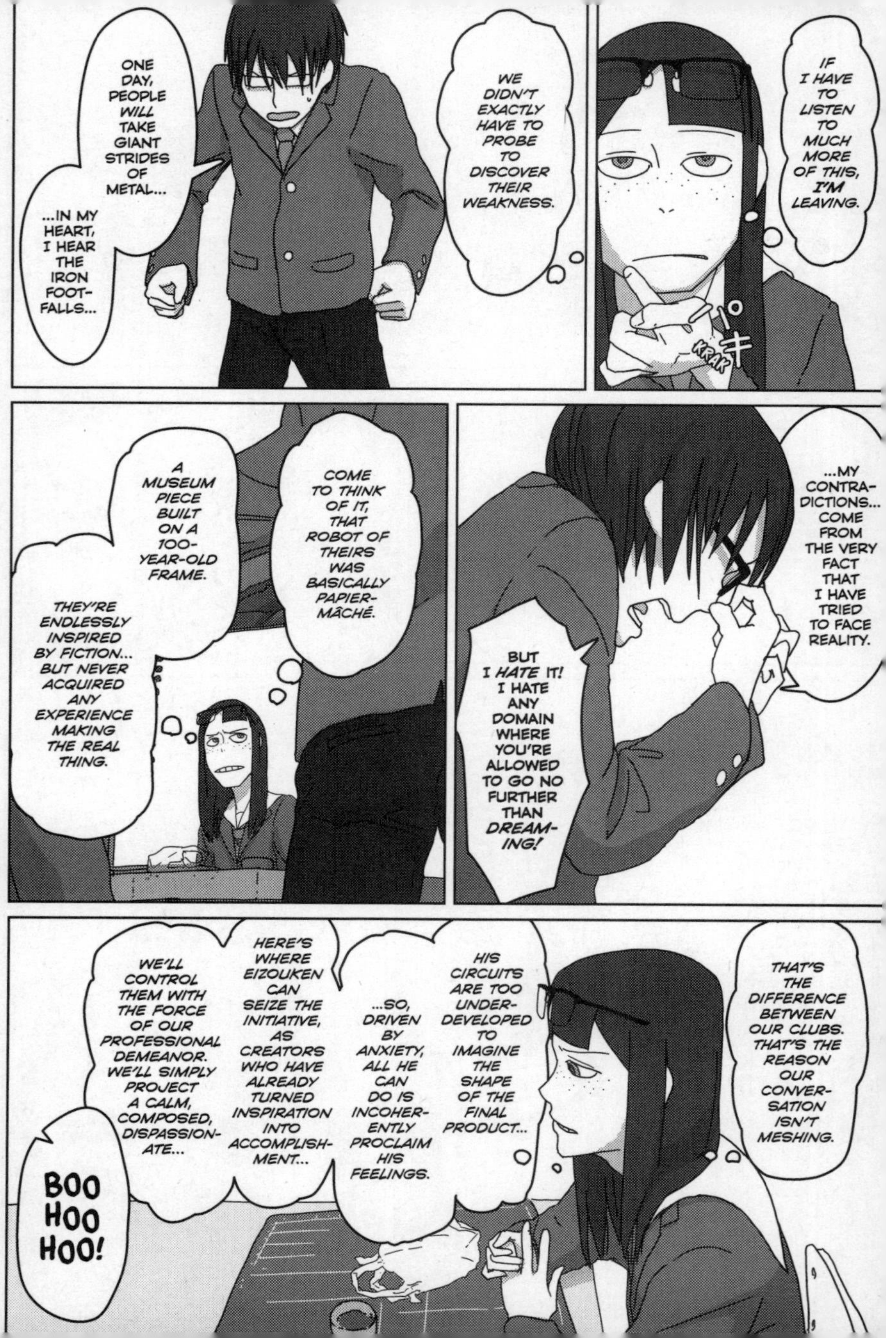
IF I HAVE TO LISTEN TO MUCH MORE OF THIS, I'M LEAVING.
WE DIDN'T EXACTLY HAVE TO PROBE TO DISCOVER THEIR WEAKNESS.
KRAK
ONE DAY, PEOPLE WILL TAKE GIANT STRIDES OF METAL...
...IN MY HEART, I HEAR THE IRON FOOT-FALLS...
...MY CONTRA-DICTIONS... COME FROM THE VERY FACT THAT I HAVE TRIED TO FACE REALITY.
BUT I HATE IT! I HATE ANY DOMAIN WHERE YOU'RE ALLOWED TO GO NO FURTHER THAN DREAM-ING!
COME TO THINK OF IT, THAT ROBOT OF THEIRS WAS BASICALLY PAPIER-MÂCHÉ.
A MUSEUM PIECE BUILT ON A 100-YEAR-OLD FRAME.
THEY'RE ENDLESSLY INSPIRED BY FICTION... BUT NEVER ACQUIRED ANY EXPERIENCE MAKING THE REAL THING.
THAT'S THE DIFFERENCE BETWEEN OUR CLUBS. THAT'S THE REASON OUR CONVER-SATION ISN'T MESHING.
HIS CIRCUITS ARE TOO UNDER-DEVELOPED TO IMAGINE THE SHAPE OF THE FINAL PRODUCT...
...SO, DRIVEN BY ANXIETY, ALL HE CAN DO IS INCOHER-ENTLY PROCLAIM HIS FEELINGS.
HERE'S WHERE EIZOUKEN CAN SEIZE THE INITIATIVE, AS CREATORS WHO HAVE ALREADY TURNED INSPIRATION INTO ACCOMPLISH-MENT...
WE'LL CONTROL THEM WITH THE FORCE OF OUR PROFESSIONAL DEMEANOR. WE'LL SIMPLY PROJECT A CALM, COMPOSED, DISPASSION-ATE...
BOO HOO HOO!

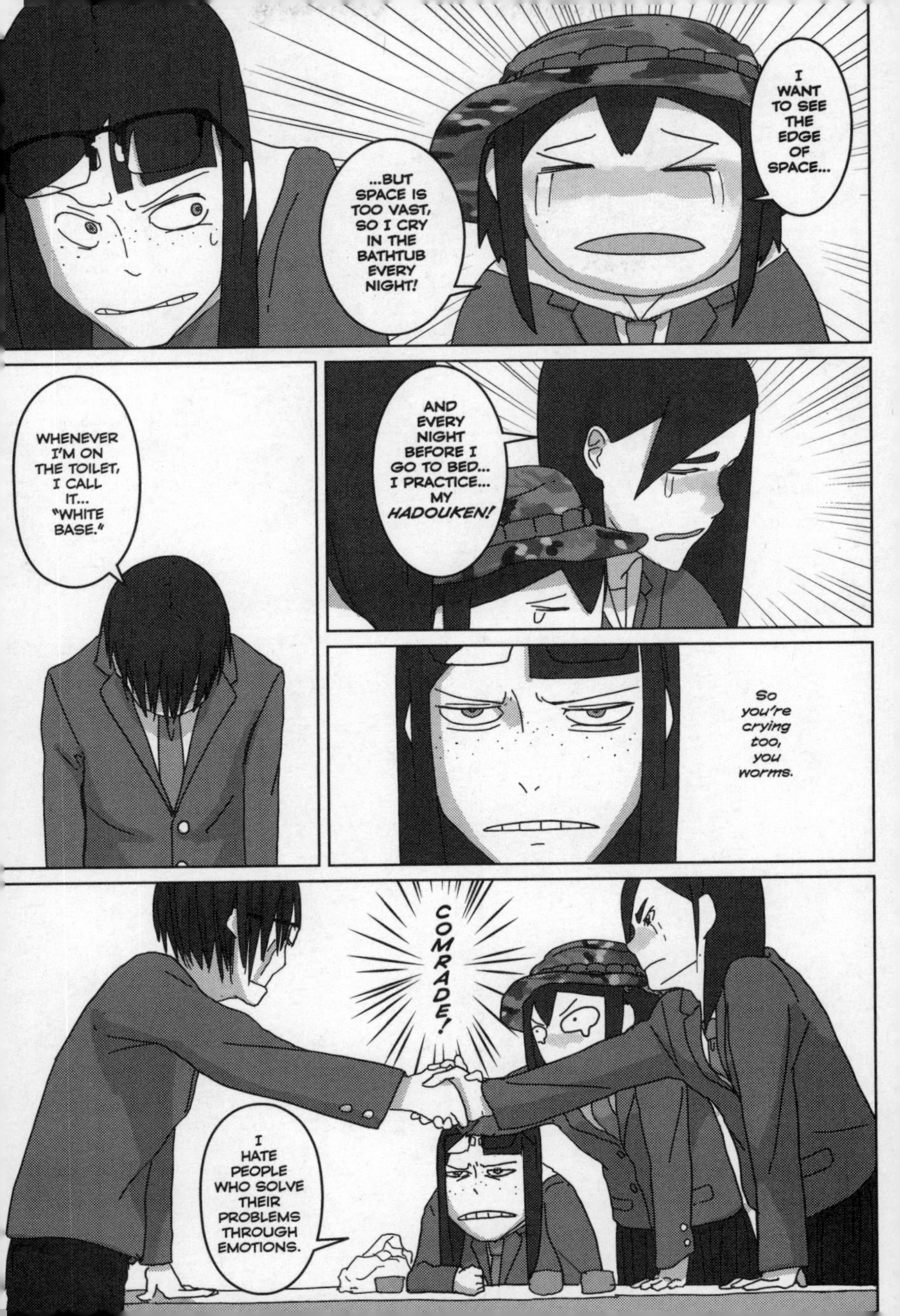
I WANT TO SEE THE EDGE OF SPACE...
...BUT SPACE IS TOO VAST, SO I CRY IN THE BATHTUB EVERY NIGHT!
AND EVERY NIGHT BEFORE I GO TO BED... I PRACTICE... MY *HADOUKEN!*
So you're crying too, you worms.
WHENEVER I'M ON THE TOILET, I CALL IT... "WHITE BASE."
COMRADE!
I HATE PEOPLE WHO SOLVE THEIR PROBLEMS THROUGH EMOTIONS.

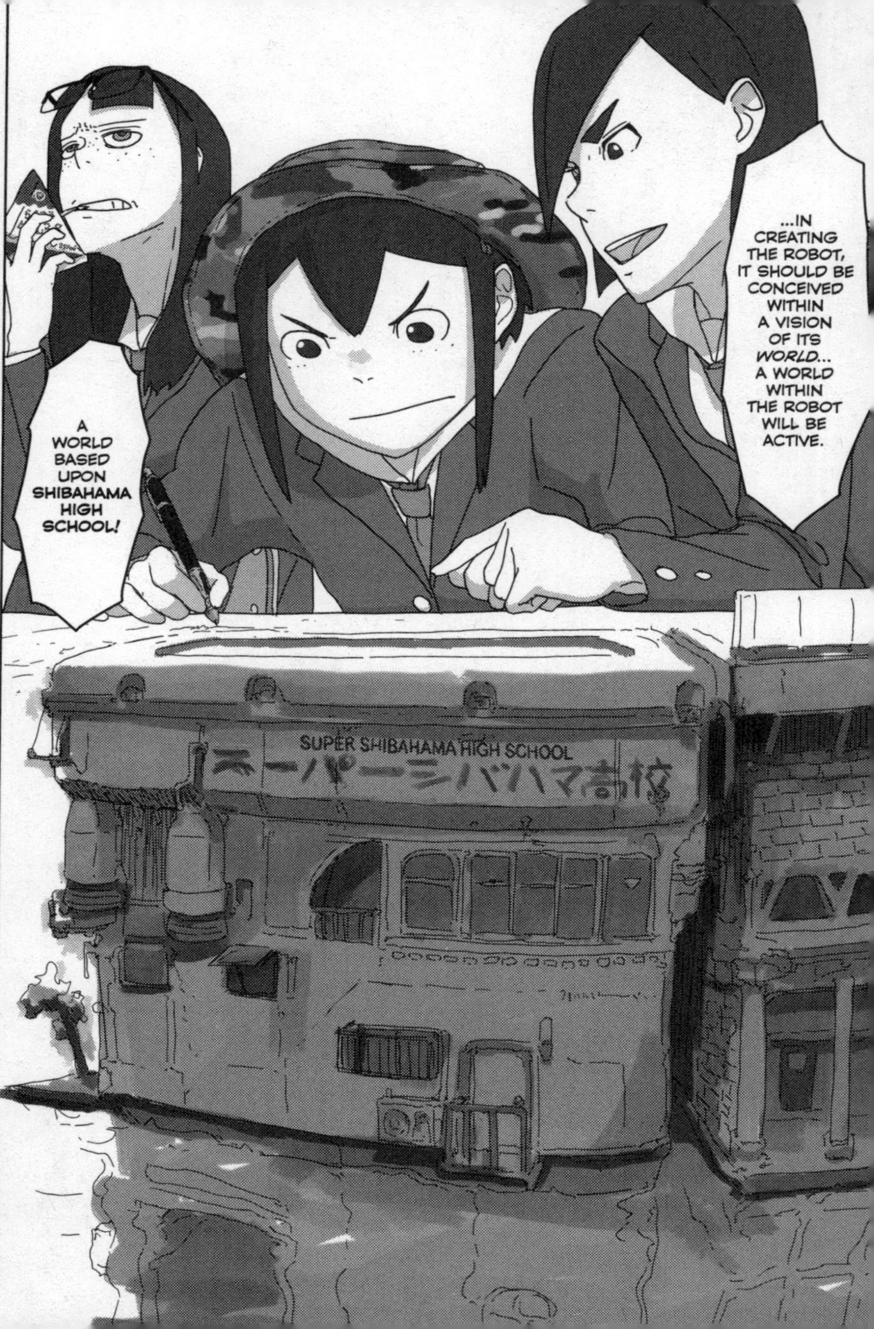
...IN CREATING THE ROBOT, IT SHOULD BE CONCEIVED WITHIN A VISION OF ITS *WORLD*... A WORLD WITHIN THE ROBOT WILL BE ACTIVE.
A WORLD BASED UPON SHIBAHAMA HIGH SCHOOL!
SUPER SHIBAHAMA HIGH SCHOOL
スーパーシバハマ高校

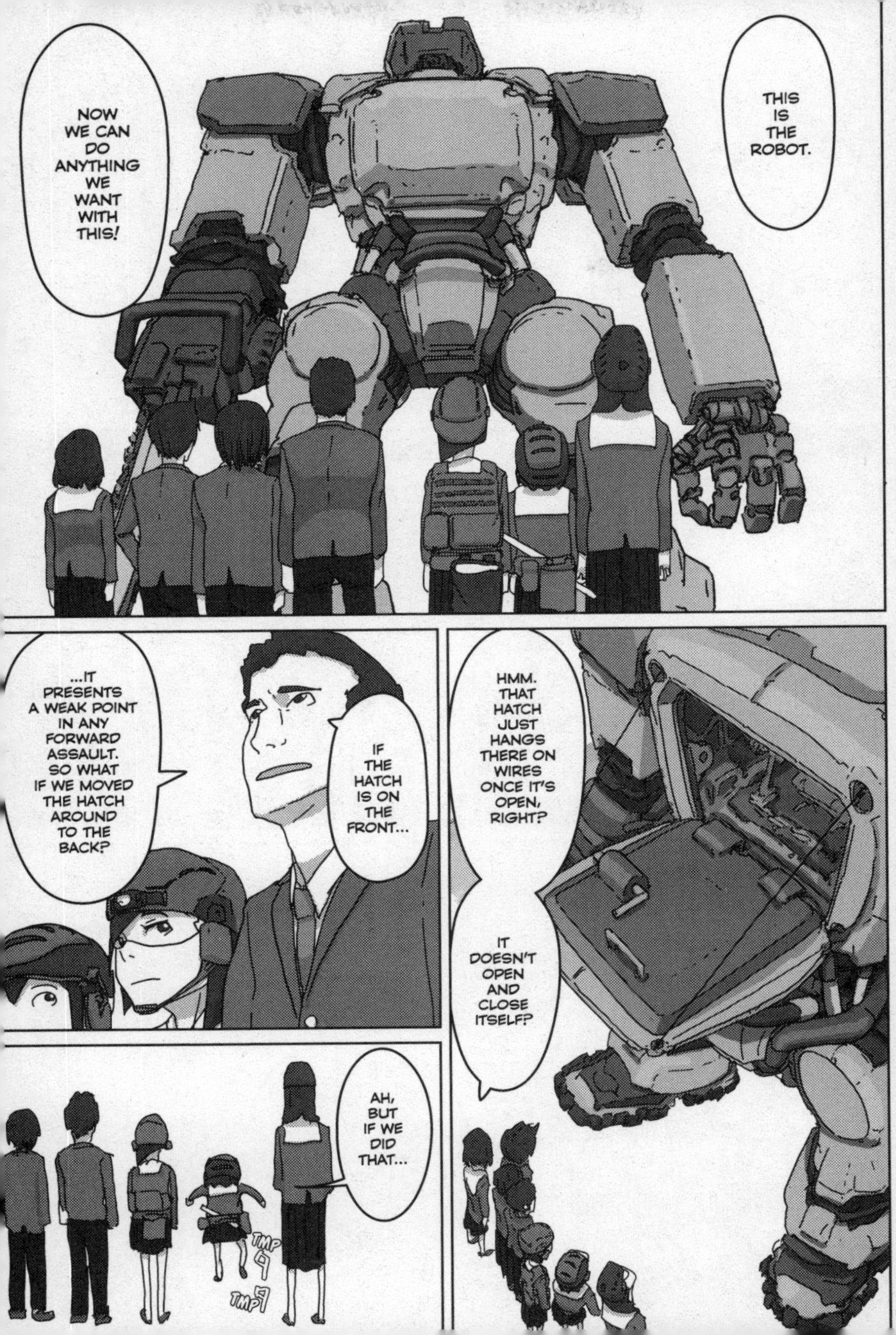
THIS IS THE ROBOT.
NOW WE CAN DO ANYTHING WE WANT WITH THIS!
HMM. THAT HATCH JUST HANGS THERE ON WIRES ONCE IT'S OPEN, RIGHT?
IT DOESN'T OPEN AND CLOSE ITSELF?
IF THE HATCH IS ON THE FRONT...
...IT PRESENTS A WEAK POINT IN ANY FORWARD ASSAULT. SO WHAT IF WE MOVED THE HATCH AROUND TO THE BACK?
AH, BUT IF WE DID THAT...
TMP
TMP

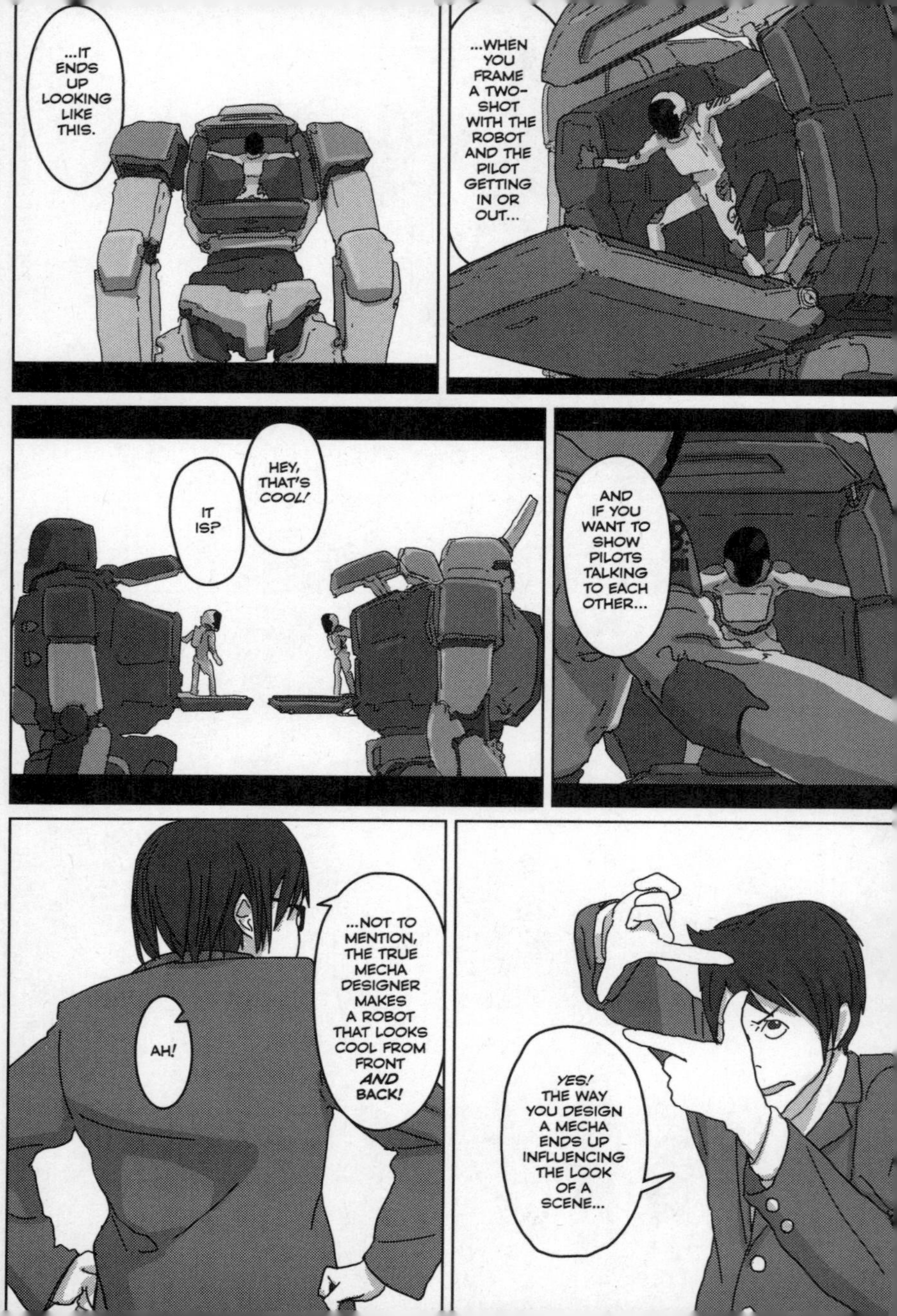
...WHEN YOU FRAME A TWO-SHOT WITH THE ROBOT AND THE PILOT GETTING IN OR OUT...
...IT ENDS UP LOOKING LIKE THIS.
AND IF YOU WANT TO SHOW PILOTS TALKING TO EACH OTHER...
HEY, THAT'S *COOL!*
IT IS?
YES! THE WAY YOU DESIGN A MECHA ENDS UP INFLUENCING THE LOOK OF A SCENE...
...NOT TO MENTION, THE TRUE MECHA DESIGNER MAKES A ROBOT THAT LOOKS COOL FROM FRONT ***AND*** BACK!
AH!

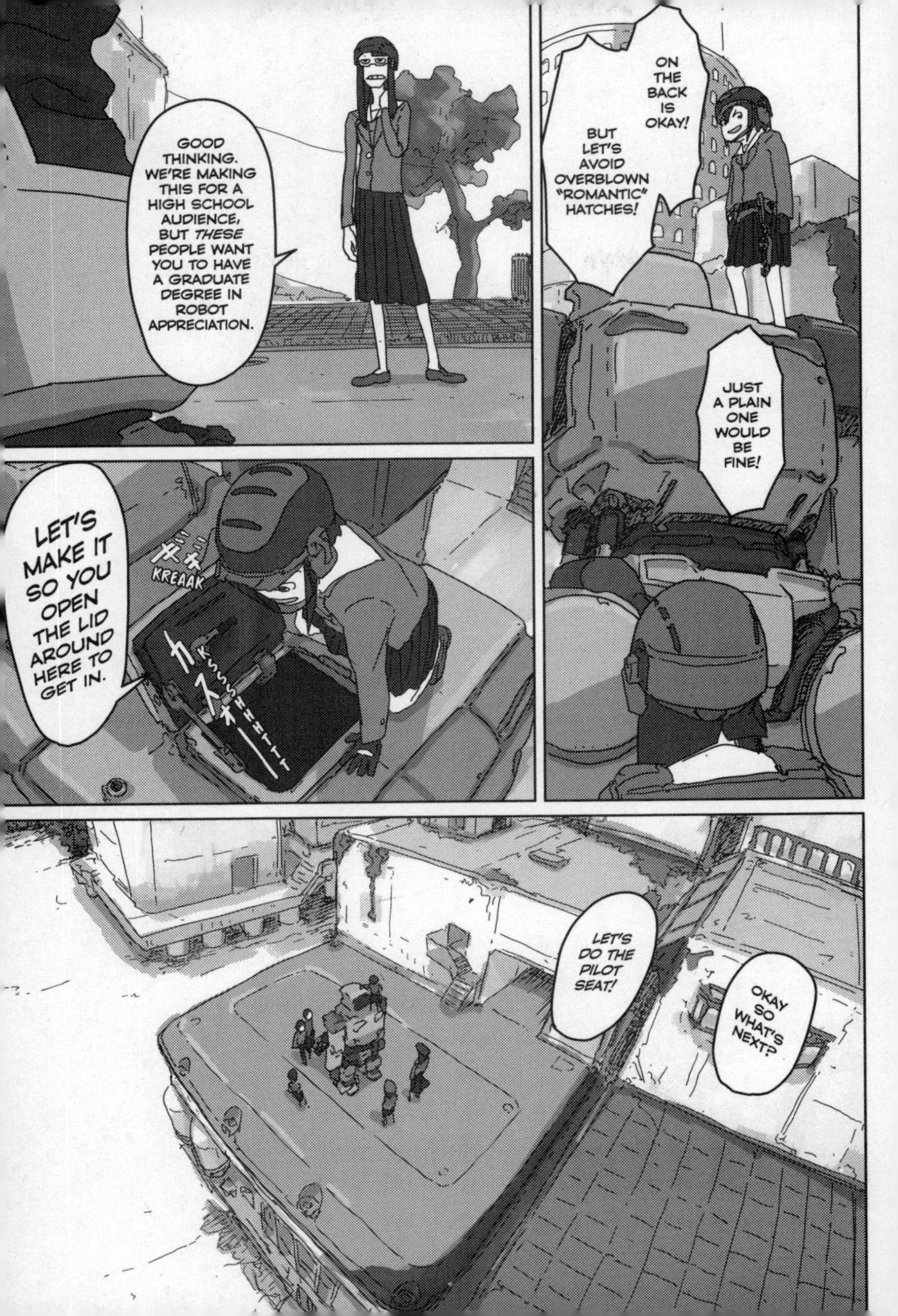
ON THE BACK IS OKAY!
BUT LET'S AVOID OVERBLOWN "ROMANTIC" HATCHES!
JUST A PLAIN ONE WOULD BE FINE!
GOOD THINKING. WE'RE MAKING THIS FOR A HIGH SCHOOL AUDIENCE, BUT *THESE* PEOPLE WANT YOU TO HAVE A GRADUATE DEGREE IN ROBOT APPRECIATION.
LET'S MAKE IT SO YOU OPEN THE LID AROUND HERE TO GET IN.
KREAAK
KSSSSHHHTTTT
OKAY SO WHAT'S NEXT?
LET'S DO THE PILOT SEAT!

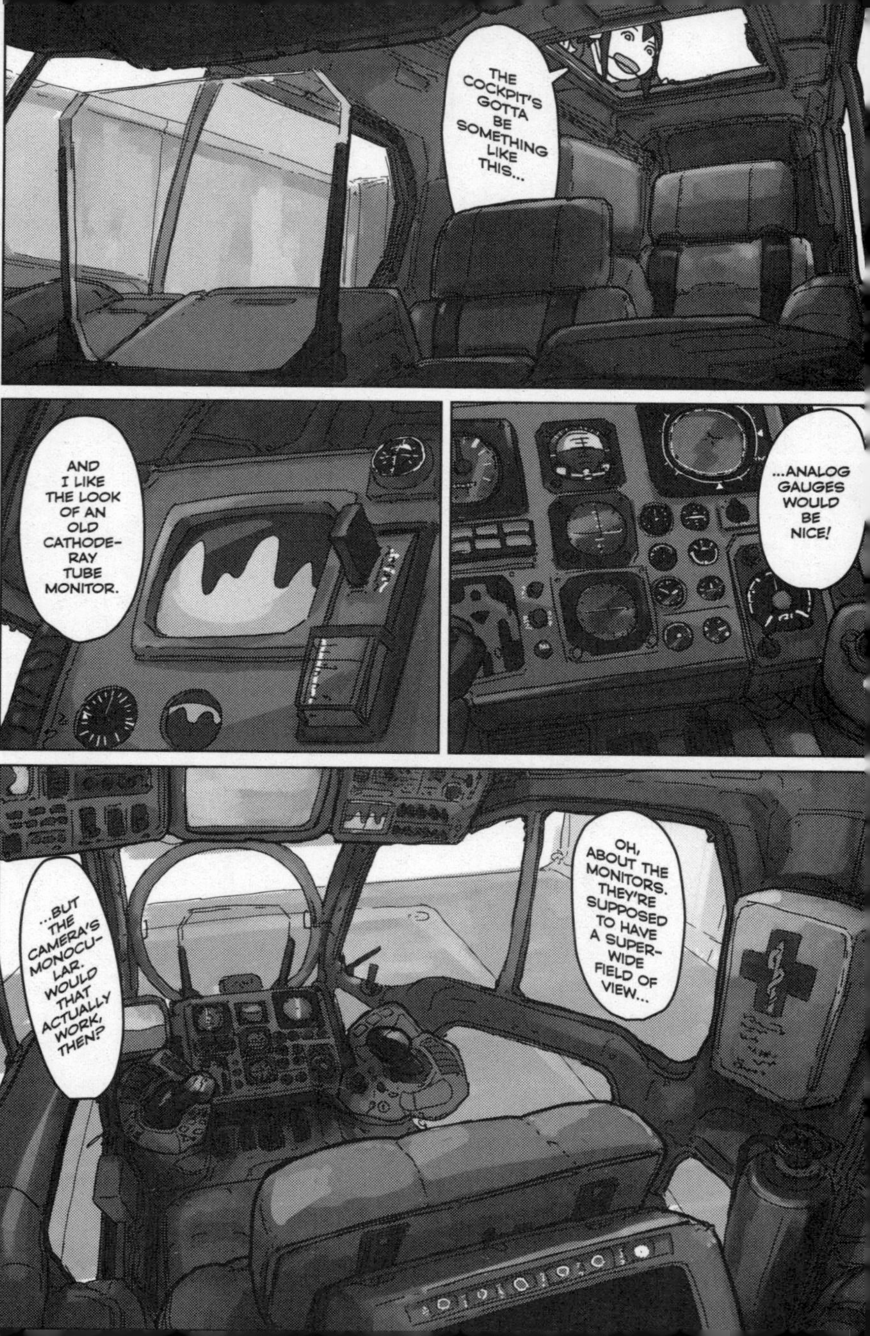
THE COCKPIT'S GOTTA BE SOMETHING LIKE THIS...
...ANALOG GAUGES WOULD BE NICE!
AND I LIKE THE LOOK OF AN OLD CATHODE-RAY TUBE MONITOR.
OH, ABOUT THE MONITORS. THEY'RE SUPPOSED TO HAVE A SUPER-WIDE FIELD OF VIEW...
...BUT THE CAMERA'S MONOCULAR. WOULD THAT ACTUALLY WORK, THEN?

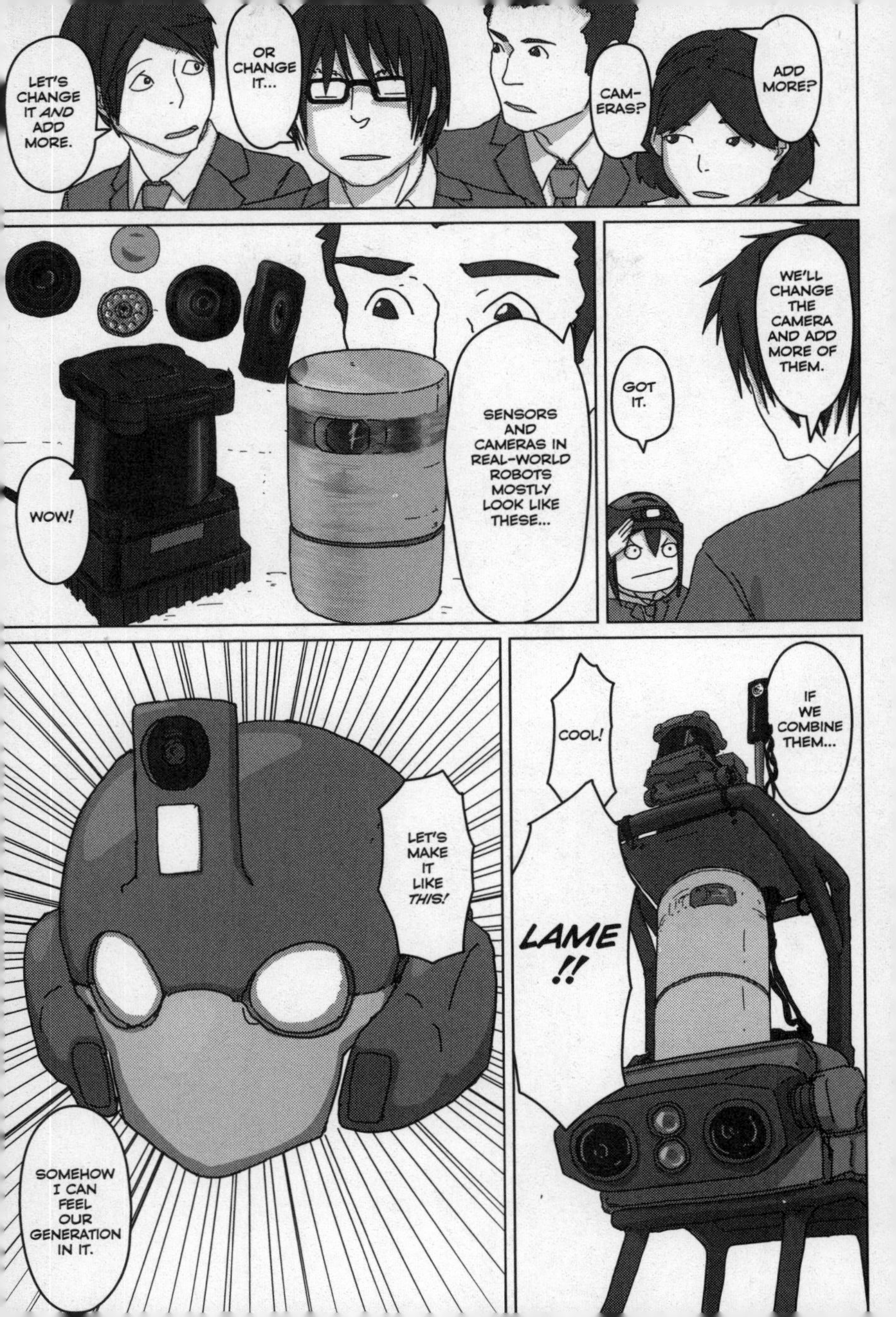
ADD MORE?
CAM-ERAS?
OR CHANGE IT...
LET'S CHANGE IT AND ADD MORE.
WE'LL CHANGE THE CAMERA AND ADD MORE OF THEM.
GOT IT.
SENSORS AND CAMERAS IN REAL-WORLD ROBOTS MOSTLY LOOK LIKE THESE...
WOW!
IF WE COMBINE THEM...
COOL!
LAME !!
LET'S MAKE IT LIKE THIS!
SOMEHOW I CAN FEEL OUR GENERATION IN IT.

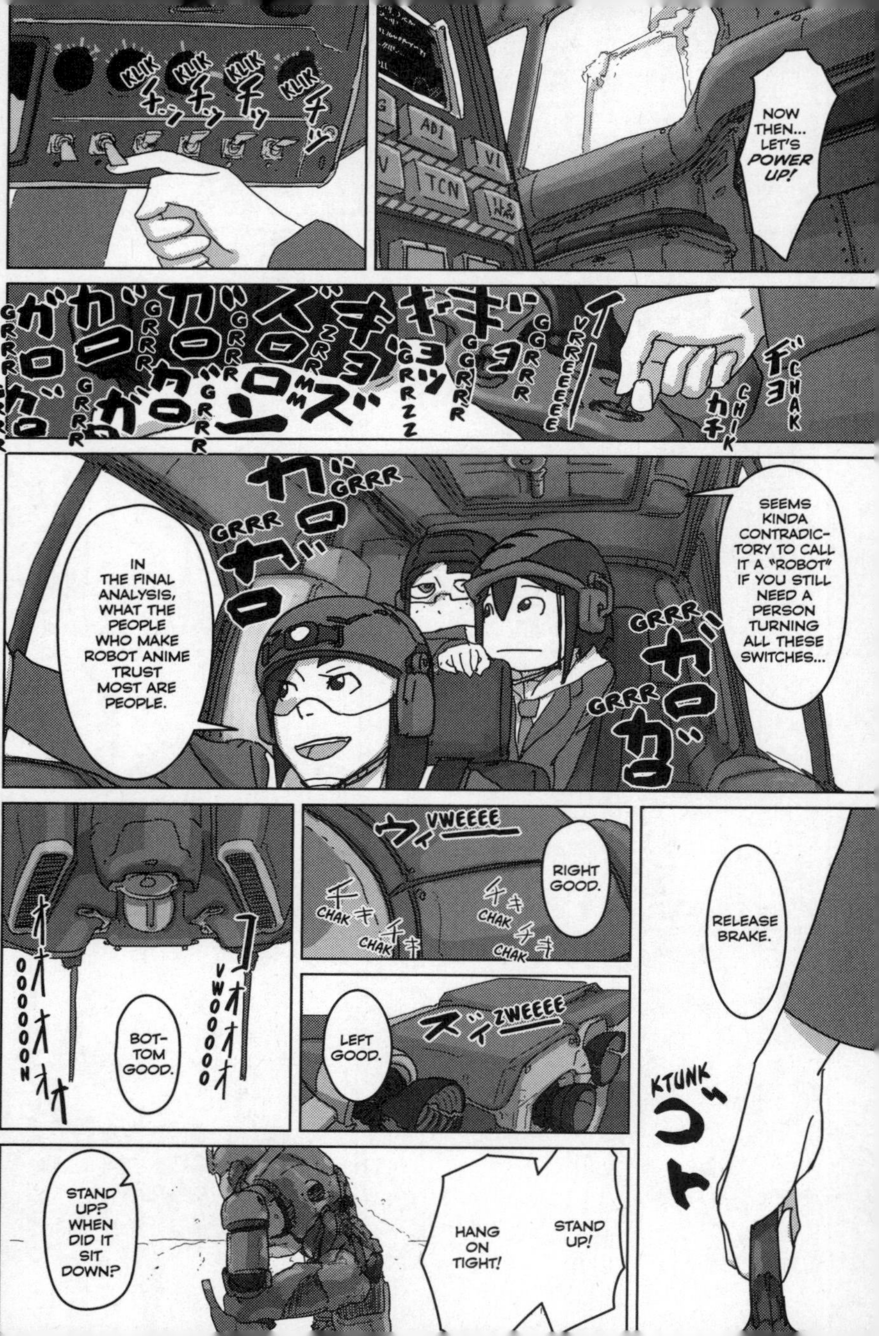
NOW THEN... LET'S POWER UP!
KLIK
KLIK
KLIK
KLIK
CHAK
CHIK
VRREEEEEE
GGRRR
GGRRR
GRRZZ
ZRRMM
GRRR
GRRR
GRRR
GRRR
GRRR
GRRR
SEEMS KINDA CONTRADICTORY TO CALL IT A "ROBOT" IF YOU STILL NEED A PERSON TURNING ALL THESE SWITCHES...
GRRR
GRRR
GRRR
GRRR
IN THE FINAL ANALYSIS, WHAT THE PEOPLE WHO MAKE ROBOT ANIME TRUST MOST ARE PEOPLE.
RELEASE BRAKE.
KTUNK
VWEEEE
RIGHT GOOD.
CHAK
CHAK
CHAK
CHAK
ZWEEEE
LEFT GOOD.
VWOOOOOO
BOT-TOM GOOD.
OOOOOOON
STAND UP!
HANG ON TIGHT!
STAND UP? WHEN DID IT SIT DOWN?

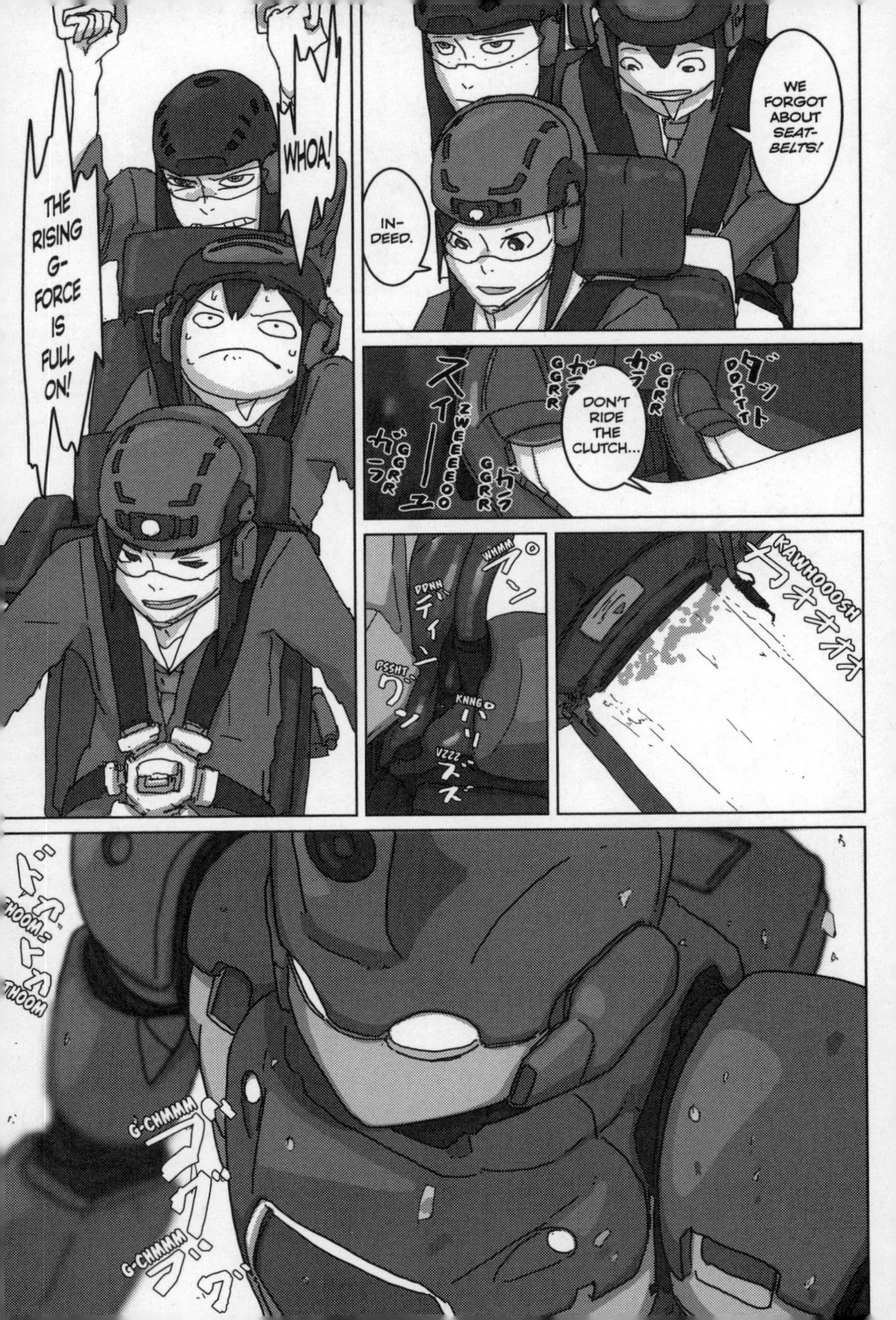

WE FORGOT ABOUT SEAT-BELTS!
IN-DEED.
DDITTT
GGRR
GGRR
DON'T RIDE THE CLUTCH...
GGRR
ZWEEEEEOO
GGRR
KAWHOOOSH
WHMMM
DDNN
PSSHT
KNNG
VZZZ
WHOA!
THE RISING G-FORCE IS FULL ON!
THOOM THOOM
G-CHMMM
G-CHMMM

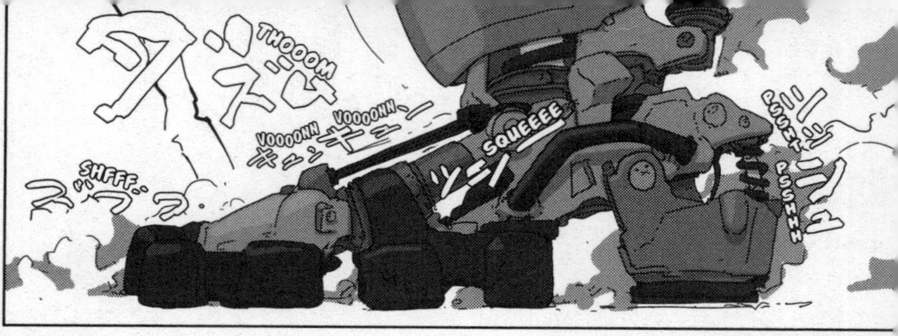
PSSHT
PSSHH
THOOOM
VOOOONN
VOOOONN
SQUEEEE
SHFFF
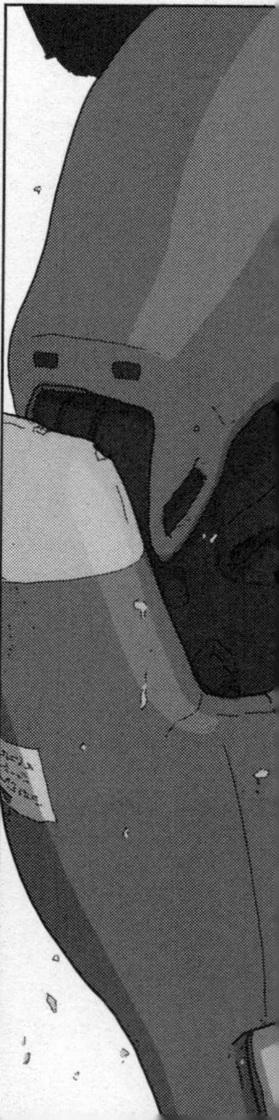
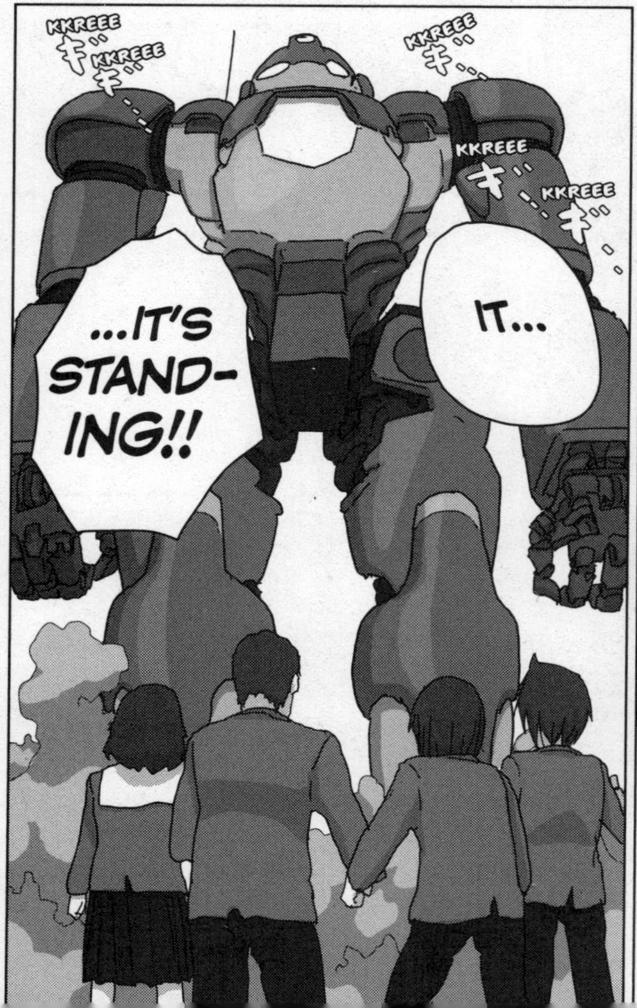
KKREEE
KKREEE
KKREEE
KKREEE
KKREEE
IT...
...IT'S STAND-ING!!

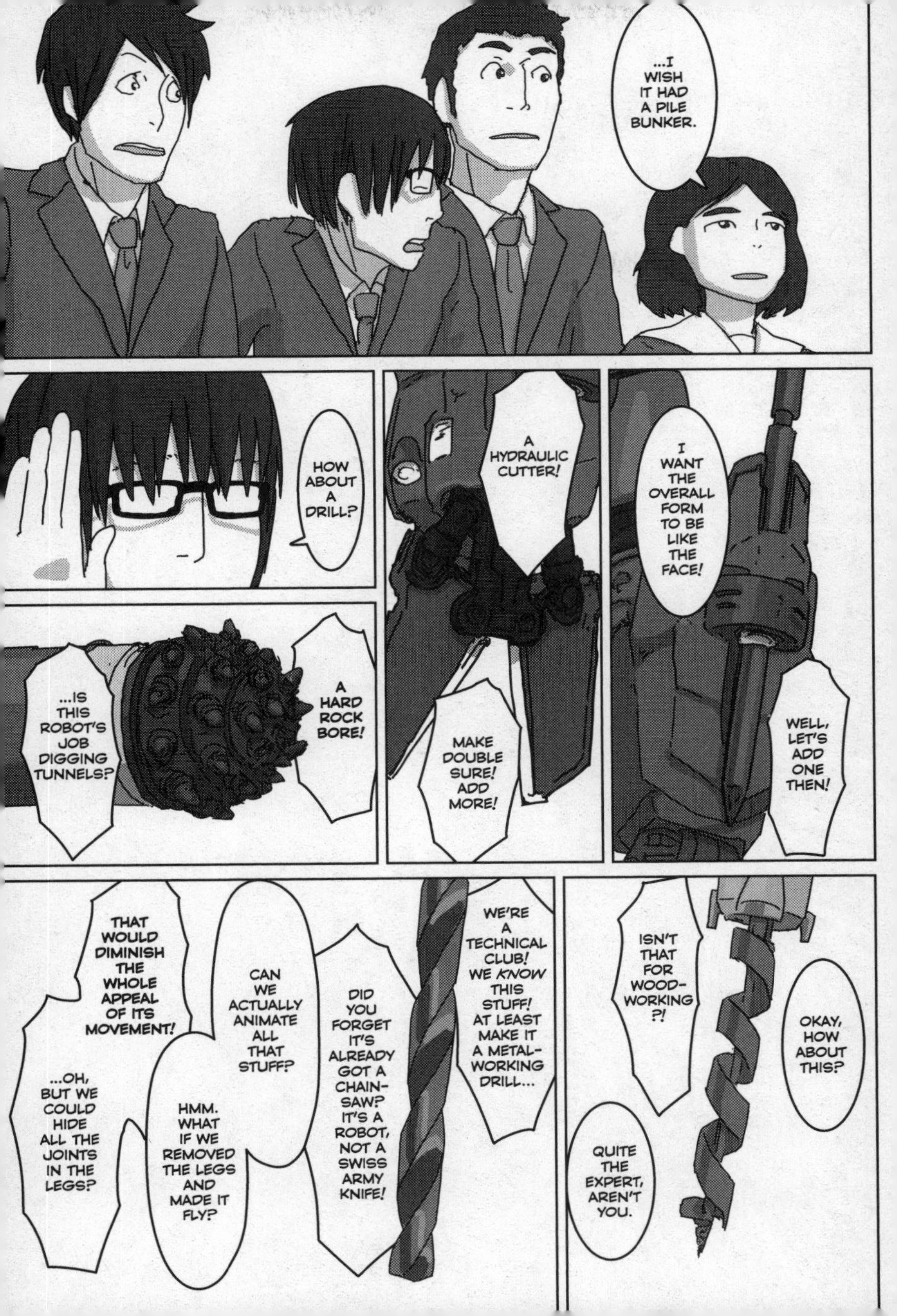
...I WISH IT HAD A PILE BUNKER.
I WANT THE OVERALL FORM TO BE LIKE THE FACE!
WELL, LET'S ADD ONE THEN!
A HYDRAULIC CUTTER!
MAKE DOUBLE SURE! ADD MORE!
HOW ABOUT A DRILL?
A HARD ROCK BORE!
...IS THIS ROBOT'S JOB DIGGING TUNNELS?
OKAY, HOW ABOUT THIS?
ISN'T THAT FOR WOOD-WORKING?!
QUITE THE EXPERT, AREN'T YOU.
WE'RE A TECHNICAL CLUB! WE *KNOW* THIS STUFF! AT LEAST MAKE IT A METAL-WORKING DRILL...
DID YOU FORGET IT'S ALREADY GOT A CHAIN-SAW? IT'S A ROBOT, NOT A SWISS ARMY KNIFE!
CAN WE ACTUALLY ANIMATE ALL THAT STUFF?
HMM. WHAT IF WE REMOVED THE LEGS AND MADE IT FLY?
THAT WOULD DIMINISH THE WHOLE APPEAL OF ITS MOVEMENT!
...OH, BUT WE COULD HIDE ALL THE JOINTS IN THE LEGS?

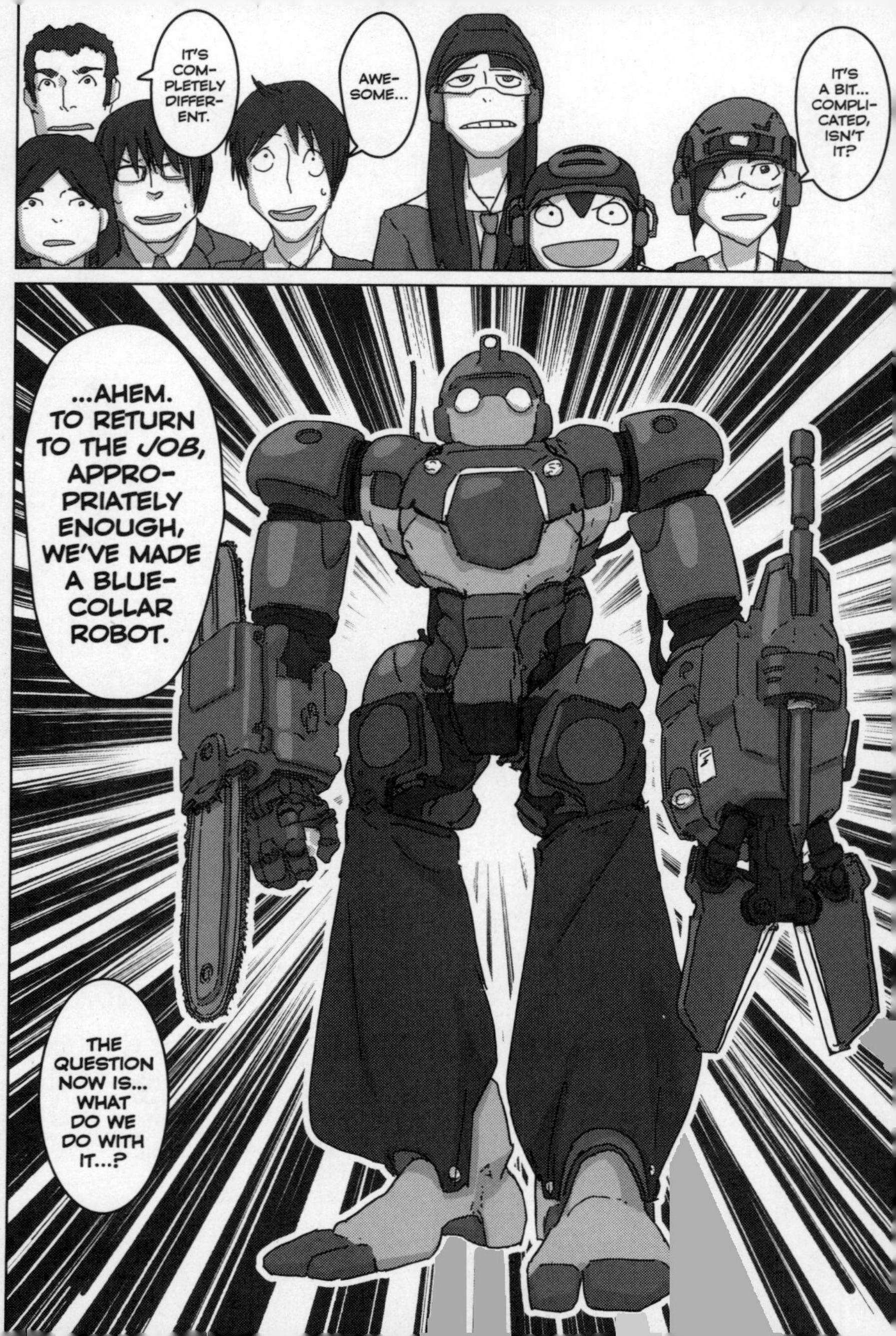
IT'S A BIT... COMPLICATED, ISN'T IT?
AWE-SOME...
IT'S COM-PLETELY DIFFER-ENT.
...AHEM. TO RETURN TO THE *JOB*, APPRO-PRIATELY ENOUGH, WE'VE MADE A BLUE-COLLAR ROBOT.
THE QUESTION NOW IS... WHAT DO WE DO WITH IT...?

CHAPTER 11: COMPENSATION FOR HARD WORK

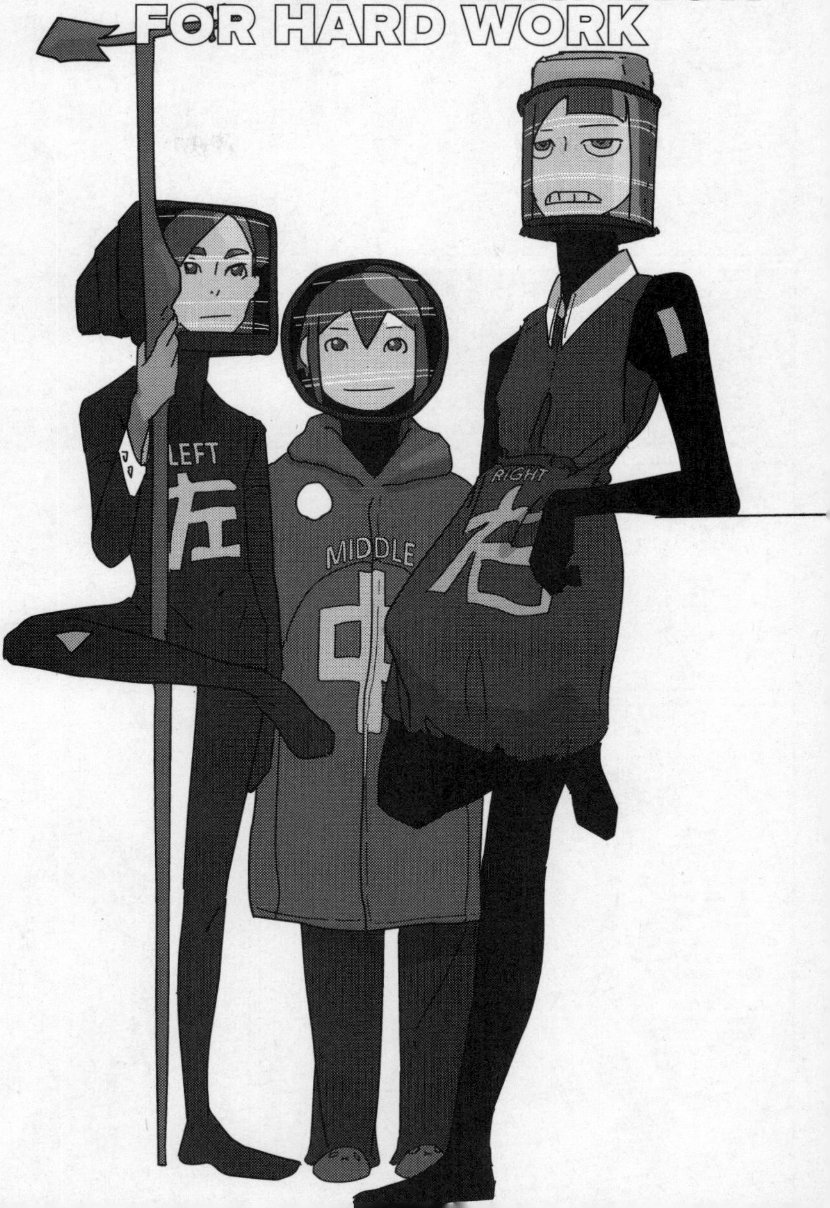
LEFT
左
MIDDLE
中
RIGHT
右

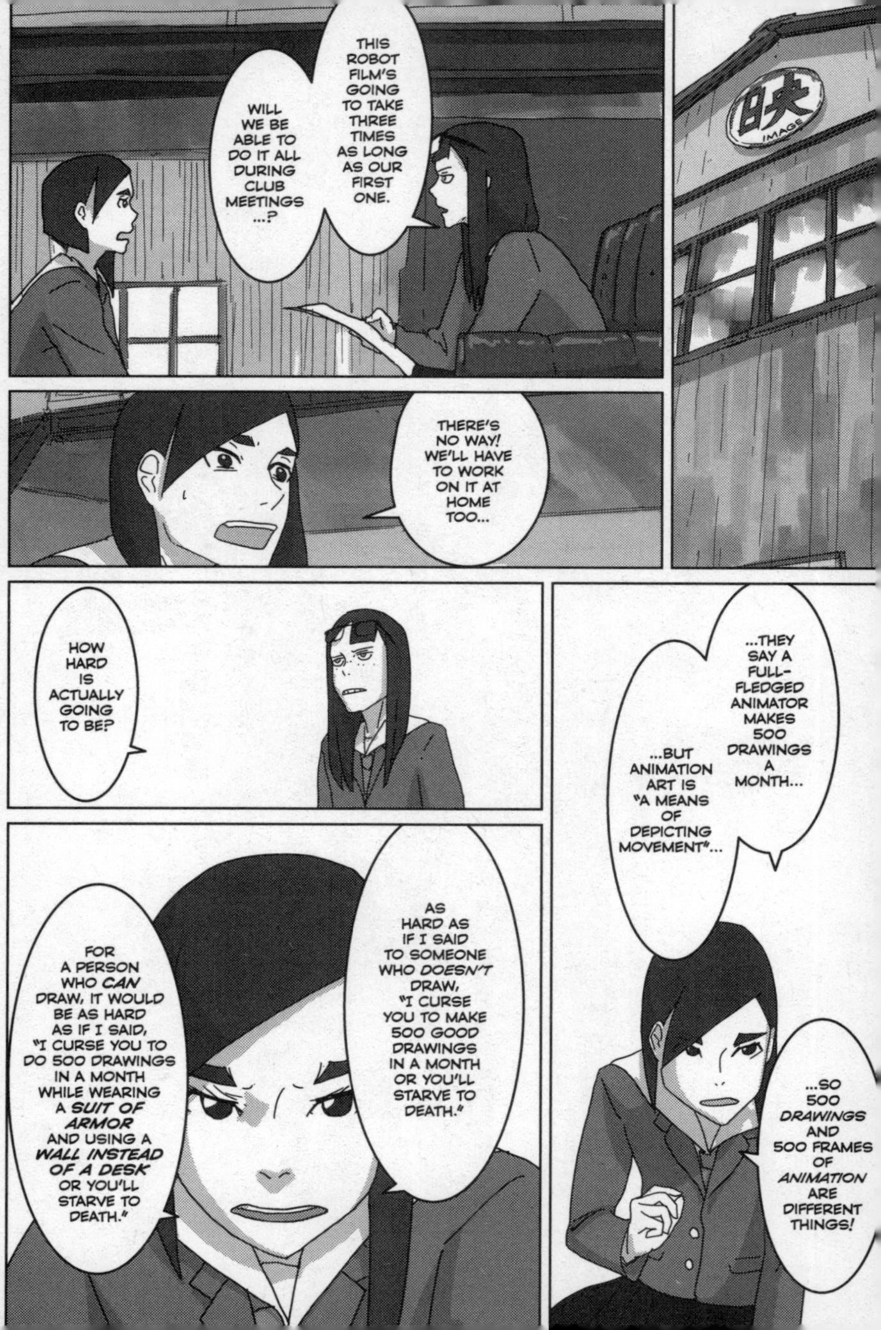

映
IMAGE
THIS ROBOT FILM'S GOING TO TAKE THREE TIMES AS LONG AS OUR FIRST ONE.
WILL WE BE ABLE TO DO IT ALL DURING CLUB MEETINGS ...?
THERE'S NO WAY! WE'LL HAVE TO WORK ON IT AT HOME TOO...
...THEY SAY A FULL-FLEDGED ANIMATOR MAKES 500 DRAWINGS A MONTH...
...BUT ANIMATION ART IS "A MEANS OF DEPICTING MOVEMENT"...
...SO 500 *DRAWINGS* AND 500 FRAMES OF *ANIMATION* ARE DIFFERENT THINGS!
HOW HARD IS ACTUALLY GOING TO BE?
AS HARD AS IF I SAID TO SOMEONE WHO *DOESN'T* DRAW, "I CURSE YOU TO MAKE 500 GOOD DRAWINGS IN A MONTH OR YOU'LL STARVE TO DEATH."
FOR A PERSON WHO ***CAN*** DRAW, IT WOULD BE AS HARD AS IF I SAID, "I CURSE YOU TO DO 500 DRAWINGS IN A MONTH WHILE WEARING A ***SUIT OF ARMOR*** AND USING A ***WALL INSTEAD OF A DESK*** OR YOU'LL STARVE TO DEATH."

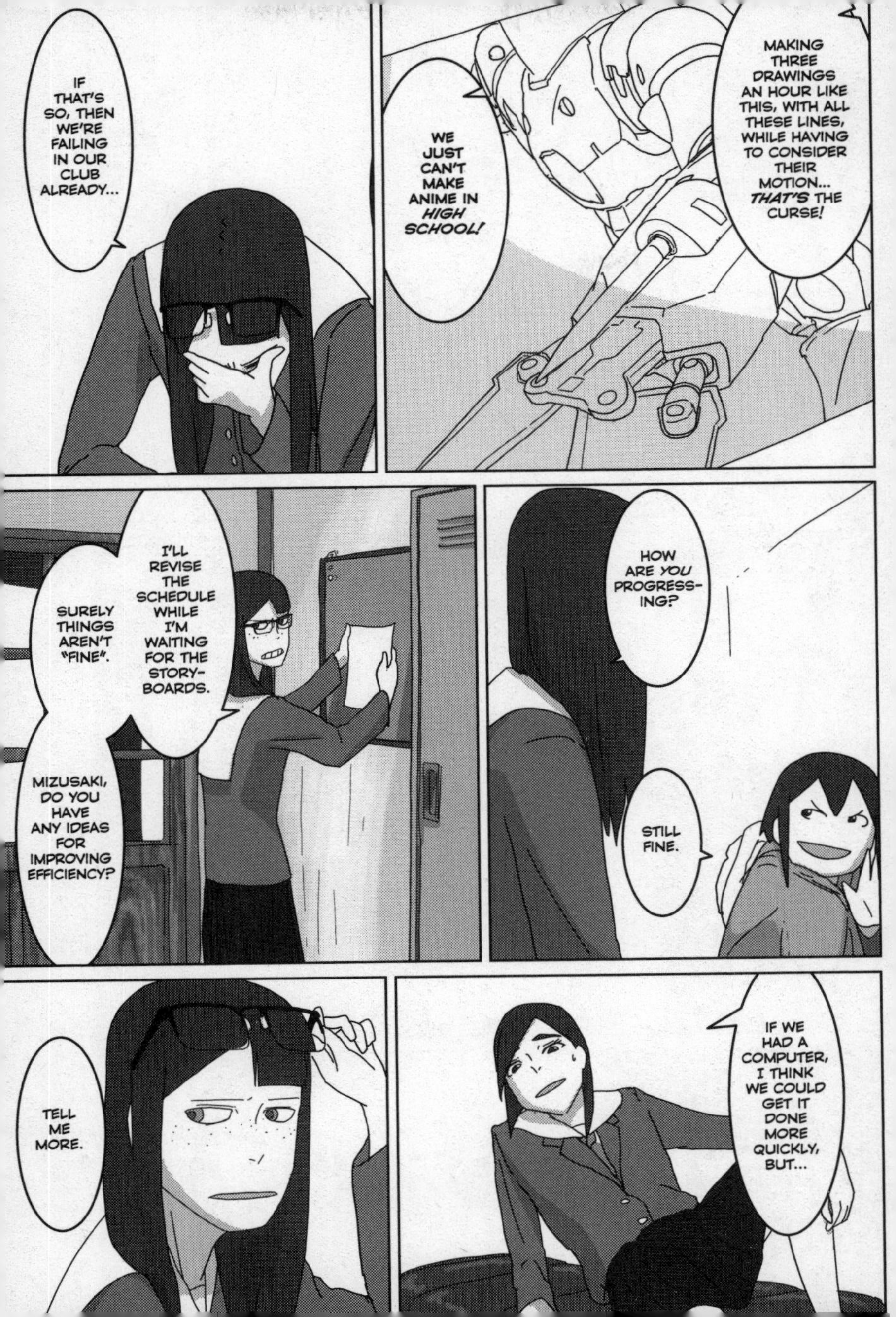
MAKING THREE DRAWINGS AN HOUR LIKE THIS, WITH ALL THESE LINES, WHILE HAVING TO CONSIDER THEIR MOTION... *THAT'S* THE CURSE!
WE JUST CAN'T MAKE ANIME IN *HIGH SCHOOL!*
IF THAT'S SO, THEN WE'RE FAILING IN OUR CLUB ALREADY...
HOW ARE *YOU* PROGRESSING?
STILL FINE.
I'LL REVISE THE SCHEDULE WHILE I'M WAITING FOR THE STORY-BOARDS.
SURELY THINGS AREN'T "FINE".
MIZUSAKI, DO YOU HAVE ANY IDEAS FOR IMPROVING EFFICIENCY?
IF WE HAD A COMPUTER, I THINK WE COULD GET IT DONE MORE QUICKLY, BUT...
TELL ME MORE.

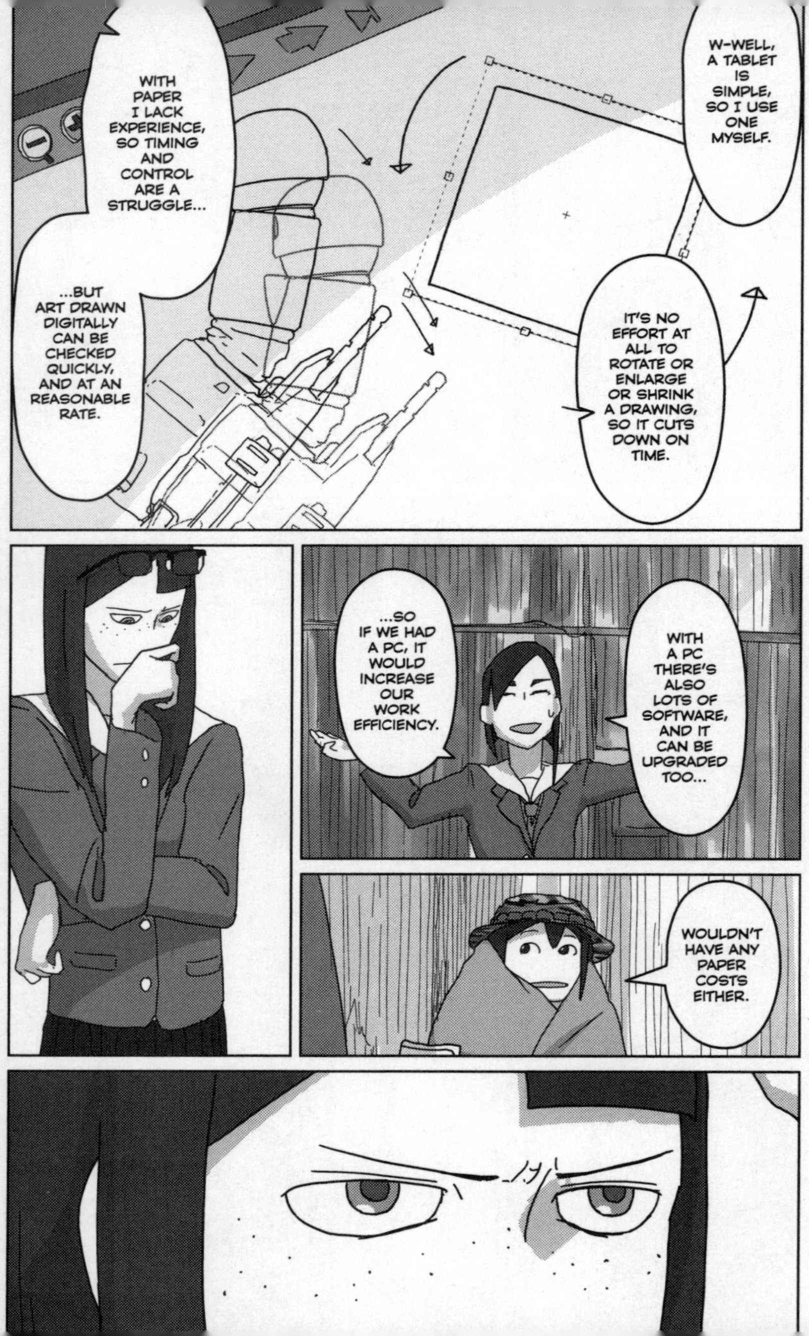
W-WELL, A TABLET IS SIMPLE, SO I USE ONE MYSELF.
IT'S NO EFFORT AT ALL TO ROTATE OR ENLARGE OR SHRINK A DRAWING, SO IT CUTS DOWN ON TIME.
WITH PAPER I LACK EXPERIENCE, SO TIMING AND CONTROL ARE A STRUGGLE...
...BUT ART DRAWN DIGITALLY CAN BE CHECKED QUICKLY, AND AT AN REASONABLE RATE.
WITH A PC THERE'S ALSO LOTS OF SOFTWARE, AND IT CAN BE UPGRADED TOO...
...SO IF WE HAD A PC, IT WOULD INCREASE OUR WORK EFFICIENCY.
WOULDN'T HAVE ANY PAPER COSTS EITHER.

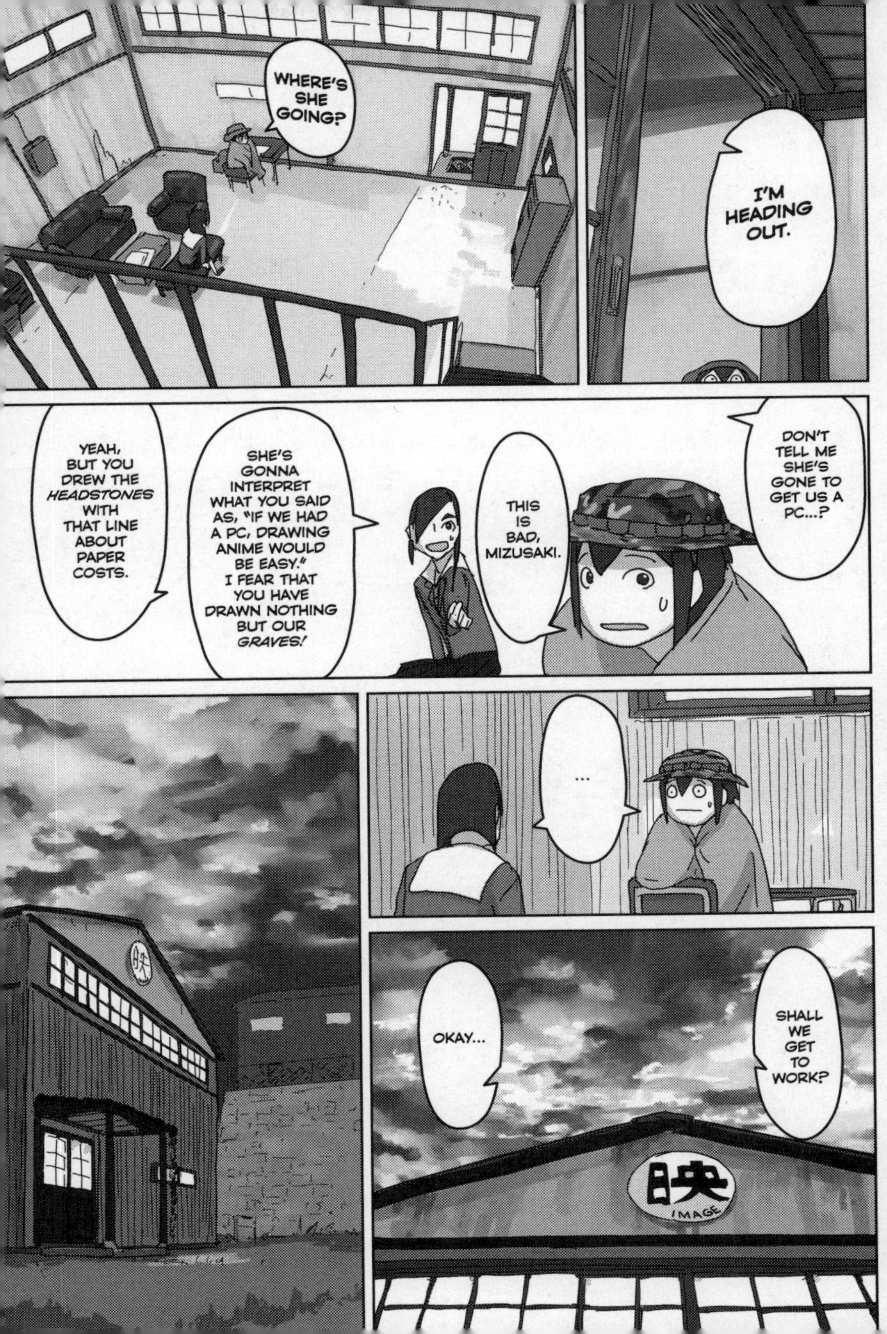
I'M HEADING OUT.
WHERE'S SHE GOING?
DON'T TELL ME SHE'S GONE TO GET US A PC...?
THIS IS BAD, MIZUSAKI.
SHE'S GONNA INTERPRET WHAT YOU SAID AS, "IF WE HAD A PC, DRAWING ANIME WOULD BE EASY." I FEAR THAT YOU HAVE DRAWN NOTHING BUT OUR *GRAVES!*
YEAH, BUT YOU DREW THE *HEADSTONES* WITH THAT LINE ABOUT PAPER COSTS.
...
SHALL WE GET TO WORK?
OKAY...
映
IMAGE

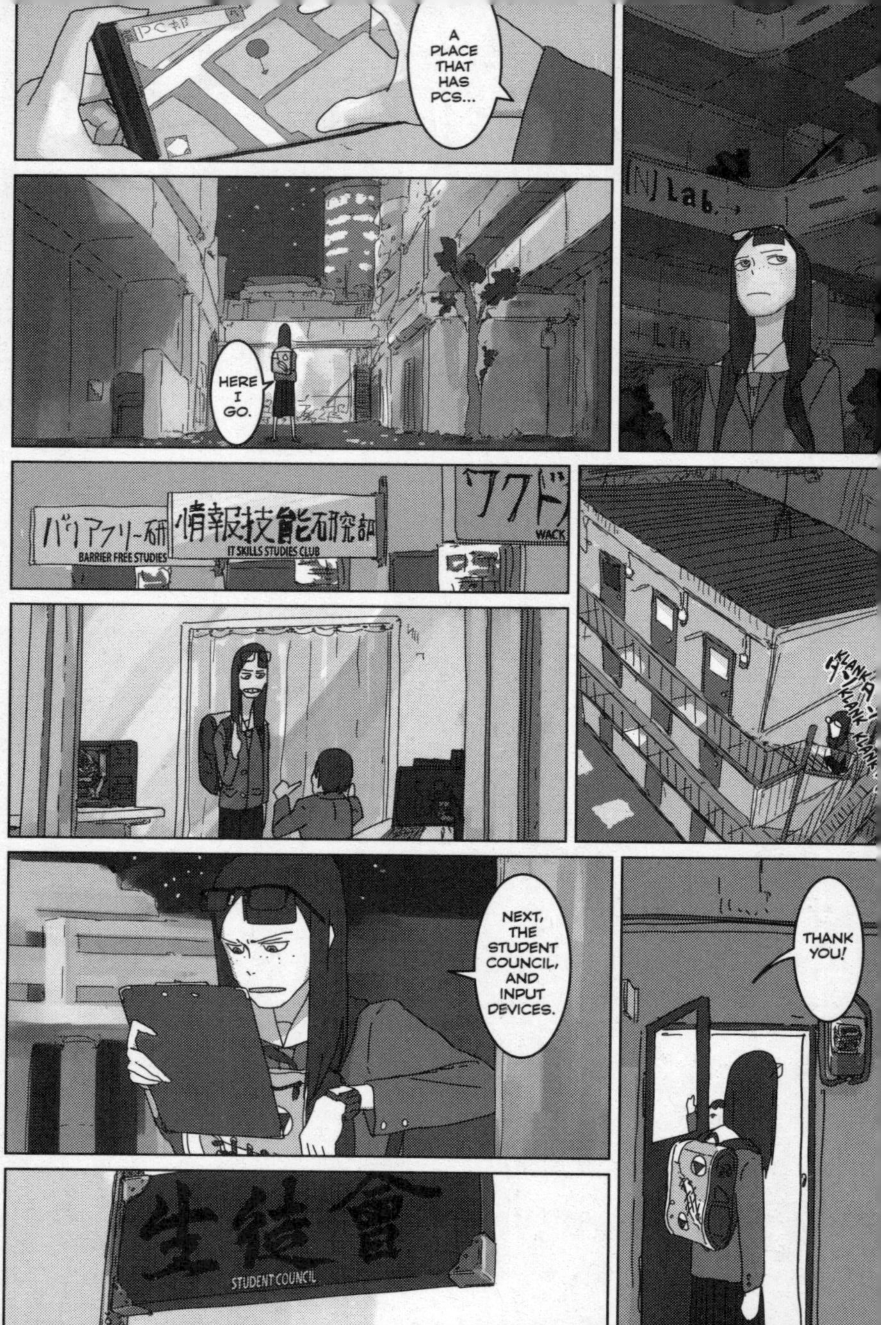
A PLACE THAT HAS PCS...
HERE I GO.
KLANK KLANK KLANK
ワクド
WACK
情報技能研究部
IT SKILLS STUDIES CLUB
バリアフリー研
BARRIER FREE STUDIES
THANK YOU!
NEXT, THE STUDENT COUNCIL, AND INPUT DEVICES.
生徒會
STUDENT COUNCIL

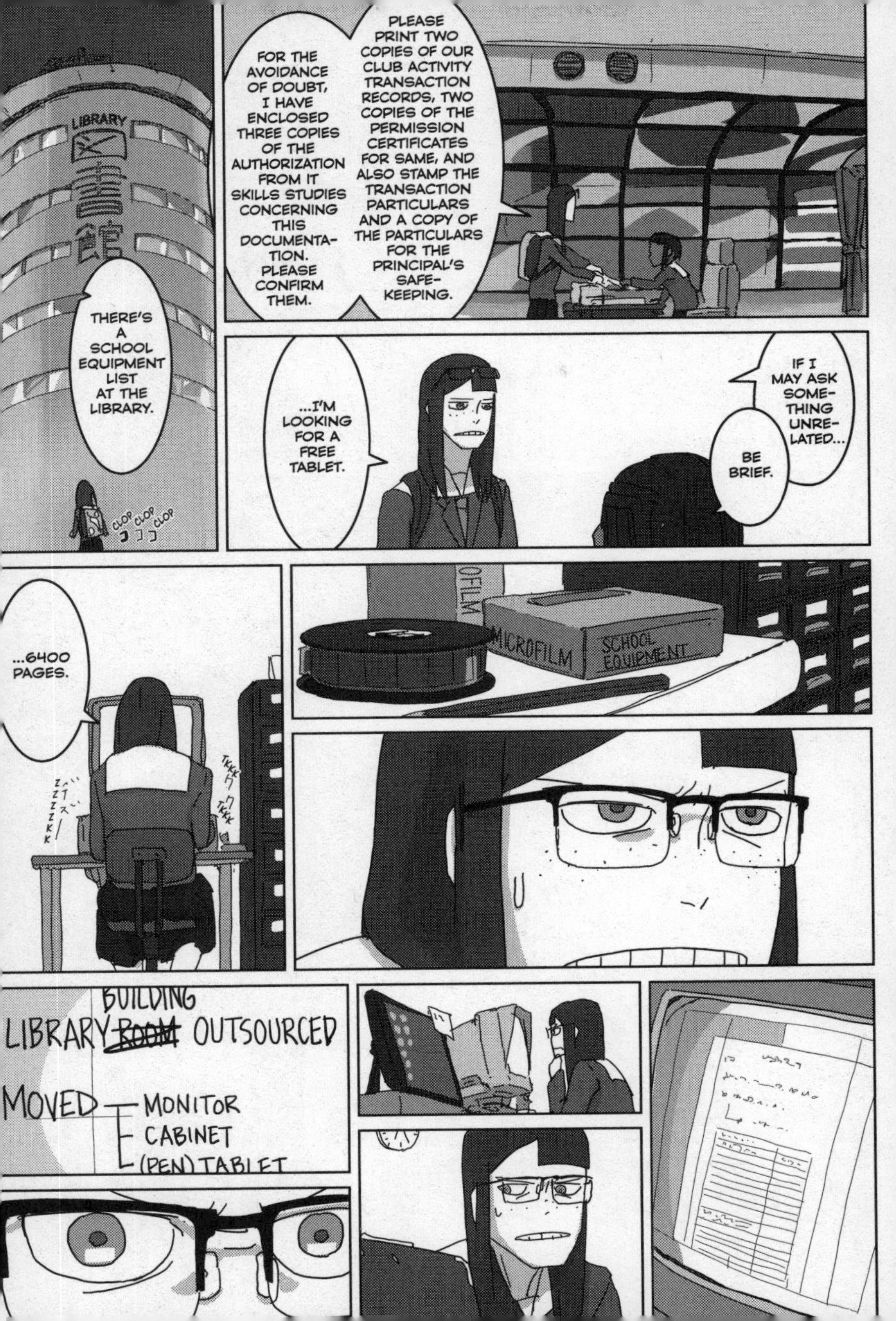
PLEASE PRINT TWO COPIES OF OUR CLUB ACTIVITY TRANSACTION RECORDS, TWO COPIES OF THE PERMISSION CERTIFICATES FOR SAME, AND ALSO STAMP THE TRANSACTION PARTICULARS AND A COPY OF THE PARTICULARS FOR THE PRINCIPAL'S SAFE-KEEPING.
FOR THE AVOIDANCE OF DOUBT, I HAVE ENCLOSED THREE COPIES OF THE AUTHORIZATION FROM IT SKILLS STUDIES CONCERNING THIS DOCUMENTA-TION. PLEASE CONFIRM THEM.
IF I MAY ASK SOME-THING UNRE-LATED...
BE BRIEF.
...I'M LOOKING FOR A FREE TABLET.
LIBRARY
THERE'S A SCHOOL EQUIPMENT LIST AT THE LIBRARY.
CLOP CLOP CLOP
MICROFILM
SCHOOL EQUIPMENT
...6400 PAGES.
TKKK TKKK
ZZZZKK
LIBRARY ~~ROOM~~ BUILDING OUTSOURCED
MOVED
MONITOR
CABINET
(PEN) TABLET

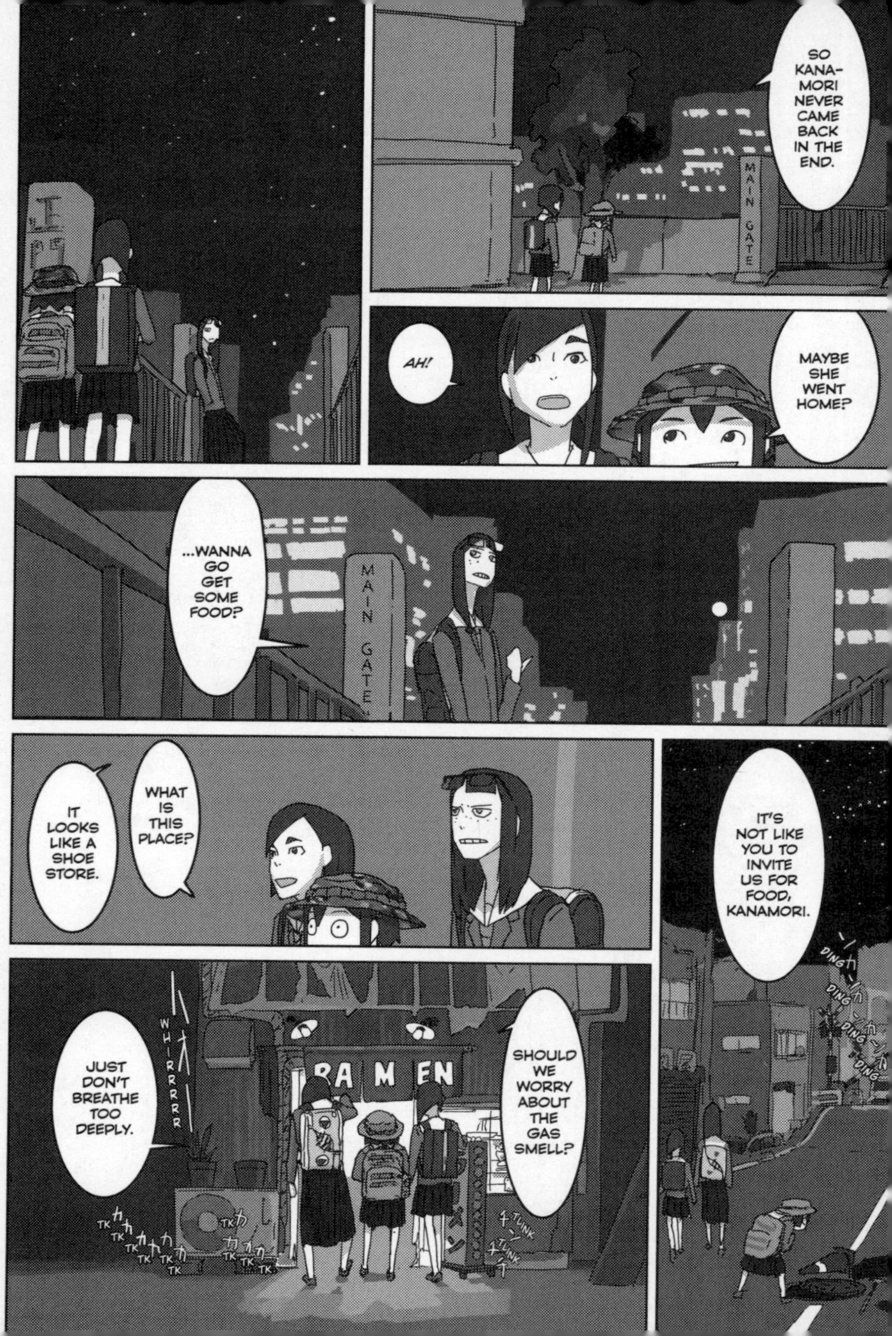
SO KANAMORI NEVER CAME BACK IN THE END.
MAIN GATE
MAYBE SHE WENT HOME?
AH!
...WANNA GO GET SOME FOOD?
MAIN GATE
IT'S NOT LIKE YOU TO INVITE US FOR FOOD, KANAMORI.
DING DING DING DING
WHAT IS THIS PLACE?
IT LOOKS LIKE A SHOE STORE.
SHOULD WE WORRY ABOUT THE GAS SMELL?
RAMEN
TLINK TLINK
JUST DON'T BREATHE TOO DEEPLY.
WHIRRRRR
TK TK TK TK TK TK TK TK TK

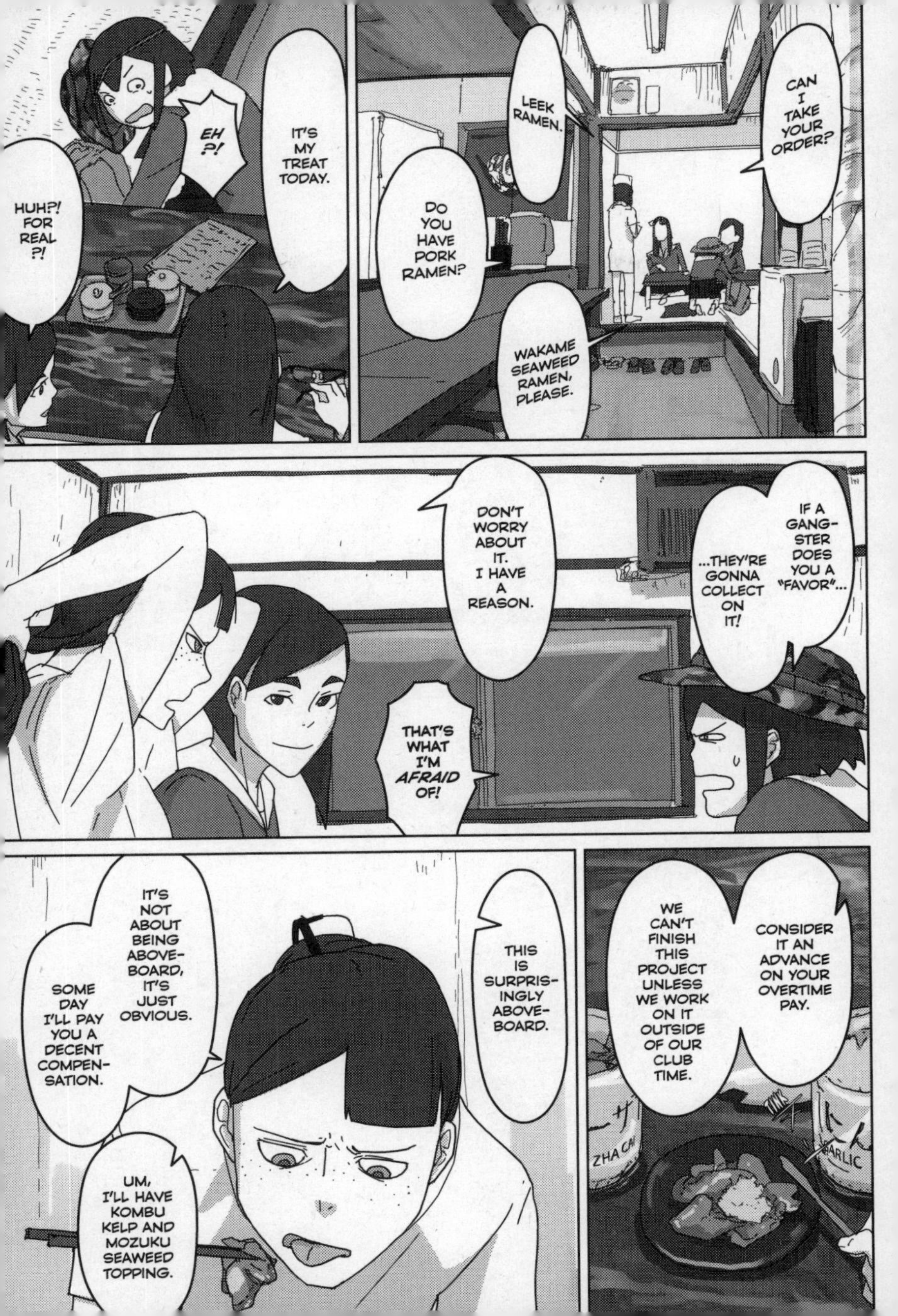

CAN I TAKE YOUR ORDER?
LEEK RAMEN.
DO YOU HAVE PORK RAMEN?
WAKAME SEAWEED RAMEN, PLEASE.
IT'S MY TREAT TODAY.
EH?!
HUH?! FOR REAL?!
IF A GANGSTER DOES YOU A "FAVOR"...
...THEY'RE GONNA COLLECT ON IT!
DON'T WORRY ABOUT IT. I HAVE A REASON.
THAT'S WHAT I'M *AFRAID* OF!
CONSIDER IT AN ADVANCE ON YOUR OVERTIME PAY.
WE CAN'T FINISH THIS PROJECT UNLESS WE WORK ON IT OUTSIDE OF OUR CLUB TIME.
ZHA CAI
GARLIC
THIS IS SURPRISINGLY ABOVEBOARD.
IT'S NOT ABOUT BEING ABOVEBOARD, IT'S JUST OBVIOUS.
SOME DAY I'LL PAY YOU A DECENT COMPENSATION.
UM, I'LL HAVE KOMBU KELP AND MOZUKU SEAWEED TOPPING.

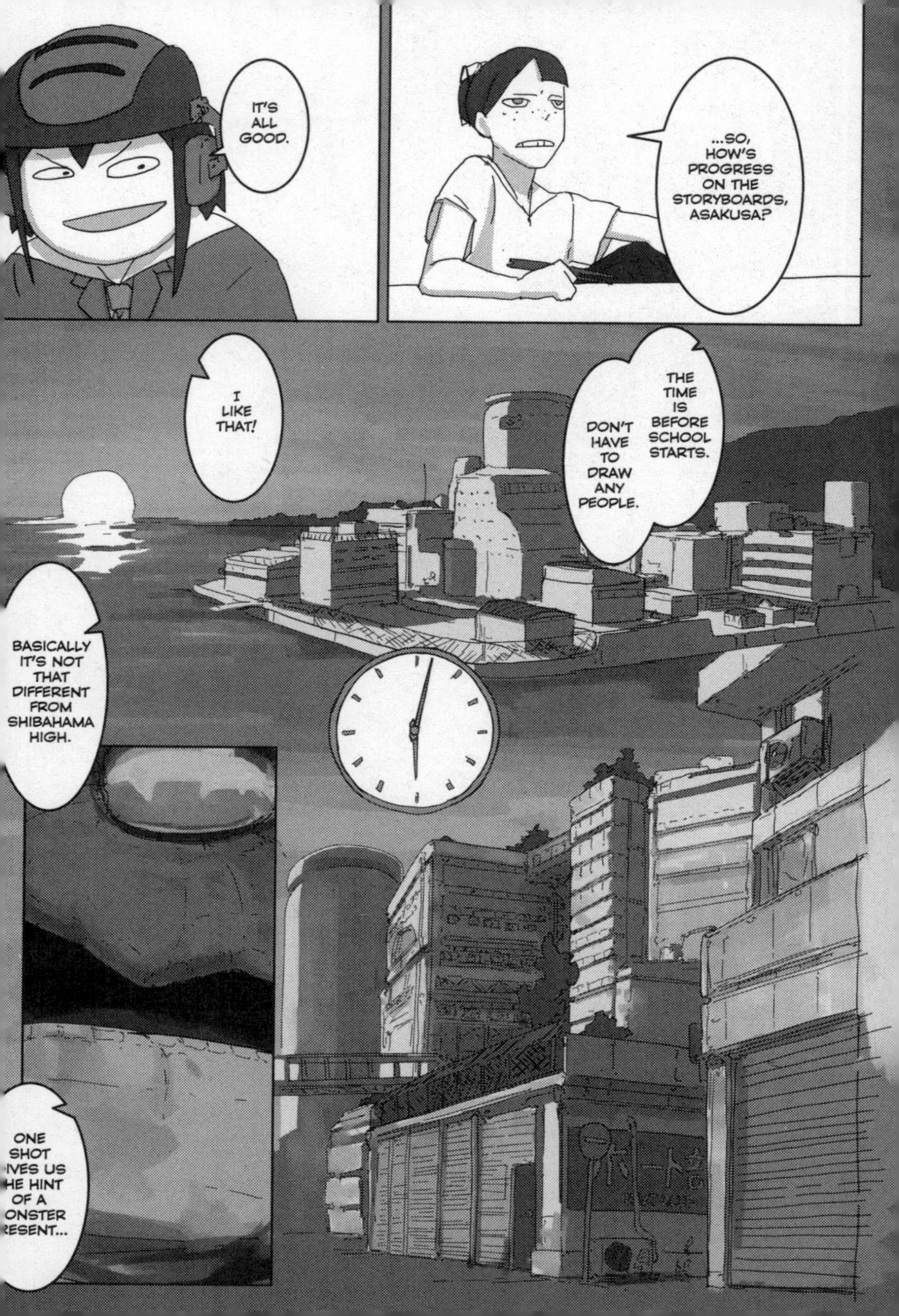
...SO, HOW'S PROGRESS ON THE STORYBOARDS, ASAKUSA?
IT'S ALL GOOD.
THE TIME IS BEFORE SCHOOL STARTS.
DON'T HAVE TO DRAW ANY PEOPLE.
I LIKE THAT!
BASICALLY IT'S NOT THAT DIFFERENT FROM SHIBAHAMA HIGH.
ONE SHOT IVES US HE HINT OF A ONSTER RESENT...

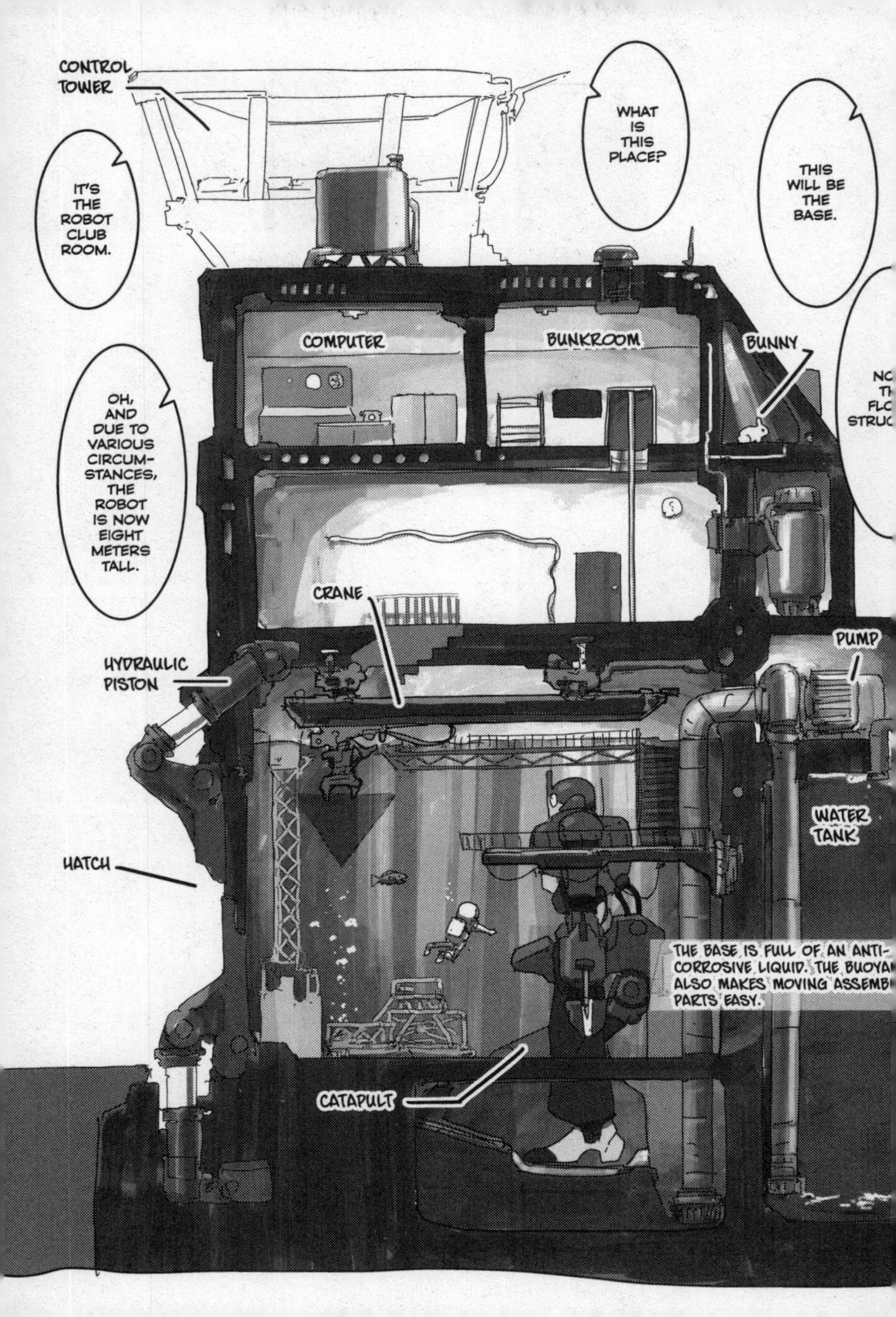
THIS WILL BE THE BASE.
WHAT IS THIS PLACE?
IT'S THE ROBOT CLUB ROOM.
CONTROL TOWER
BUNNY
BUNKROOM
COMPUTER
OH, AND DUE TO VARIOUS CIRCUMSTANCES, THE ROBOT IS NOW EIGHT METERS TALL.
PUMP
CRANE
HYDRAULIC PISTON
WATER TANK
HATCH
THE BASE IS FULL OF AN ANTI-CORROSIVE LIQUID. THE BUOYA ALSO MAKES MOVING ASSEMB PARTS EASY.
CATAPULT

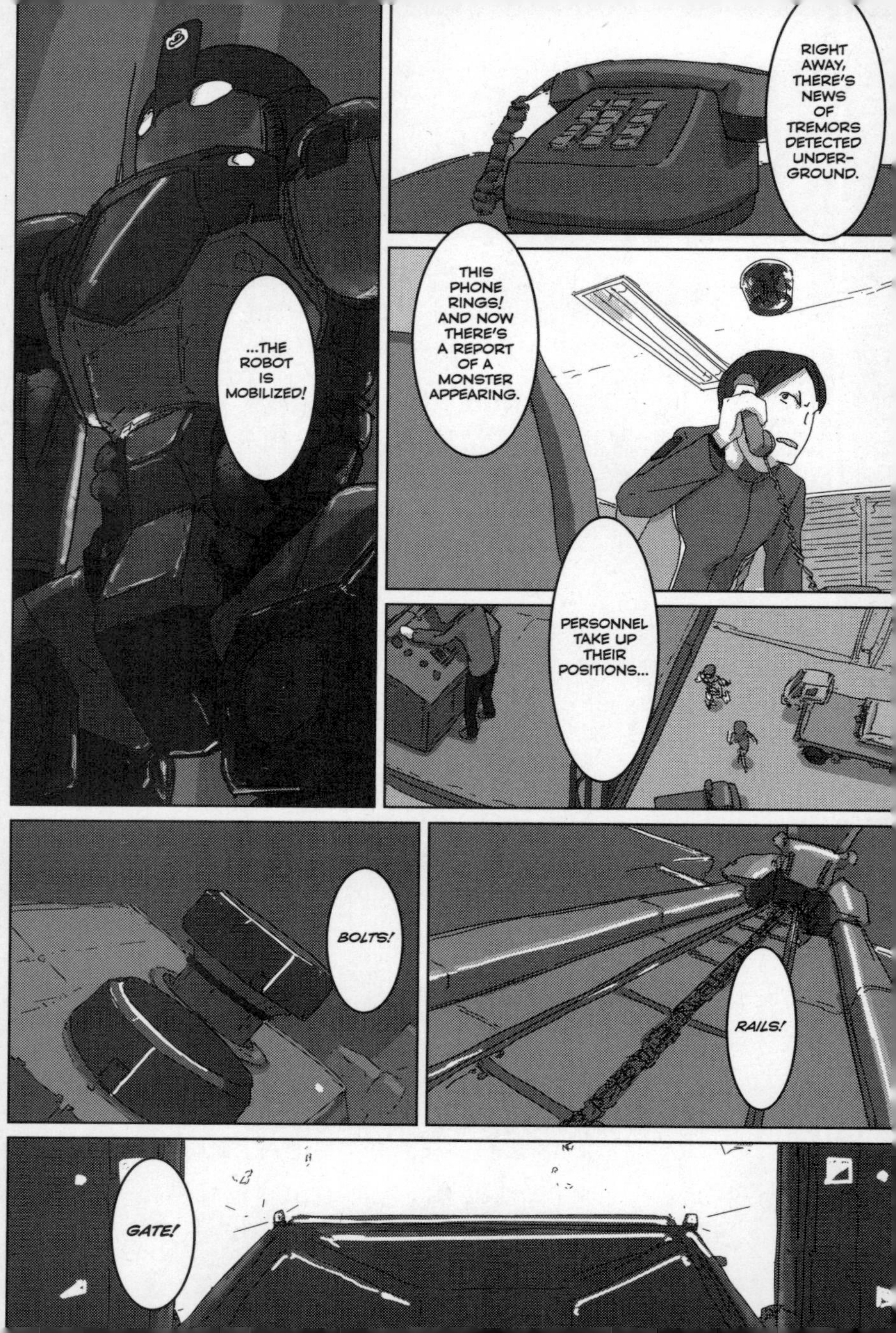
RIGHT AWAY, THERE'S NEWS OF TREMORS DETECTED UNDER-GROUND.
THIS PHONE RINGS! AND NOW THERE'S A REPORT OF A MONSTER APPEARING.
PERSONNEL TAKE UP THEIR POSITIONS...
...THE ROBOT IS MOBILIZED!
RAILS!
BOLTS!
GATE!

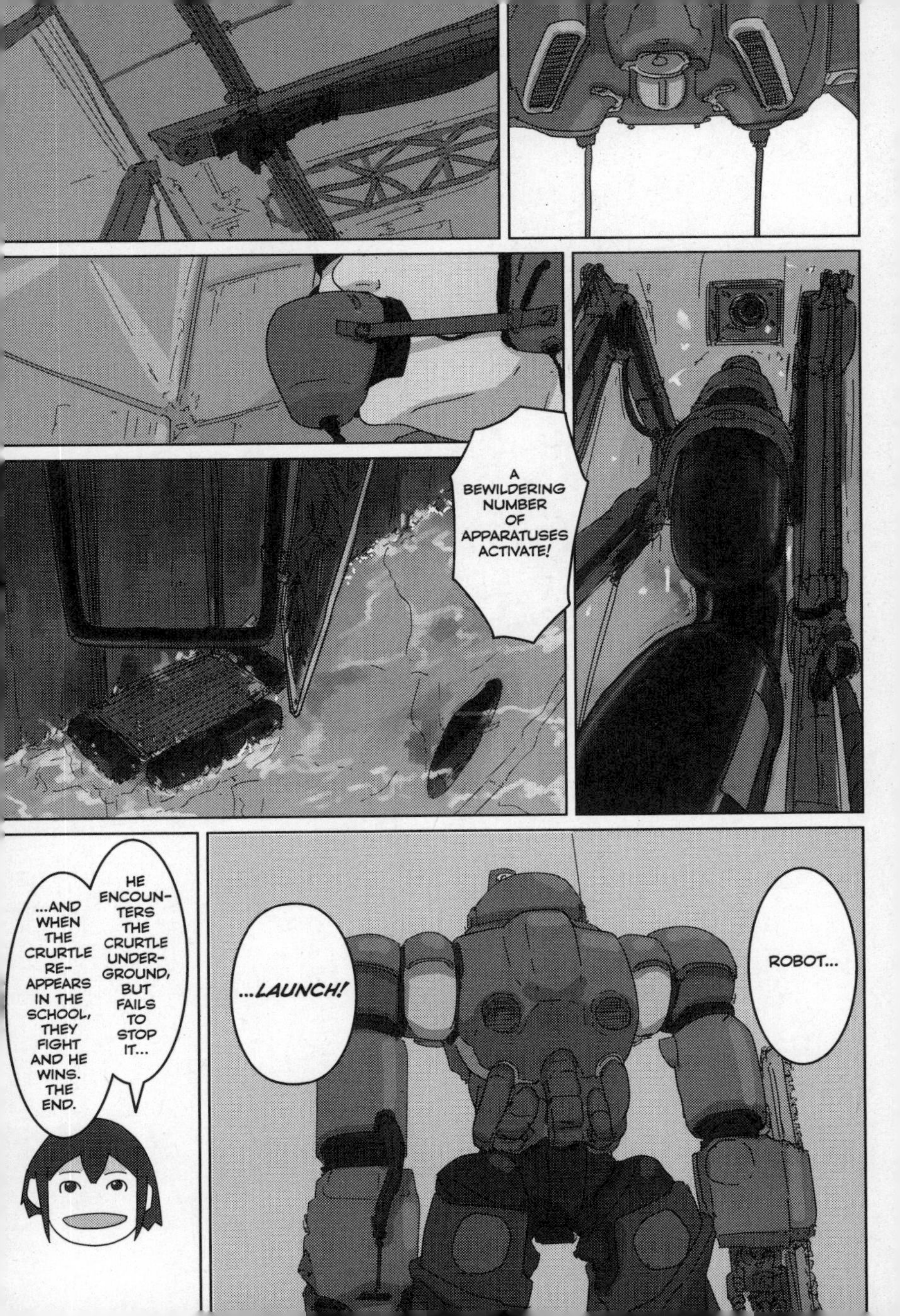
A BEWILDERING NUMBER OF APPARATUSES ACTIVATE!
ROBOT...
...LAUNCH!
HE ENCOUNTERS THE CRURTLE UNDERGROUND, BUT FAILS TO STOP IT...
...AND WHEN THE CRURTLE REAPPEARS IN THE SCHOOL, THEY FIGHT AND HE WINS. THE END.

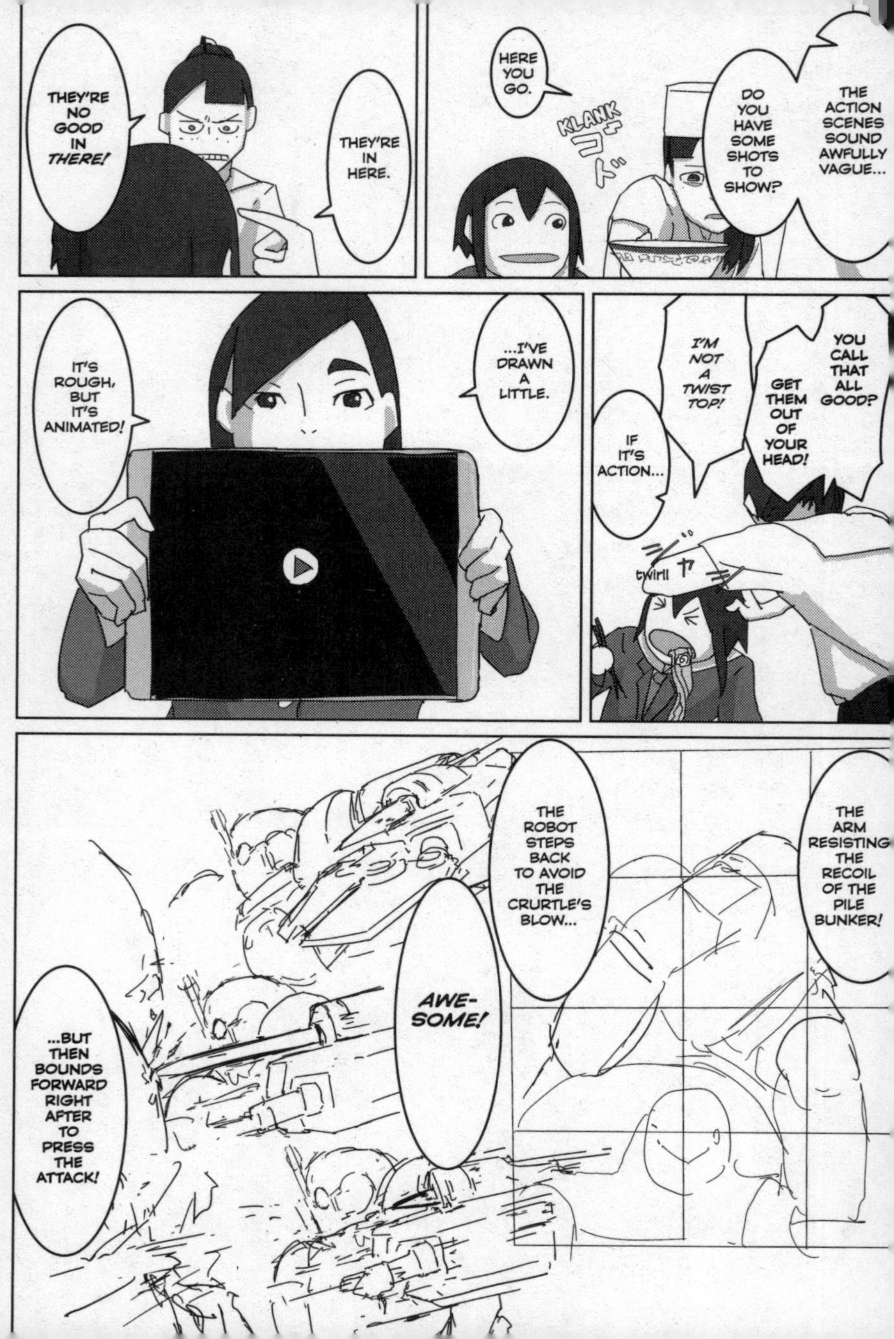
THE ACTION SCENES SOUND AWFULLY VAGUE...
DO YOU HAVE SOME SHOTS TO SHOW?
KLANK
HERE YOU GO.
THEY'RE IN HERE.
THEY'RE NO GOOD IN *THERE!*
YOU CALL THAT ALL GOOD?
GET THEM OUT OF YOUR HEAD!
I'M NOT A TWIST TOP!
IF IT'S ACTION...
twirl
...I'VE DRAWN A LITTLE.
IT'S ROUGH, BUT IT'S ANIMATED!
THE ARM RESISTING THE RECOIL OF THE PILE BUNKER!
THE ROBOT STEPS BACK TO AVOID THE CRURTLE'S BLOW...
AWESOME!
...BUT THEN BOUNDS FORWARD RIGHT AFTER TO PRESS THE ATTACK!

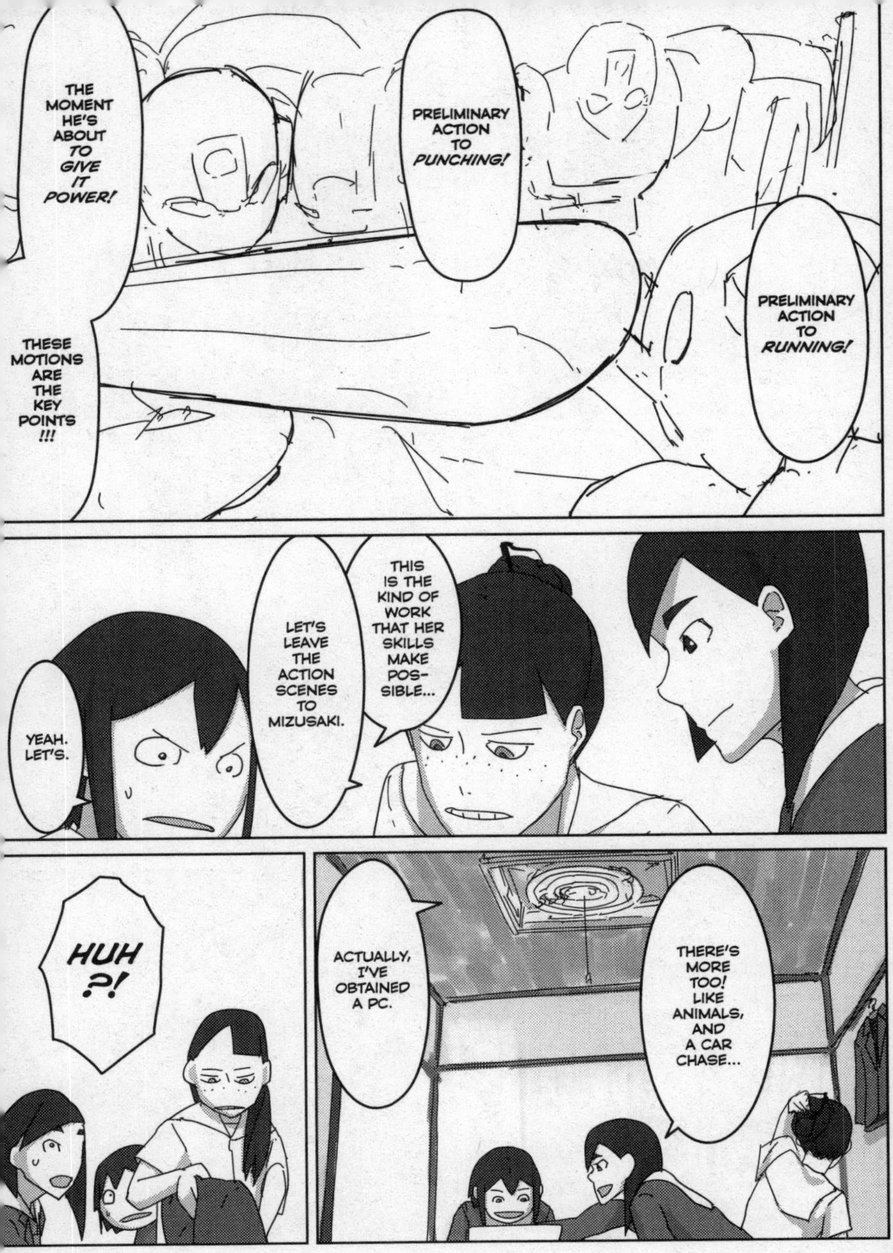
PRELIMINARY ACTION TO RUNNING!
PRELIMINARY ACTION TO PUNCHING!
THE MOMENT HE'S ABOUT TO GIVE IT POWER!
THESE MOTIONS ARE THE KEY POINTS !!!
THIS IS THE KIND OF WORK THAT HER SKILLS MAKE POSSIBLE...
LET'S LEAVE THE ACTION SCENES TO MIZUSAKI.
YEAH. LET'S.
THERE'S MORE TOO! LIKE ANIMALS, AND A CAR CHASE...
ACTUALLY, I'VE OBTAINED A PC.
HUH ?!

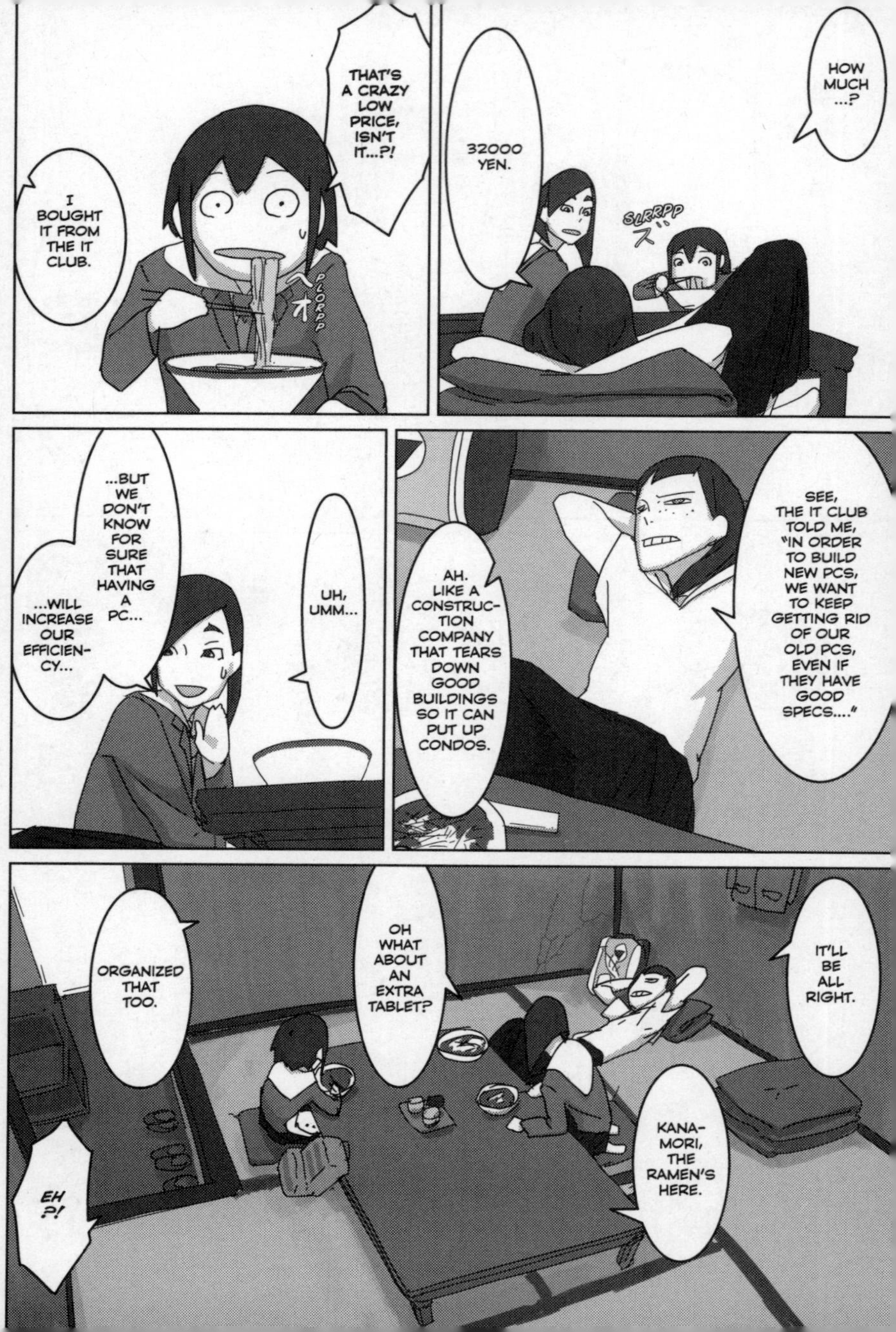
HOW MUCH ...?
32000 YEN.
SLRRPP
THAT'S A CRAZY LOW PRICE, ISN'T IT...?!
PLORPP
I BOUGHT IT FROM THE IT CLUB.
SEE, THE IT CLUB TOLD ME, "IN ORDER TO BUILD NEW PCS, WE WANT TO KEEP GETTING RID OF OUR OLD PCS, EVEN IF THEY HAVE GOOD SPECS...."
AH. LIKE A CONSTRUCTION COMPANY THAT TEARS DOWN GOOD BUILDINGS SO IT CAN PUT UP CONDOS.
UH, UMM...
...BUT WE DON'T KNOW FOR SURE THAT HAVING A PC...
...WILL INCREASE OUR EFFICIENCY...
IT'LL BE ALL RIGHT.
KANAMORI, THE RAMEN'S HERE.
OH WHAT ABOUT AN EXTRA TABLET?
ORGANIZED THAT TOO.
EH ?!

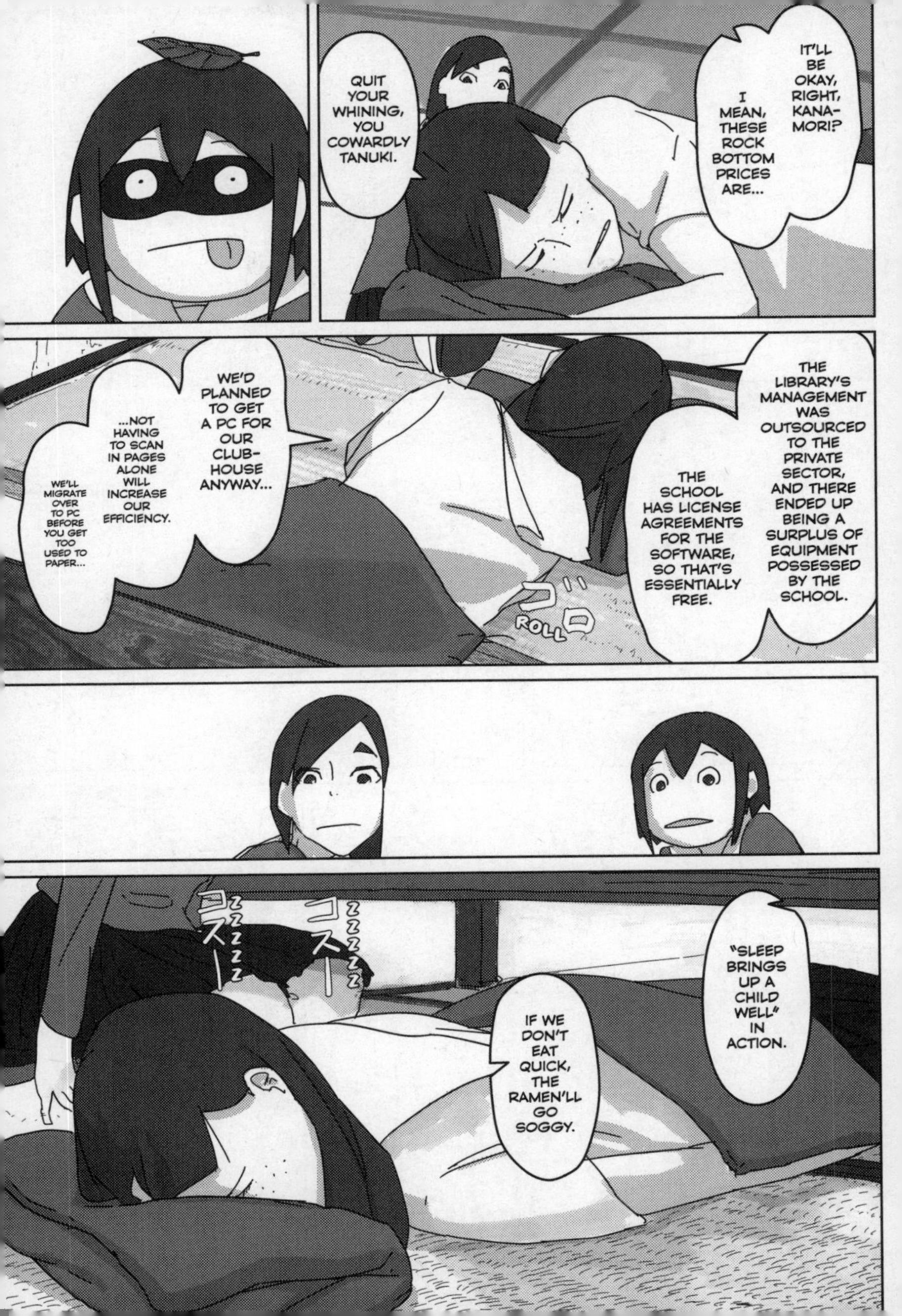
IT'LL BE OKAY, RIGHT, KANAMORI?
I MEAN, THESE ROCK BOTTOM PRICES ARE...
QUIT YOUR WHINING, YOU COWARDLY TANUKI.
THE LIBRARY'S MANAGEMENT WAS OUTSOURCED TO THE PRIVATE SECTOR, AND THERE ENDED UP BEING A SURPLUS OF EQUIPMENT POSSESSED BY THE SCHOOL.
THE SCHOOL HAS LICENSE AGREEMENTS FOR THE SOFTWARE, SO THAT'S ESSENTIALLY FREE.
コロ
ROLL
WE'D PLANNED TO GET A PC FOR OUR CLUBHOUSE ANYWAY...
...NOT HAVING TO SCAN IN PAGES ALONE WILL INCREASE OUR EFFICIENCY.
WE'LL MIGRATE OVER TO PC BEFORE YOU GET TOO USED TO PAPER...
"SLEEP BRINGS UP A CHILD WELL" IN ACTION.
IF WE DON'T EAT QUICK, THE RAMEN'LL GO SOGGY.
コスー
コスー

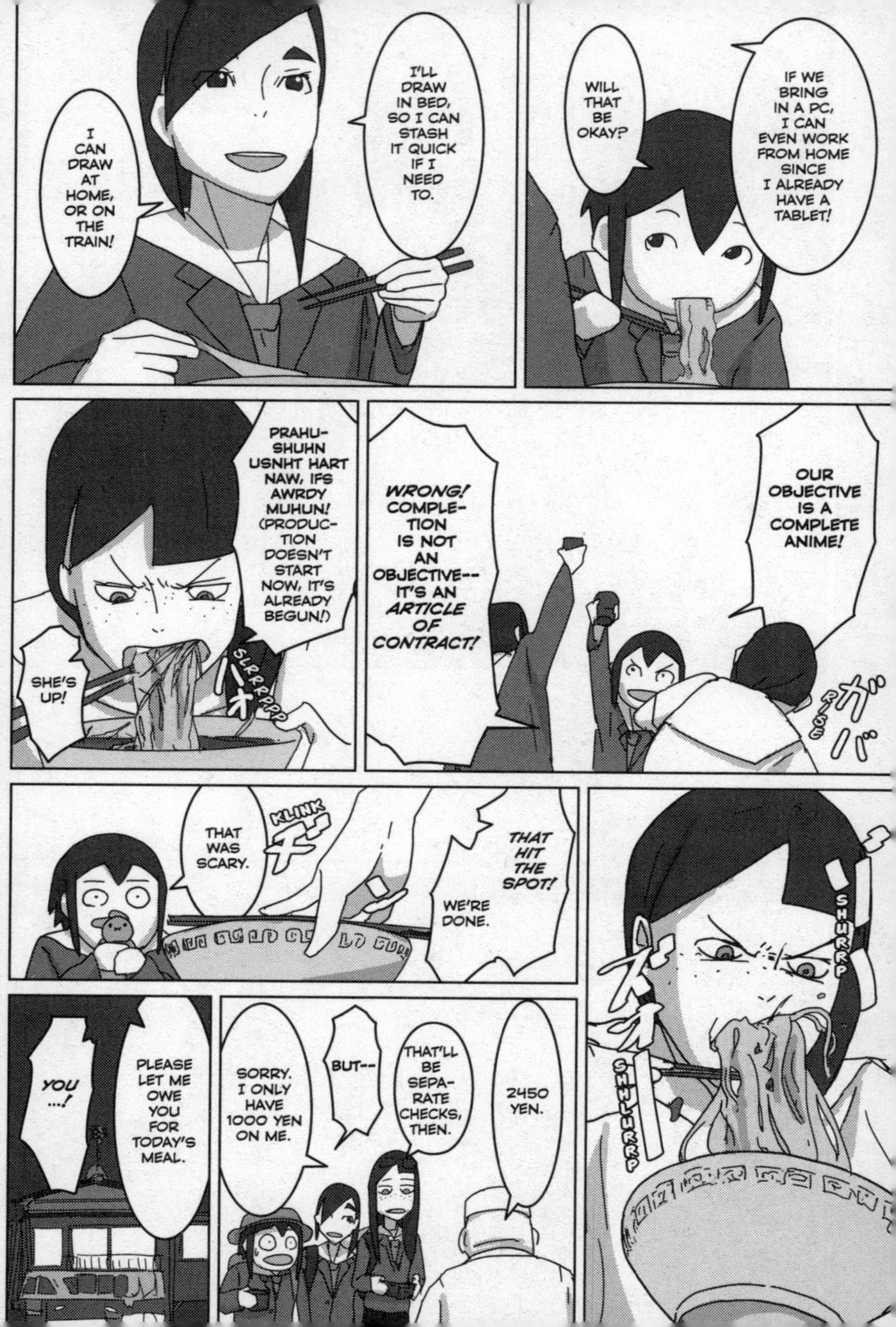
IF WE BRING IN A PC, I CAN EVEN WORK FROM HOME SINCE I ALREADY HAVE A TABLET!
WILL THAT BE OKAY?
I'LL DRAW IN BED, SO I CAN STASH IT QUICK IF I NEED TO.
I CAN DRAW AT HOME, OR ON THE TRAIN!
OUR OBJECTIVE IS A COMPLETE ANIME!
RISE
WRONG! COMPLETION IS NOT AN OBJECTIVE--IT'S AN ARTICLE OF CONTRACT!
PRAHU-SHUHN USNHT HART NAW, IFS AWRDY MUHUN! (PRODUCTION DOESN'T START NOW, IT'S ALREADY BEGUN!)
SLRRRPPP
SHE'S UP!
SHURRP
SHLURRRP
THAT HIT THE SPOT!
WE'RE DONE.
KLINK
THAT WAS SCARY.
2450 YEN.
THAT'LL BE SEPARATE CHECKS, THEN.
BUT--
SORRY. I ONLY HAVE 1000 YEN ON ME.
PLEASE LET ME OWE YOU FOR TODAY'S MEAL.
YOU ...!

CHAPTER 12:
THE PAIR'S ON-SWITCHES

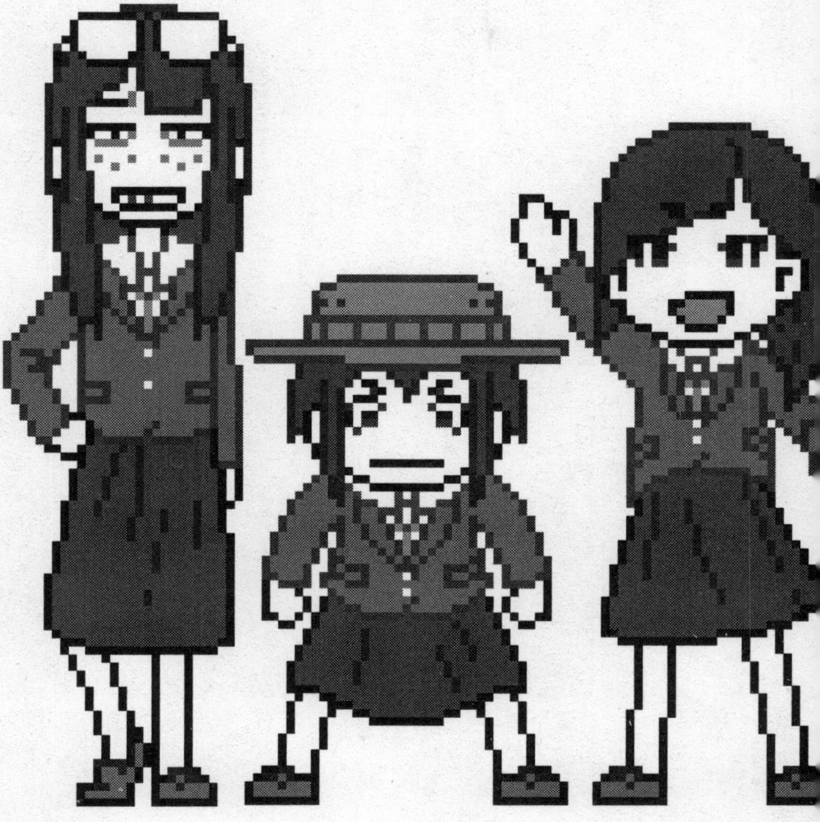

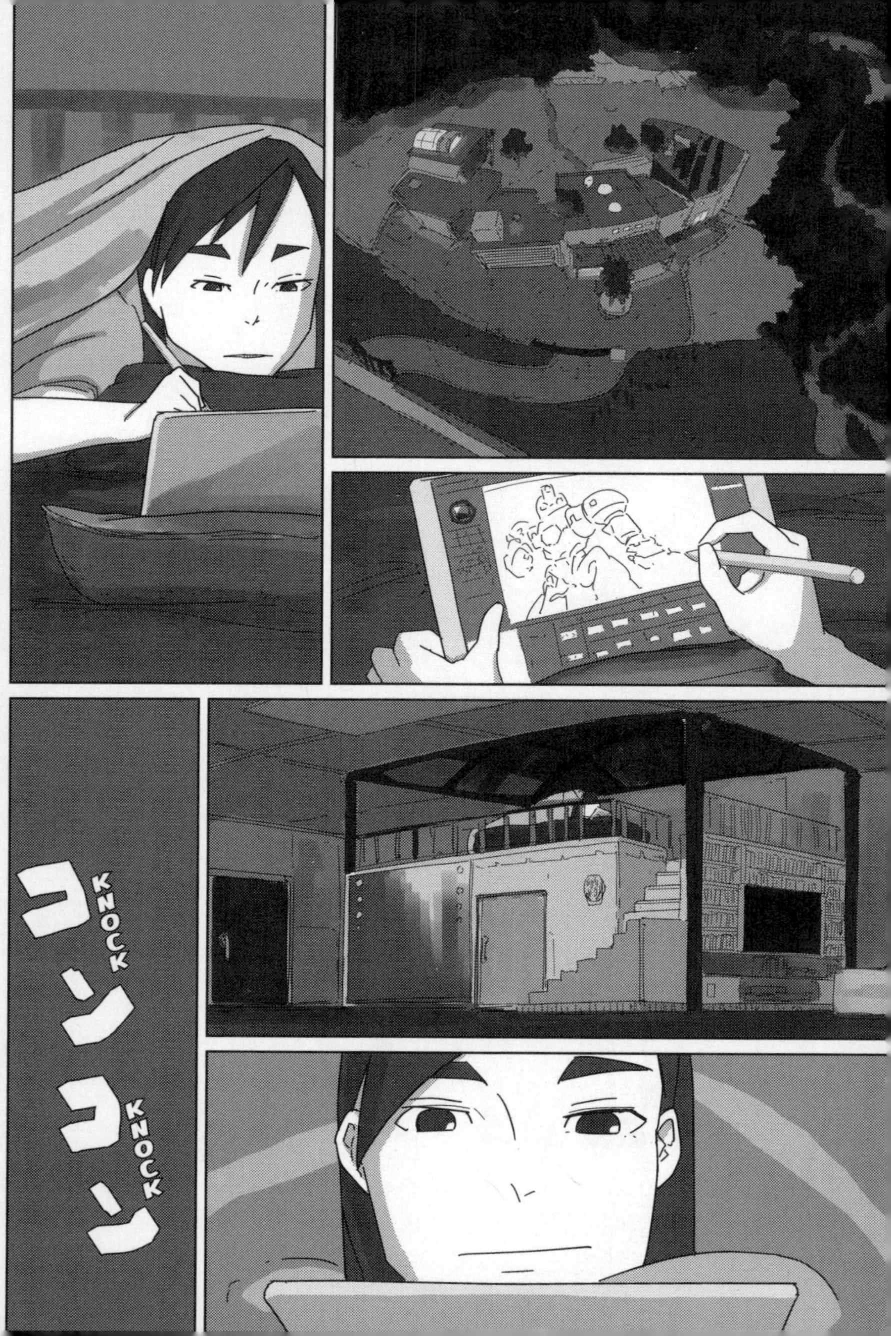
コーン
KNOCK
コーン
KNOCK

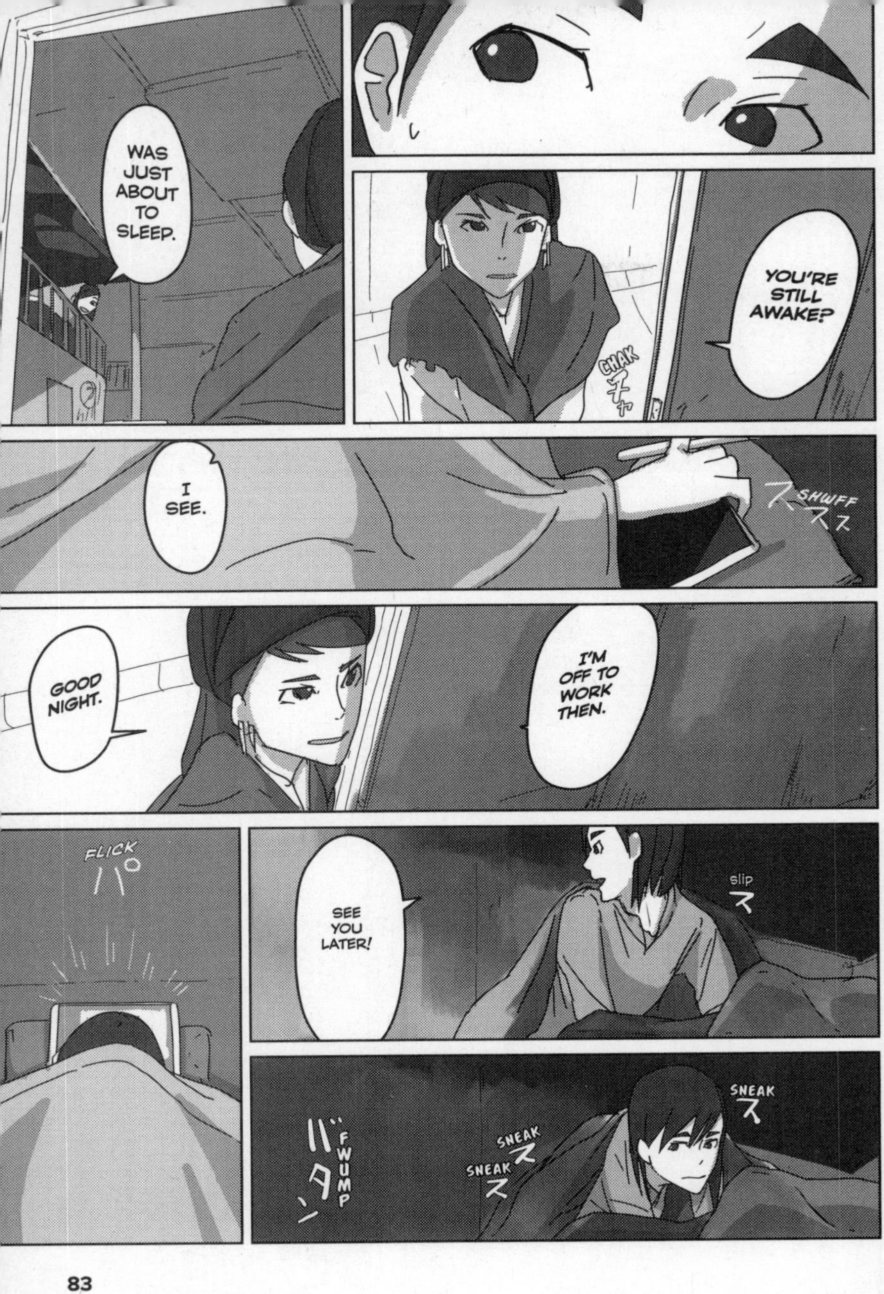
YOU'RE STILL AWAKE?
CHAK
WAS JUST ABOUT TO SLEEP.
SHWUFF
I SEE.
I'M OFF TO WORK THEN.
GOOD NIGHT.
slip
SEE YOU LATER!
SNEAK
SNEAK
SNEAK
FWUMP
FLICK

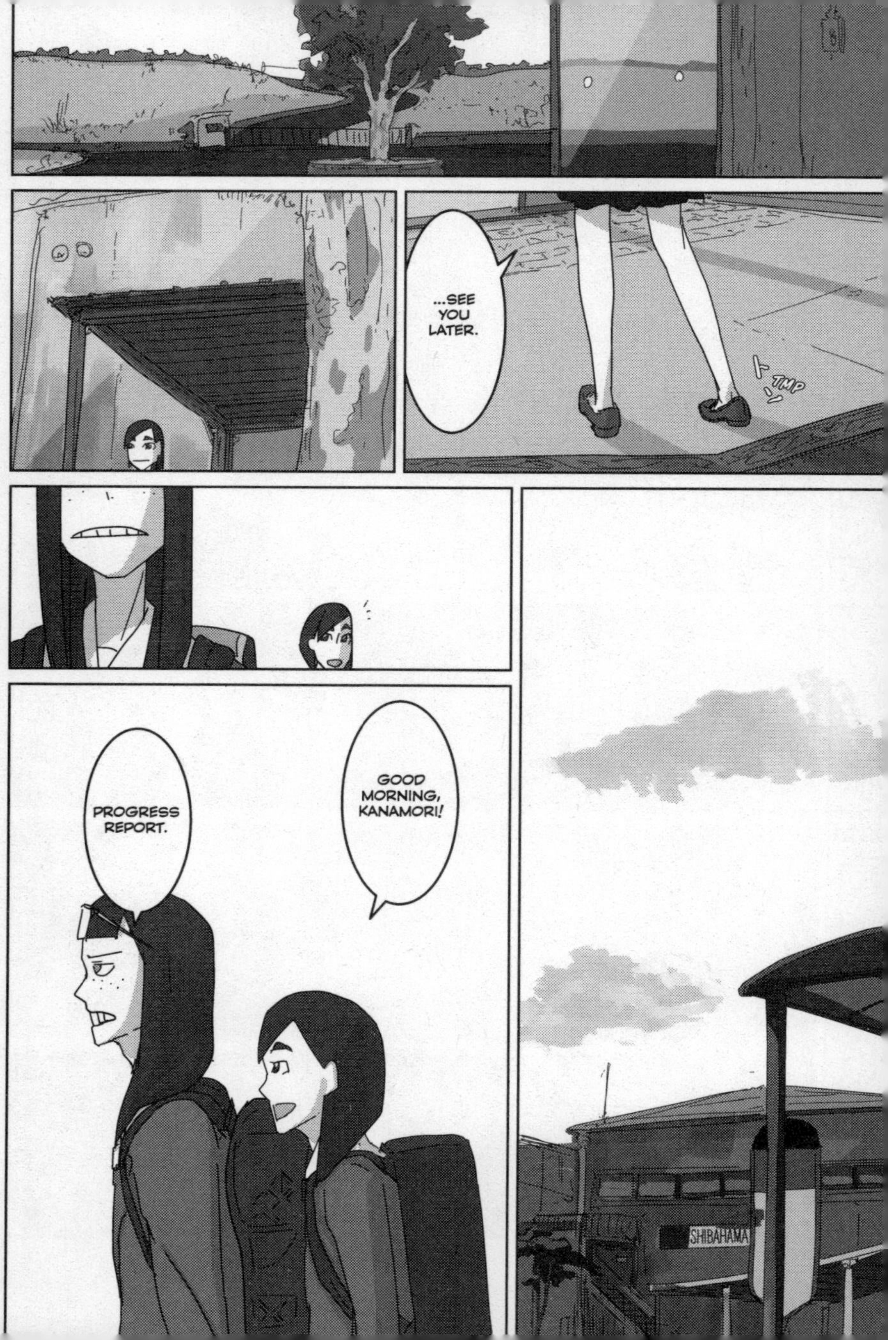
...SEE YOU LATER.
TMP
SHIBAHAMA
GOOD MORNING, KANAMORI!
PROGRESS REPORT.

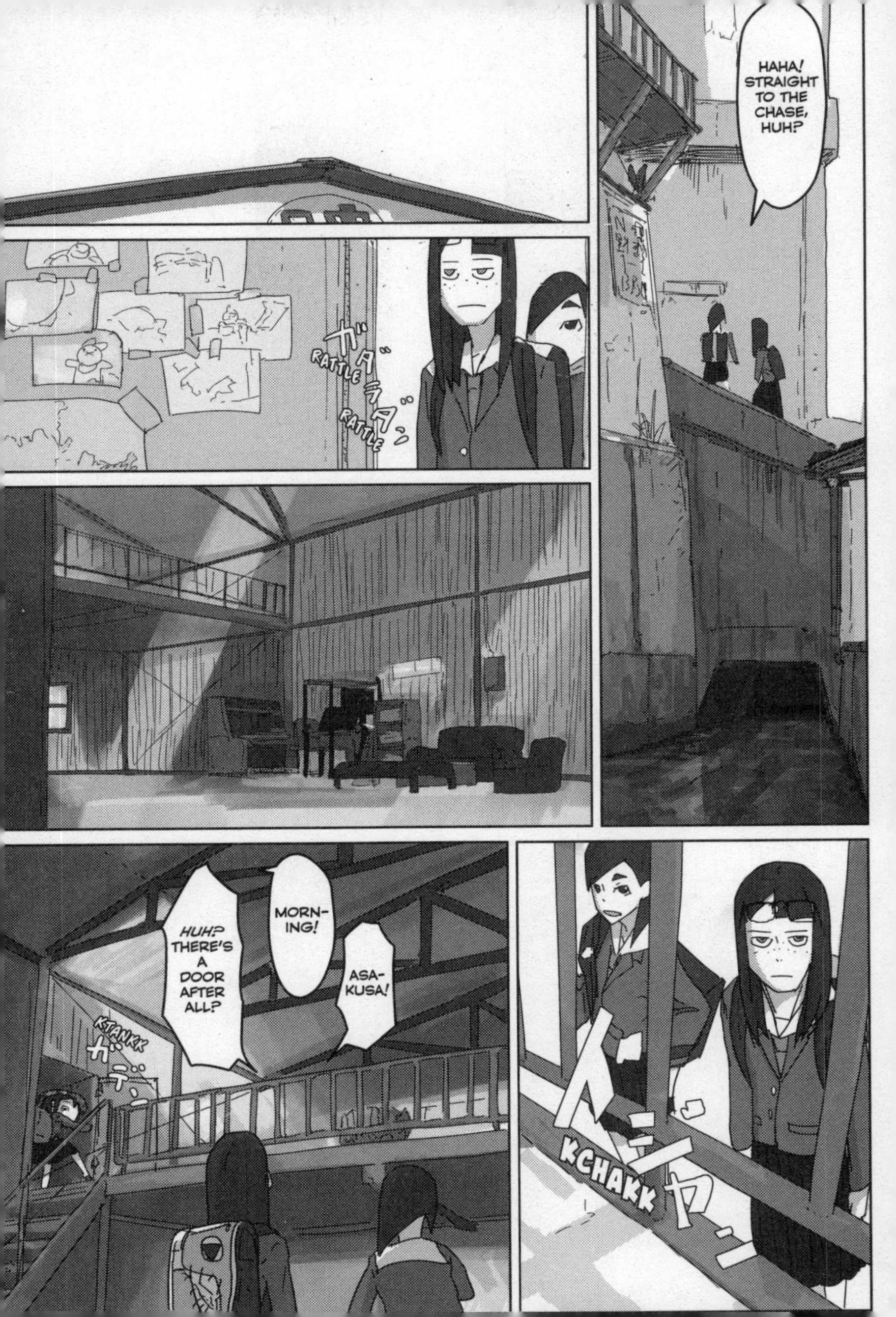
HAHA! STRAIGHT TO THE CHASE, HUH?
RATTLE RATTLE
KCHAKK
MORNING!
ASA-KUSA!
HUH? THERE'S A DOOR AFTER ALL?
KTANKK

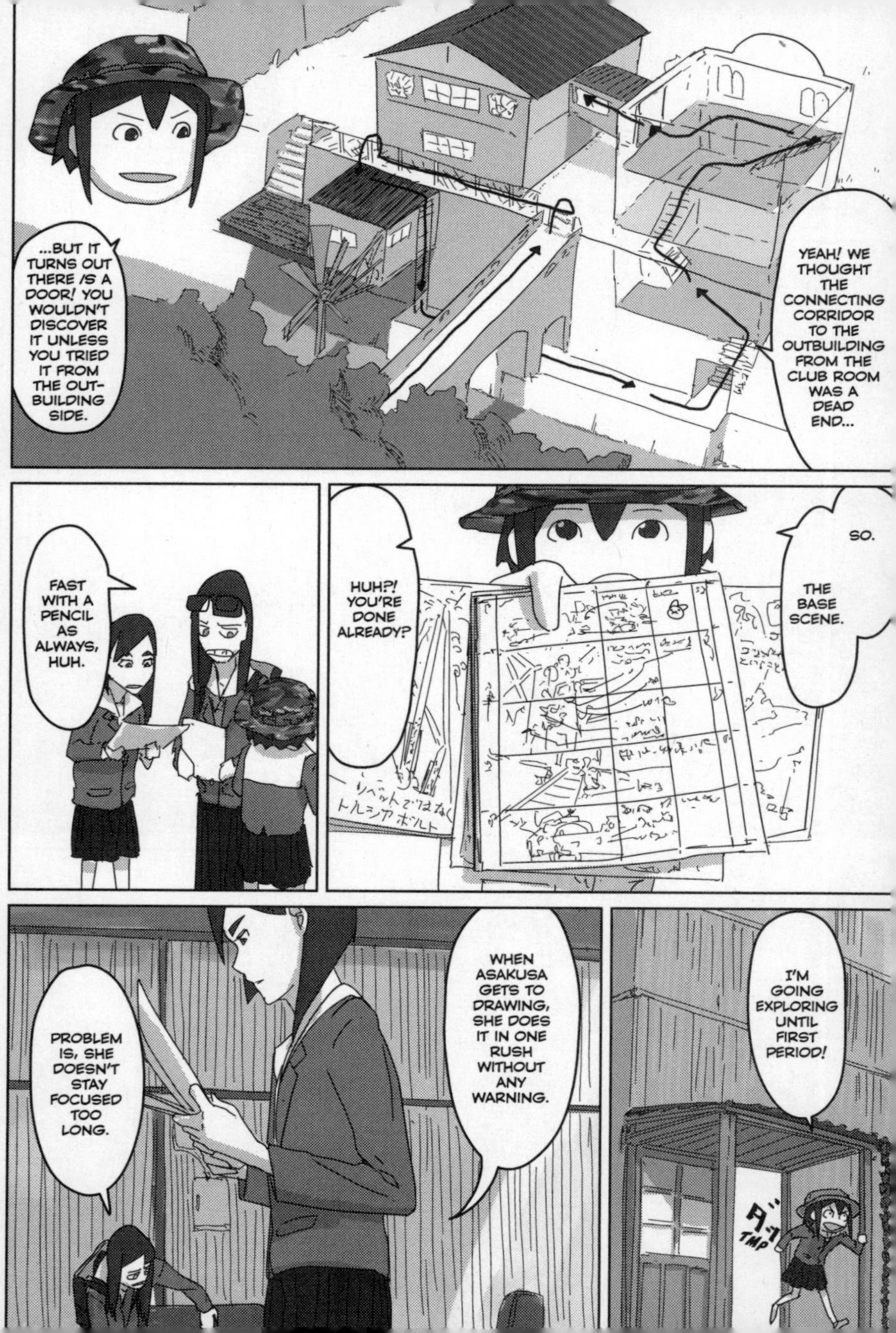
YEAH! WE THOUGHT THE CONNECTING CORRIDOR TO THE OUTBUILDING FROM THE CLUB ROOM WAS A DEAD END...
...BUT IT TURNS OUT THERE IS A DOOR! YOU WOULDN'T DISCOVER IT UNLESS YOU TRIED IT FROM THE OUT-BUILDING SIDE.
SO.
THE BASE SCENE.
HUH?! YOU'RE DONE ALREADY?
リベットではなく
トルシアボルト
FAST WITH A PENCIL AS ALWAYS, HUH.
I'M GOING EXPLORING UNTIL FIRST PERIOD!
ダッ
TMP
WHEN ASAKUSA GETS TO DRAWING, SHE DOES IT IN ONE RUSH WITHOUT ANY WARNING.
PROBLEM IS, SHE DOESN'T STAY FOCUSED TOO LONG.

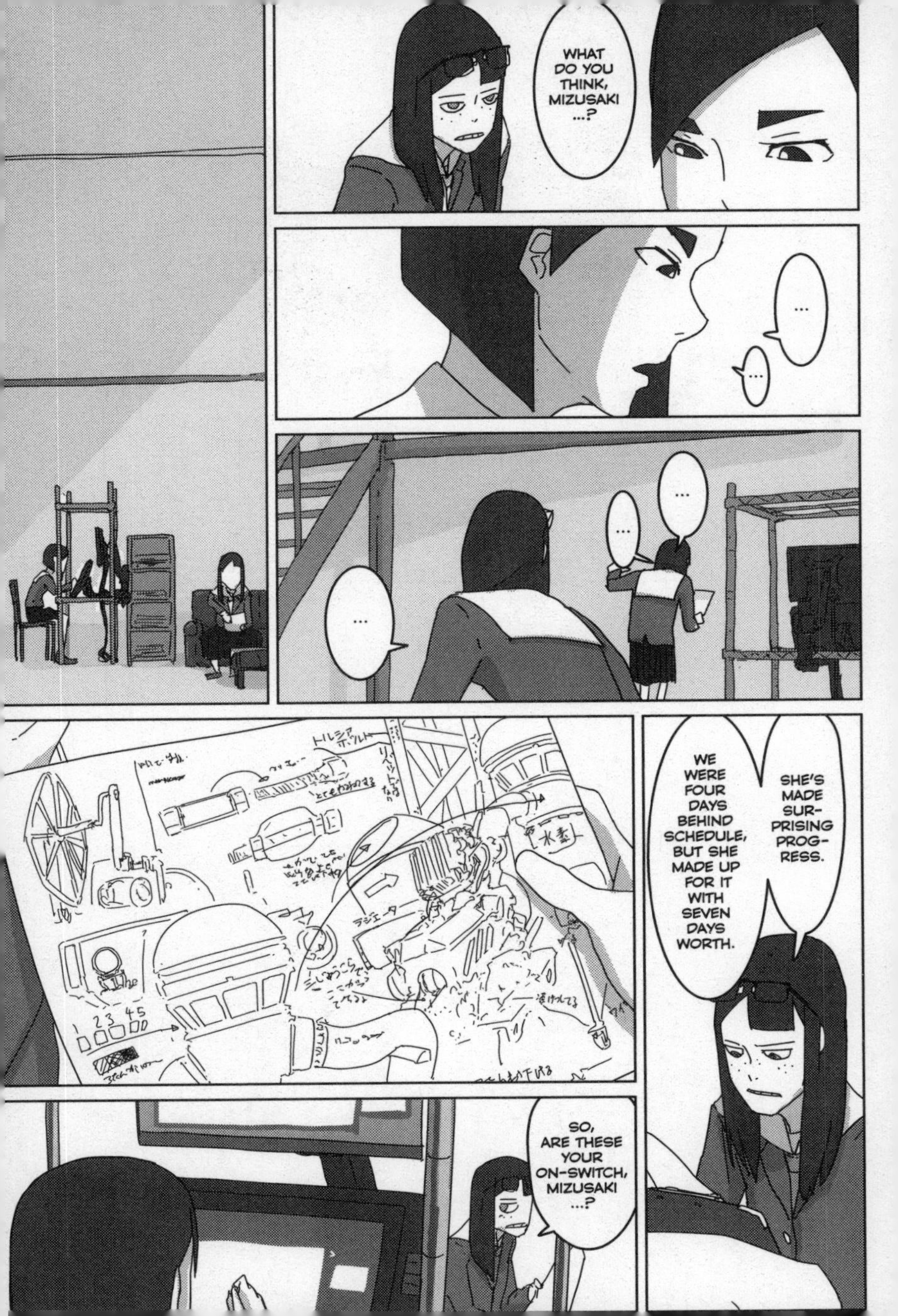
WHAT DO YOU THINK, MIZUSAKI ...?
...
...
...
...
...
SHE'S MADE SUR-PRISING PROG-RESS.
WE WERE FOUR DAYS BEHIND SCHEDULE, BUT SHE MADE UP FOR IT WITH SEVEN DAYS WORTH.
水素
ラジエーター
SO, ARE THESE YOUR ON-SWITCH, MIZUSAKI ...?

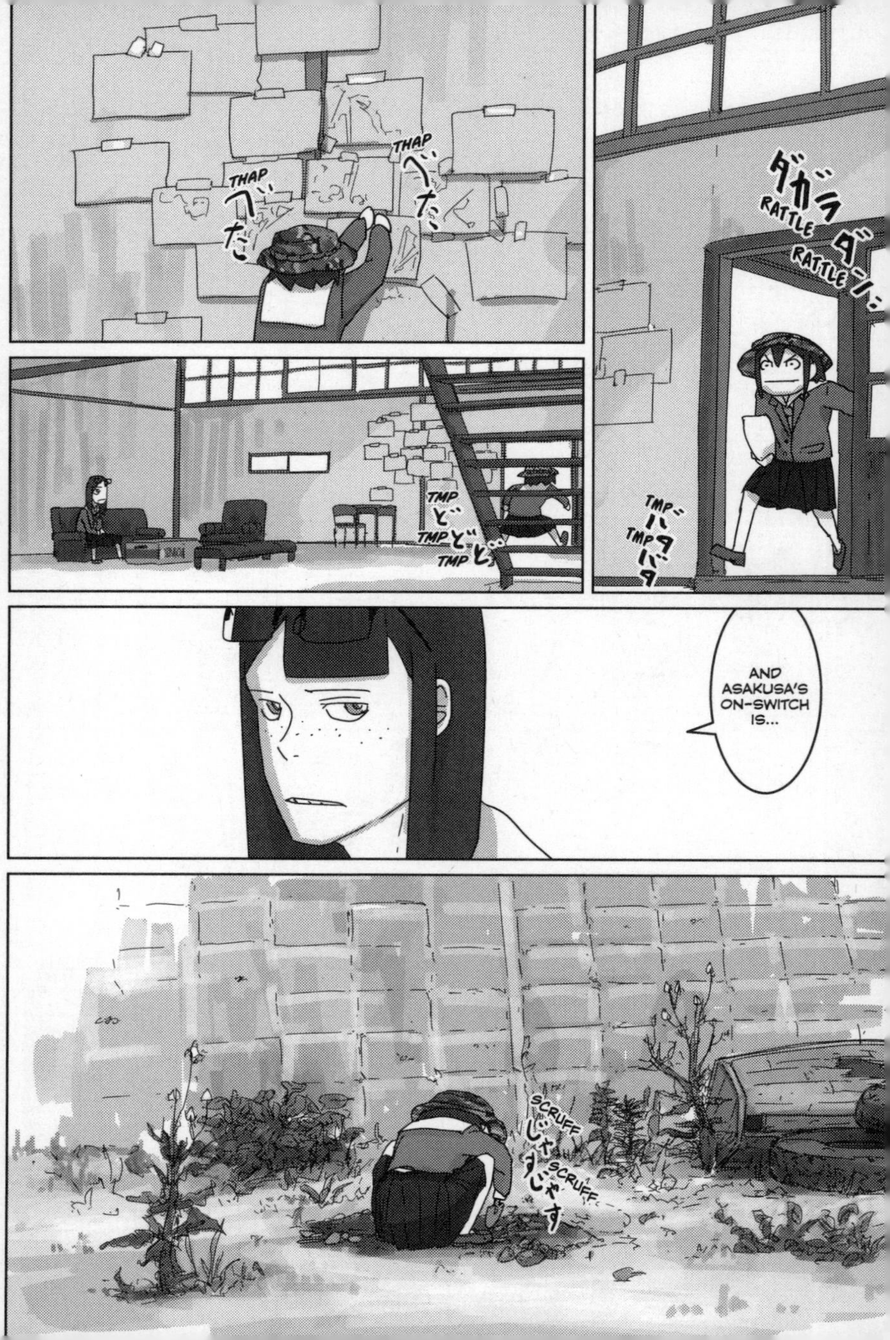
RATTLE
RATTLE
TMP
TMP
THAP
THAP
TMP
TMP
TMP
AND ASAKUSA'S ON-SWITCH IS...
SCRUFF
SCRUFF

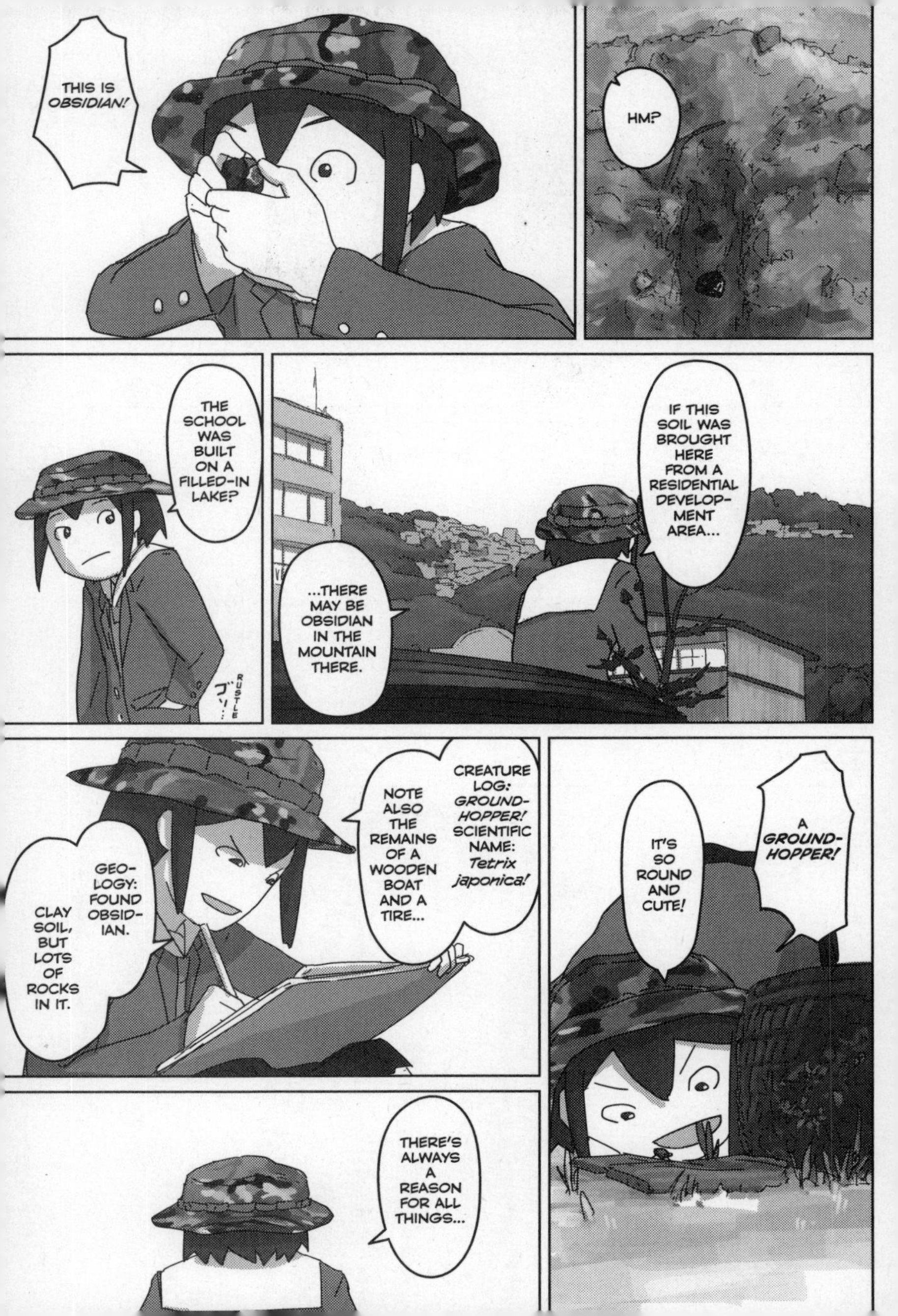
HM?
THIS IS *OBSIDIAN!*
IF THIS SOIL WAS BROUGHT HERE FROM A RESIDENTIAL DEVELOPMENT AREA...
...THERE MAY BE OBSIDIAN IN THE MOUNTAIN THERE.
THE SCHOOL WAS BUILT ON A FILLED-IN LAKE?
ゴソ
RUSTLE
A *GROUNDHOPPER!*
IT'S SO ROUND AND CUTE!
CREATURE LOG: *GROUNDHOPPER!* SCIENTIFIC NAME: *Tetrix japonica!*
NOTE ALSO THE REMAINS OF A WOODEN BOAT AND A TIRE...
GEOLOGY: FOUND OBSIDIAN.
CLAY SOIL, BUT LOTS OF ROCKS IN IT.
THERE'S ALWAYS A REASON FOR ALL THINGS...

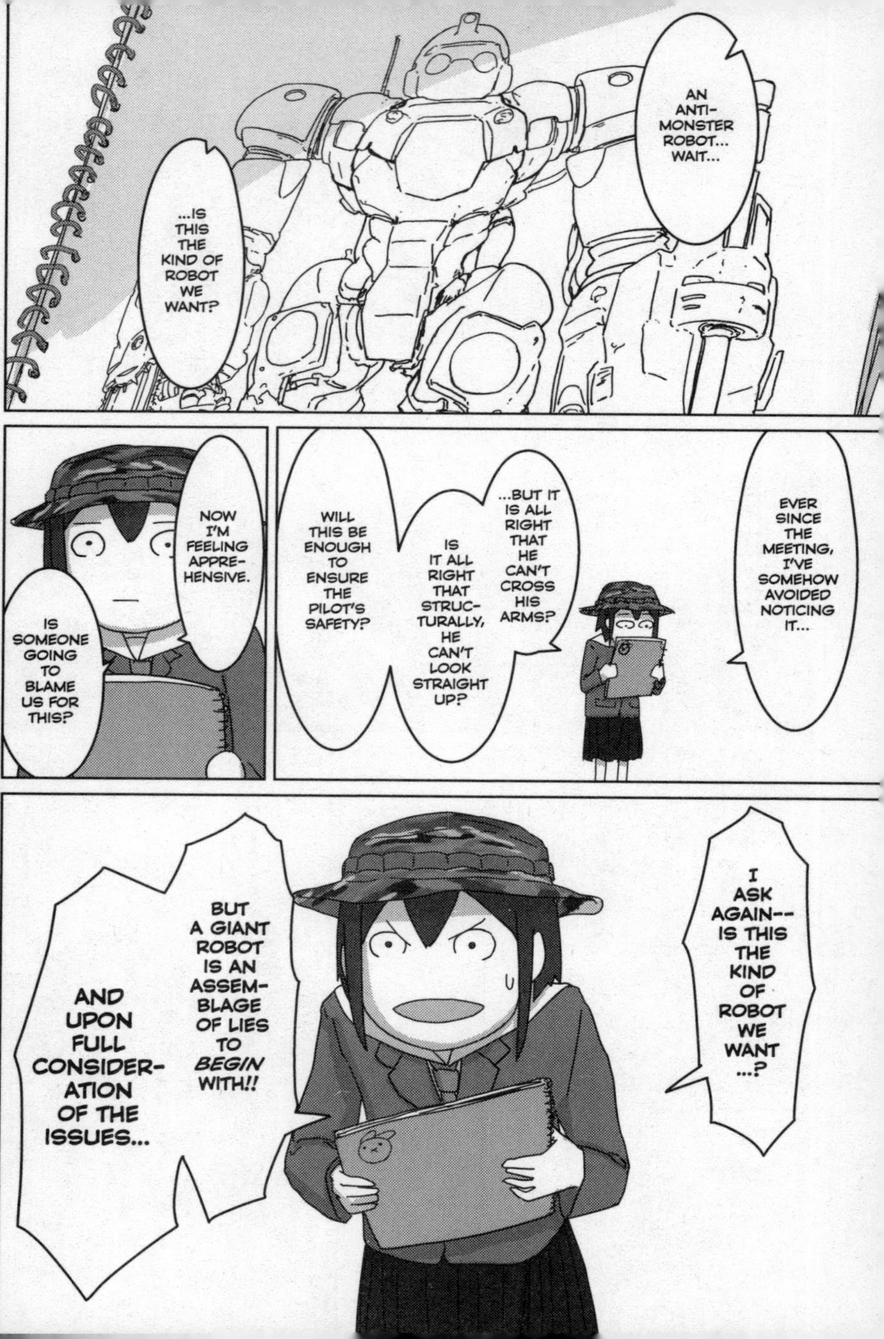
AN ANTI-MONSTER ROBOT... WAIT...
...IS THIS THE KIND OF ROBOT WE WANT?
EVER SINCE THE MEETING, I'VE SOMEHOW AVOIDED NOTICING IT...
...BUT IT IS ALL RIGHT THAT HE CAN'T CROSS HIS ARMS?
IS IT ALL RIGHT THAT STRUCTURALLY, HE CAN'T LOOK STRAIGHT UP?
WILL THIS BE ENOUGH TO ENSURE THE PILOT'S SAFETY?
NOW I'M FEELING APPREHENSIVE.
IS SOMEONE GOING TO BLAME US FOR THIS?
I ASK AGAIN-- IS THIS THE KIND OF ROBOT WE WANT ...?
BUT A GIANT ROBOT IS AN ASSEMBLAGE OF LIES TO *BEGIN* WITH!!
AND UPON FULL CONSIDERATION OF THE ISSUES...

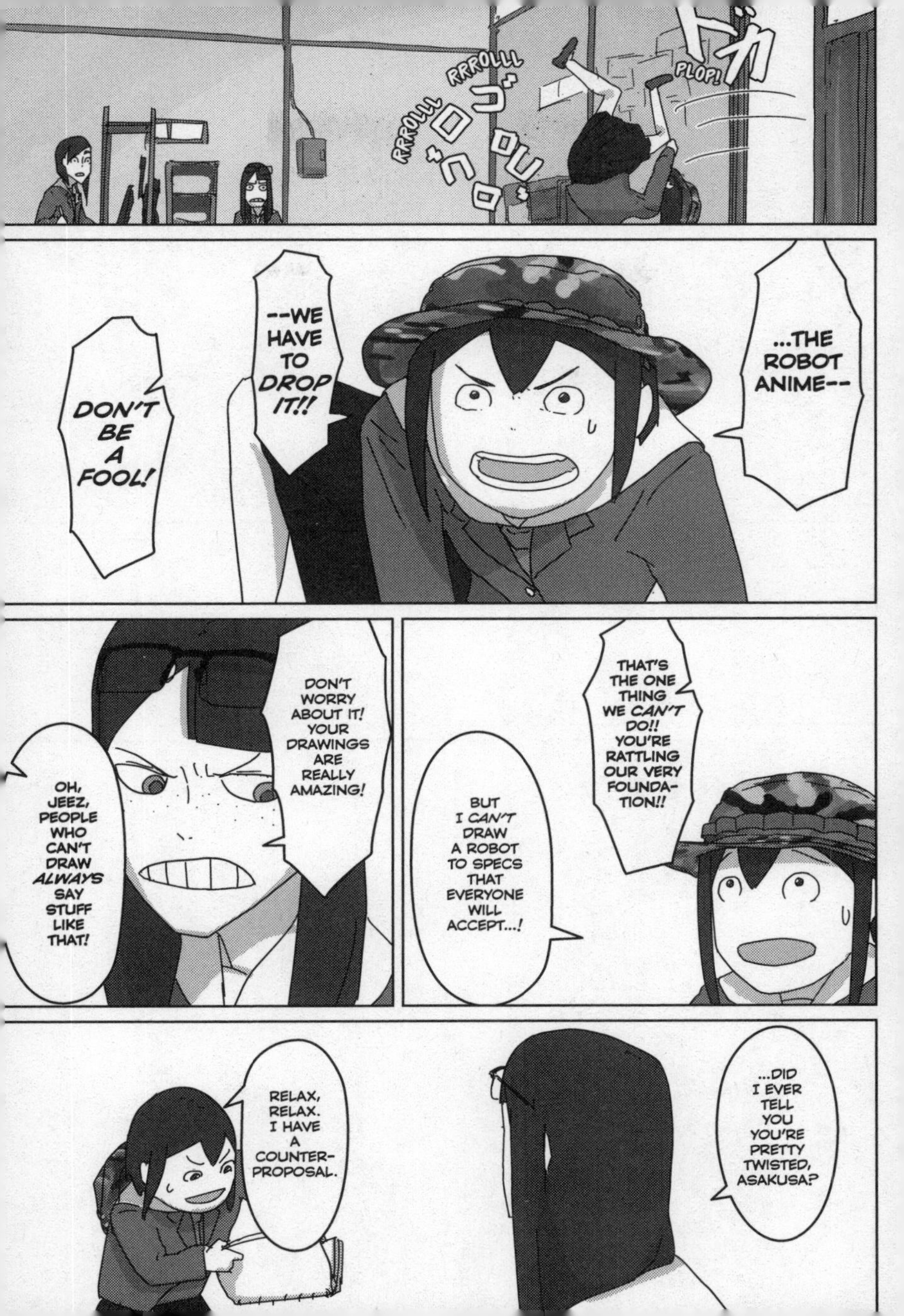
ドガ
PLOP!
RRROLLL
ゴロ
RRROLLL
ゴロ
...THE ROBOT ANIME--
--WE HAVE TO *DROP IT!!*
DON'T BE A FOOL!
THAT'S THE ONE THING WE *CAN'T* DO!! YOU'RE RATTLING OUR VERY FOUNDATION!!
BUT I *CAN'T* DRAW A ROBOT TO SPECS THAT EVERYONE WILL ACCEPT...!
DON'T WORRY ABOUT IT! YOUR DRAWINGS ARE REALLY AMAZING!
OH, JEEZ, PEOPLE WHO CAN'T DRAW *ALWAYS* SAY STUFF LIKE THAT!
...DID I EVER TELL YOU YOU'RE PRETTY TWISTED, ASAKUSA?
RELAX, RELAX. I HAVE A COUNTER-PROPOSAL.

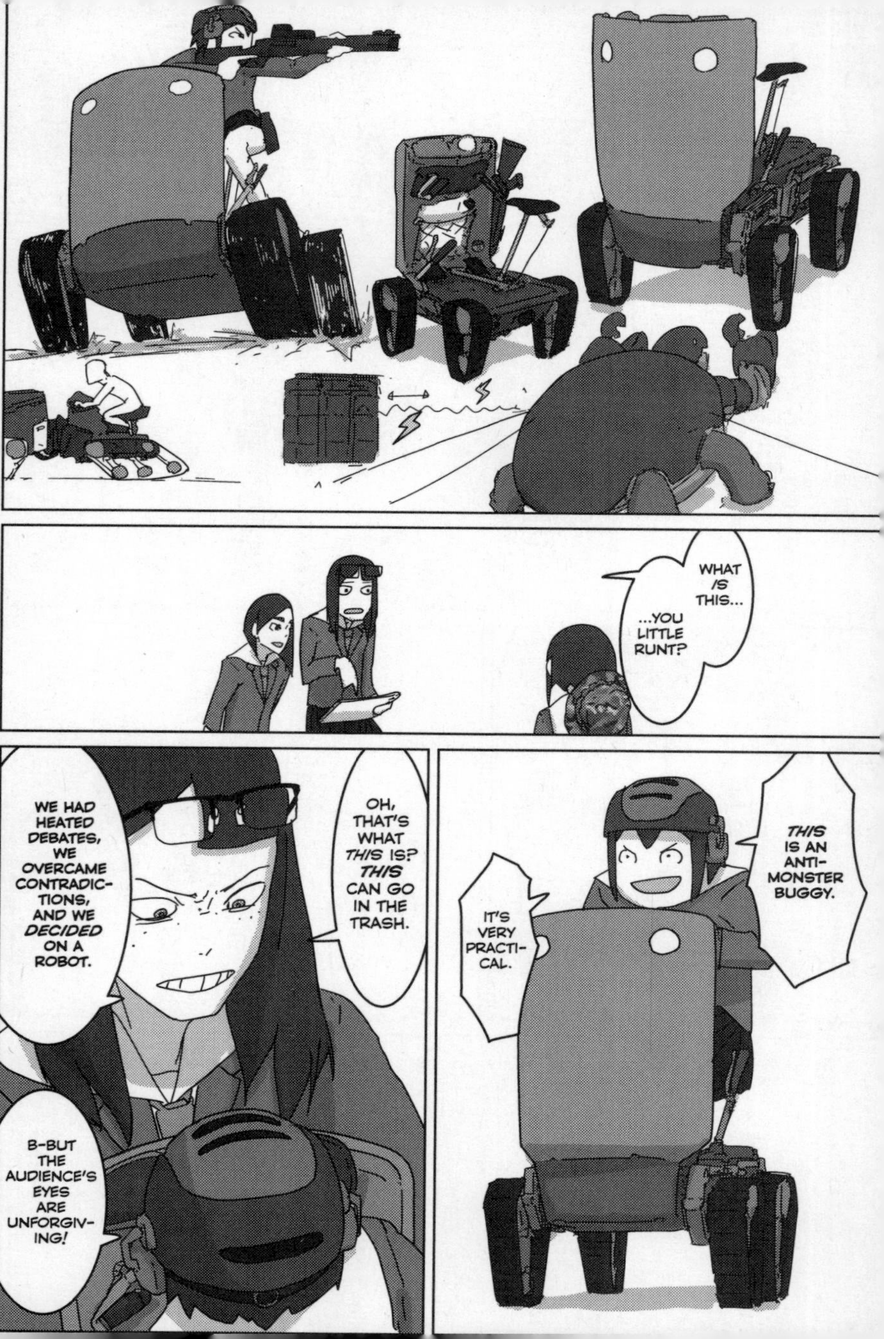
WHAT *IS* THIS...
...YOU LITTLE RUNT?
THIS IS AN ANTI-MONSTER BUGGY.
IT'S VERY PRACTICAL.
OH, THAT'S WHAT *THIS* IS? *THIS* CAN GO IN THE TRASH.
WE HAD HEATED DEBATES, WE OVERCAME CONTRADICTIONS, AND WE *DECIDED* ON A ROBOT.
B-BUT THE AUDIENCE'S EYES ARE UNFORGIVING!

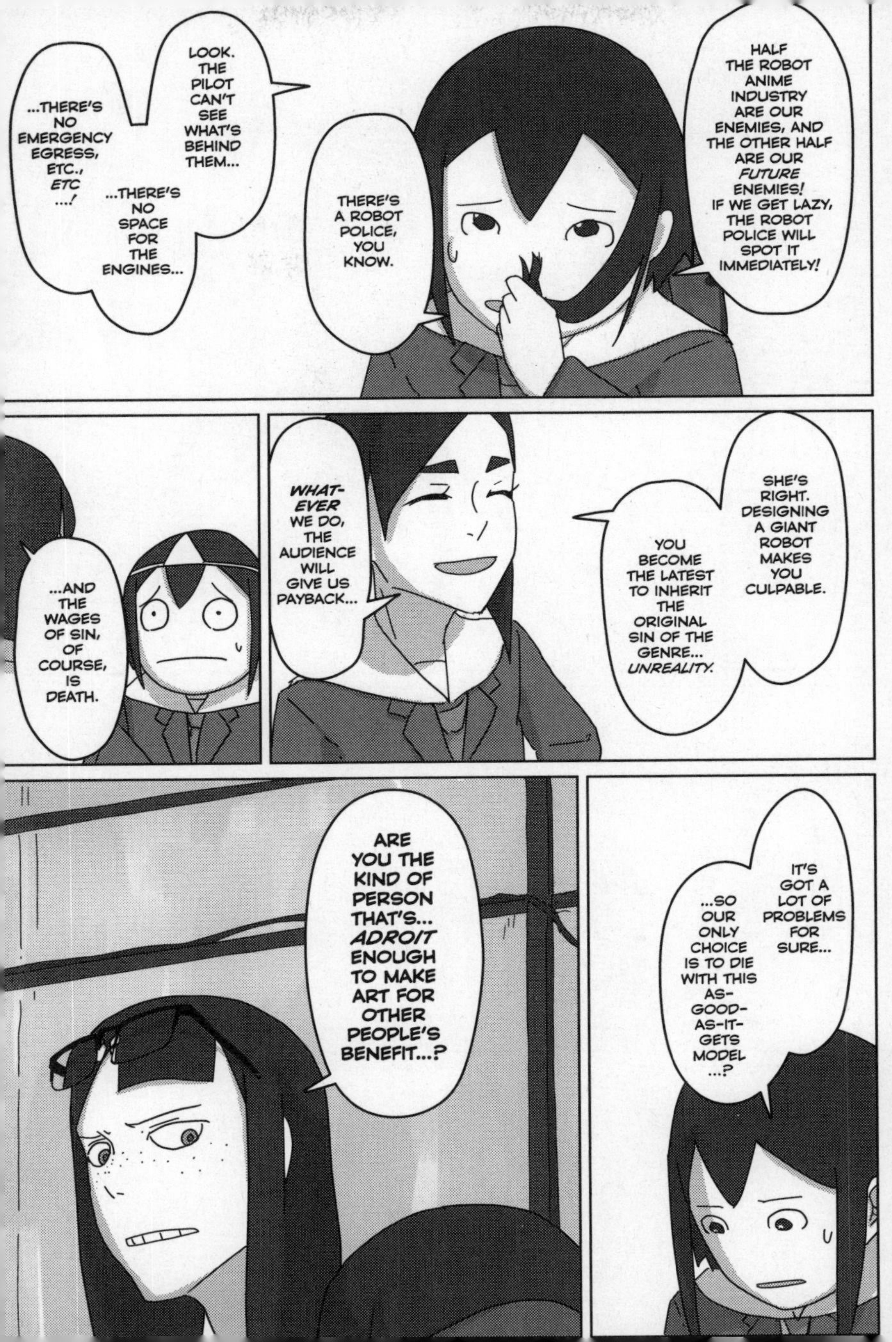
HALF THE ROBOT ANIME INDUSTRY ARE OUR ENEMIES, AND THE OTHER HALF ARE OUR *FUTURE* ENEMIES! IF WE GET LAZY, THE ROBOT POLICE WILL SPOT IT IMMEDIATELY!
THERE'S A ROBOT POLICE, YOU KNOW.
LOOK. THE PILOT CAN'T SEE WHAT'S BEHIND THEM...
...THERE'S NO SPACE FOR THE ENGINES...
...THERE'S NO EMERGENCY EGRESS, ETC., *ETC* ...!
SHE'S RIGHT. DESIGNING A GIANT ROBOT MAKES YOU CULPABLE.
YOU BECOME THE LATEST TO INHERIT THE ORIGINAL SIN OF THE GENRE... *UNREALITY.*
WHAT-EVER WE DO, THE AUDIENCE WILL GIVE US PAYBACK...
...AND THE WAGES OF SIN, OF COURSE, IS DEATH.
IT'S GOT A LOT OF PROBLEMS FOR SURE...
...SO OUR ONLY CHOICE IS TO DIE WITH THIS AS-GOOD-AS-IT-GETS MODEL ...?
ARE YOU THE KIND OF PERSON THAT'S... *ADROIT* ENOUGH TO MAKE ART FOR OTHER PEOPLE'S BENEFIT...?

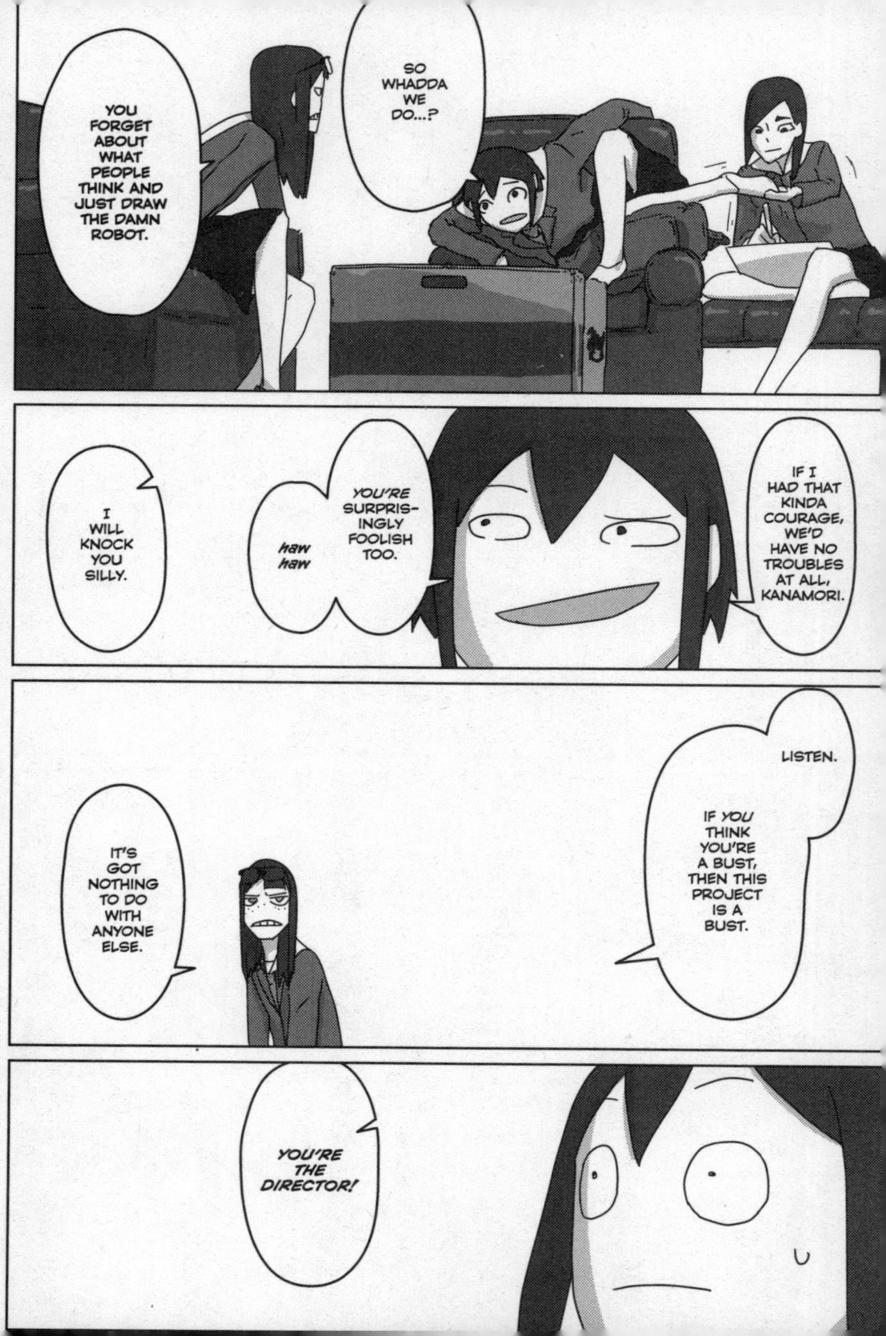
SO WHADDA WE DO...?
YOU FORGET ABOUT WHAT PEOPLE THINK AND JUST DRAW THE DAMN ROBOT.
IF I HAD THAT KINDA COURAGE, WE'D HAVE NO TROUBLES AT ALL, KANAMORI.
YOU'RE SURPRISINGLY FOOLISH TOO.
haw haw
I WILL KNOCK YOU SILLY.
LISTEN.
IF YOU THINK YOU'RE A BUST, THEN THIS PROJECT IS A BUST.
IT'S GOT NOTHING TO DO WITH ANYONE ELSE.
YOU'RE THE DIRECTOR!

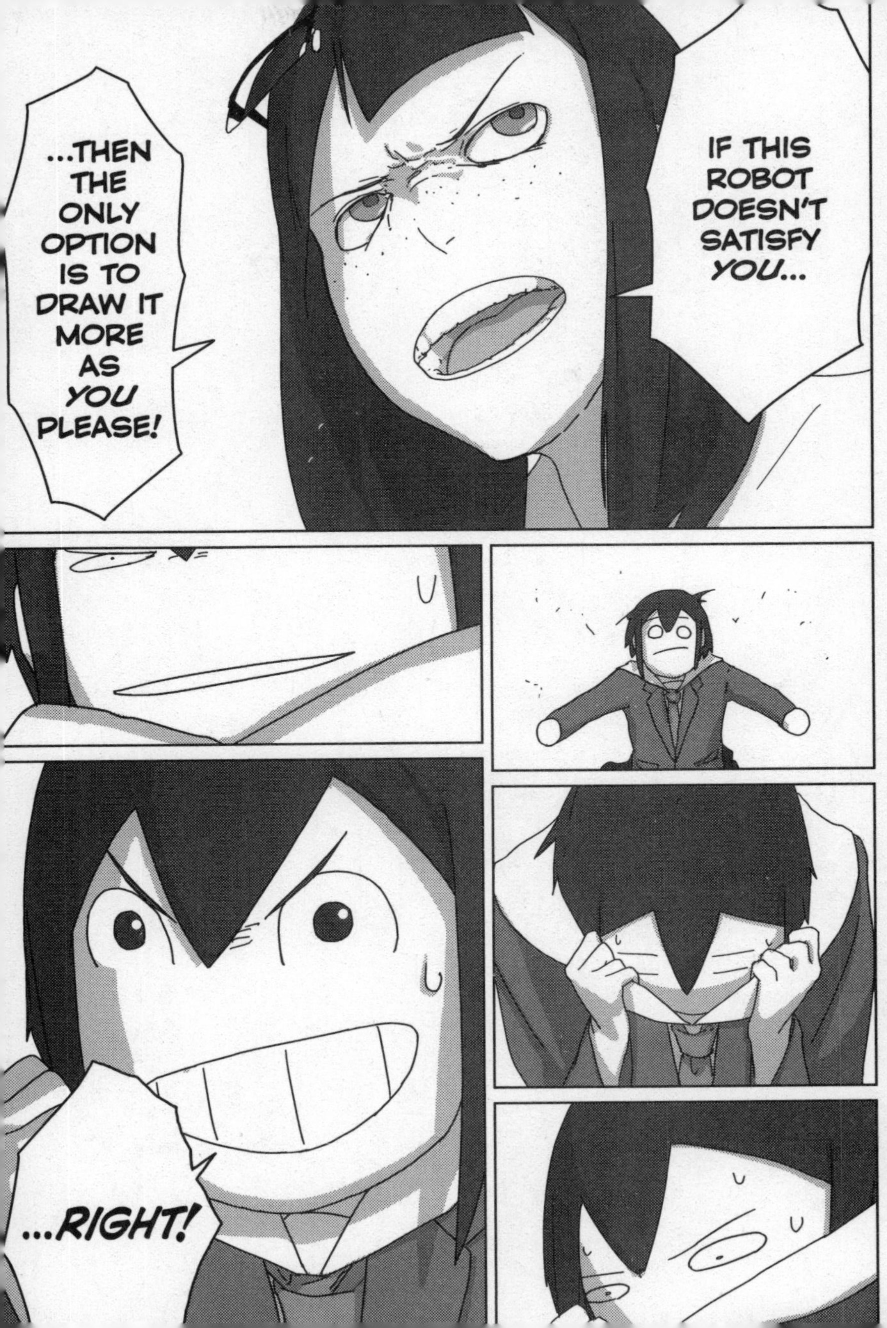
IF THIS ROBOT DOESN'T SATISFY *YOU*...
...THEN THE ONLY OPTION IS TO DRAW IT MORE AS *YOU* PLEASE!
...*RIGHT!*

SHIBA 8 #1
INTERNAL WORKINGS DIAGRAMS

Asakusa

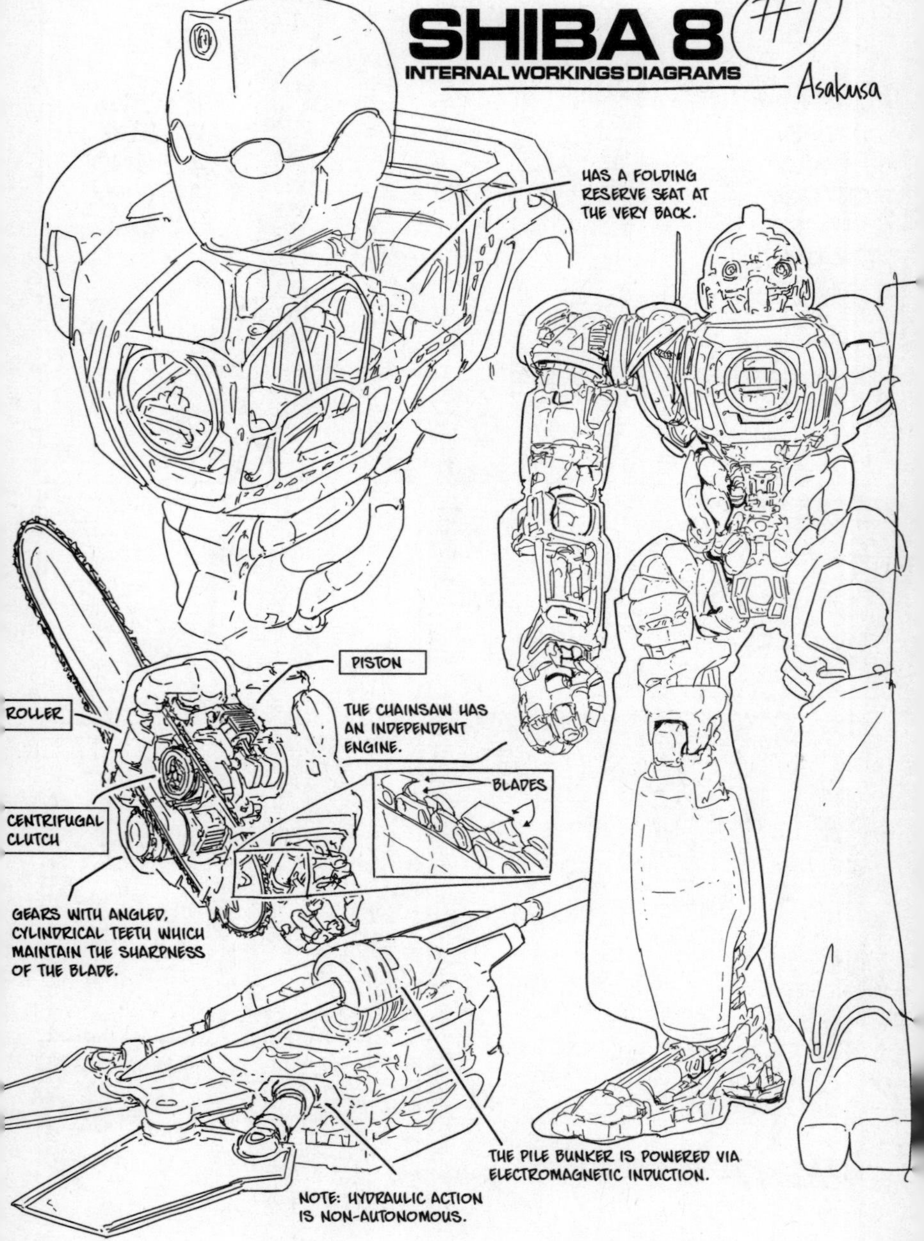

HAS A FOLDING RESERVE SEAT AT THE VERY BACK.
PISTON
ROLLER
THE CHAINSAW HAS AN INDEPENDENT ENGINE.
BLADES
CENTRIFUGAL CLUTCH
GEARS WITH ANGLED, CYLINDRICAL TEETH WHICH MAINTAIN THE SHARPNESS OF THE BLADE.
THE PILE BUNKER IS POWERED VIA ELECTROMAGNETIC INDUCTION.
NOTE: HYDRAULIC ACTION IS NON-AUTONOMOUS.

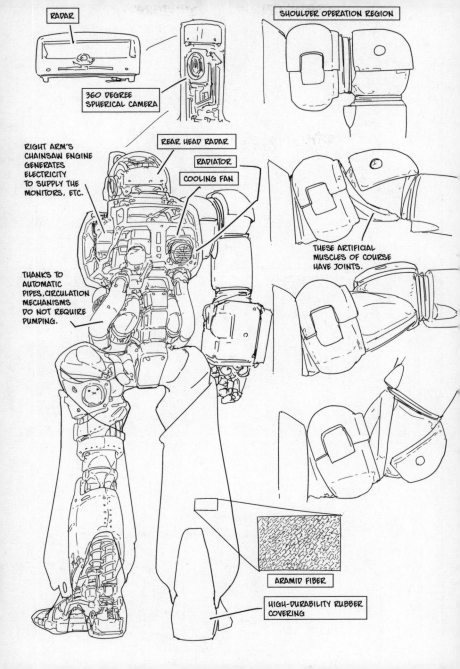

RADAR

360 DEGREE SPHERICAL CAMERA

SHOULDER OPERATION REGION

RIGHT ARM'S CHAINSAW ENGINE GENERATES ELECTRICITY TO SUPPLY THE MONITORS, ETC.

REAR HEAD RADAR

RADIATOR

COOLING FAN

THESE ARTIFICIAL MUSCLES OF COURSE HAVE JOINTS.

THANKS TO AUTOMATIC PIPES, CIRCULATION MECHANISMS DO NOT REQUIRE PUMPING.

ARAMID FIBER

HIGH-DURABILITY RUBBER COVERING

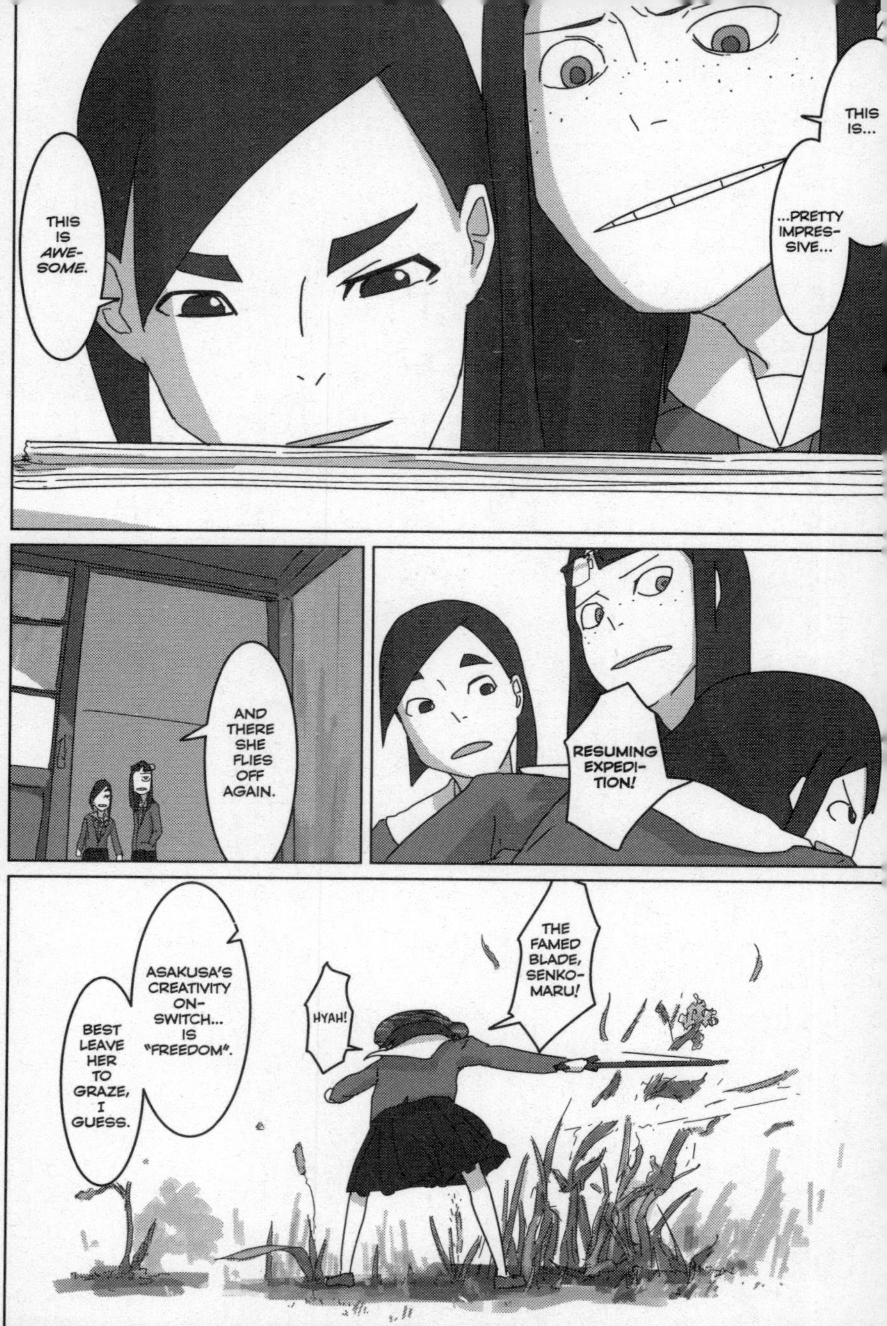
THIS IS...
...PRETTY IMPRESSIVE...
THIS IS AWESOME.
RESUMING EXPEDITION!
AND THERE SHE FLIES OFF AGAIN.
THE FAMED BLADE, SENKO-MARU!
HYAH!
ASAKUSA'S CREATIVITY ON-SWITCH... IS "FREEDOM".
BEST LEAVE HER TO GRAZE, I GUESS.

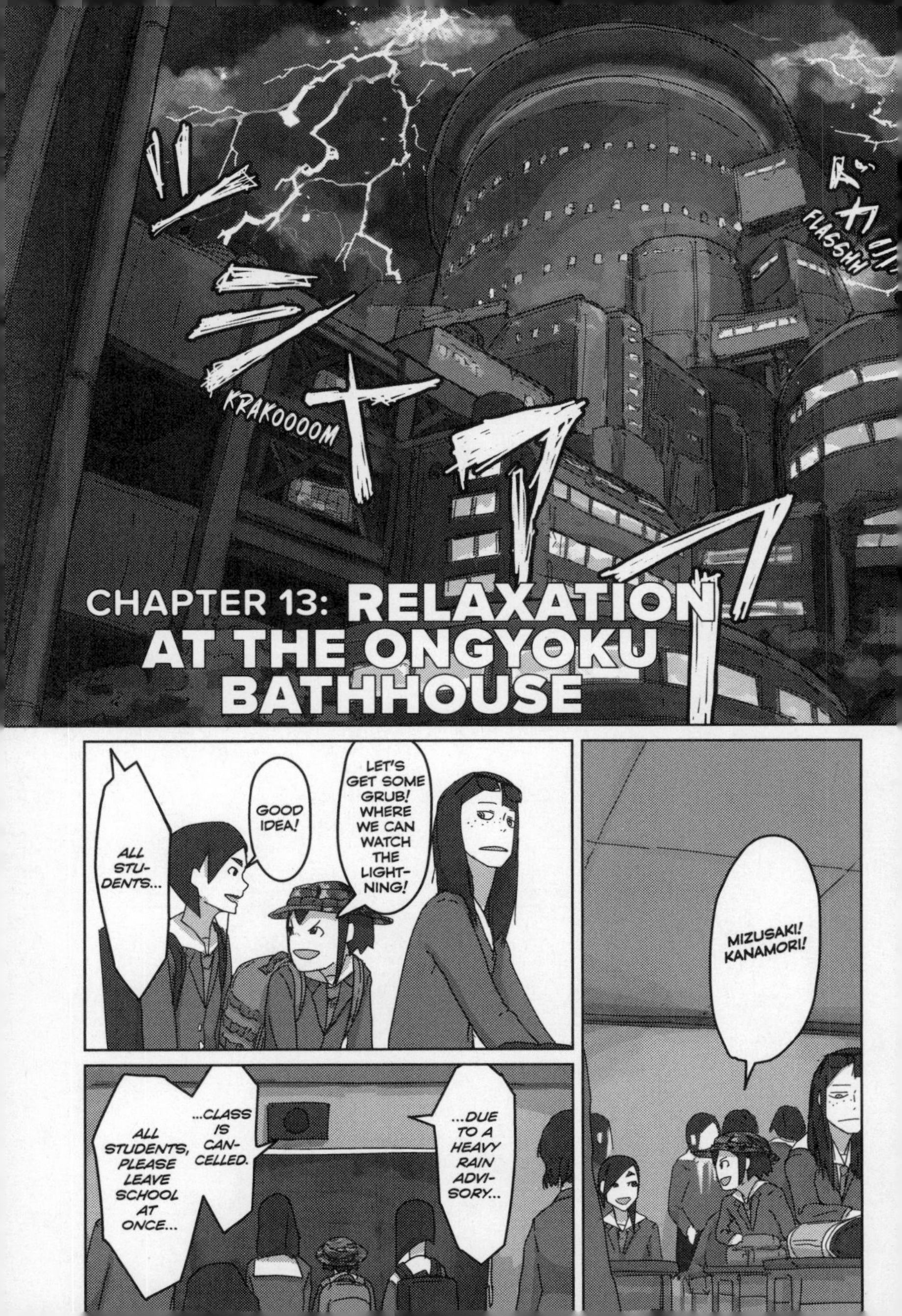
FLASSHH
KRAKOOOOM
CHAPTER 13: RELAXATION AT THE ONGYOKU BATHHOUSE
MIZUSAKI! KANAMORI!
LET'S GET SOME GRUB! WHERE WE CAN WATCH THE LIGHT-NING!
GOOD IDEA!
ALL STU-DENTS...
...DUE TO A HEAVY RAIN ADVI-SORY...
...CLASS IS CAN-CELLED.
ALL STUDENTS, PLEASE LEAVE SCHOOL AT ONCE...

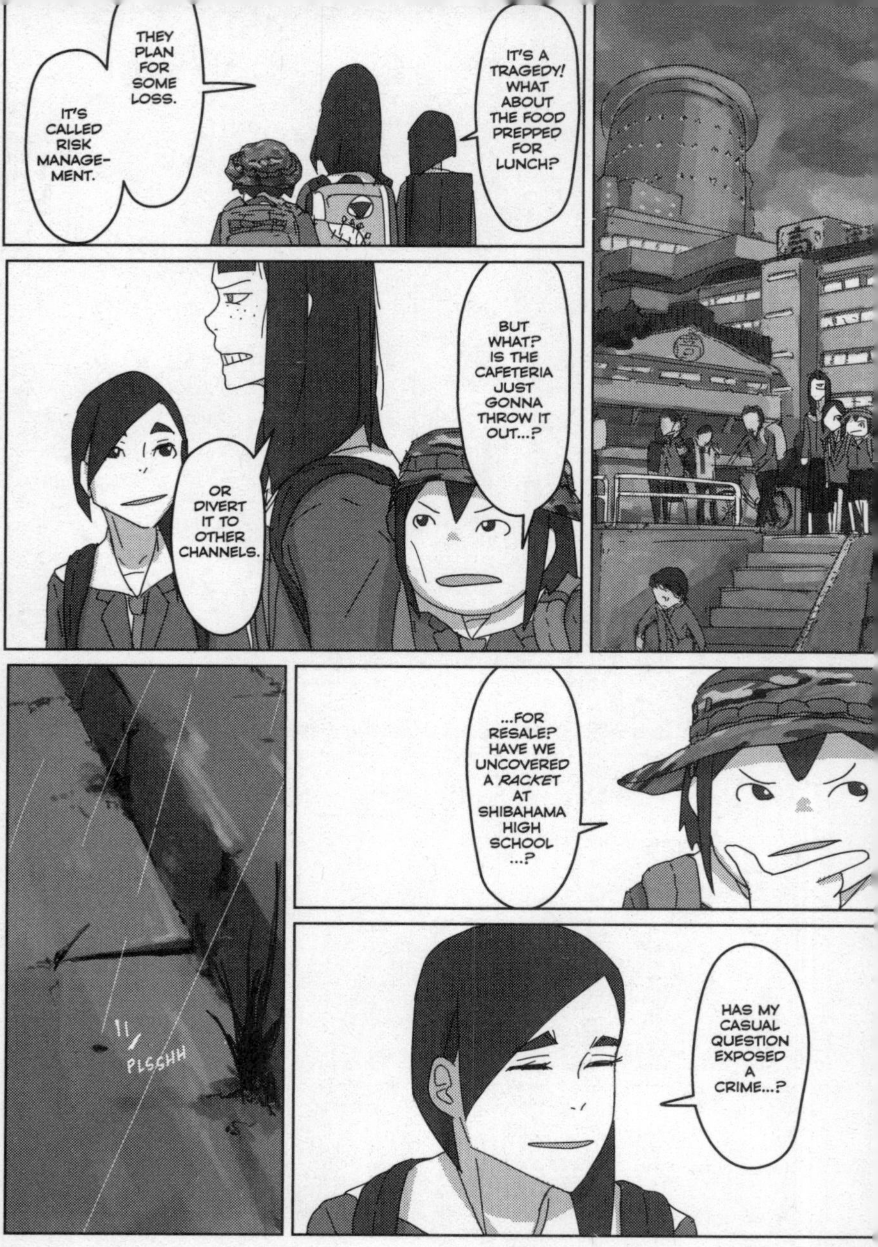
IT'S A TRAGEDY! WHAT ABOUT THE FOOD PREPPED FOR LUNCH?
THEY PLAN FOR SOME LOSS.
IT'S CALLED RISK MANAGEMENT.
BUT WHAT? IS THE CAFETERIA JUST GONNA THROW IT OUT...?
OR DIVERT IT TO OTHER CHANNELS.
...FOR RESALE? HAVE WE UNCOVERED A *RACKET* AT SHIBAHAMA HIGH SCHOOL ...?
HAS MY CASUAL QUESTION EXPOSED A CRIME...?
PLSSHH

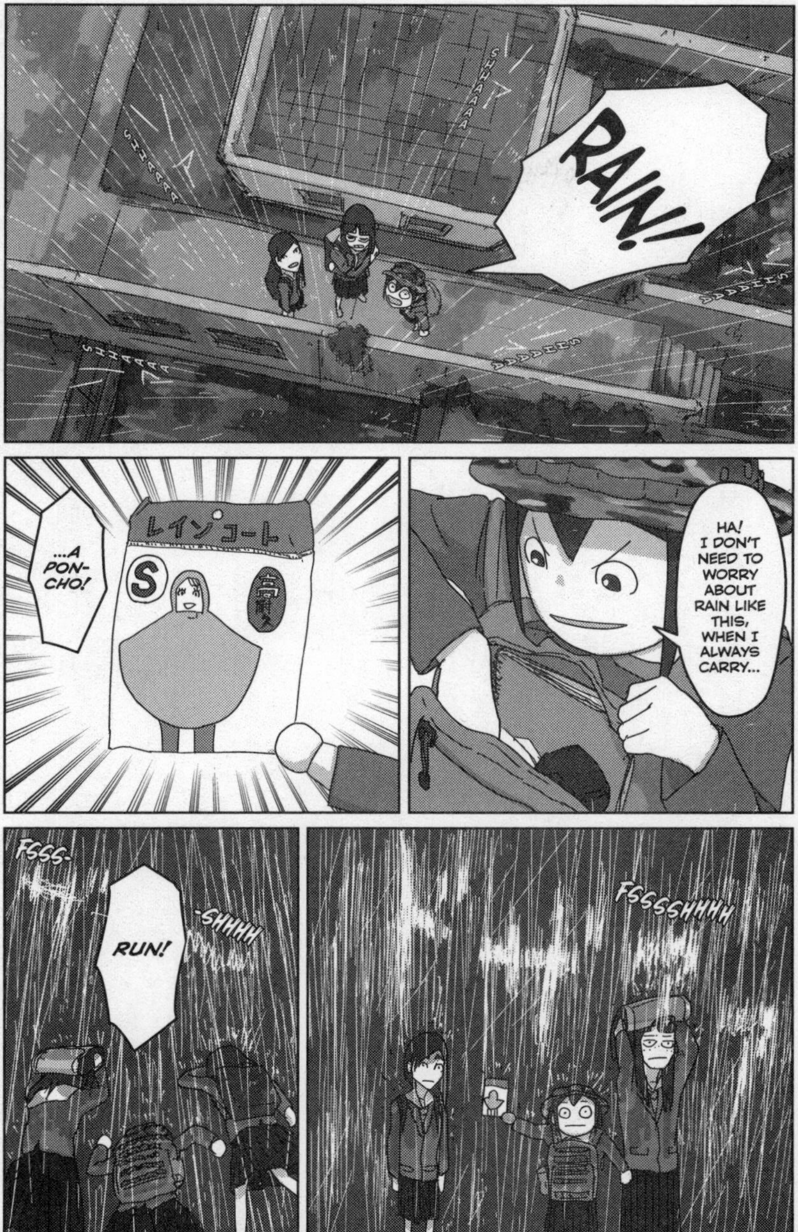

RAIN!
HA! I DON'T NEED TO WORRY ABOUT RAIN LIKE THIS, WHEN I ALWAYS CARRY...
レインコート
S
...A PONCHO!
FSSSSHHHH
FSSS-
-SHHHH
RUN!

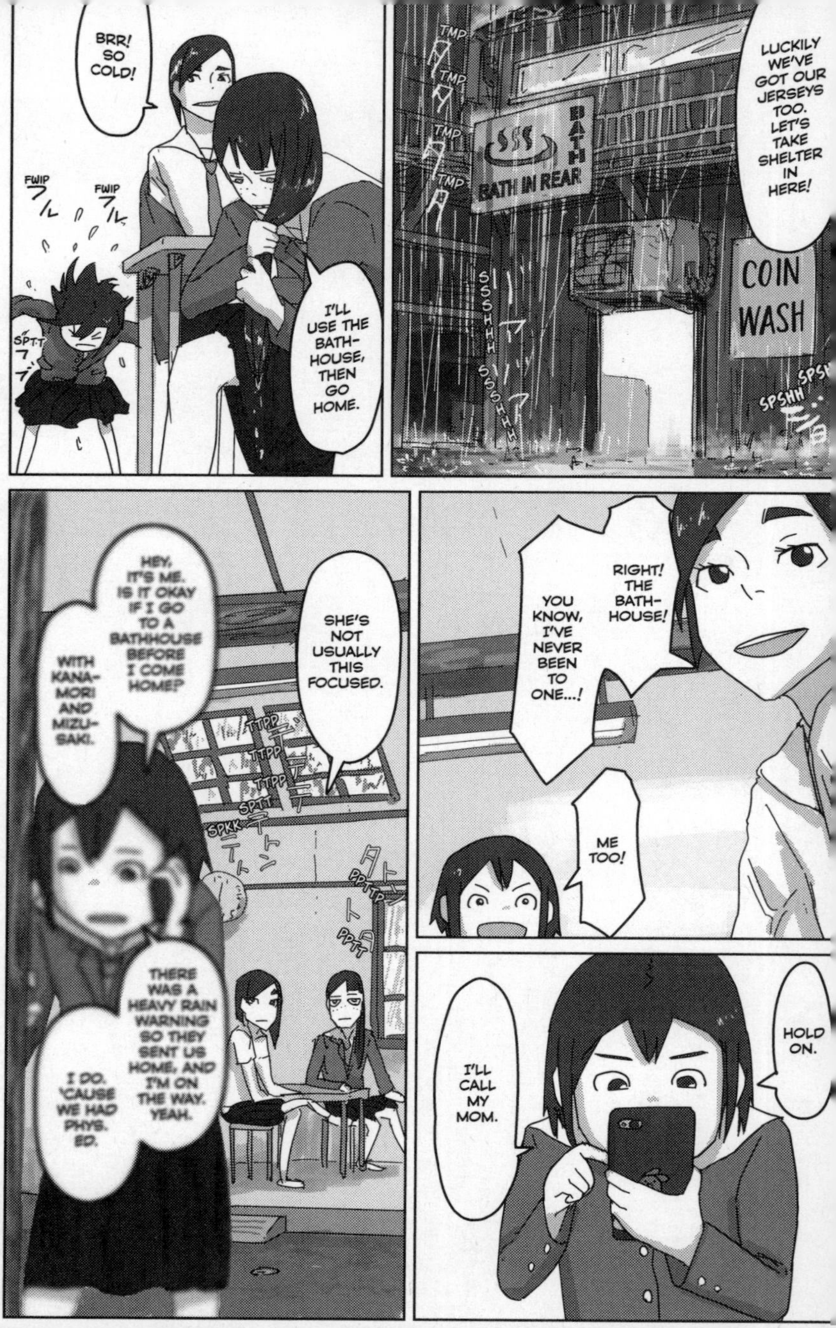
TMP
TMP
TMP
TMP
BATH
BATH IN REAR
LUCKILY WE'VE GOT OUR JERSEYS TOO. LET'S TAKE SHELTER IN HERE!
COIN WASH
SSSHHH
SSSHHH
SPSHH
SPSH
BRR! SO COLD!
FWIP
FWIP
SPTT
I'LL USE THE BATH-HOUSE, THEN GO HOME.
RIGHT! THE BATH-HOUSE!
YOU KNOW, I'VE NEVER BEEN TO ONE...!
ME TOO!
HOLD ON.
I'LL CALL MY MOM.
SHE'S NOT USUALLY THIS FOCUSED.
HEY, IT'S ME. IS IT OKAY IF I GO TO A BATHHOUSE BEFORE I COME HOME?
WITH KANAMORI AND MIZUSAKI.
TTPP
TTPP
TTPP
SPTT
SPKK
PPTTP
PPTT
THERE WAS A HEAVY RAIN WARNING SO THEY SENT US HOME, AND I'M ON THE WAY. YEAH.
I DO. 'CAUSE WE HAD PHYS. ED.

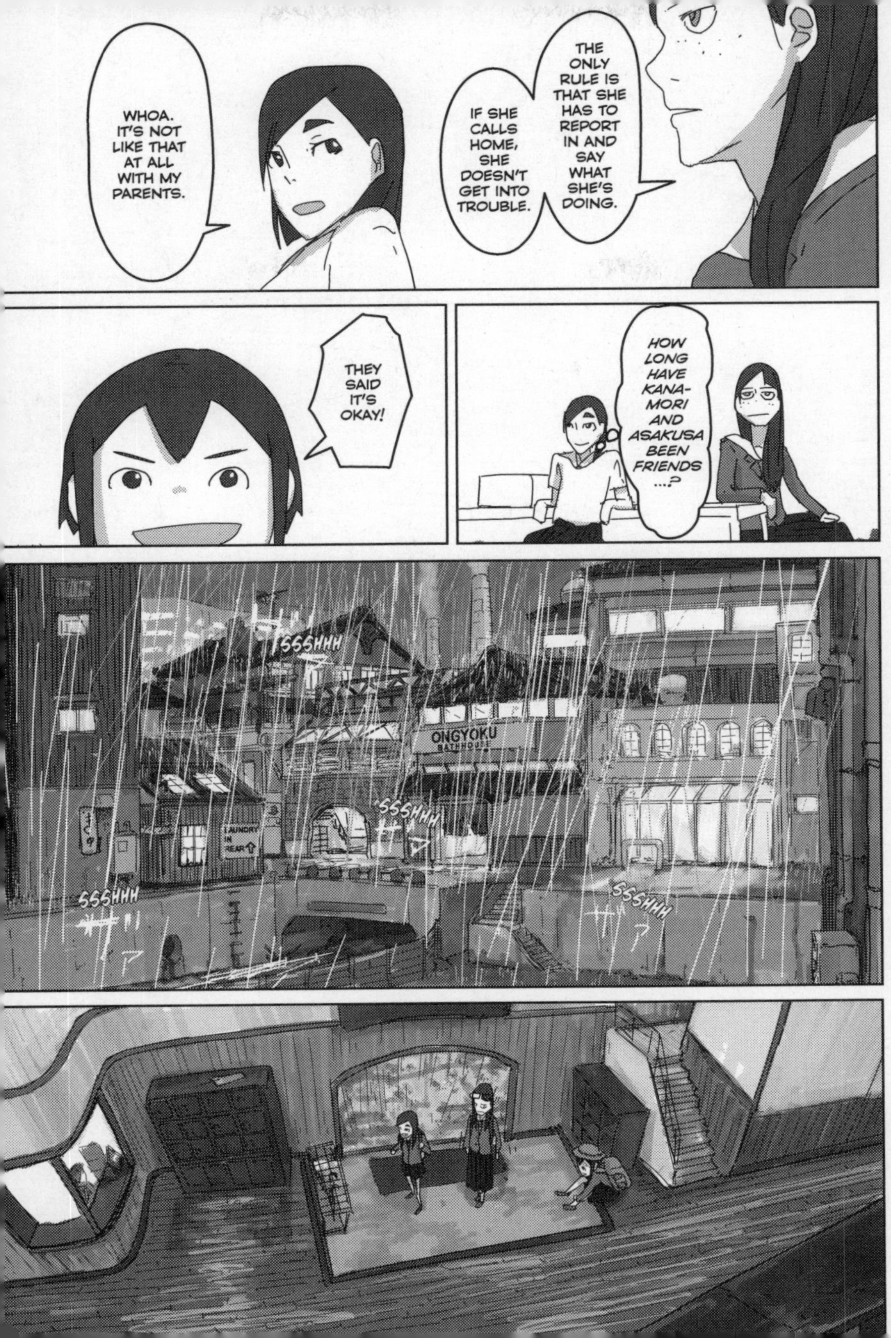
THE ONLY RULE IS THAT SHE HAS TO REPORT IN AND SAY WHAT SHE'S DOING.
IF SHE CALLS HOME, SHE DOESN'T GET INTO TROUBLE.
WHOA. IT'S NOT LIKE THAT AT ALL WITH MY PARENTS.
HOW LONG HAVE KANAMORI AND ASAKUSA BEEN FRIENDS...?
THEY SAID IT'S OKAY!
SSSHHH
ONGYOKU
BATHHOUSE
SSSHHH
LAUNDRY IN REAR
SSSHHH
SSSHHH

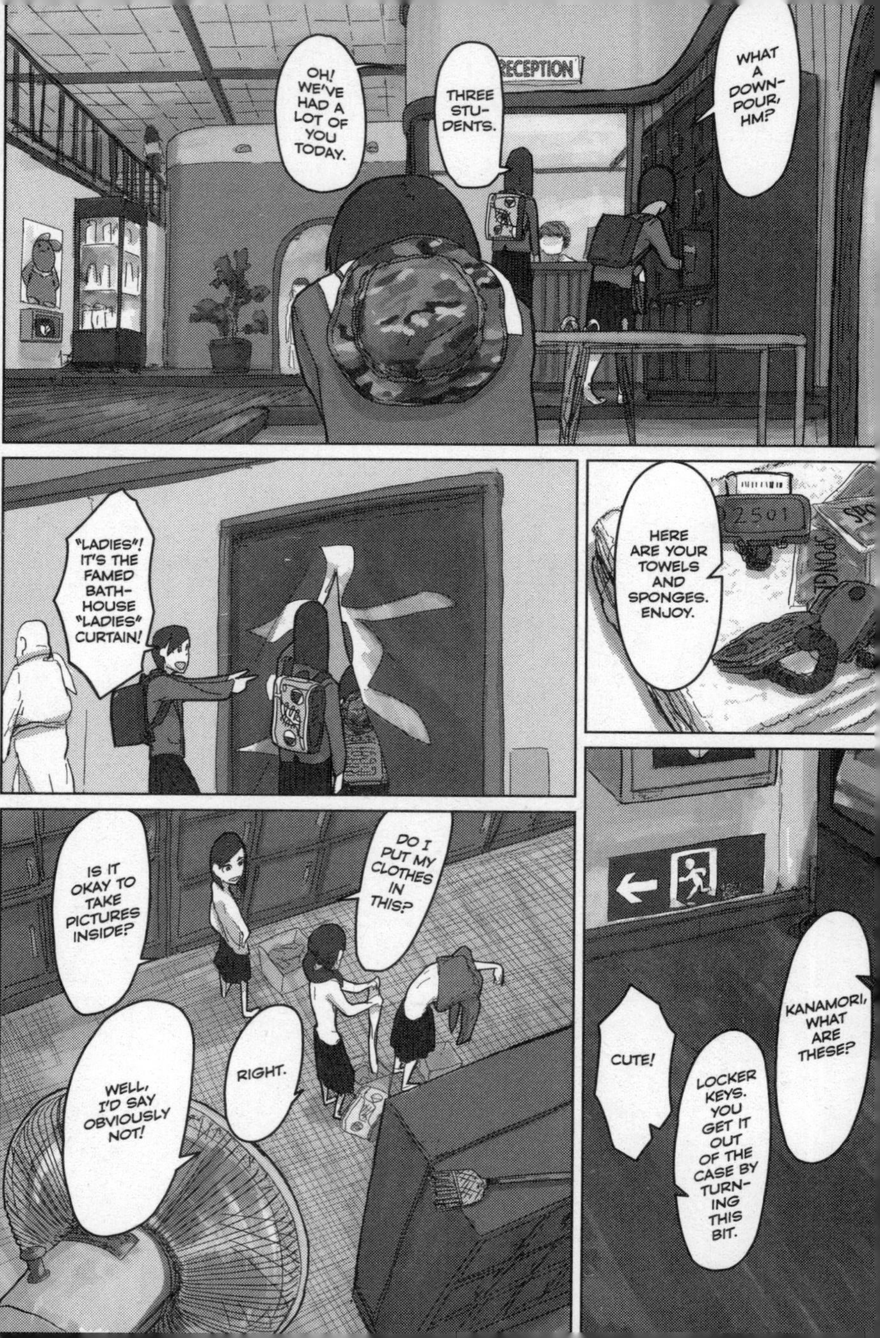
RECEPTION
WHAT A DOWNPOUR, HM?
THREE STUDENTS.
OH! WE'VE HAD A LOT OF YOU TODAY.
HERE ARE YOUR TOWELS AND SPONGES. ENJOY.
"LADIES"! IT'S THE FAMED BATHHOUSE "LADIES" CURTAIN!
KANAMORI, WHAT ARE THESE?
CUTE!
LOCKER KEYS. YOU GET IT OUT OF THE CASE BY TURNING THIS BIT.
DO I PUT MY CLOTHES IN THIS?
IS IT OKAY TO TAKE PICTURES INSIDE?
RIGHT.
WELL, I'D SAY OBVIOUSLY NOT!

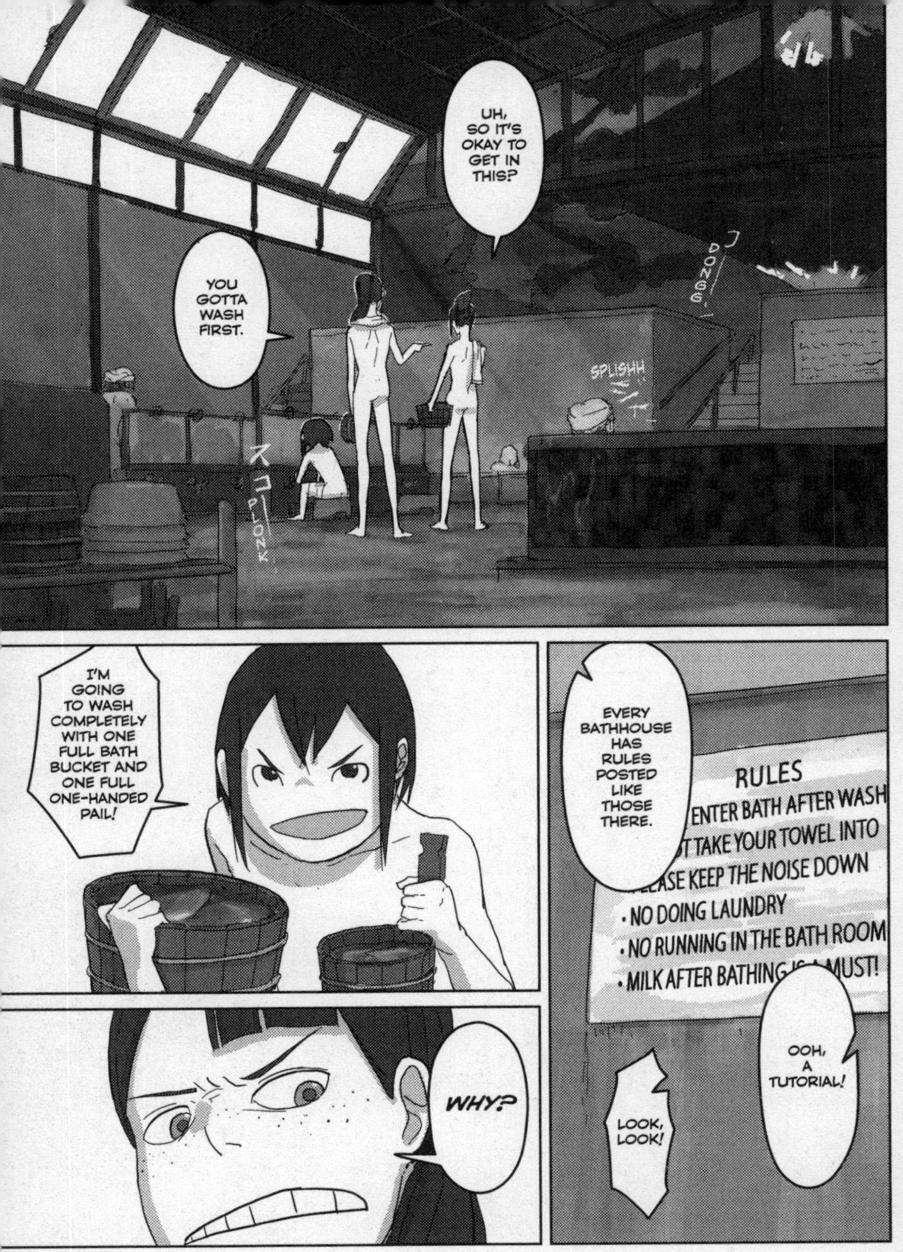
UH, SO IT'S OKAY TO GET IN THIS?
YOU GOTTA WASH FIRST.
DONGG
SPLISHH
PLONK
EVERY BATHHOUSE HAS RULES POSTED LIKE THOSE THERE.
RULES
ENTER BATH AFTER WASH
T TAKE YOUR TOWEL INTO
EASE KEEP THE NOISE DOWN
• NO DOING LAUNDRY
• NO RUNNING IN THE BATH ROOM
• MILK AFTER BATHING
MUST!
OOH, A TUTORIAL!
LOOK, LOOK!
I'M GOING TO WASH COMPLETELY WITH ONE FULL BATH BUCKET AND ONE FULL ONE-HANDED PAIL!
WHY?

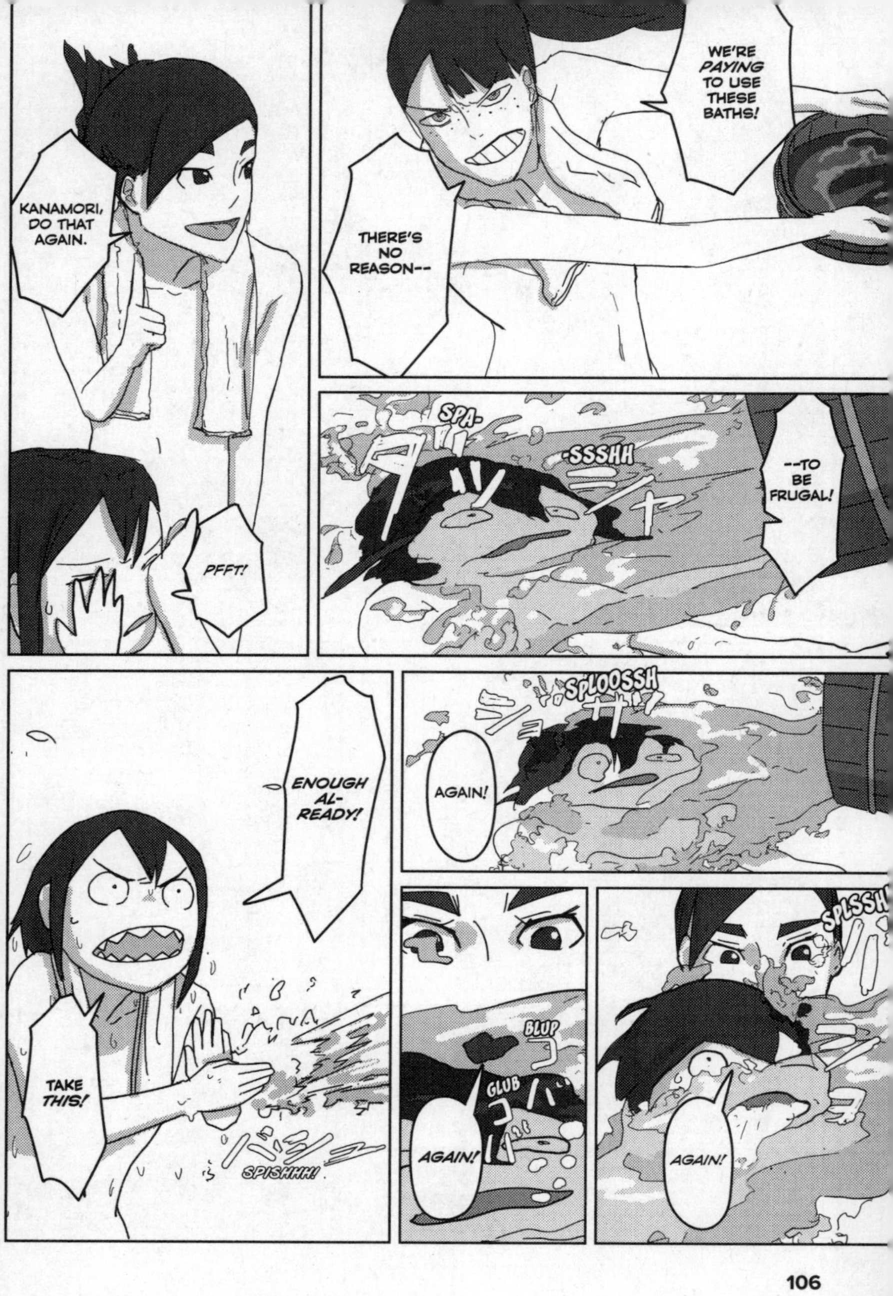
WE'RE PAYING TO USE THESE BATHS!
THERE'S NO REASON--
SPA-
-SSSHH
--TO BE FRUGAL!
KANAMORI, DO THAT AGAIN.
PFFT!
SPLOOSSH
AGAIN!
SPLSSH
AGAIN!
BLUP
GLUB
AGAIN!
ENOUGH AL-READY!
TAKE THIS!
SPISHHH!

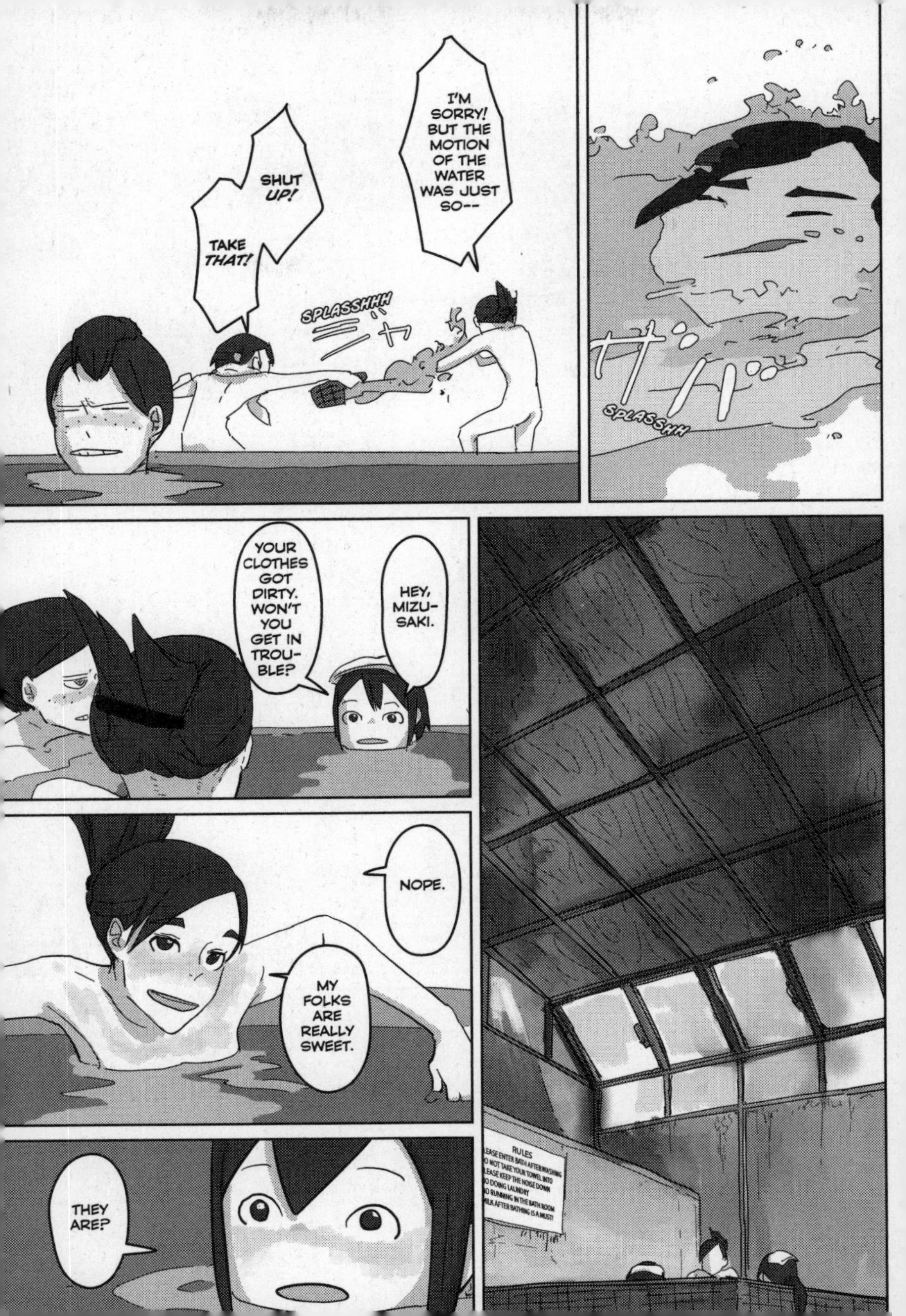
ザバ
SPLASSHH
I'M SORRY! BUT THE MOTION OF THE WATER WAS JUST SO--
SHUT UP!
TAKE THAT!
SPLASSHHH
ジャ
RULES
LEASE ENTER BATH AFTER WASHING
O NOT TAKE YOUR TOWEL INTO
LEASE KEEP THE NOISE DOWN
O DOING LAUNDRY
O RUNNING IN THE BATH ROOM
MILK AFTER BATHING IS A MUST!
HEY, MIZUSAKI.
YOUR CLOTHES GOT DIRTY. WON'T YOU GET IN TROUBLE?
NOPE.
MY FOLKS ARE REALLY SWEET.
THEY ARE?

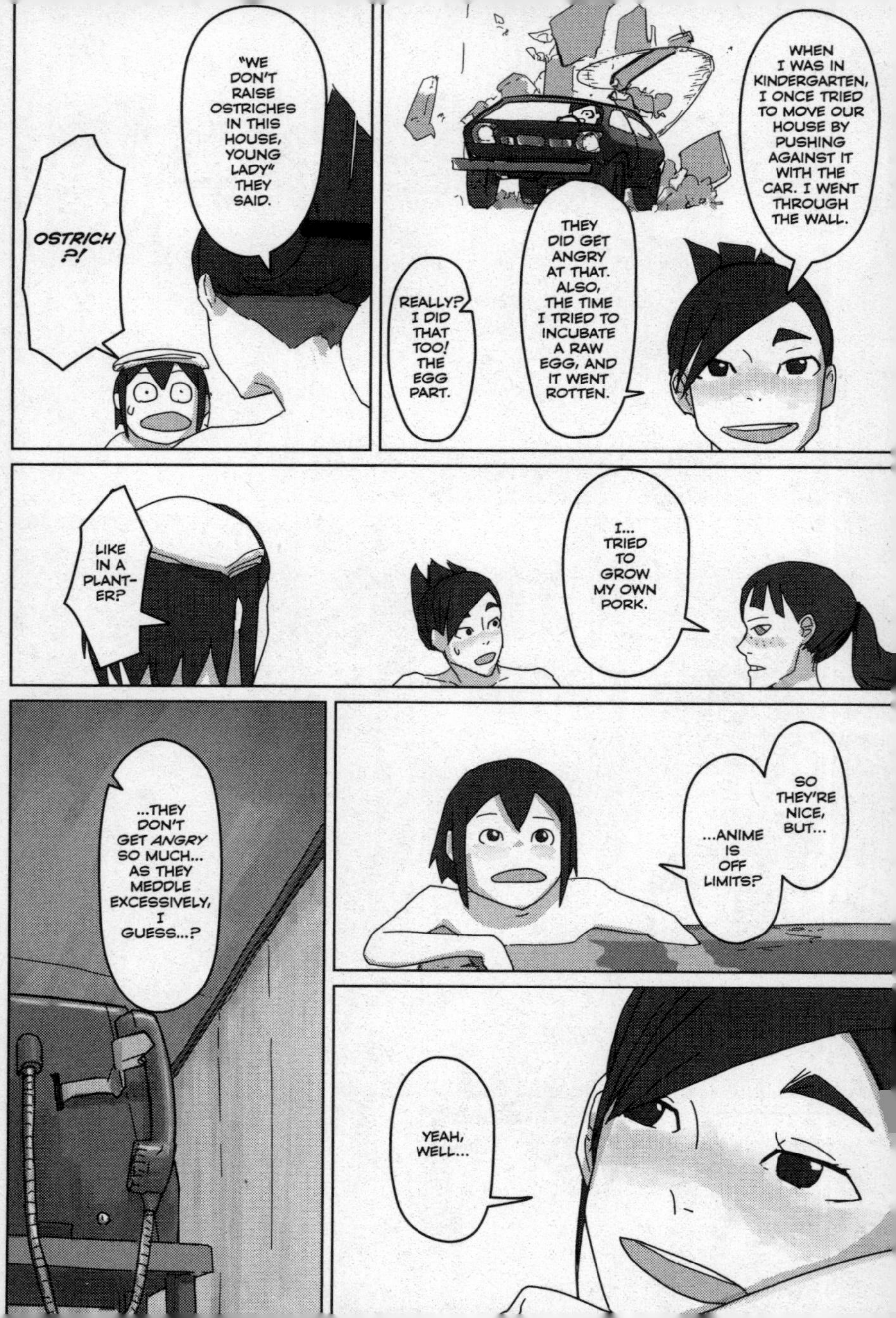
WHEN I WAS IN KINDERGARTEN, I ONCE TRIED TO MOVE OUR HOUSE BY PUSHING AGAINST IT WITH THE CAR. I WENT THROUGH THE WALL.
THEY DID GET ANGRY AT THAT. ALSO, THE TIME I TRIED TO INCUBATE A RAW EGG, AND IT WENT ROTTEN.
REALLY? I DID THAT TOO! THE EGG PART.
"WE DON'T RAISE OSTRICHES IN THIS HOUSE, YOUNG LADY" THEY SAID.
OSTRICH?!
I... TRIED TO GROW MY OWN PORK.
LIKE IN A PLANTER?
SO THEY'RE NICE, BUT...
...ANIME IS OFF LIMITS?
YEAH, WELL...
...THEY DON'T GET ANGRY SO MUCH... AS THEY MEDDLE EXCESSIVELY, I GUESS...?

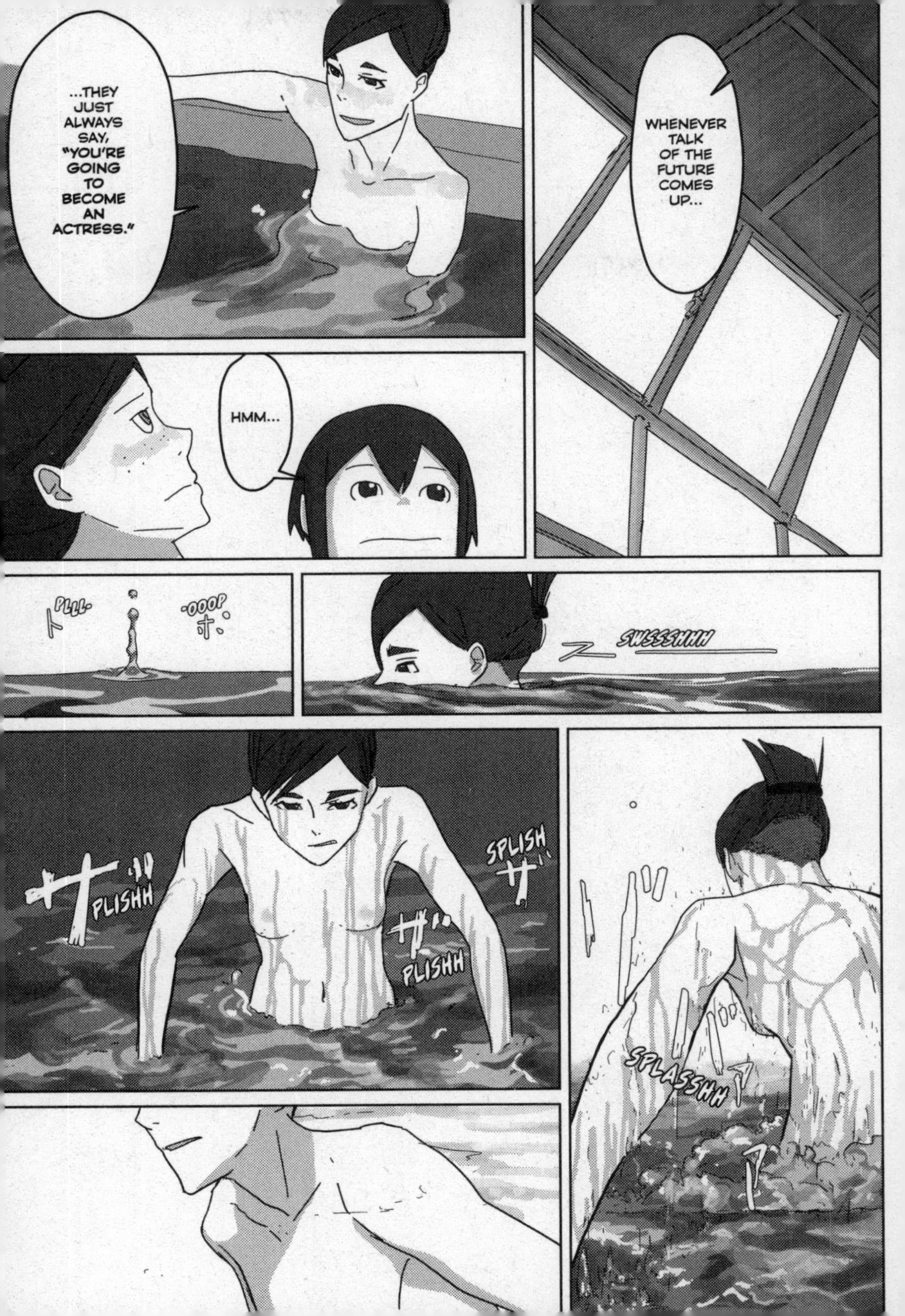
WHENEVER TALK OF THE FUTURE COMES UP...
...THEY JUST ALWAYS SAY, "YOU'RE GOING TO BECOME AN ACTRESS."
HMM...
SWSSSHHH
PLLL-
-OOOP
SPLASSHH
SPLISH
PLISHH
PLISHH

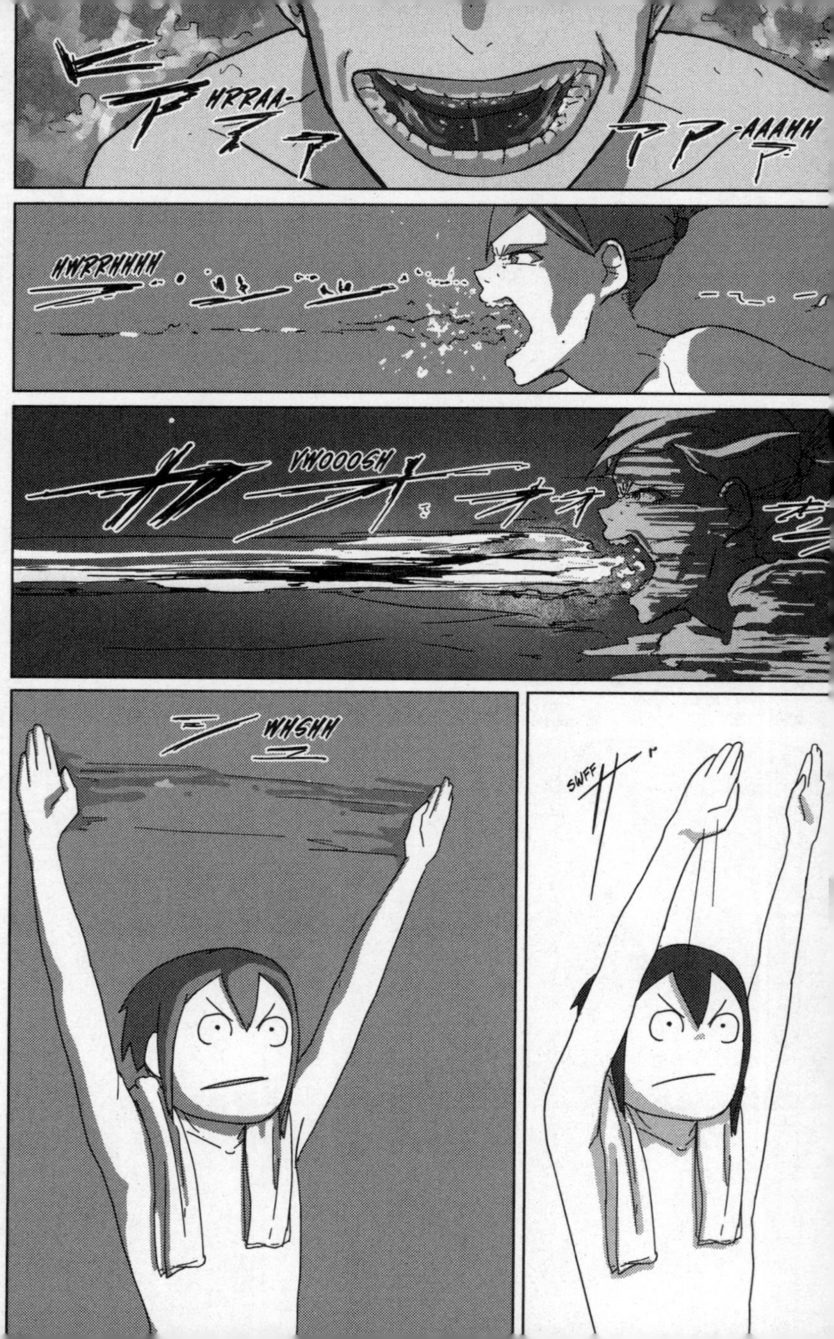
HRRAA-
-AAAHH
HWRRHHHH
VWOOOSH
SWFF
WHSHH

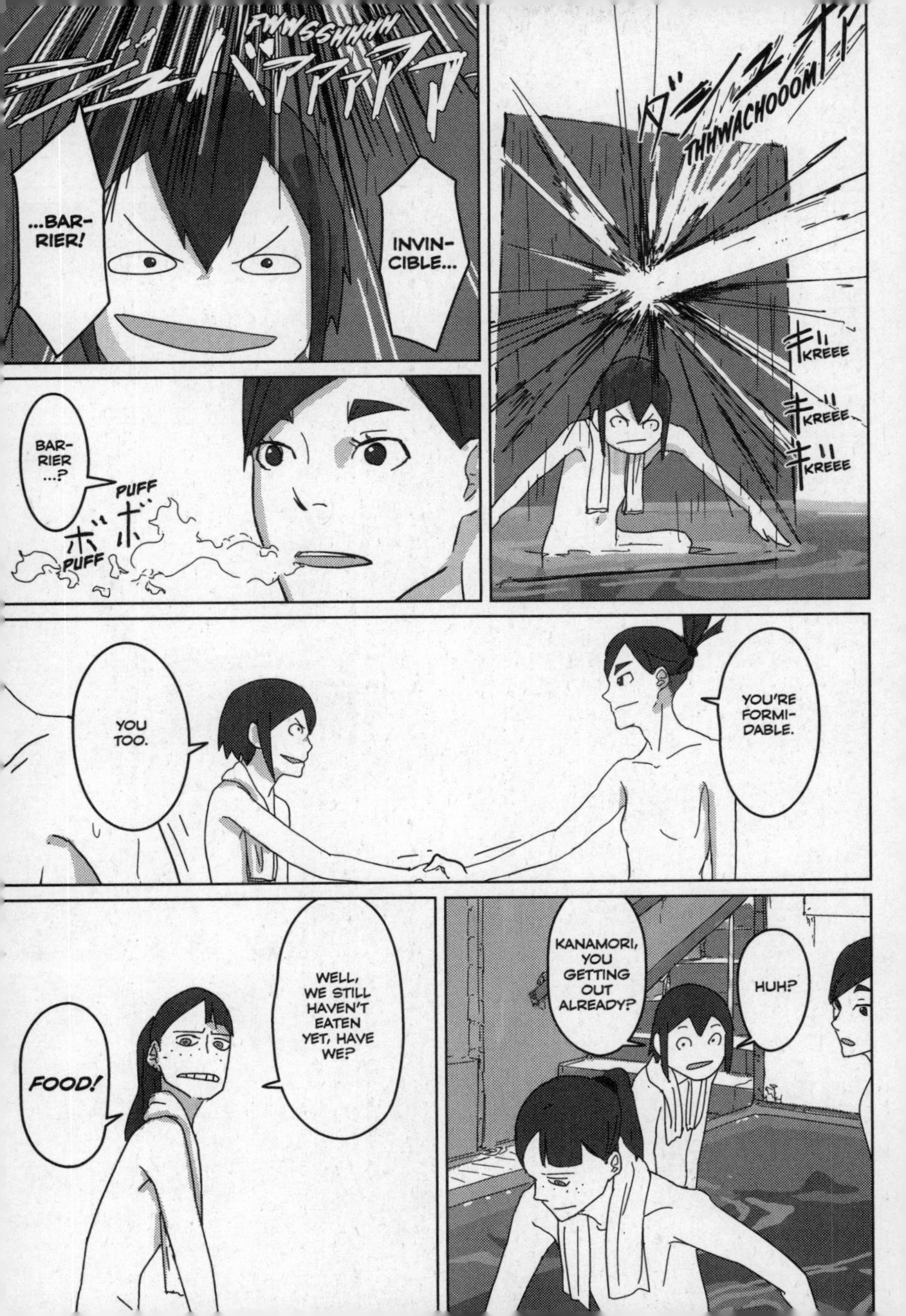
THHWACHOOOM
KREEE
KREEE
KREEE
FWWSSHHHH
INVINCIBLE...
...BARRIER!
PUFF
BARRIER ...?
PUFF
YOU'RE FORMIDABLE.
YOU TOO.
HUH?
KANAMORI, YOU GETTING OUT ALREADY?
WELL, WE STILL HAVEN'T EATEN YET, HAVE WE?
FOOD!

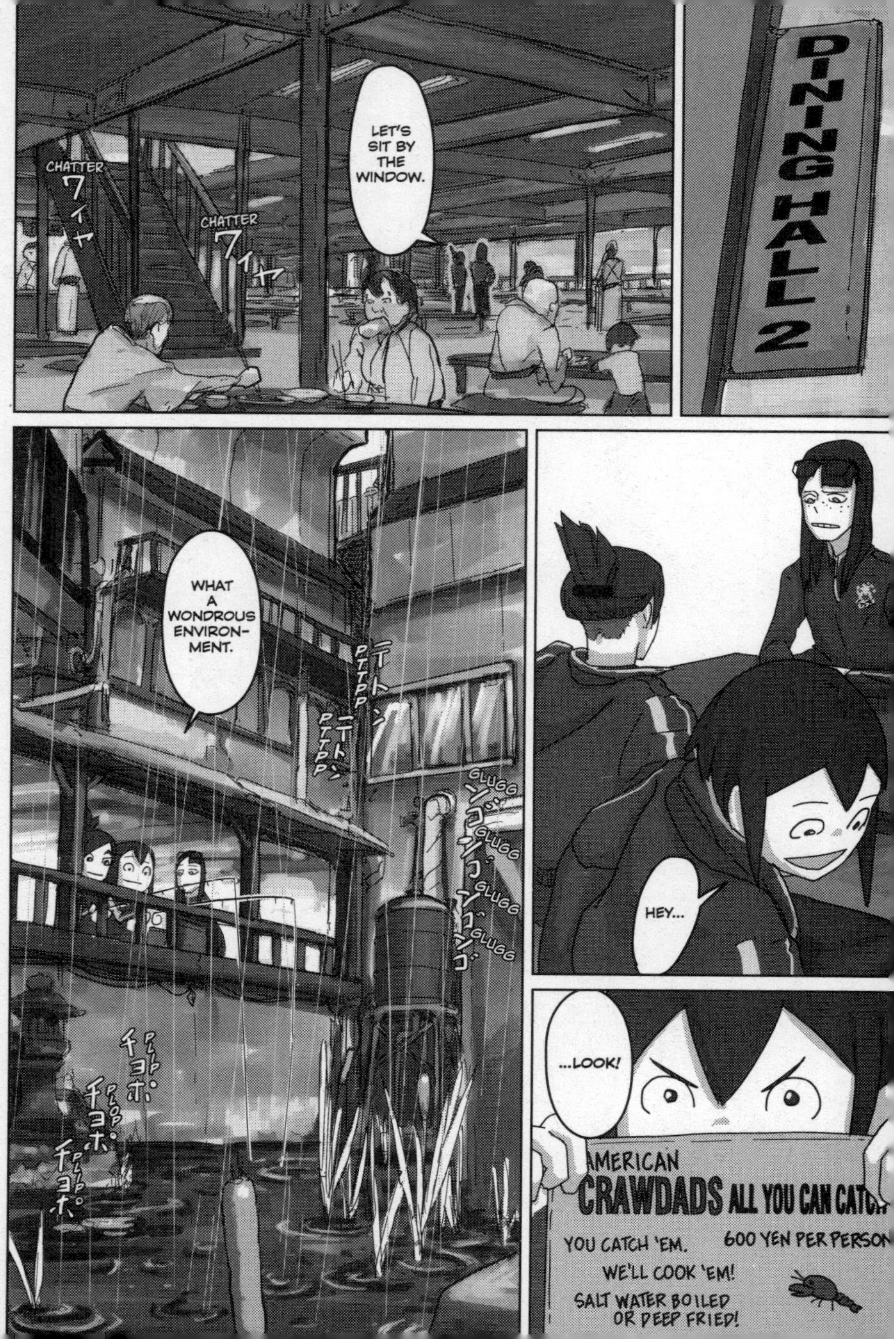

DINING HALL 2
CHATTER
CHATTER
LET'S SIT BY THE WINDOW.
HEY...
...LOOK!
AMERICAN CRAWDADS ALL YOU CAN CATCH
YOU CATCH 'EM. WE'LL COOK 'EM!
600 YEN PER PERSON
SALT WATER BOILED OR DEEP FRIED!
WHAT A WONDROUS ENVIRON-MENT.
PTTPP
PTTPP
GLUGG
GLUGG
GLUGG
GLUGG
PLOP
PLOP
PLOP

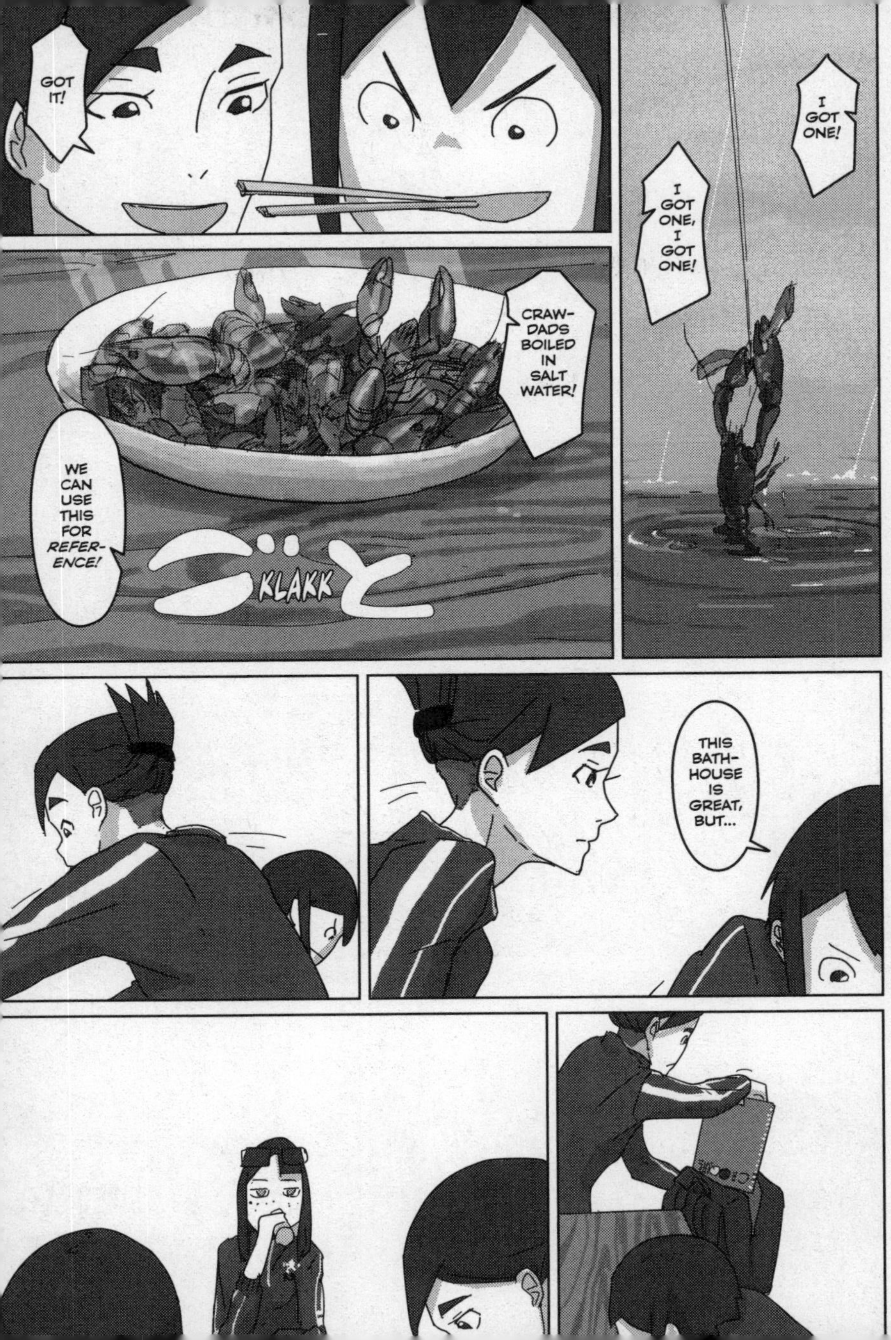
I GOT ONE!
I GOT ONE, I GOT ONE!
GOT IT!
CRAW-DADS BOILED IN SALT WATER!
WE CAN USE THIS FOR *REFERENCE!*
KLAKK
THIS BATH-HOUSE IS GREAT, BUT...

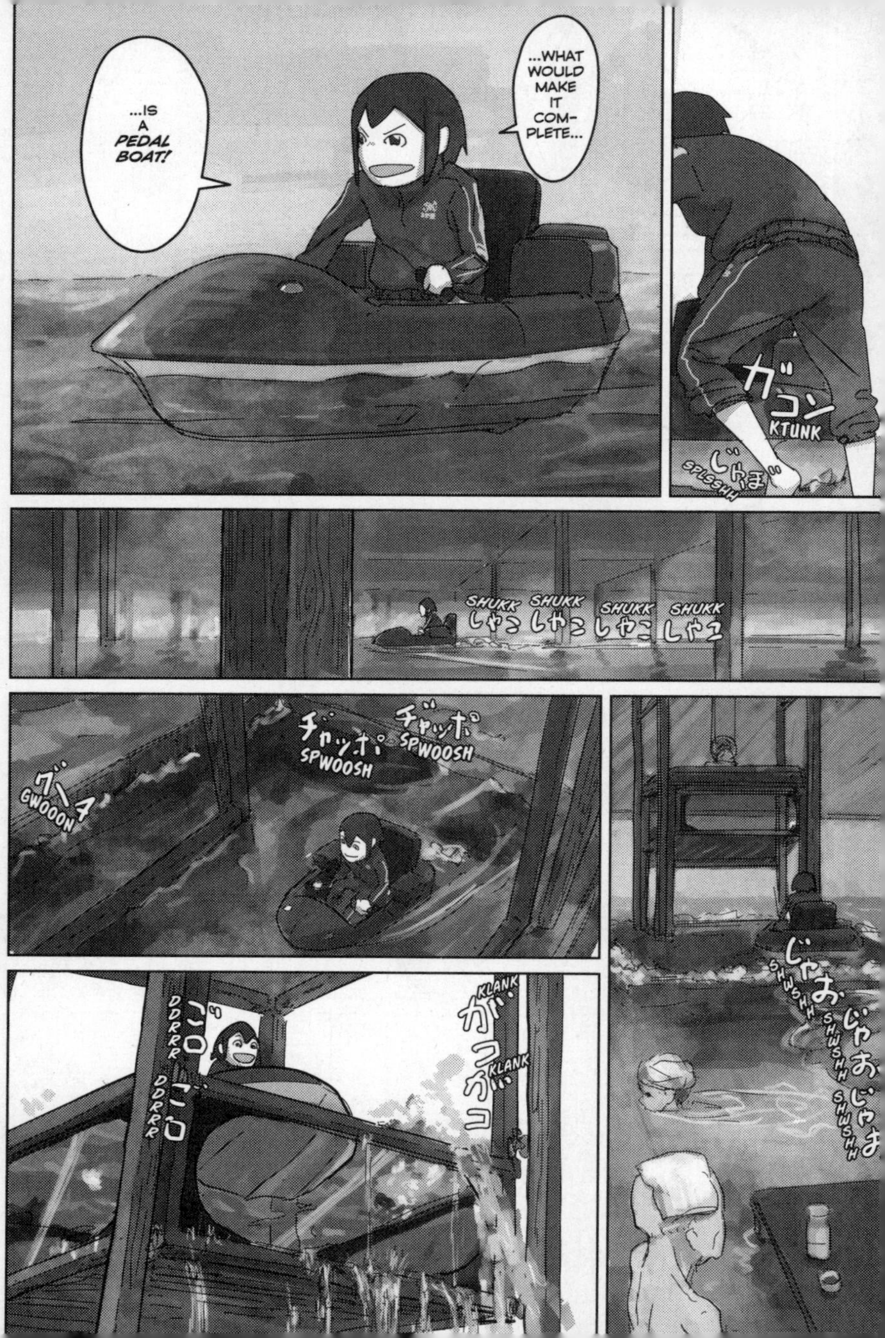
ガコン
KTUNK
じゃぼ
SPLSSHH
...WHAT WOULD MAKE IT COMPLETE...
...IS A PEDAL BOAT!
SHUKK SHUKK SHUKK SHUKK
しゃこしゃこしゃこしゃこ
じゃおじゃおじゃお
SHWSHH SHWSHH SHWSHH
SPWOOSH
SPWOOSH
GWOOON
KLANK KLANK
がコがコ
ごロごロ
DDRRR DDRRR

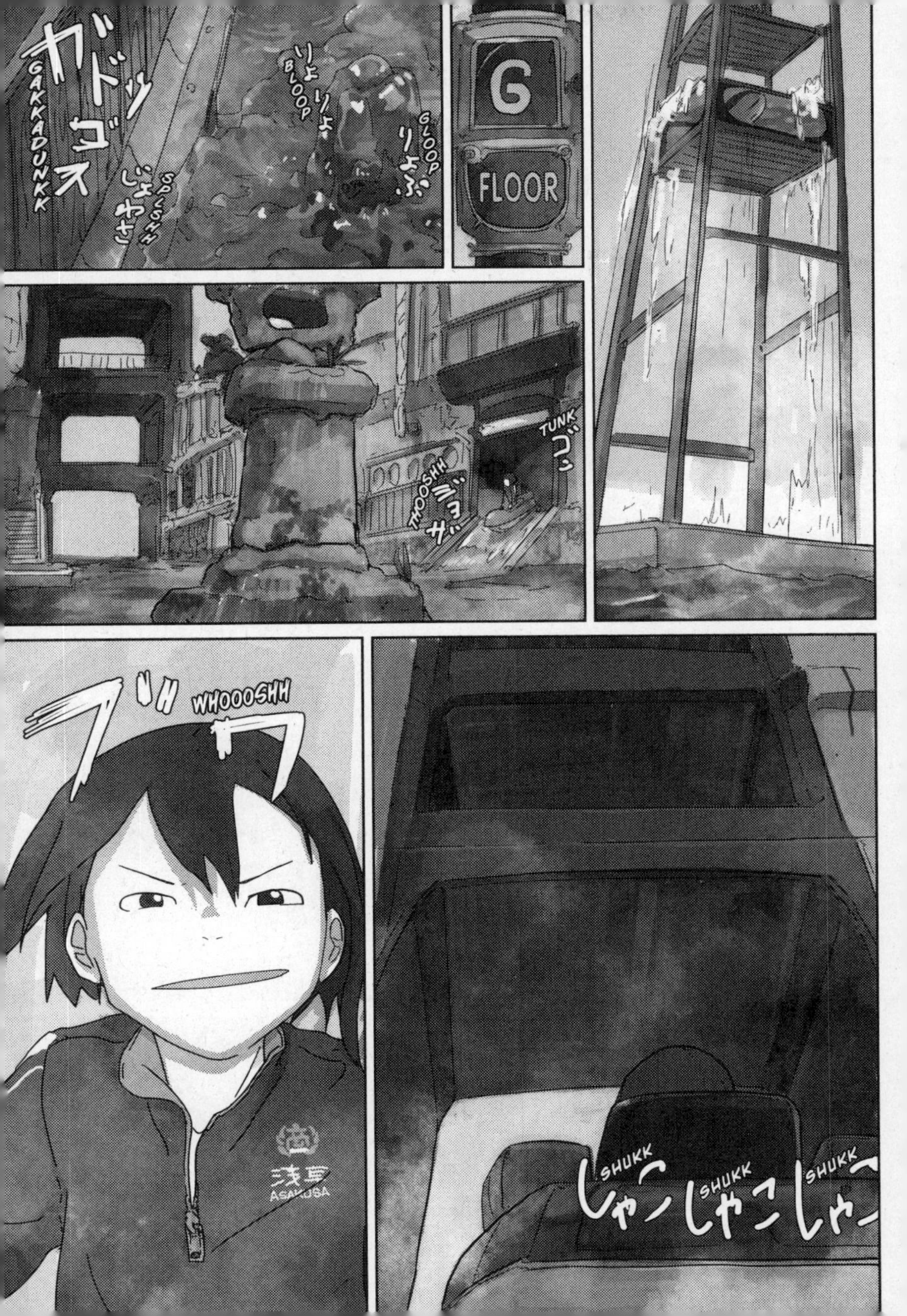

G
FLOOR
GLOOP
BLOOP
SPLSHH
GAKKADUNKK
TUNK
THOOSHH
SHUKK
SHUKK
SHUKK
WHOOOSHH
浅草
ASAKUSA

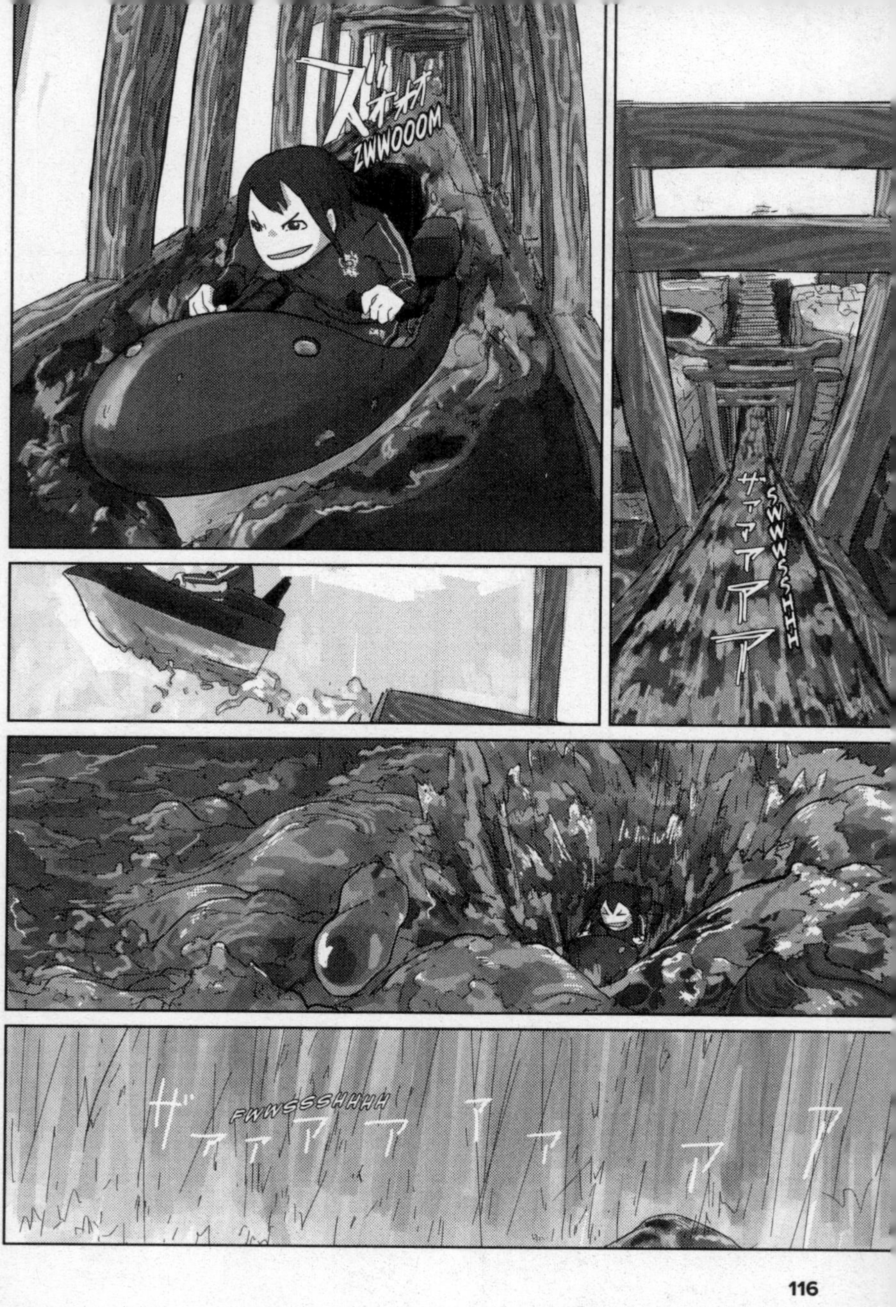
SWWWSSHHH
ZWWOOOM
FWWSSSHHHH

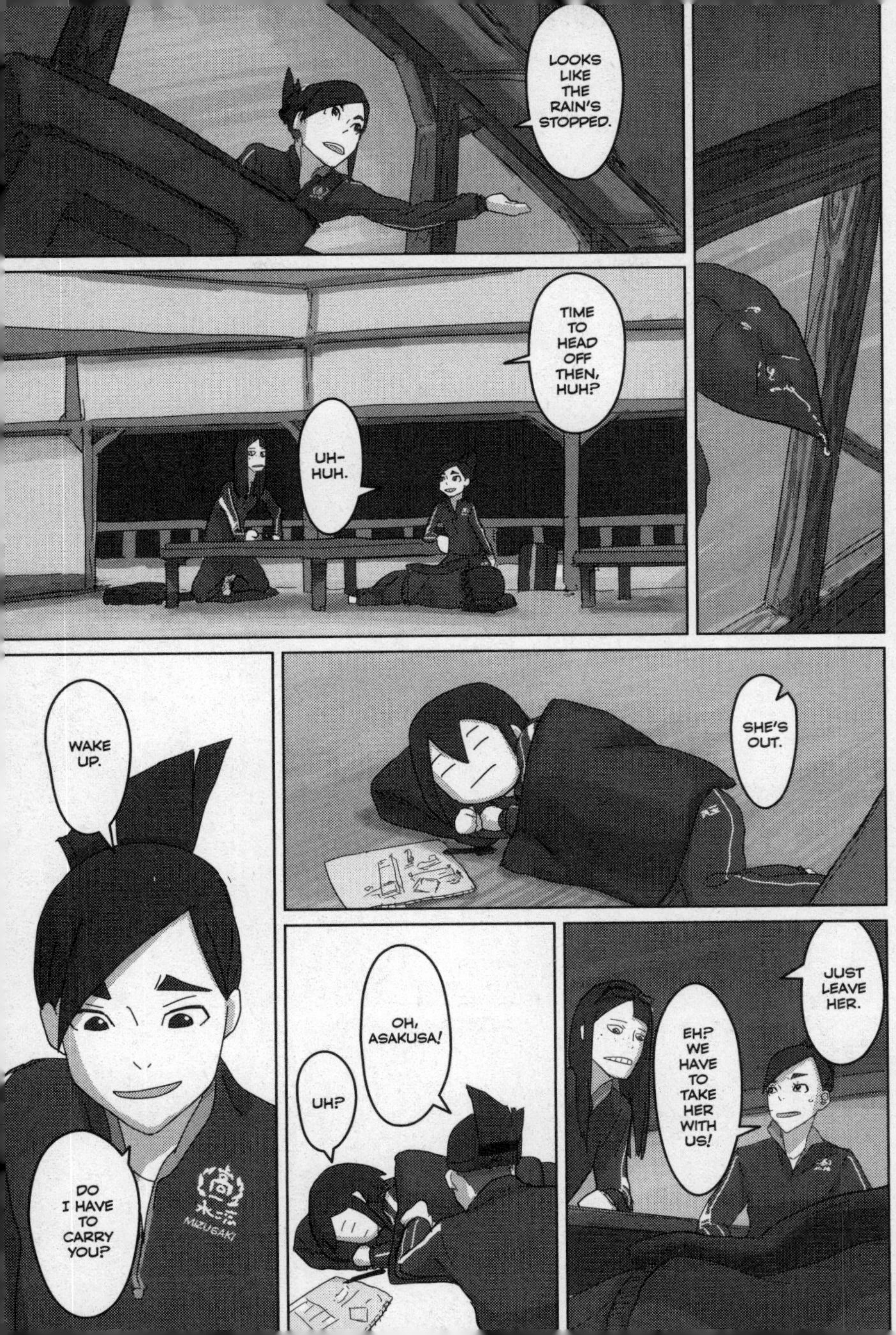
LOOKS LIKE THE RAIN'S STOPPED.
TIME TO HEAD OFF THEN, HUH?
UH-HUH.
SHE'S OUT.
JUST LEAVE HER.
EH? WE HAVE TO TAKE HER WITH US!
OH, ASAKUSA!
UH?
WAKE UP.
DO I HAVE TO CARRY YOU?
MIZUSAKI

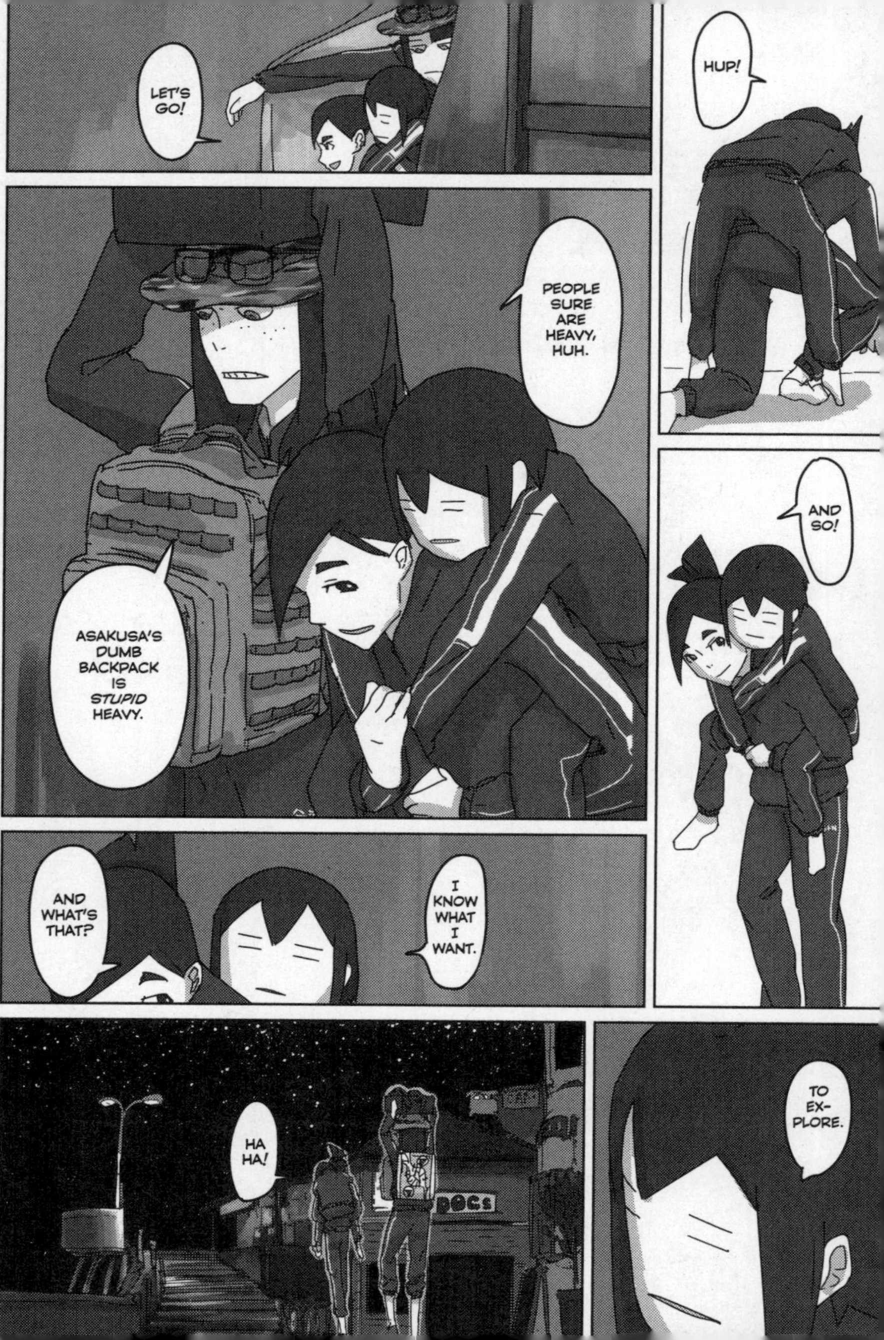
HUP!
AND SO!
LET'S GO!
PEOPLE SURE ARE HEAVY, HUH.
ASAKUSA'S DUMB BACKPACK IS *STUPID* HEAVY.
I KNOW WHAT I WANT.
AND WHAT'S THAT?
TO EXPLORE.
HA HA!

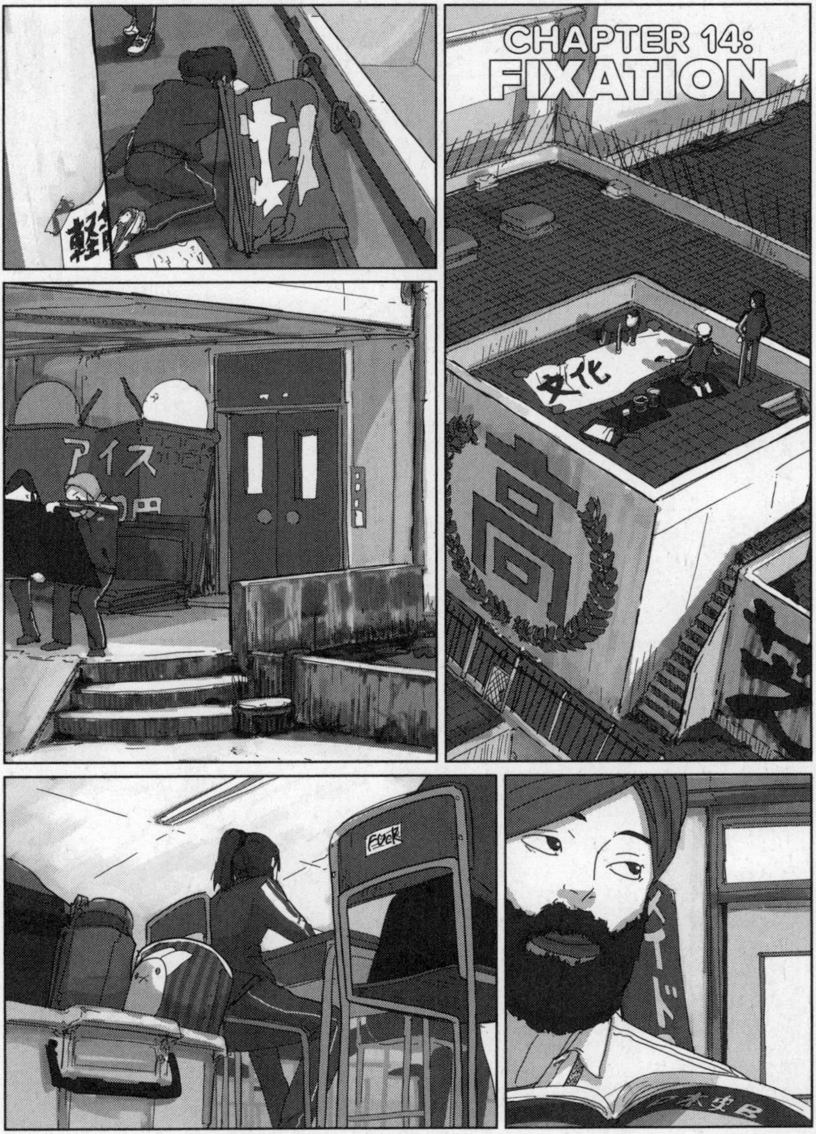
CHAPTER 14:
FIXATION
文化
アイス

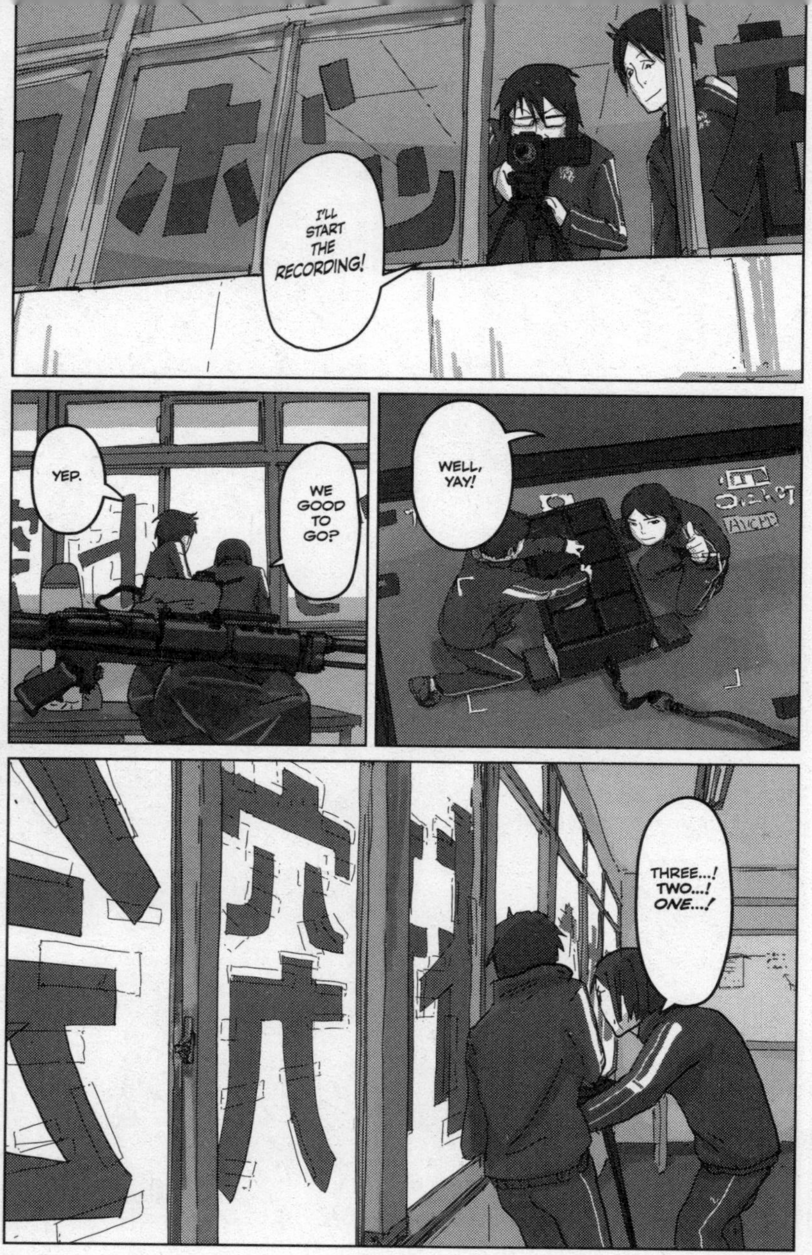
I'LL START THE RECORDING!
WELL, YAY!
WE GOOD TO GO?
YEP.
THREE...! TWO...! ONE...!

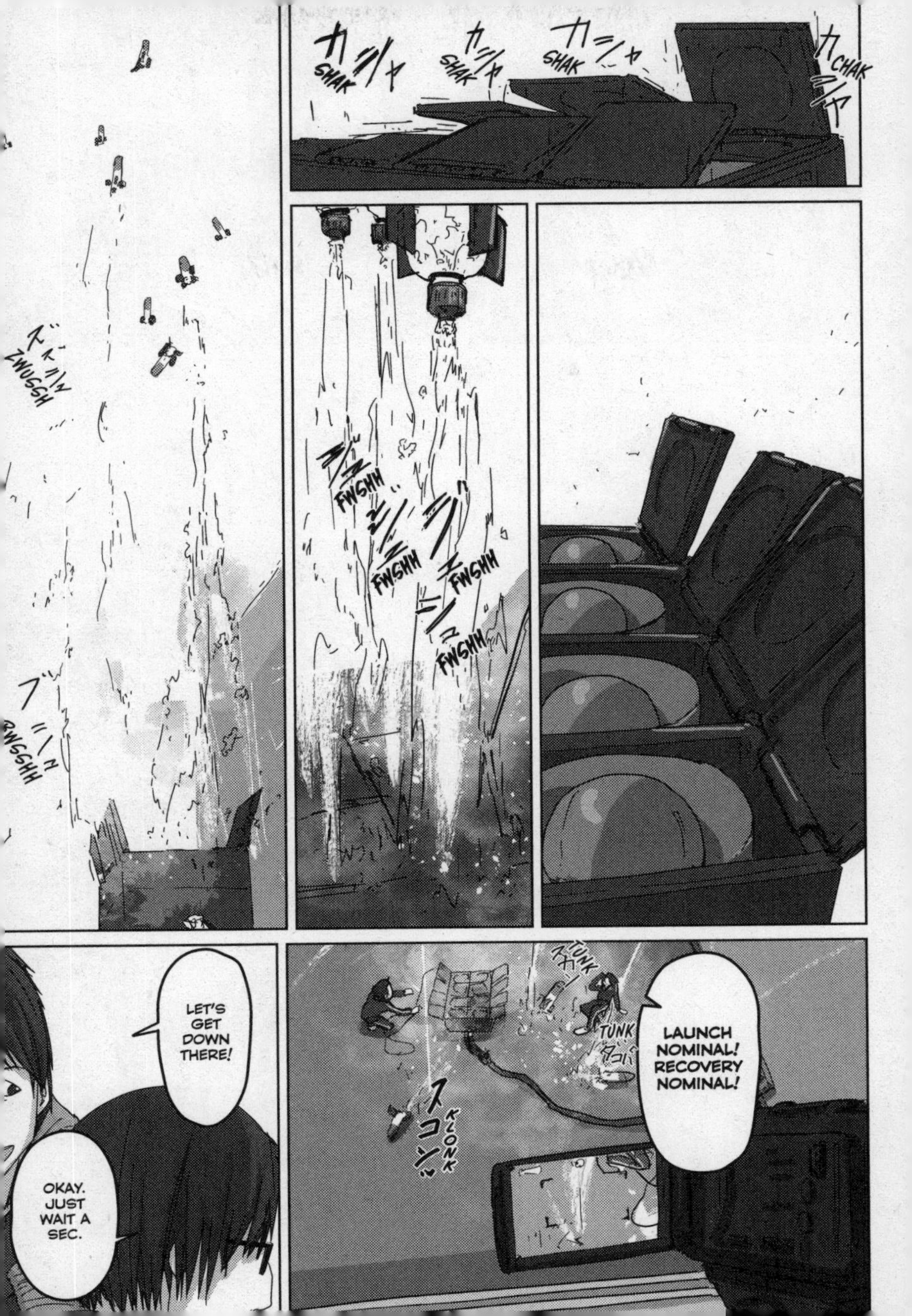
CHAK
SHAK
SHAK
SHAK
FWSHH
FWSHH
FWSHH
FWSHH
ZWUGSHH
BWSSHH
TUNK
TUNK
LAUNCH NOMINAL! RECOVERY NOMINAL!
KLONK
LET'S GET DOWN THERE!
OKAY. JUST WAIT A SEC.

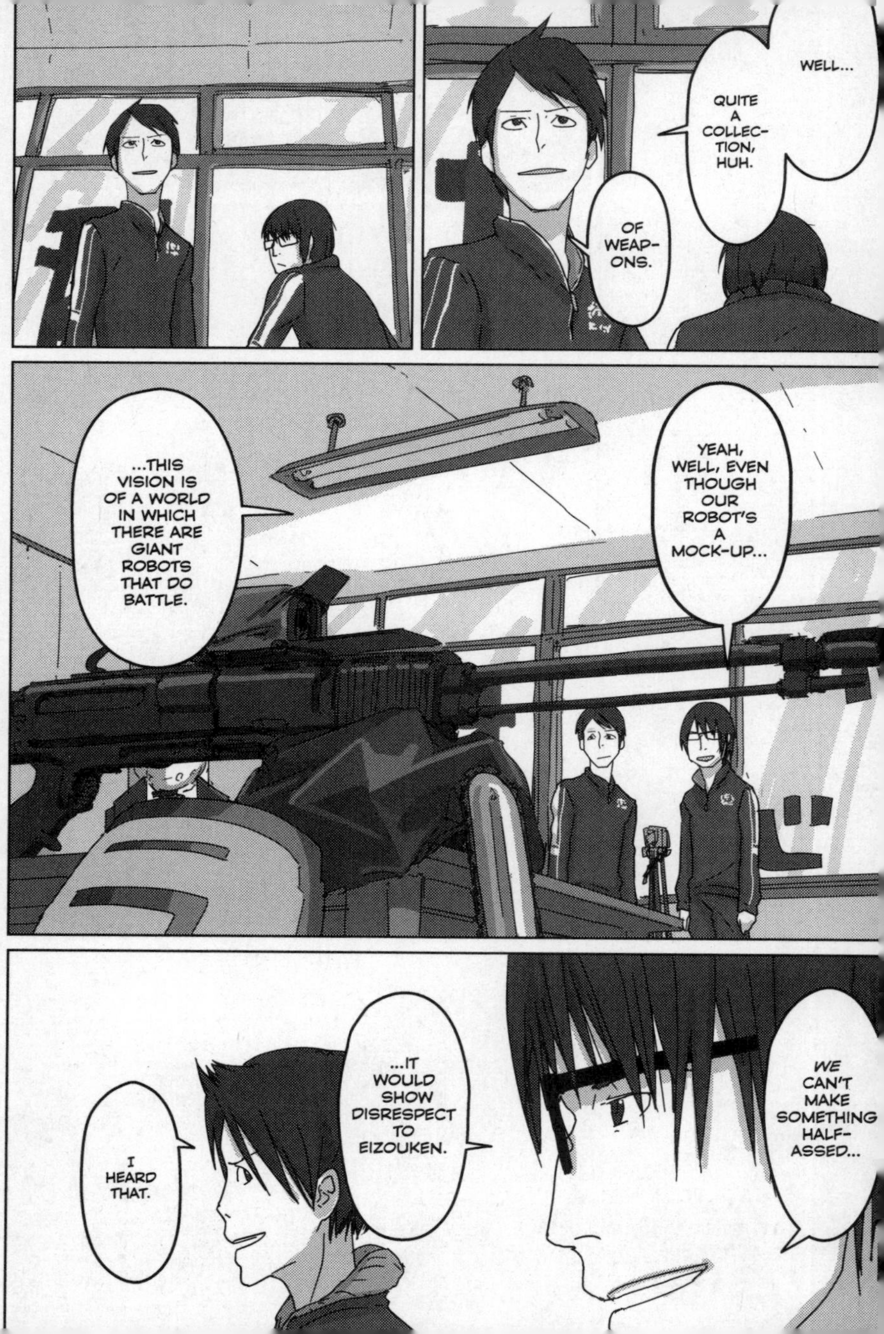
WELL... QUITE A COLLECTION, HUH.
OF WEAPONS.
YEAH, WELL, EVEN THOUGH OUR ROBOT'S A MOCK-UP...
...THIS VISION IS OF A WORLD IN WHICH THERE ARE GIANT ROBOTS THAT DO BATTLE.
WE CAN'T MAKE SOMETHING HALF-ASSED...
...IT WOULD SHOW DISRESPECT TO EIZOUKEN.
I HEARD THAT.

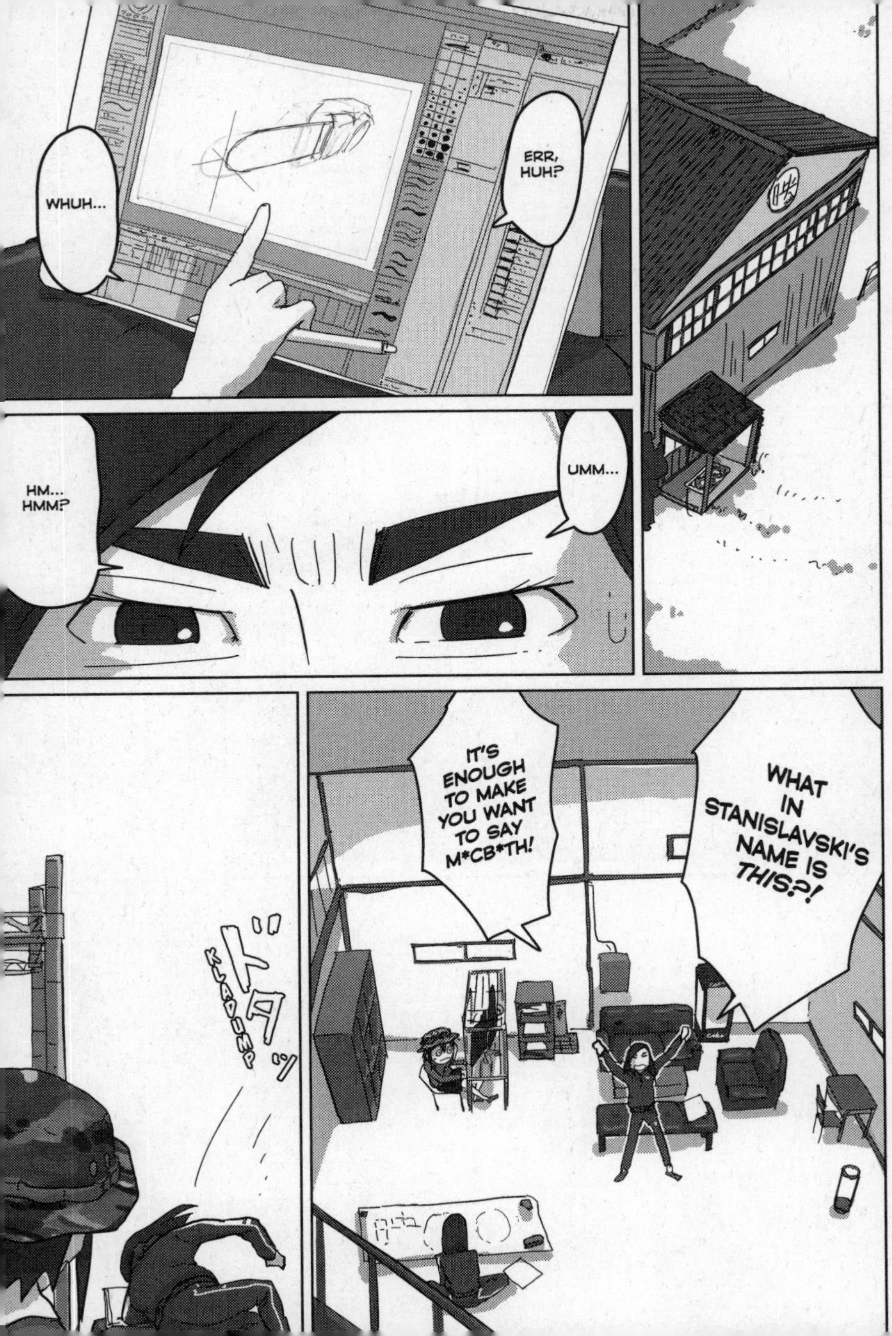
ERR, HUH?
WHUH...
UMM...
HM... HMM?
WHAT IN STANISLAVSKI'S NAME IS *THIS?!*
IT'S ENOUGH TO MAKE YOU WANT TO SAY M*CB*TH!
ドタッ
KLADUMP

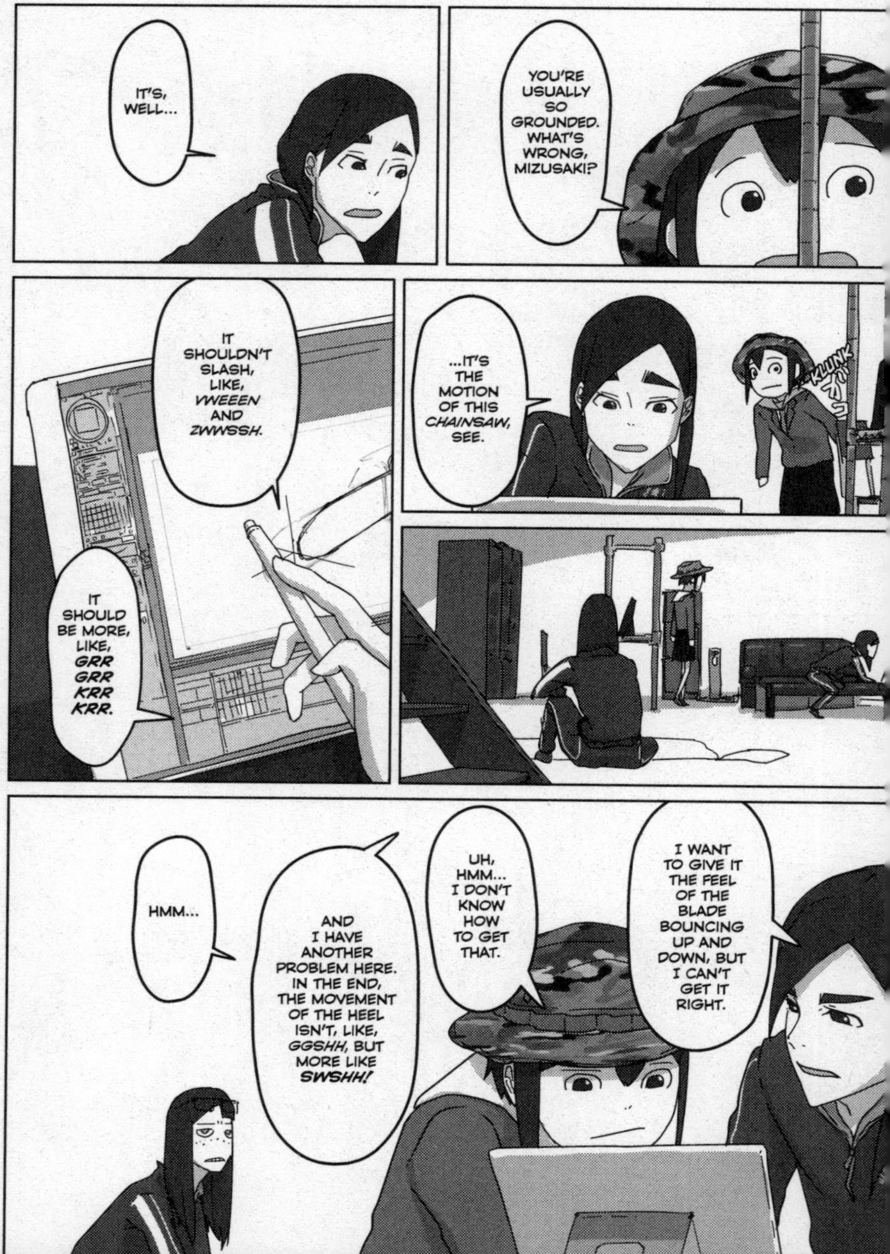
YOU'RE USUALLY SO GROUNDED. WHAT'S WRONG, MIZUSAKI!?
IT'S, WELL...
KLUNK
...IT'S THE MOTION OF THIS CHAINSAW, SEE.
IT SHOULDN'T SLASH, LIKE, VWEEEN AND ZWWSSH.
IT SHOULD BE MORE, LIKE, GRR GRR KRR KRR.
I WANT TO GIVE IT THE FEEL OF THE BLADE BOUNCING UP AND DOWN, BUT I CAN'T GET IT RIGHT.
UH, HMM... I DON'T KNOW HOW TO GET THAT.
AND I HAVE ANOTHER PROBLEM HERE. IN THE END, THE MOVEMENT OF THE HEEL ISN'T, LIKE, GGSHH, BUT MORE LIKE SWSHH!
HMM...

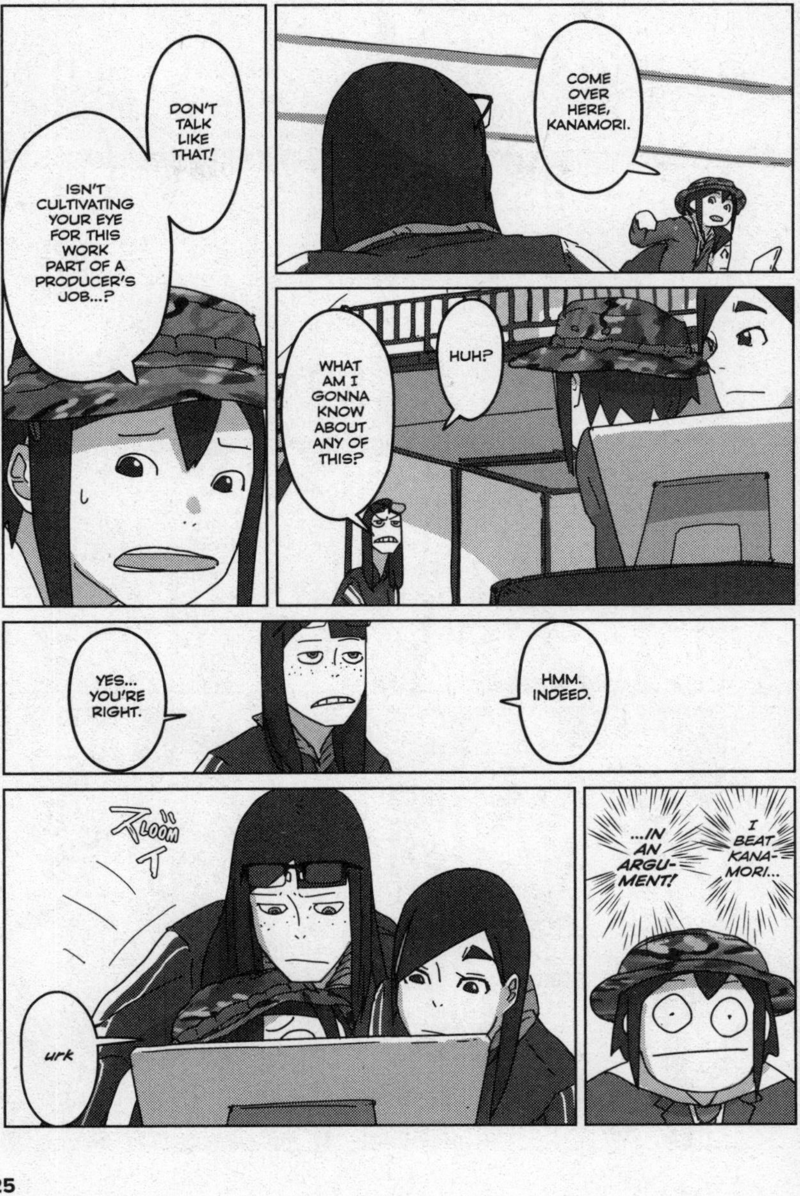
COME OVER HERE, KANAMORI.
HUH?
WHAT AM I GONNA KNOW ABOUT ANY OF THIS?
DON'T TALK LIKE THAT!
ISN'T CULTIVATING YOUR EYE FOR THIS WORK PART OF A PRODUCER'S JOB...?
HMM. INDEED.
YES... YOU'RE RIGHT.
I BEAT KANAMORI...
...IN AN ARGUMENT!
urk

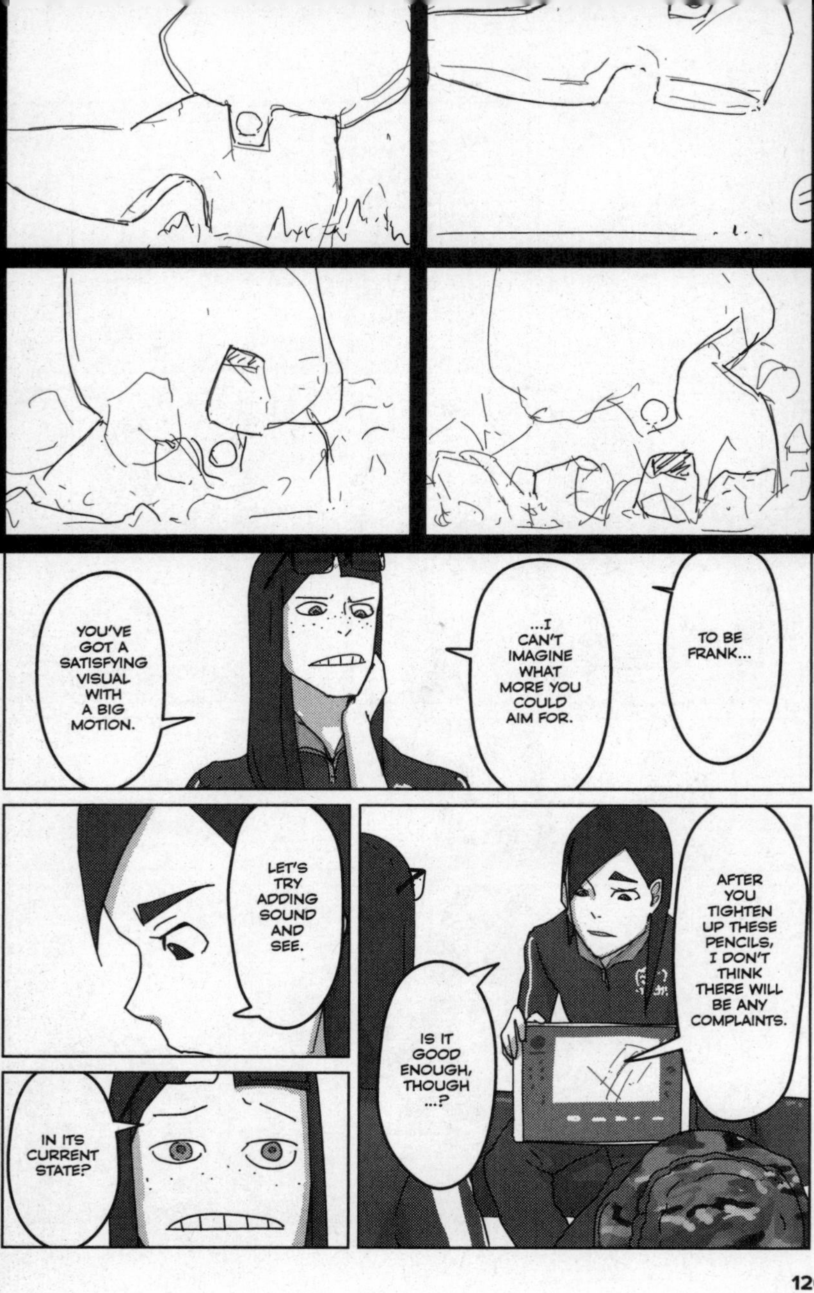
TO BE FRANK...
...I CAN'T IMAGINE WHAT MORE YOU COULD AIM FOR.
YOU'VE GOT A SATISFYING VISUAL WITH A BIG MOTION.
AFTER YOU TIGHTEN UP THESE PENCILS, I DON'T THINK THERE WILL BE ANY COMPLAINTS.
IS IT GOOD ENOUGH, THOUGH ...?
LET'S TRY ADDING SOUND AND SEE.
IN ITS CURRENT STATE?

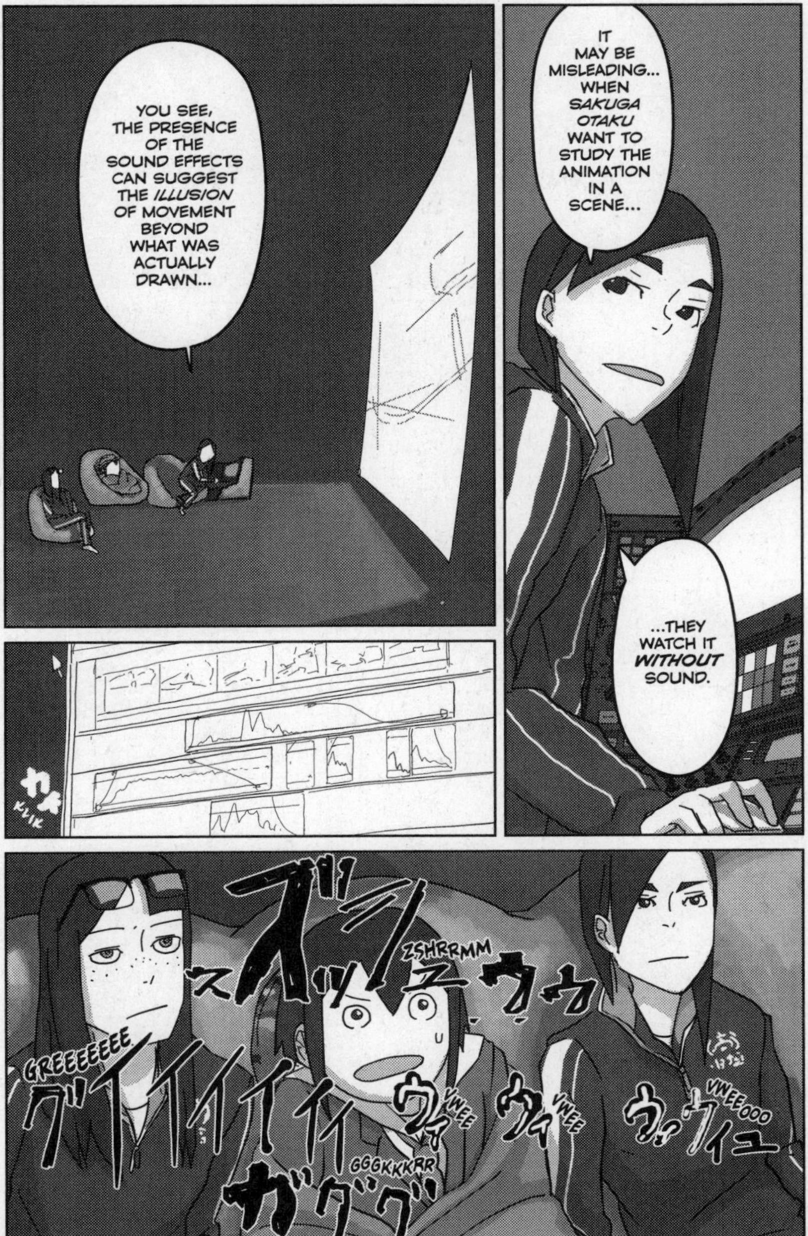
IT MAY BE MISLEADING... WHEN *SAKUGA OTAKU* WANT TO STUDY THE ANIMATION IN A SCENE...
...THEY WATCH IT ***WITHOUT*** SOUND.
YOU SEE, THE PRESENCE OF THE SOUND EFFECTS CAN SUGGEST THE *ILLUSION* OF MOVEMENT BEYOND WHAT WAS ACTUALLY DRAWN...
KLIK
ZSHRRMM
VWEEOOO
VWEE
VWEE
GREEEEEEE
GGGKKKRR

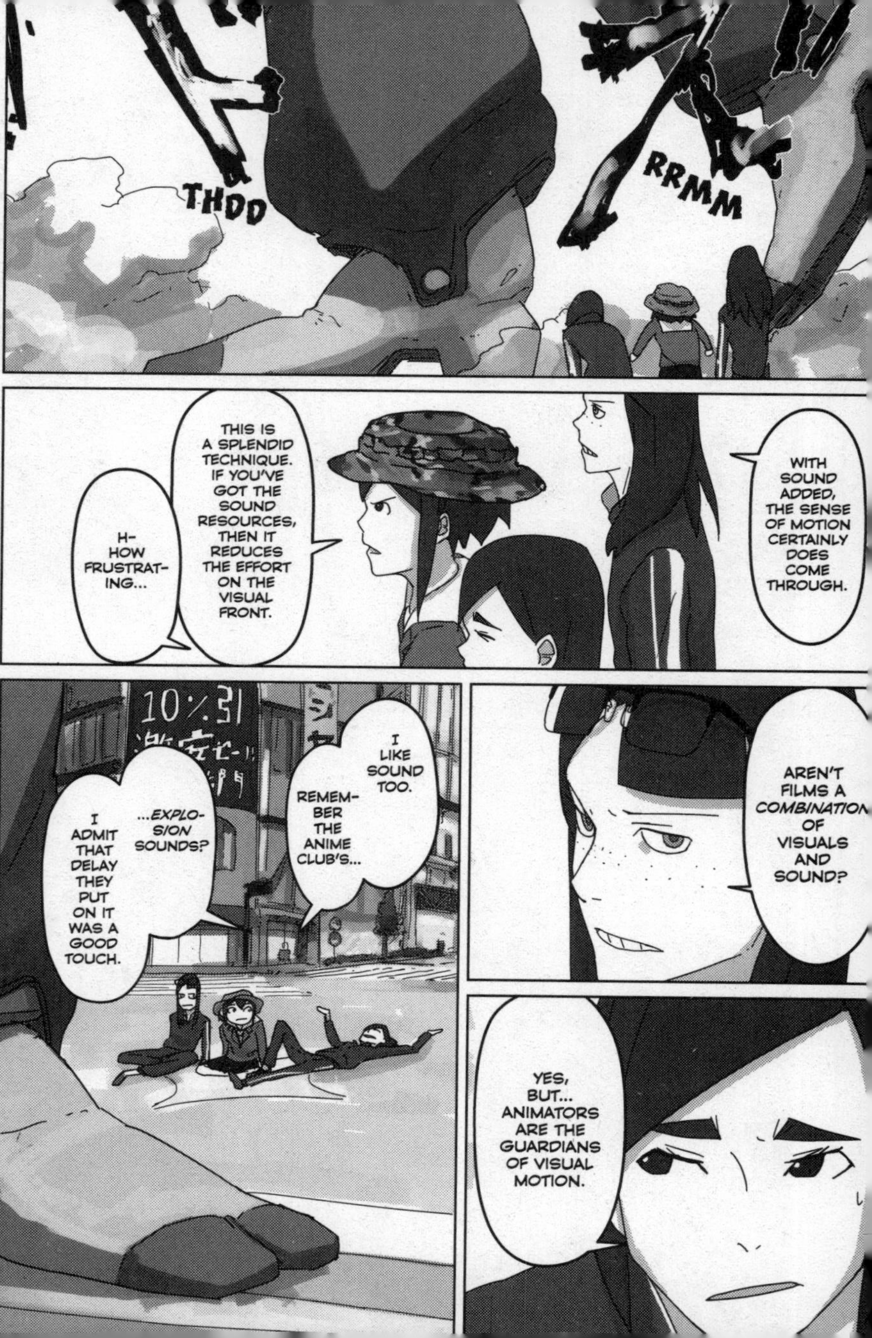
RRMM
THDD
WITH SOUND ADDED, THE SENSE OF MOTION CERTAINLY DOES COME THROUGH.
THIS IS A SPLENDID TECHNIQUE. IF YOU'VE GOT THE SOUND RESOURCES, THEN IT REDUCES THE EFFORT ON THE VISUAL FRONT.
H-HOW FRUSTRATING...
AREN'T FILMS A *COMBINATION* OF VISUALS AND SOUND?
YES, BUT... ANIMATORS ARE THE GUARDIANS OF VISUAL MOTION.
10%引
I LIKE SOUND TOO.
REMEMBER THE ANIME CLUB'S...
...*EXPLOSION SOUNDS?*
I ADMIT THAT DELAY THEY PUT ON IT WAS A GOOD TOUCH.

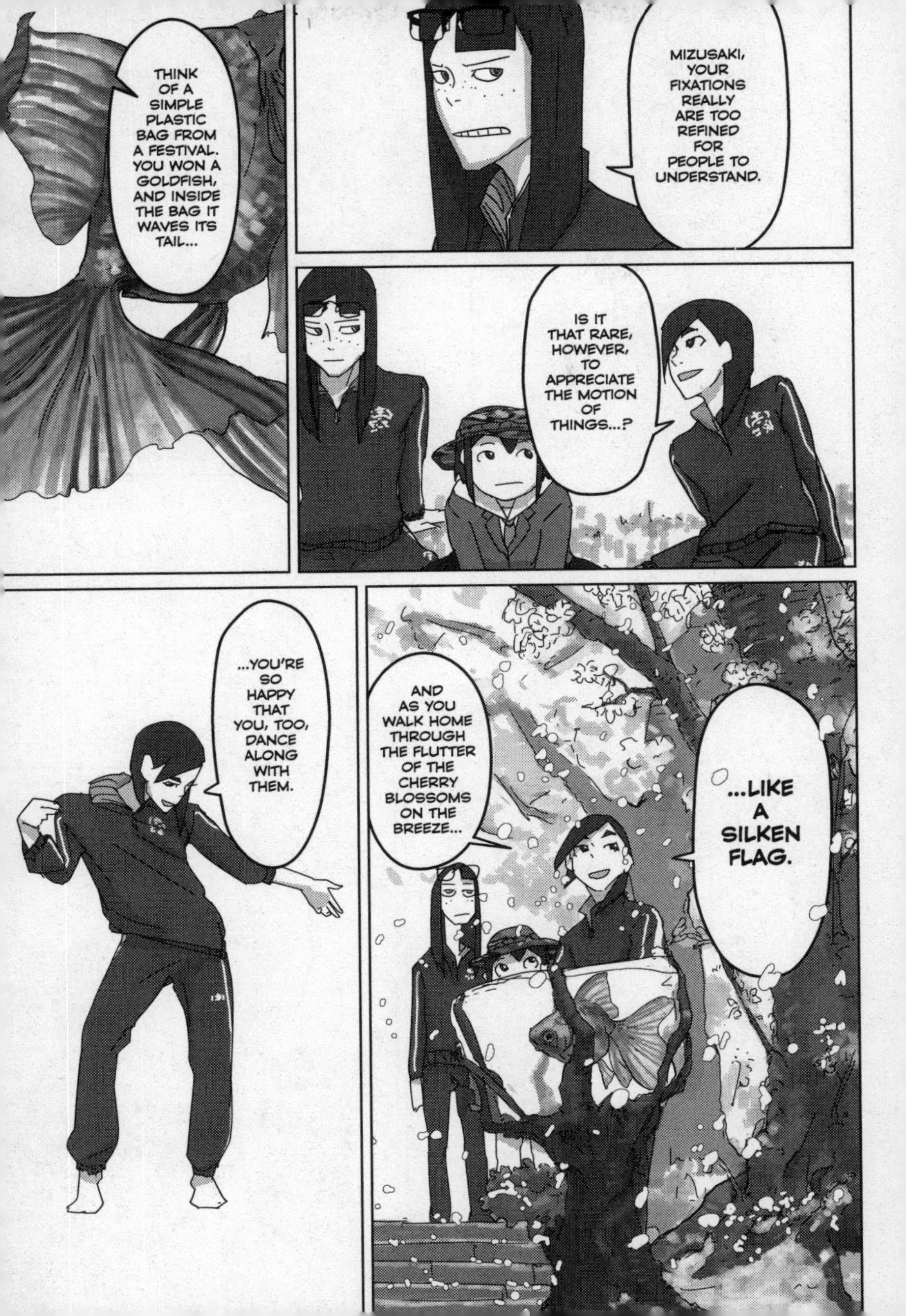
MIZUSAKI, YOUR FIXATIONS REALLY ARE TOO REFINED FOR PEOPLE TO UNDERSTAND.
IS IT THAT RARE, HOWEVER, TO APPRECIATE THE MOTION OF THINGS...?
THINK OF A SIMPLE PLASTIC BAG FROM A FESTIVAL. YOU WON A GOLDFISH, AND INSIDE THE BAG IT WAVES ITS TAIL...
...LIKE A SILKEN FLAG.
AND AS YOU WALK HOME THROUGH THE FLUTTER OF THE CHERRY BLOSSOMS ON THE BREEZE...
...YOU'RE SO HAPPY THAT YOU, TOO, DANCE ALONG WITH THEM.

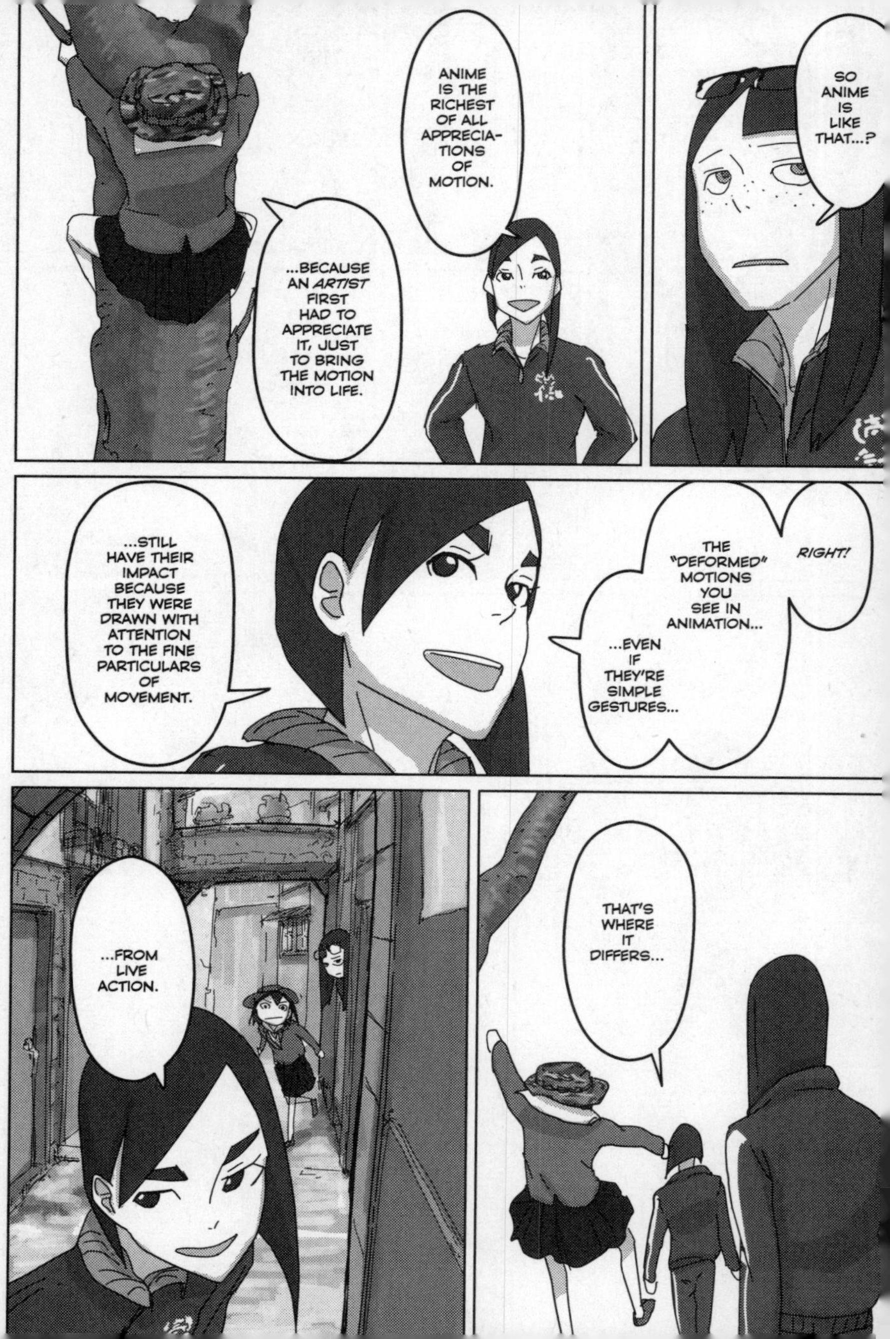

SO ANIME IS LIKE THAT...?
ANIME IS THE RICHEST OF ALL APPRECIA-TIONS OF MOTION.
...BECAUSE AN *ARTIST* FIRST HAD TO APPRECIATE IT, JUST TO BRING THE MOTION INTO LIFE.
RIGHT!
THE "DEFORMED" MOTIONS YOU SEE IN ANIMATION...
...EVEN IF THEY'RE SIMPLE GESTURES...
...STILL HAVE THEIR IMPACT BECAUSE THEY WERE DRAWN WITH ATTENTION TO THE FINE PARTICULARS OF MOVEMENT.
THAT'S WHERE IT DIFFERS...
...FROM LIVE ACTION.

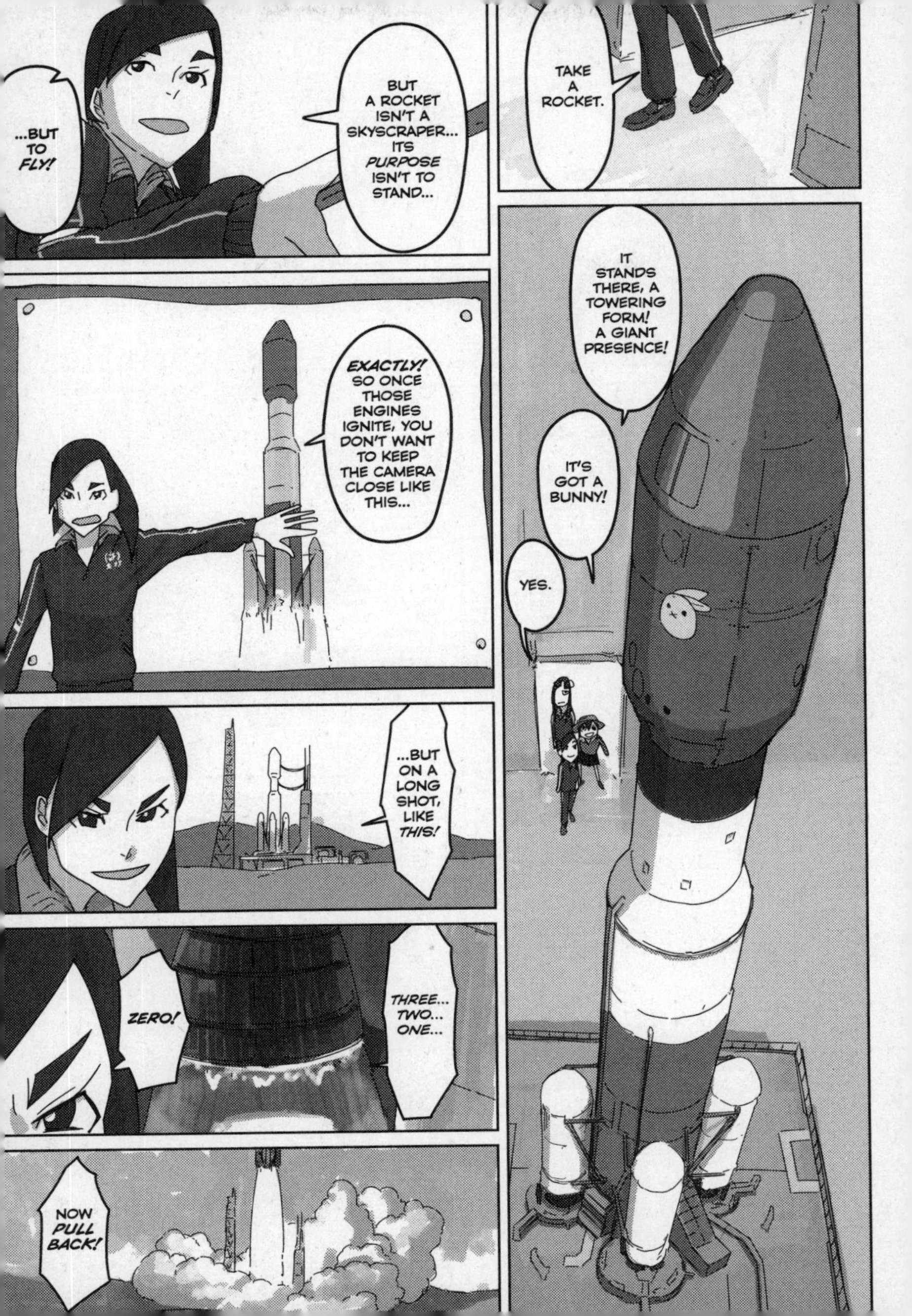
TAKE A ROCKET.
BUT A ROCKET ISN'T A SKYSCRAPER... ITS *PURPOSE* ISN'T TO STAND...
...BUT TO *FLY!*
IT STANDS THERE, A TOWERING FORM! A GIANT PRESENCE!
IT'S GOT A BUNNY!
YES.
EXACTLY! SO ONCE THOSE ENGINES IGNITE, YOU DON'T WANT TO KEEP THE CAMERA CLOSE LIKE THIS...
...BUT ON A LONG SHOT, LIKE *THIS!*
THREE... TWO... ONE...
ZERO!
NOW *PULL BACK!*

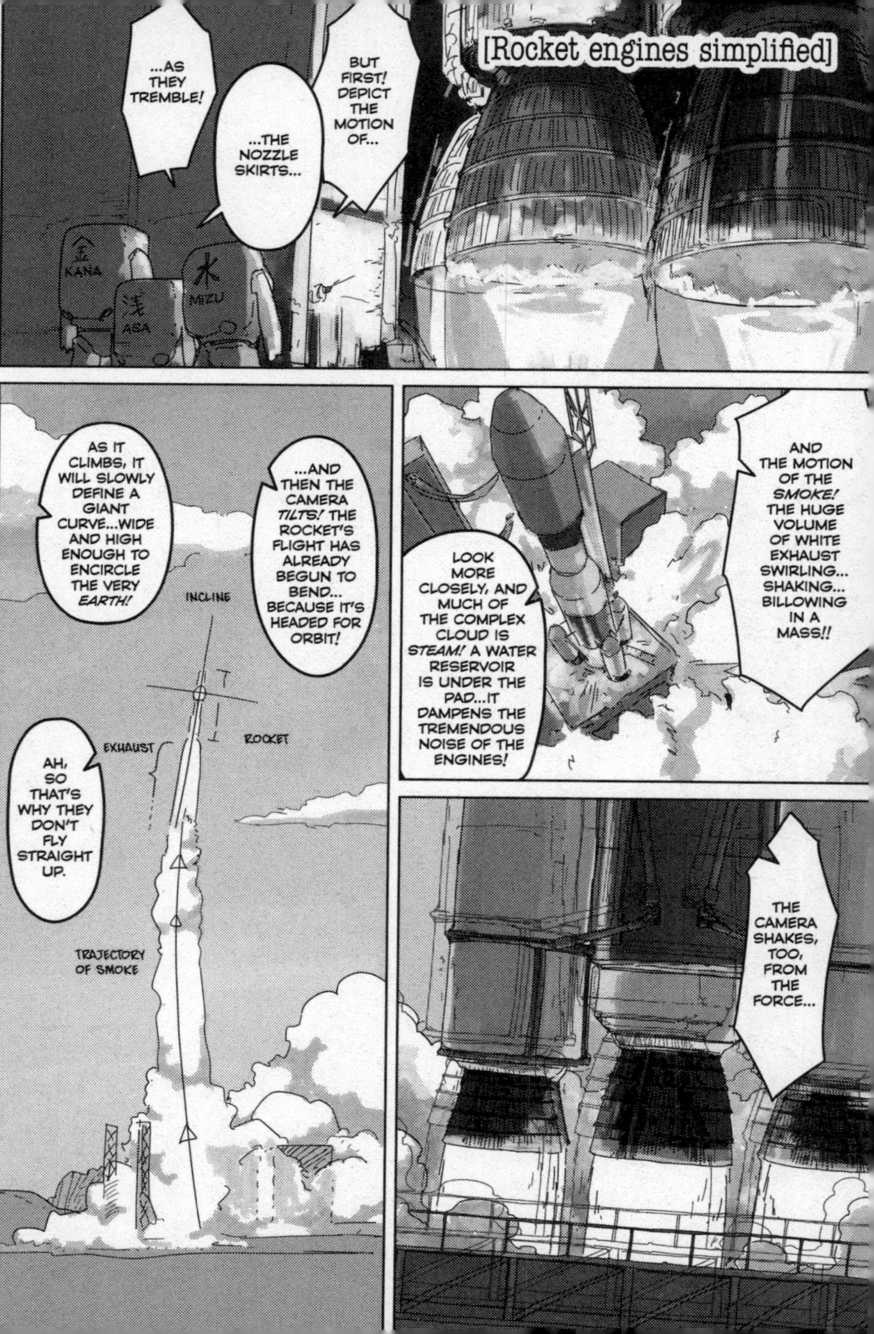
[Rocket engines simplified]
BUT FIRST! DEPICT THE MOTION OF...
...THE NOZZLE SKIRTS...
...AS THEY TREMBLE!
金 KANA
浅 ASA
水 MIZU
AND THE MOTION OF THE *SMOKE!* THE HUGE VOLUME OF WHITE EXHAUST SWIRLING... SHAKING... BILLOWING IN A MASS!!
LOOK MORE CLOSELY, AND MUCH OF THE COMPLEX CLOUD IS *STEAM!* A WATER RESERVOIR IS UNDER THE PAD...IT DAMPENS THE TREMENDOUS NOISE OF THE ENGINES!
THE CAMERA SHAKES, TOO, FROM THE FORCE...
...AND THEN THE CAMERA *TILTS!* THE ROCKET'S FLIGHT HAS ALREADY BEGUN TO BEND... BECAUSE IT'S HEADED FOR ORBIT!
AS IT CLIMBS, IT WILL SLOWLY DEFINE A GIANT CURVE...WIDE AND HIGH ENOUGH TO ENCIRCLE THE VERY *EARTH!*
INCLINE
ROCKET
EXHAUST
AH, SO THAT'S WHY THEY DON'T FLY STRAIGHT UP.
TRAJECTORY OF SMOKE

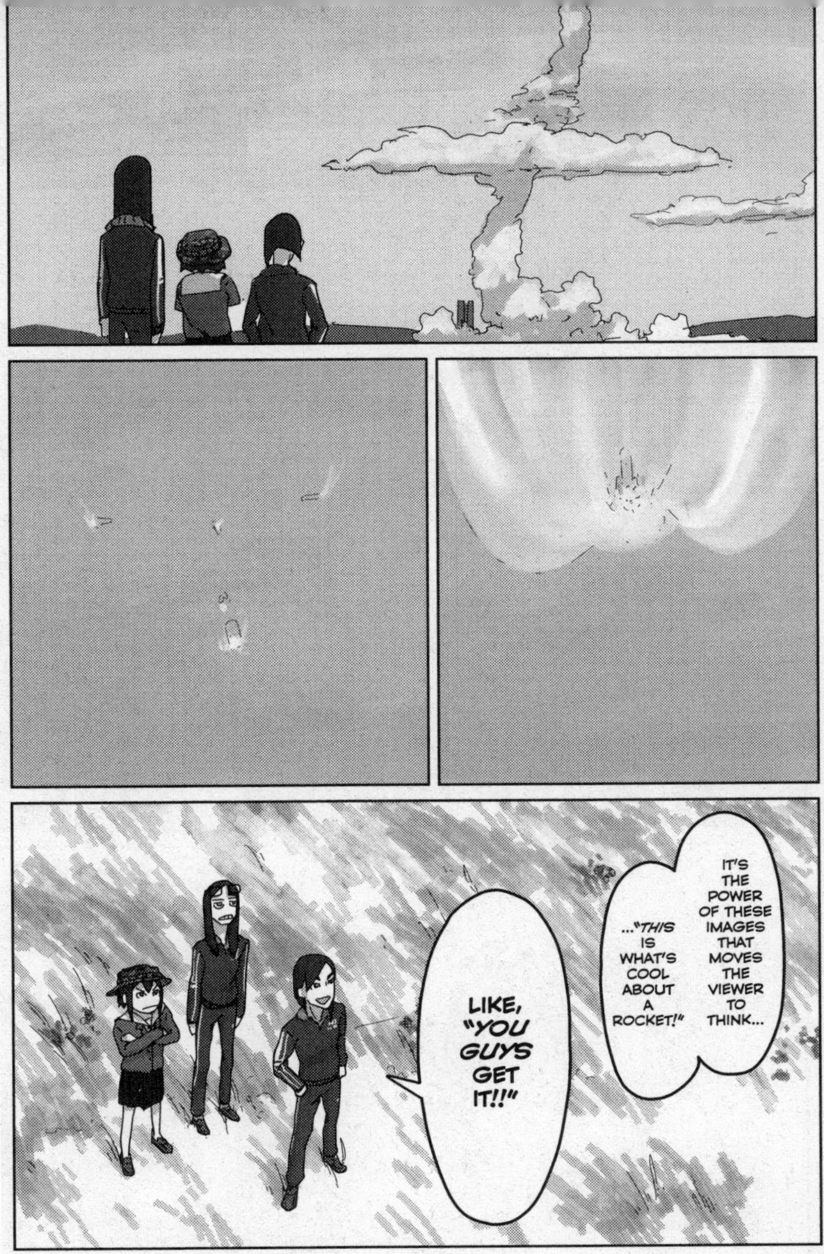
IT'S THE POWER OF THESE IMAGES THAT MOVES THE VIEWER TO THINK...
..."THIS IS WHAT'S COOL ABOUT A ROCKET!"
LIKE, "YOU GUYS GET IT!!"

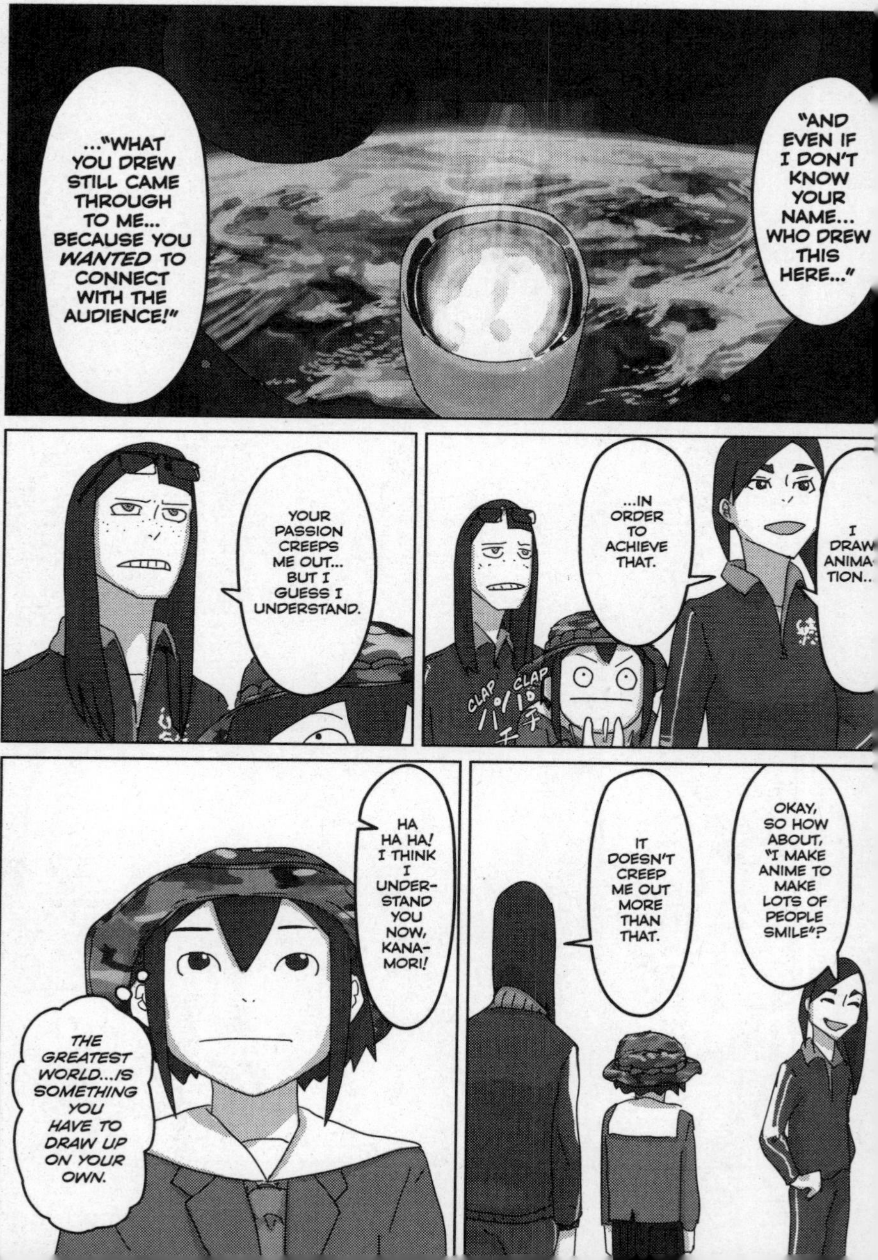
"AND EVEN IF I DON'T KNOW YOUR NAME... WHO DREW THIS HERE..."
..."WHAT YOU DREW STILL CAME THROUGH TO ME... BECAUSE YOU *WANTED* TO CONNECT WITH THE AUDIENCE!"
I DRAW ANIMA TION..
...IN ORDER TO ACHIEVE THAT.
CLAP CLAP
YOUR PASSION CREEPS ME OUT... BUT I GUESS I UNDERSTAND.
OKAY, SO HOW ABOUT, "I MAKE ANIME TO MAKE LOTS OF PEOPLE SMILE"?
IT DOESN'T CREEP ME OUT MORE THAN THAT.
HA HA HA! I THINK I UNDER-STAND YOU NOW, KANA-MORI!
THE GREATEST WORLD...IS SOMETHING YOU HAVE TO DRAW UP ON YOUR OWN.

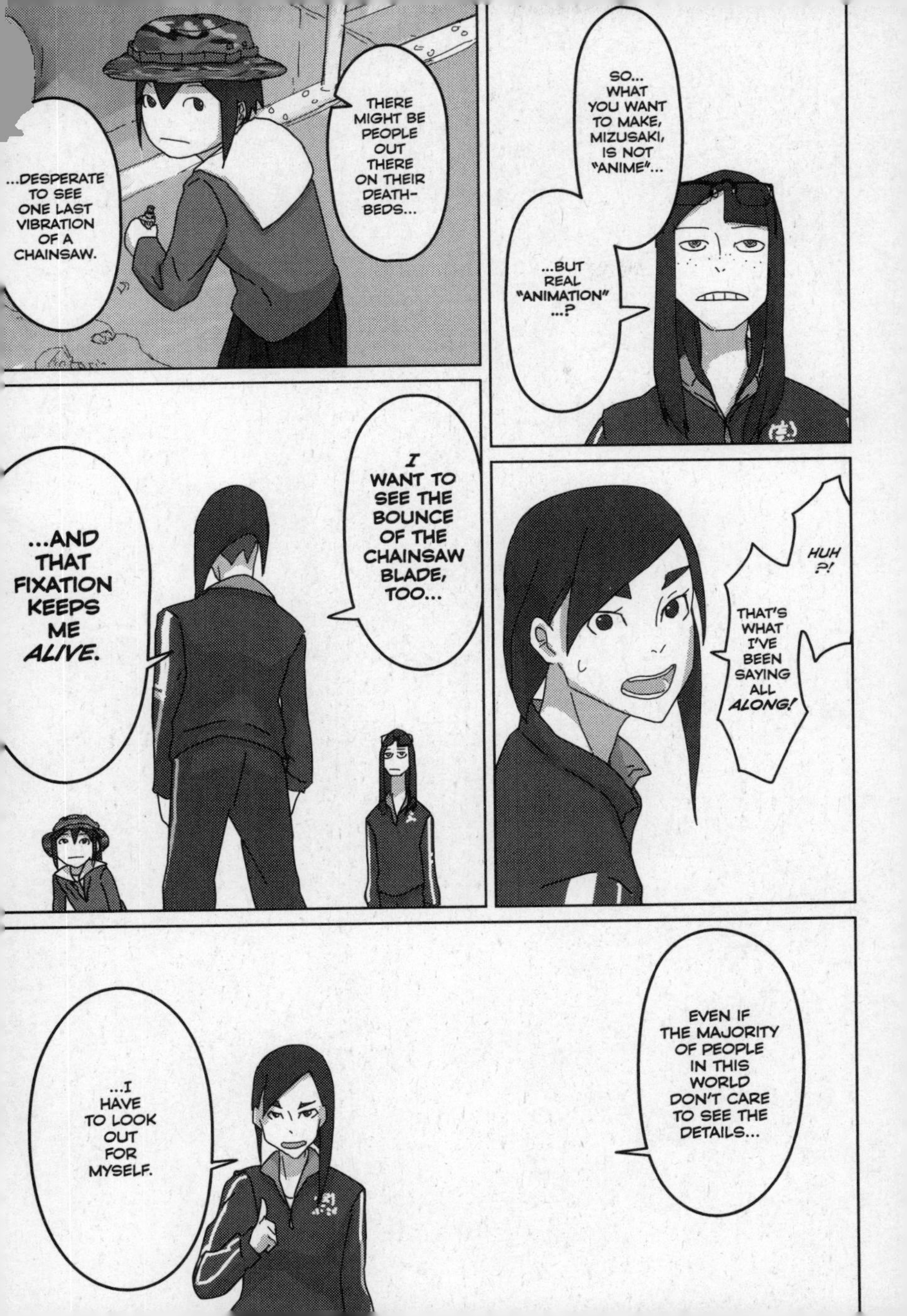
SO... WHAT YOU WANT TO MAKE, MIZUSAKI, IS NOT "ANIME"...
...BUT REAL "ANIMATION" ...?
THERE MIGHT BE PEOPLE OUT THERE ON THEIR DEATH-BEDS...
...DESPERATE TO SEE ONE LAST VIBRATION OF A CHAINSAW.
HUH ?!
THAT'S WHAT I'VE BEEN SAYING ALL *ALONG!*
I WANT TO SEE THE BOUNCE OF THE CHAINSAW BLADE, TOO...
...AND THAT FIXATION KEEPS ME *ALIVE*.
EVEN IF THE MAJORITY OF PEOPLE IN THIS WORLD DON'T CARE TO SEE THE DETAILS...
...I HAVE TO LOOK OUT FOR MYSELF.

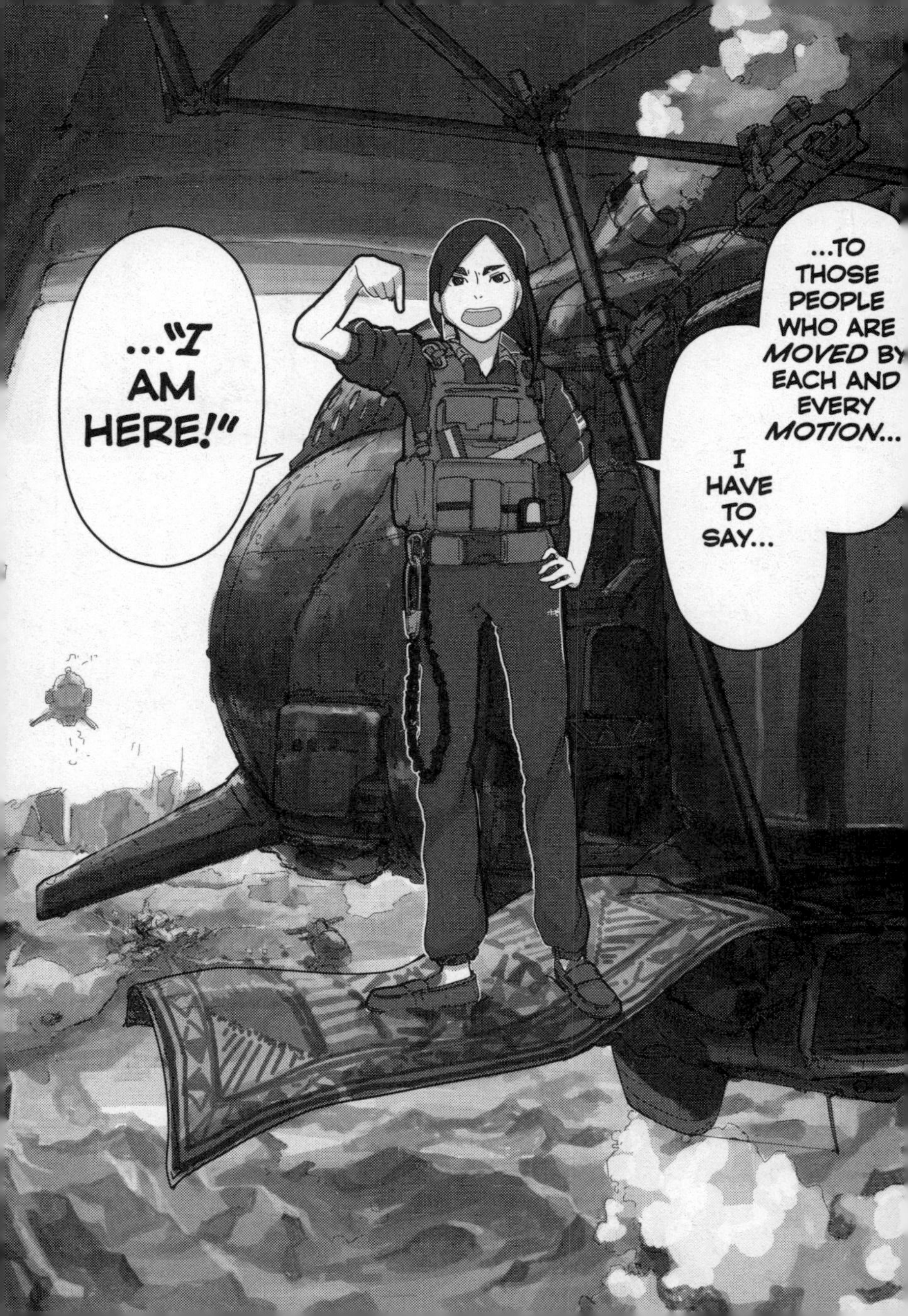
...TO THOSE PEOPLE WHO ARE *MOVED* BY EACH AND EVERY *MOTION*...
I HAVE TO SAY...
..."*I* AM HERE!"

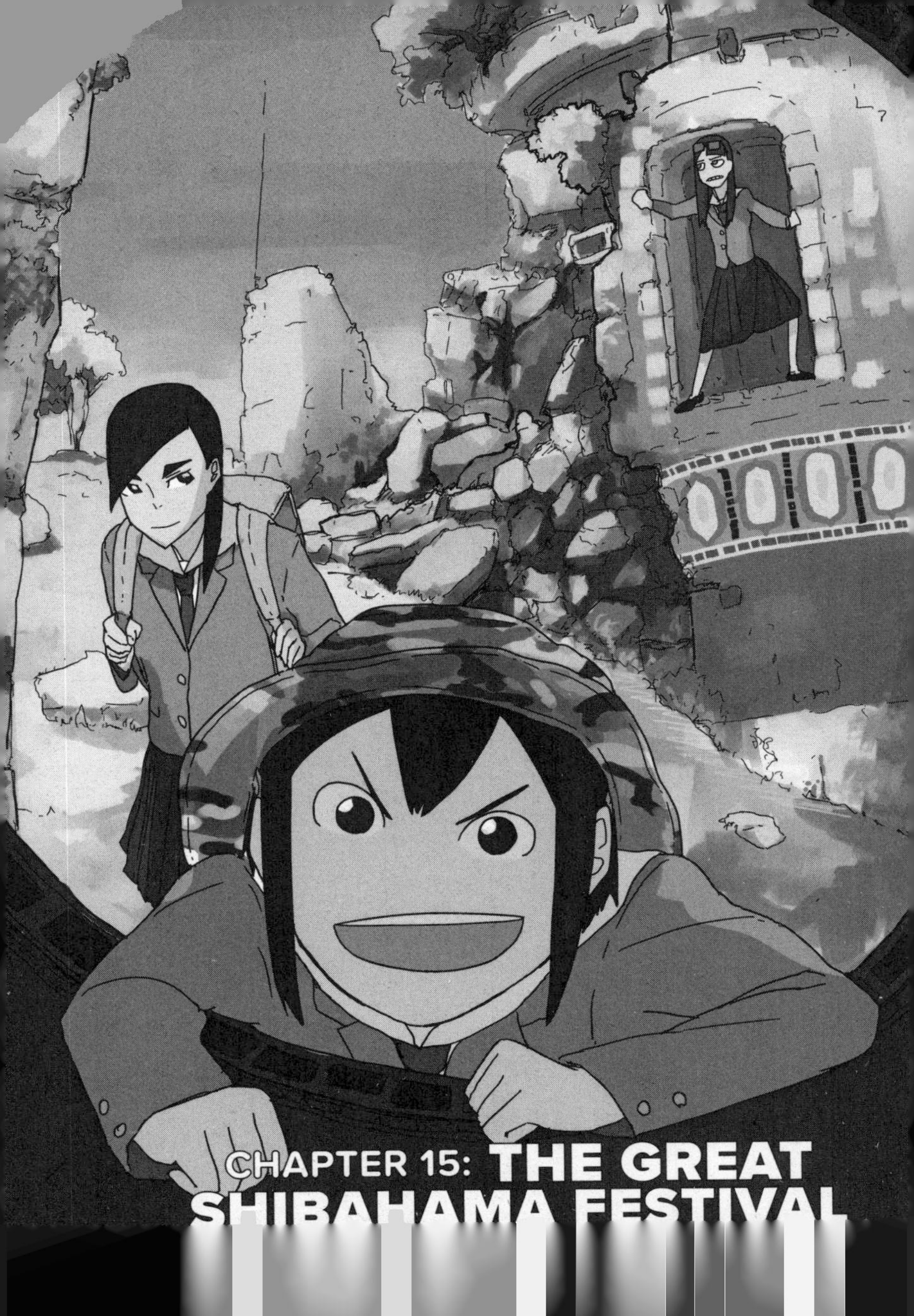

CHAPTER 15: THE GREAT SHIBAHAMA FESTIVAL

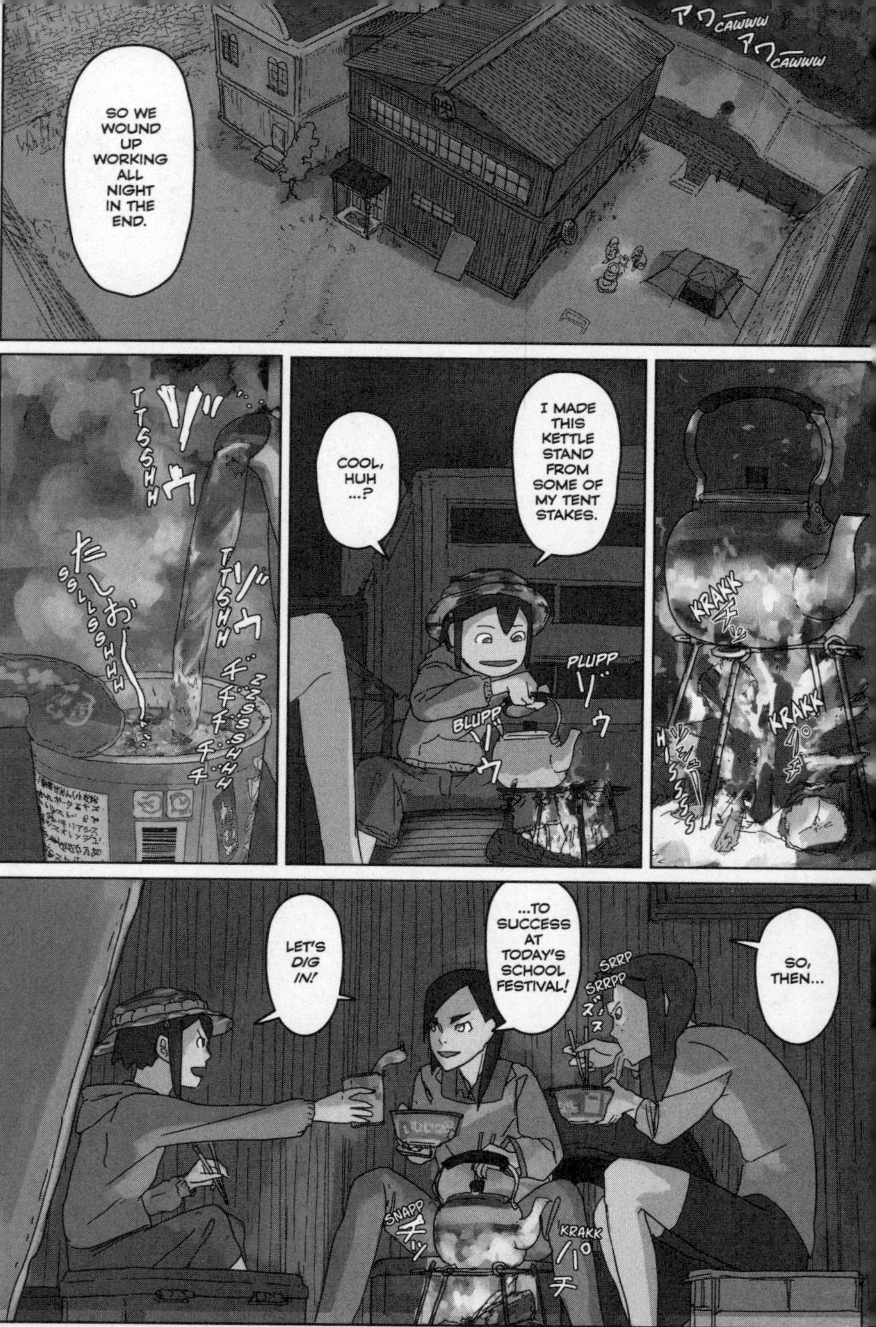
アワ CAWWW
アワ CAWWW
SO WE WOUND UP WORKING ALL NIGHT IN THE END.
KRAKK
KRAKK
I MADE THIS KETTLE STAND FROM SOME OF MY TENT STAKES.
COOL, HUH ...?
PLUPP
BLUPP
TTSSHH
TTSSHH
SSLLSSHHH
ZSSSHH
SO, THEN...
SRRP
SRRPP
...TO SUCCESS AT TODAY'S SCHOOL FESTIVAL!
LET'S DIG IN!
SNAPP
KRAKK

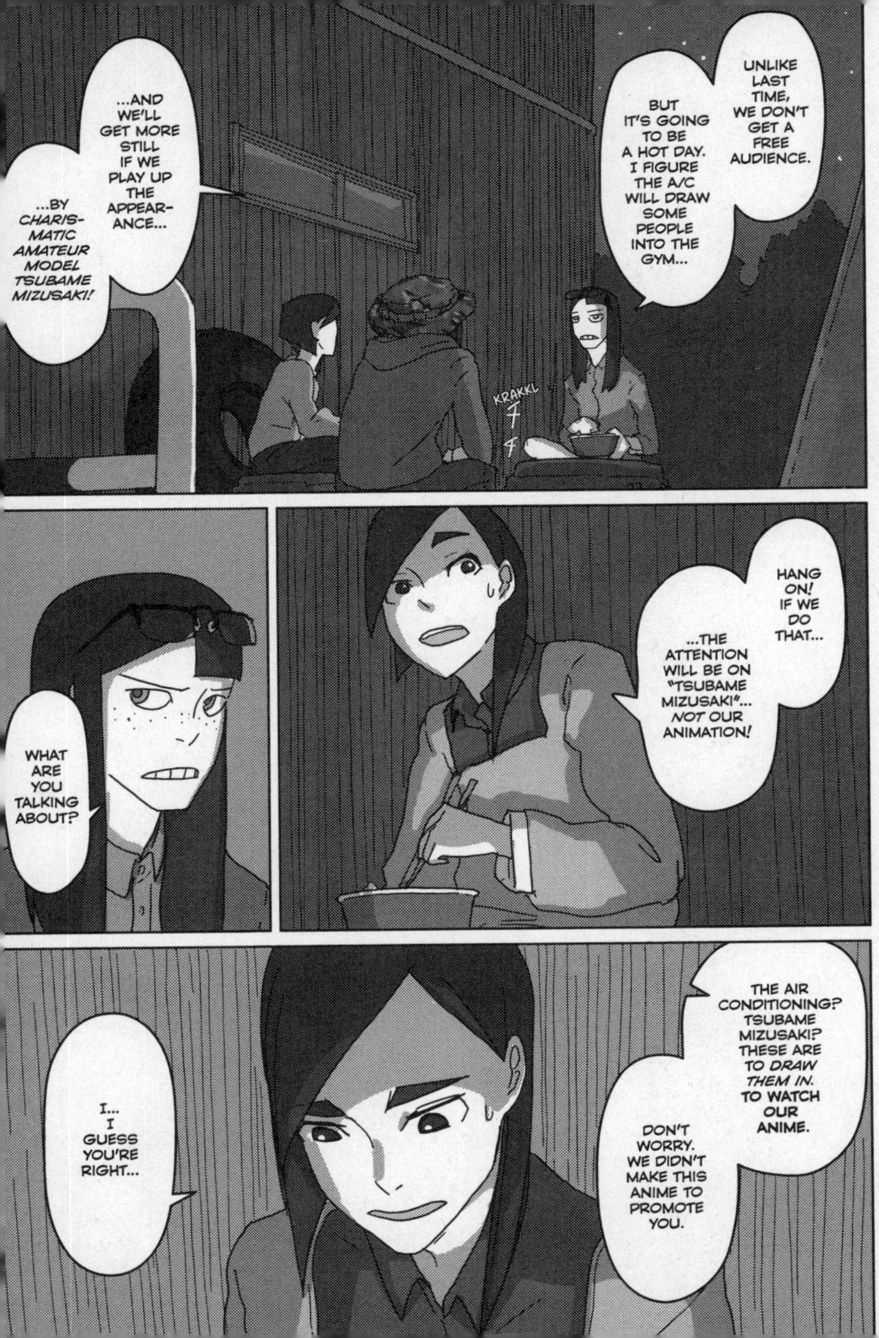
UNLIKE LAST TIME, WE DON'T GET A FREE AUDIENCE.
BUT IT'S GOING TO BE A HOT DAY. I FIGURE THE A/C WILL DRAW SOME PEOPLE INTO THE GYM...
...AND WE'LL GET MORE STILL IF WE PLAY UP THE APPEAR-ANCE...
...BY *CHARIS-MATIC AMATEUR MODEL TSUBAME MIZUSAKI!*
KRAKKL
HANG ON! IF WE DO THAT...
...THE ATTENTION WILL BE ON "TSUBAME MIZUSAKI"... *NOT* OUR ANIMATION!
WHAT ARE YOU TALKING ABOUT?
THE AIR CONDITIONING? TSUBAME MIZUSAKI? THESE ARE TO *DRAW THEM IN.* TO WATCH OUR ANIME.
DON'T WORRY. WE DIDN'T MAKE THIS ANIME TO PROMOTE YOU.
I... I GUESS YOU'RE RIGHT...

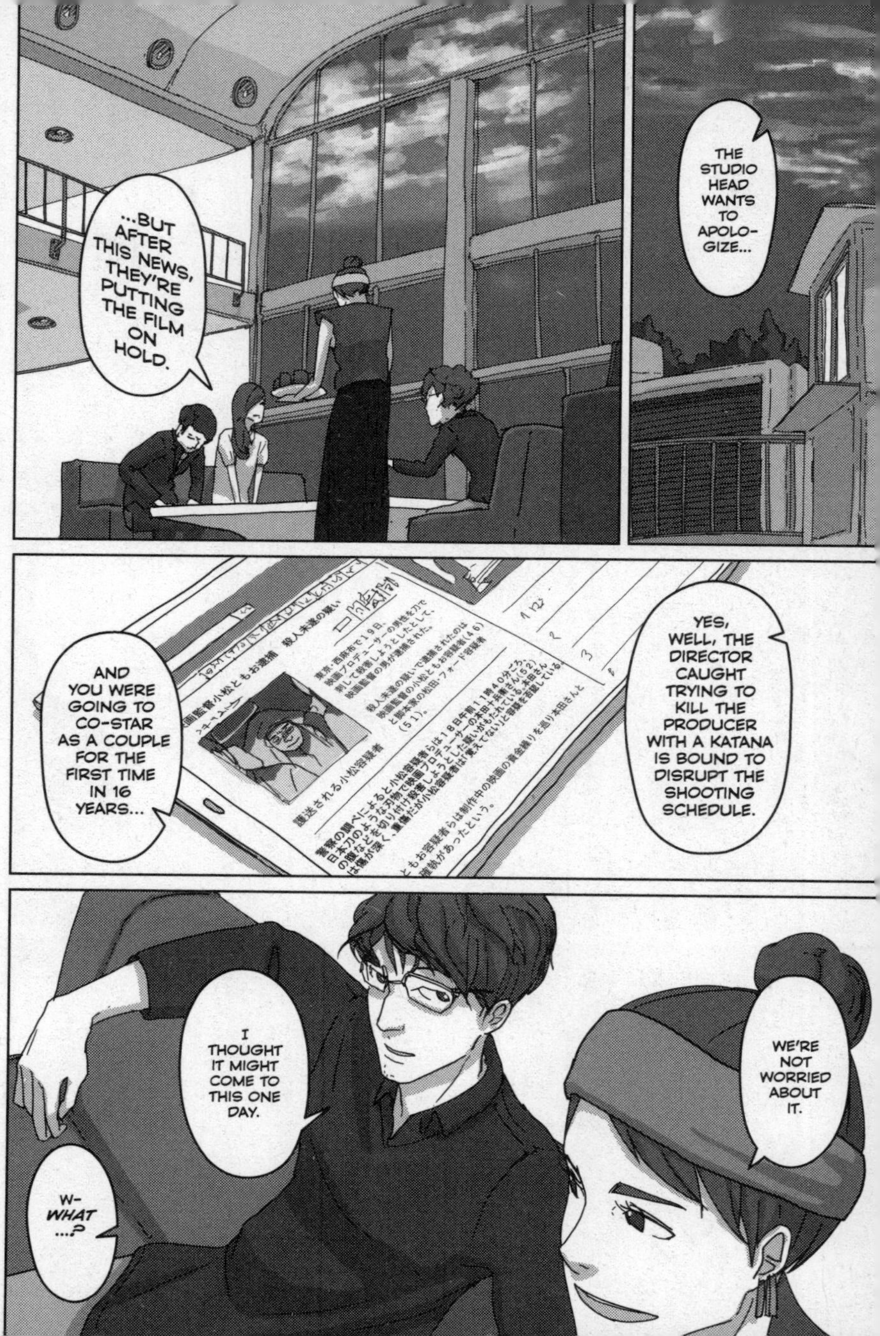
THE STUDIO HEAD WANTS TO APOLOGIZE...
...BUT AFTER THIS NEWS, THEY'RE PUTTING THE FILM ON HOLD.
YES, WELL, THE DIRECTOR CAUGHT TRYING TO KILL THE PRODUCER WITH A KATANA IS BOUND TO DISRUPT THE SHOOTING SCHEDULE.
AND YOU WERE GOING TO CO-STAR AS A COUPLE FOR THE FIRST TIME IN 16 YEARS...
WE'RE NOT WORRIED ABOUT IT.
I THOUGHT IT MIGHT COME TO THIS ONE DAY.
W-*WHAT*...?

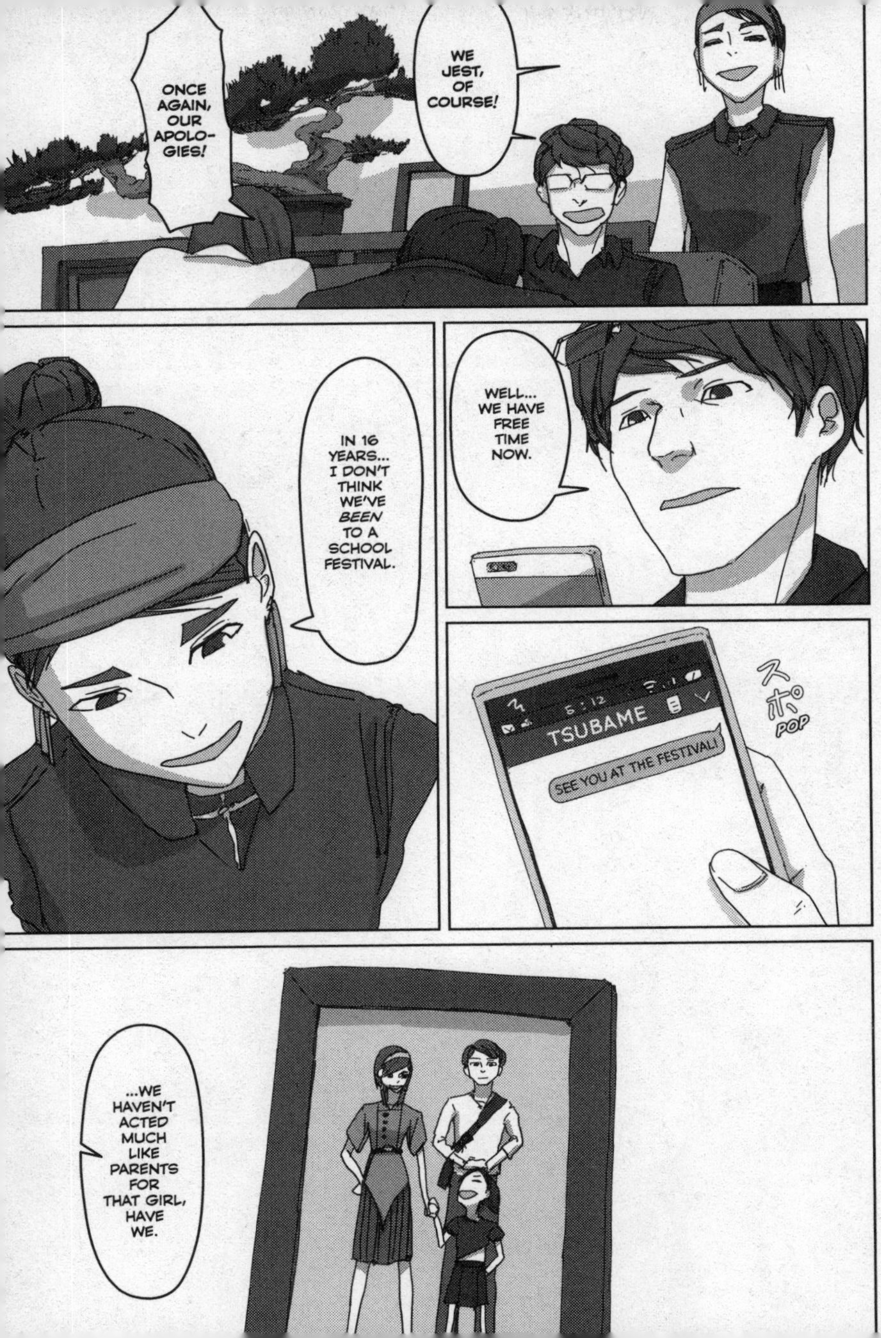
WE JEST, OF COURSE!
ONCE AGAIN, OUR APOLOGIES!
WELL... WE HAVE FREE TIME NOW.
5:12
TSUBAME
SEE YOU AT THE FESTIVAL!
スポ
POP
IN 16 YEARS... I DON'T THINK WE'VE *BEEN* TO A SCHOOL FESTIVAL.
...WE HAVEN'T ACTED MUCH LIKE PARENTS FOR THAT GIRL, HAVE WE.

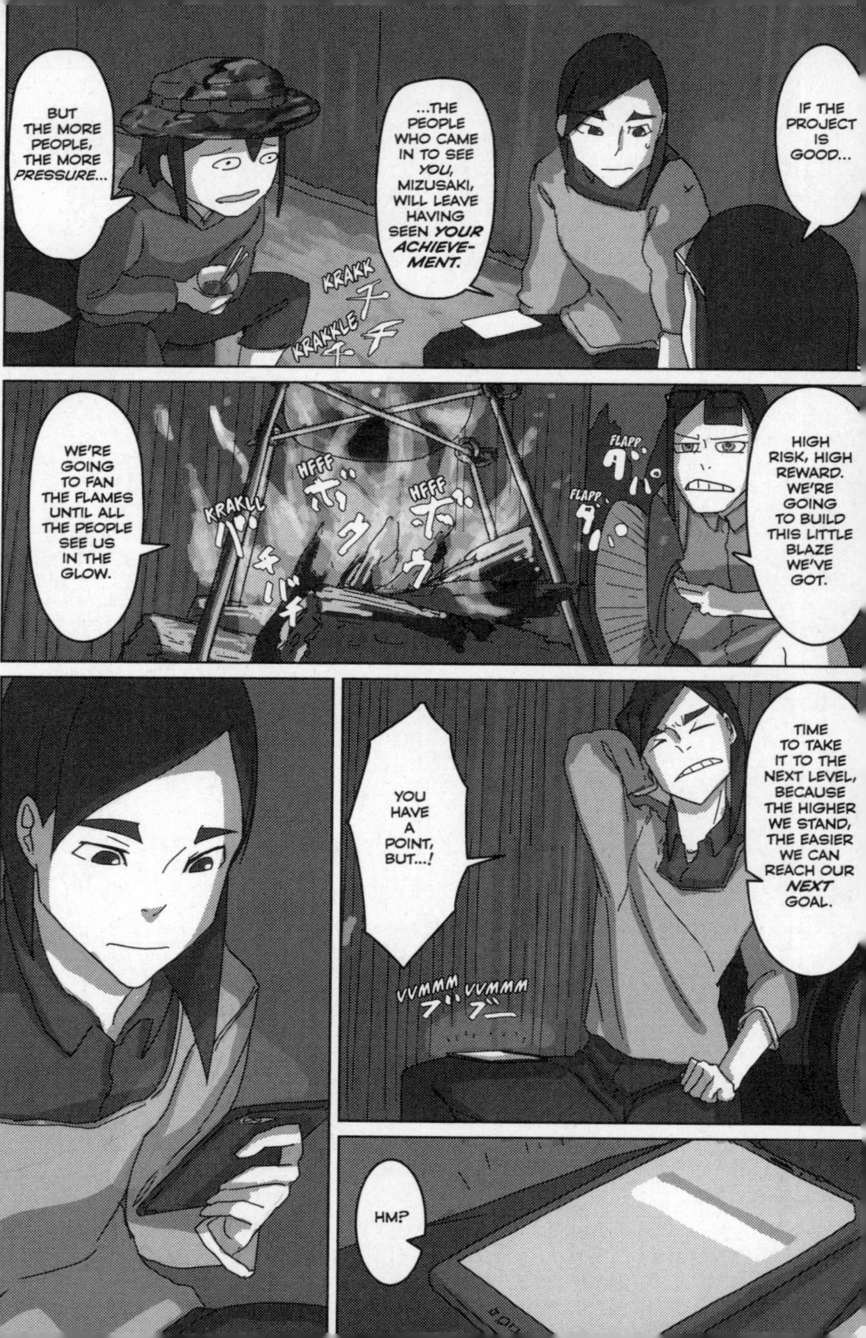
IF THE PROJECT IS GOOD...
...THE PEOPLE WHO CAME IN TO SEE *YOU*, MIZUSAKI, WILL LEAVE HAVING SEEN ***YOUR ACHIEVEMENT.***
KRAKK
KRAKKLE
BUT THE MORE PEOPLE, THE MORE *PRESSURE*...
HIGH RISK, HIGH REWARD. WE'RE GOING TO BUILD THIS LITTLE BLAZE WE'VE GOT.
FLAPP
FLAPP
HFFF
HFFF
KRAKLL
WE'RE GOING TO FAN THE FLAMES UNTIL ALL THE PEOPLE SEE US IN THE GLOW.
TIME TO TAKE IT TO THE NEXT LEVEL, BECAUSE THE HIGHER WE STAND, THE EASIER WE CAN REACH OUR ***NEXT*** GOAL.
YOU HAVE A POINT, BUT...!
VVMMM VVMMM
HM?

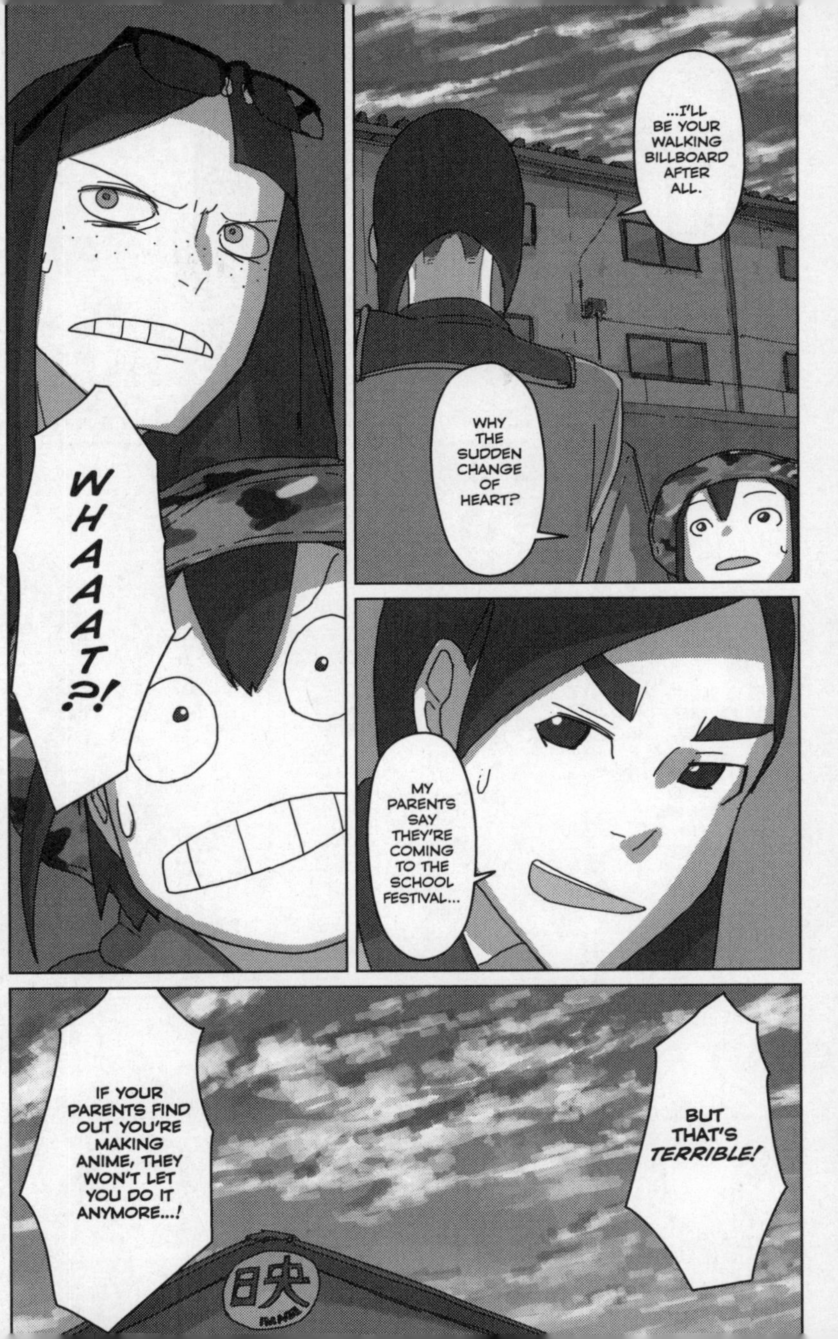
...I'LL BE YOUR WALKING BILLBOARD AFTER ALL.
WHY THE SUDDEN CHANGE OF HEART?
MY PARENTS SAY THEY'RE COMING TO THE SCHOOL FESTIVAL...
WHAAAAT?!
BUT THAT'S *TERRIBLE!*
IF YOUR PARENTS FIND OUT YOU'RE MAKING ANIME, THEY WON'T LET YOU DO IT ANYMORE...!

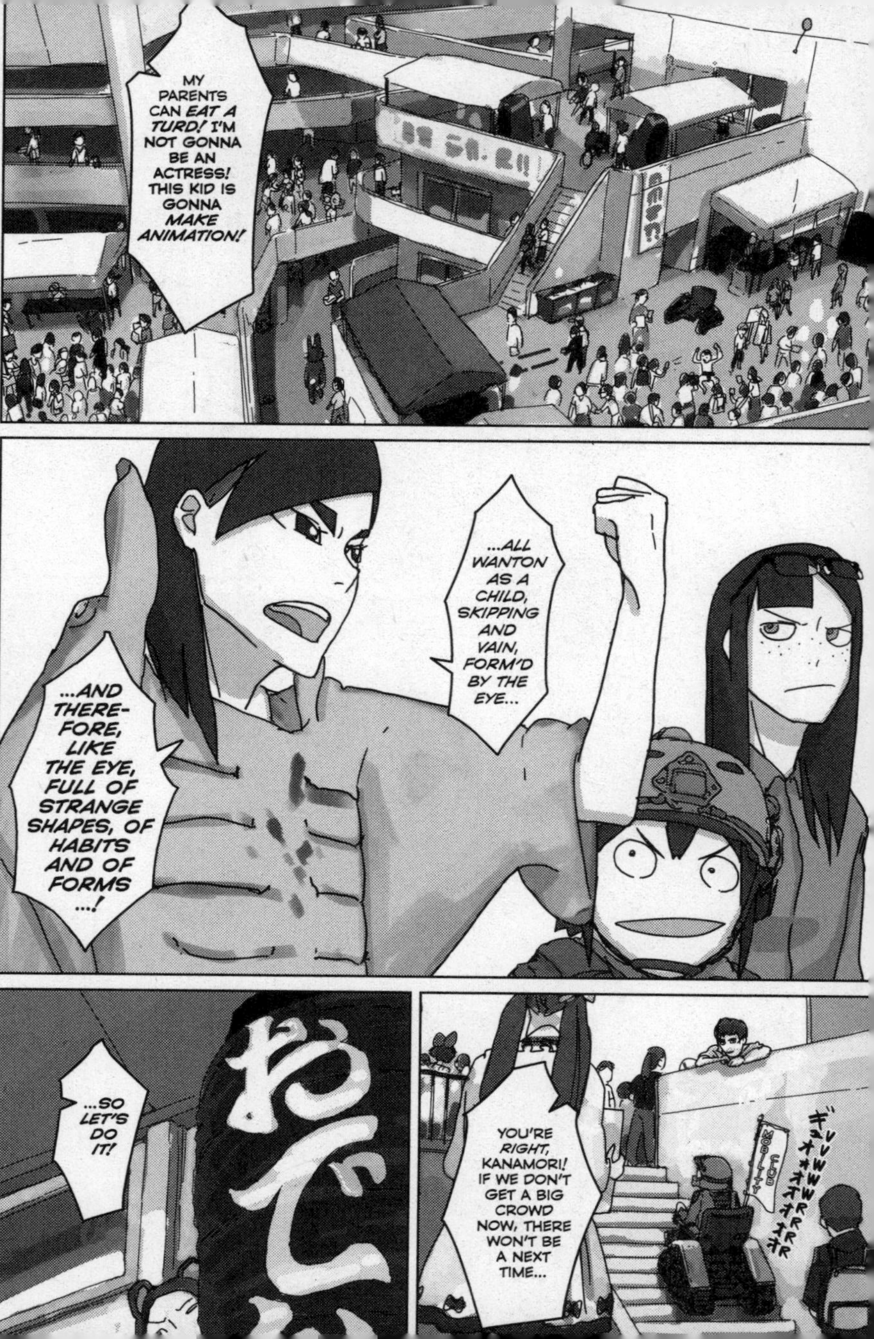
MY PARENTS CAN *EAT A TURD!* I'M NOT GONNA BE AN ACTRESS! THIS KID IS GONNA *MAKE ANIMATION!*
...ALL WANTON AS A CHILD, SKIPPING AND VAIN, FORM'D BY THE EYE...
...AND THEREFORE, LIKE THE EYE, FULL OF STRANGE SHAPES, OF HABITS AND OF FORMS ...!
YOU'RE *RIGHT,* KANAMORI! IF WE DON'T GET A BIG CROWD NOW, THERE WON'T BE A NEXT TIME...
MOBILITY CLUB
VVWWWRRR
...SO *LET'S* DO *IT!*

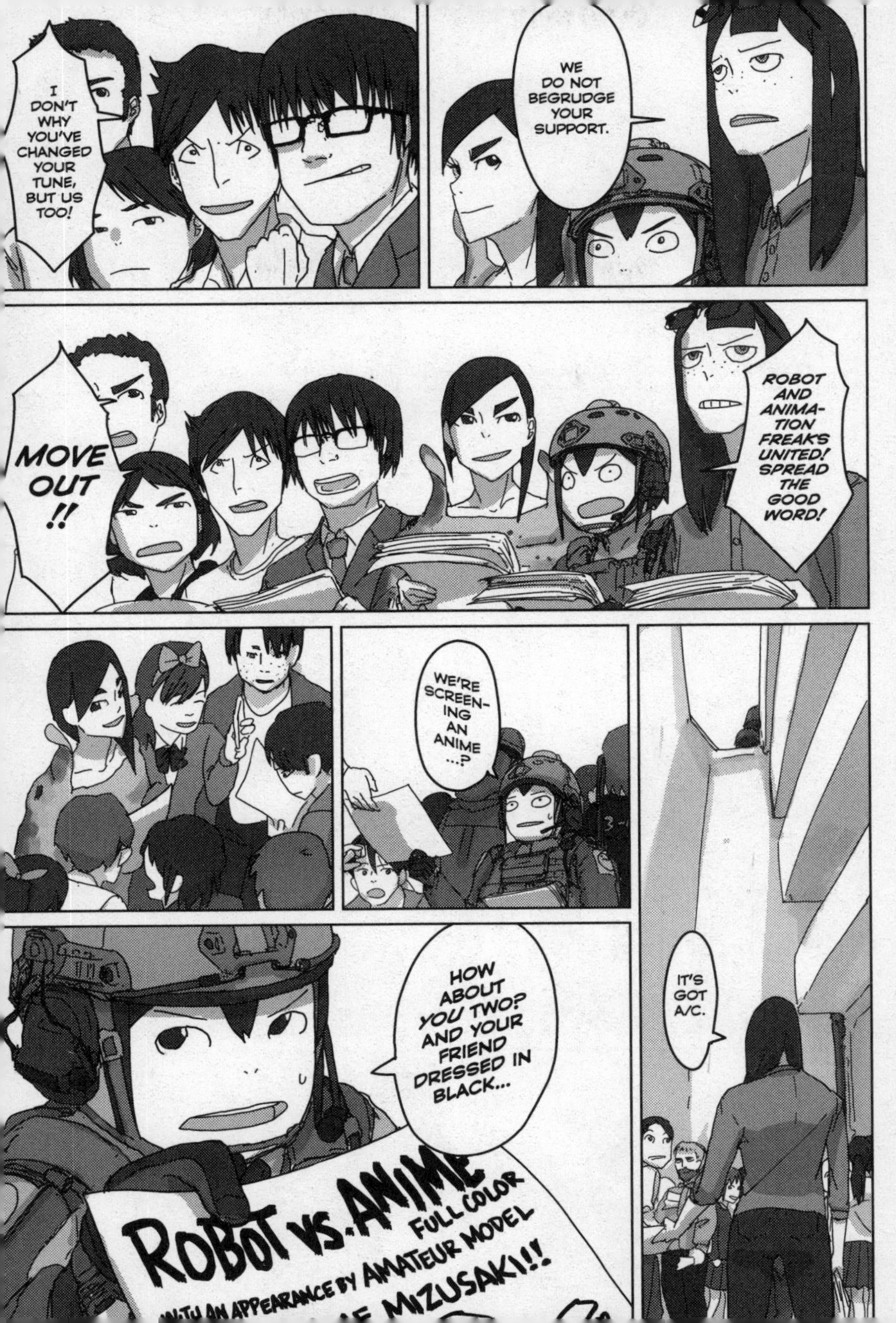
WE DO NOT BEGRUDGE YOUR SUPPORT.
I DON'T WHY YOU'VE CHANGED YOUR TUNE, BUT US TOO!
ROBOT AND ANIMATION FREAKS UNITED! SPREAD THE GOOD WORD!
MOVE OUT!!
IT'S GOT A/C.
WE'RE SCREENING AN ANIME...?
HOW ABOUT YOU TWO? AND YOUR FRIEND DRESSED IN BLACK...
ROBOT VS. ANIME
FULL COLOR
WITH AN APPEARANCE BY AMATEUR MODEL
MIZUSAKI!!

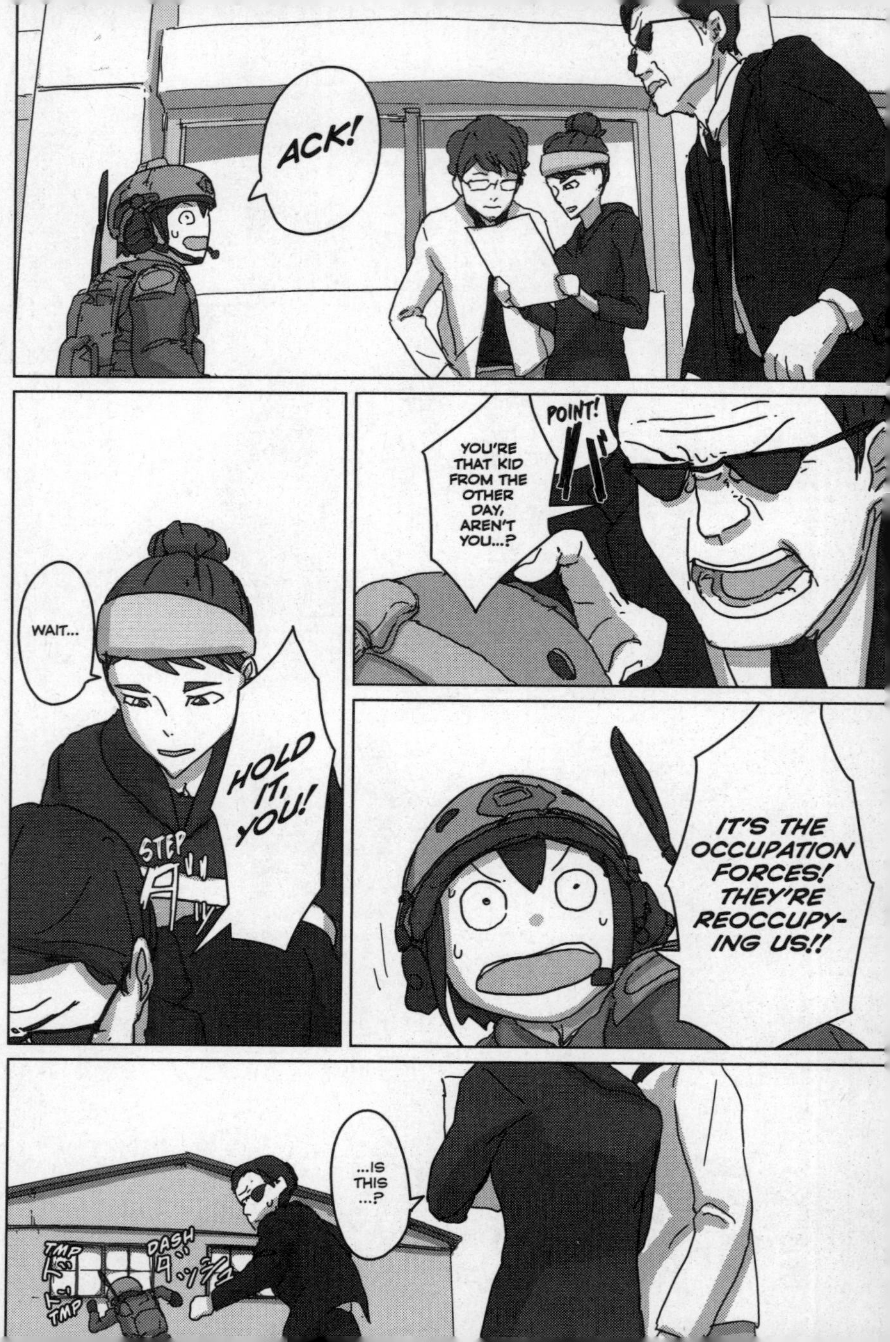
ACK!
POINT!
YOU'RE THAT KID FROM THE OTHER DAY, AREN'T YOU...?
IT'S THE OCCUPATION FORCES! THEY'RE REOCCUPY-ING US!!
WAIT...
HOLD IT, YOU!
STEP
...IS THIS ...?
DASH
TMP
TMP

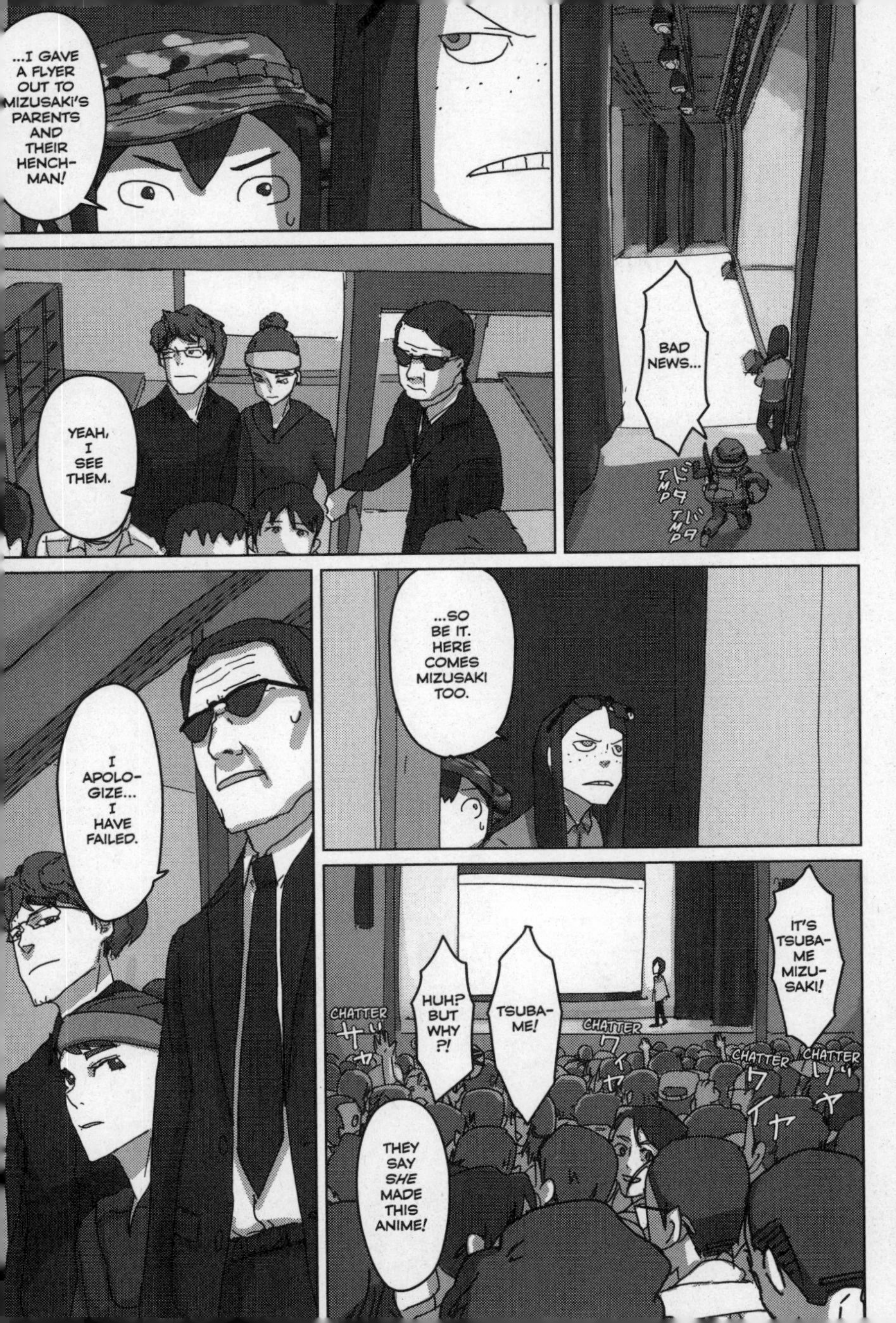
BAD NEWS...
TMP TMP
TMP TMP
...I GAVE A FLYER OUT TO MIZUSAKI'S PARENTS AND THEIR HENCH-MAN!
YEAH, I SEE THEM.
...SO BE IT. HERE COMES MIZUSAKI TOO.
IT'S TSUBA-ME MIZU-SAKI!
CHATTER
CHATTER
CHATTER
TSUBA-ME!
HUH? BUT WHY ?!
CHATTER
THEY SAY *SHE* MADE THIS ANIME!
I APOLO-GIZE... I HAVE FAILED.

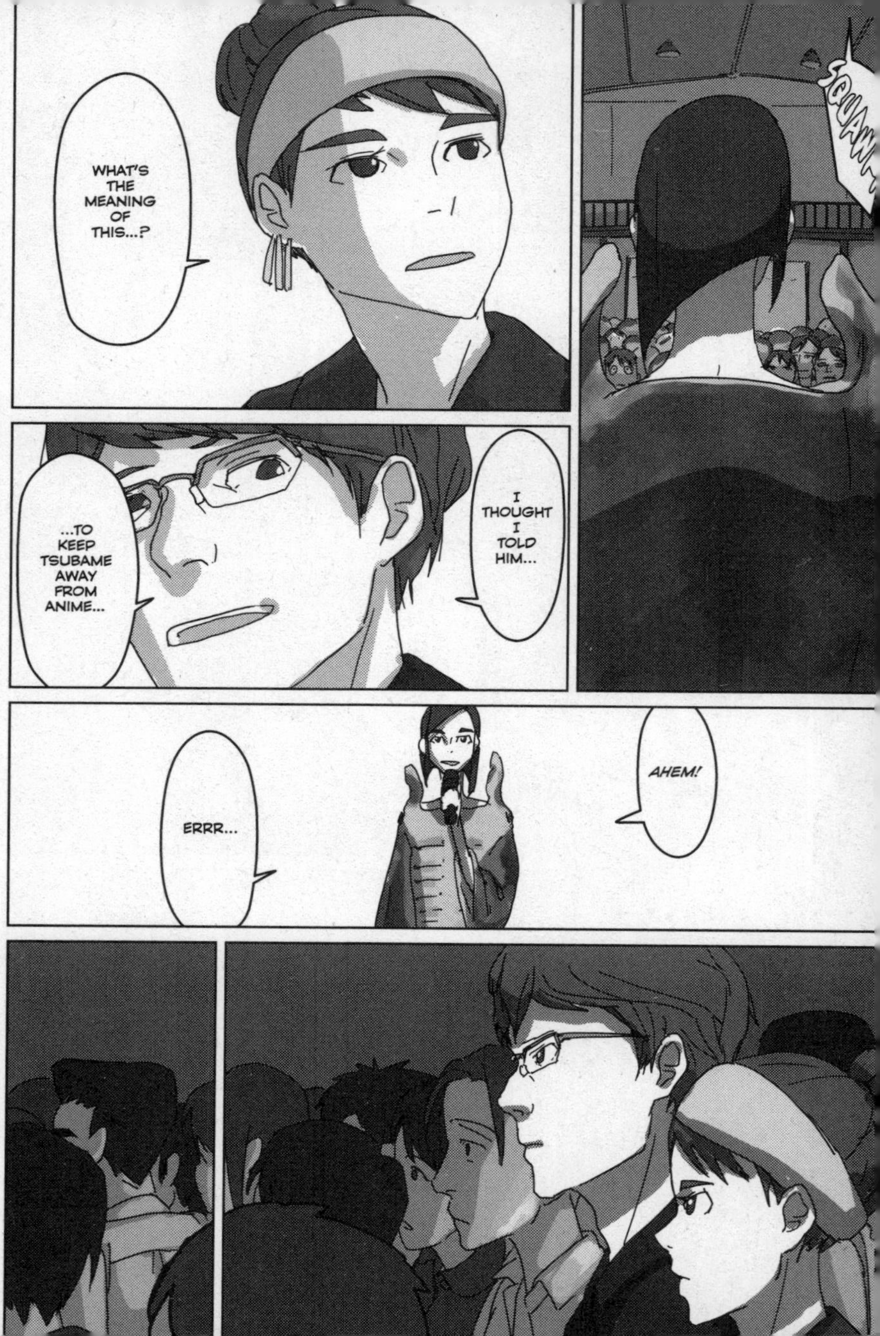
SQUAW
WHAT'S THE MEANING OF THIS...?
I THOUGHT I TOLD HIM...
...TO KEEP TSUBAME AWAY FROM ANIME...
AHEM!
ERRR...

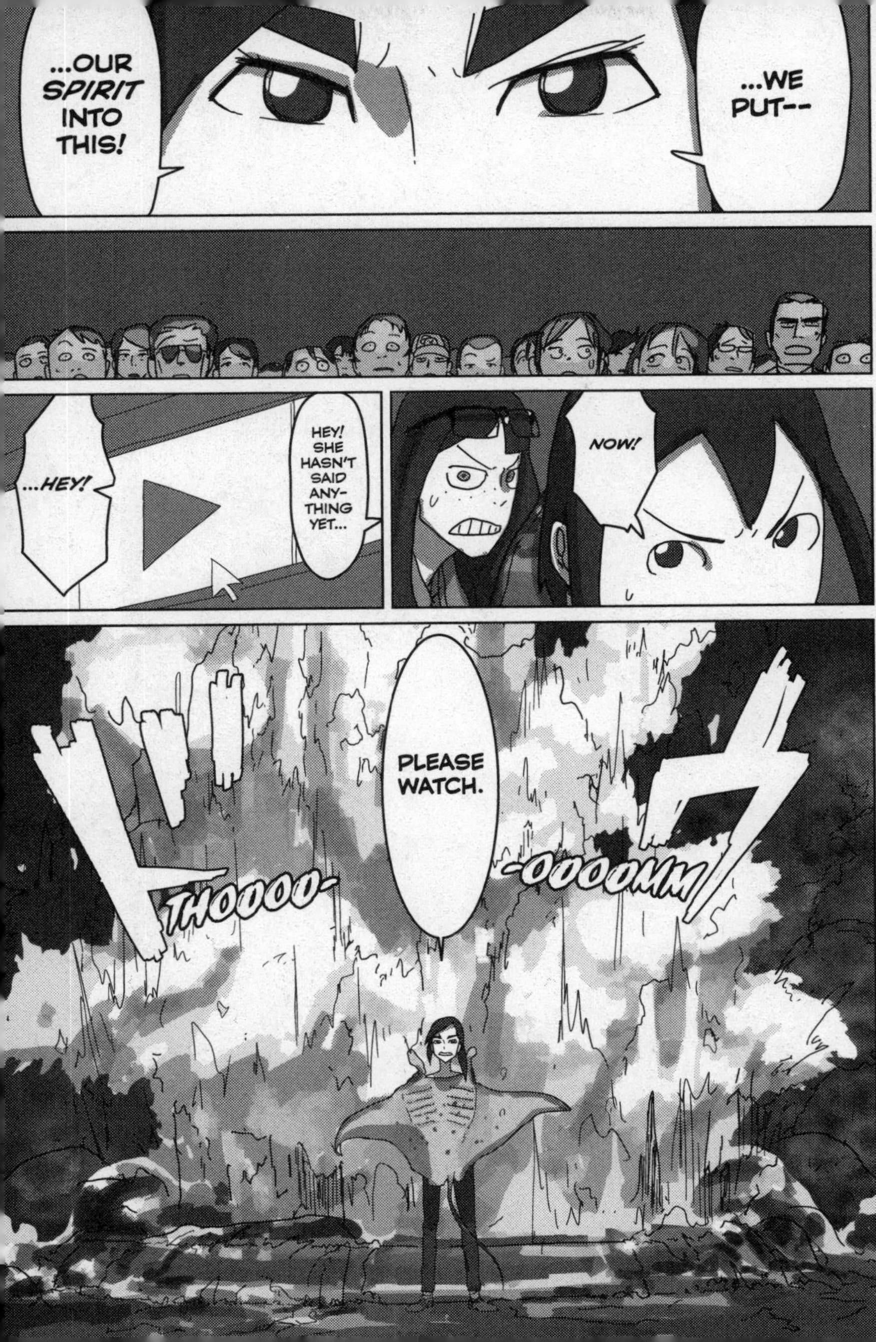
...WE PUT--
...OUR SPIRIT INTO THIS!
NOW!
HEY! SHE HASN'T SAID ANYTHING YET...
...HEY!
PLEASE WATCH.
THOOOO-
-OOOOMM

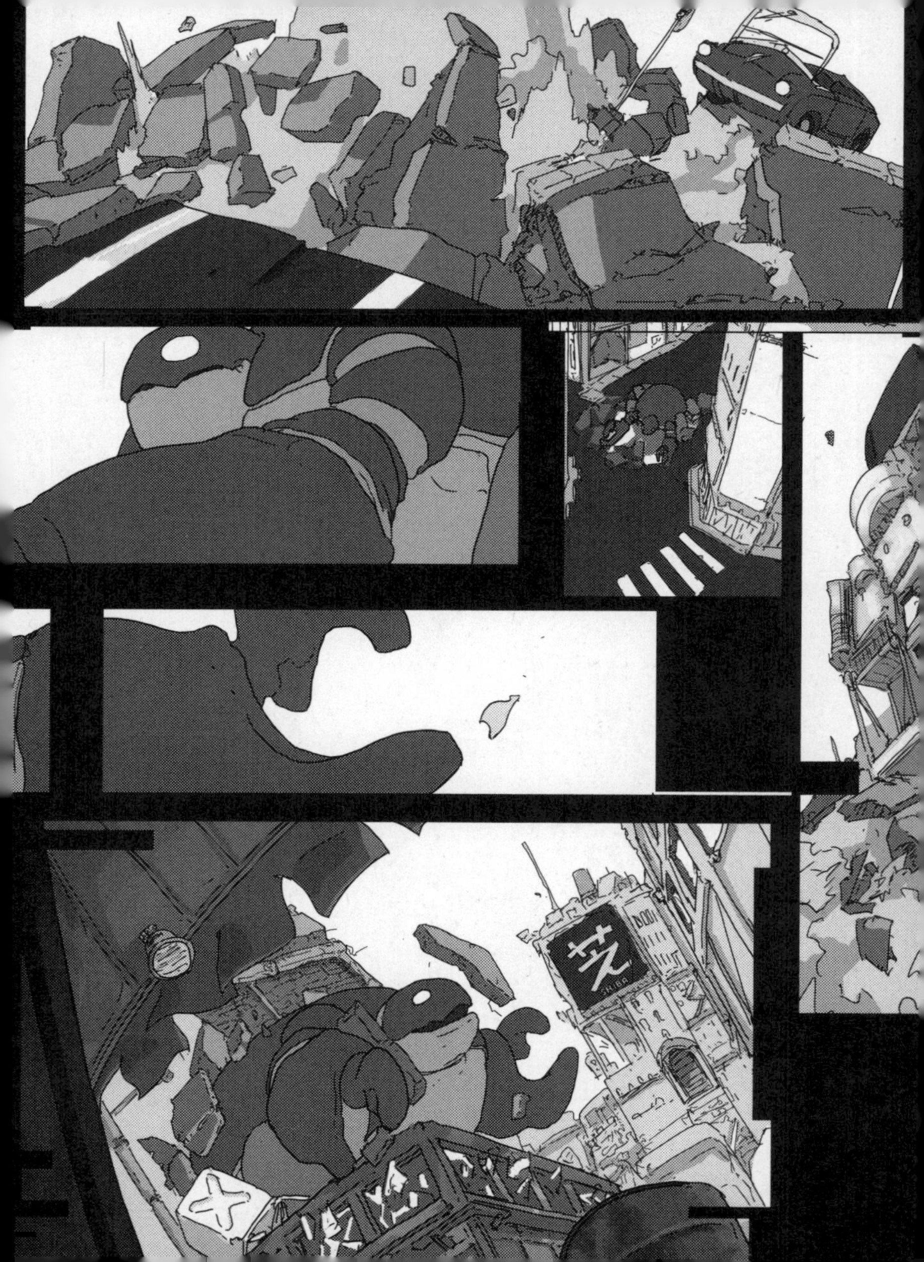
芝
SHIBA

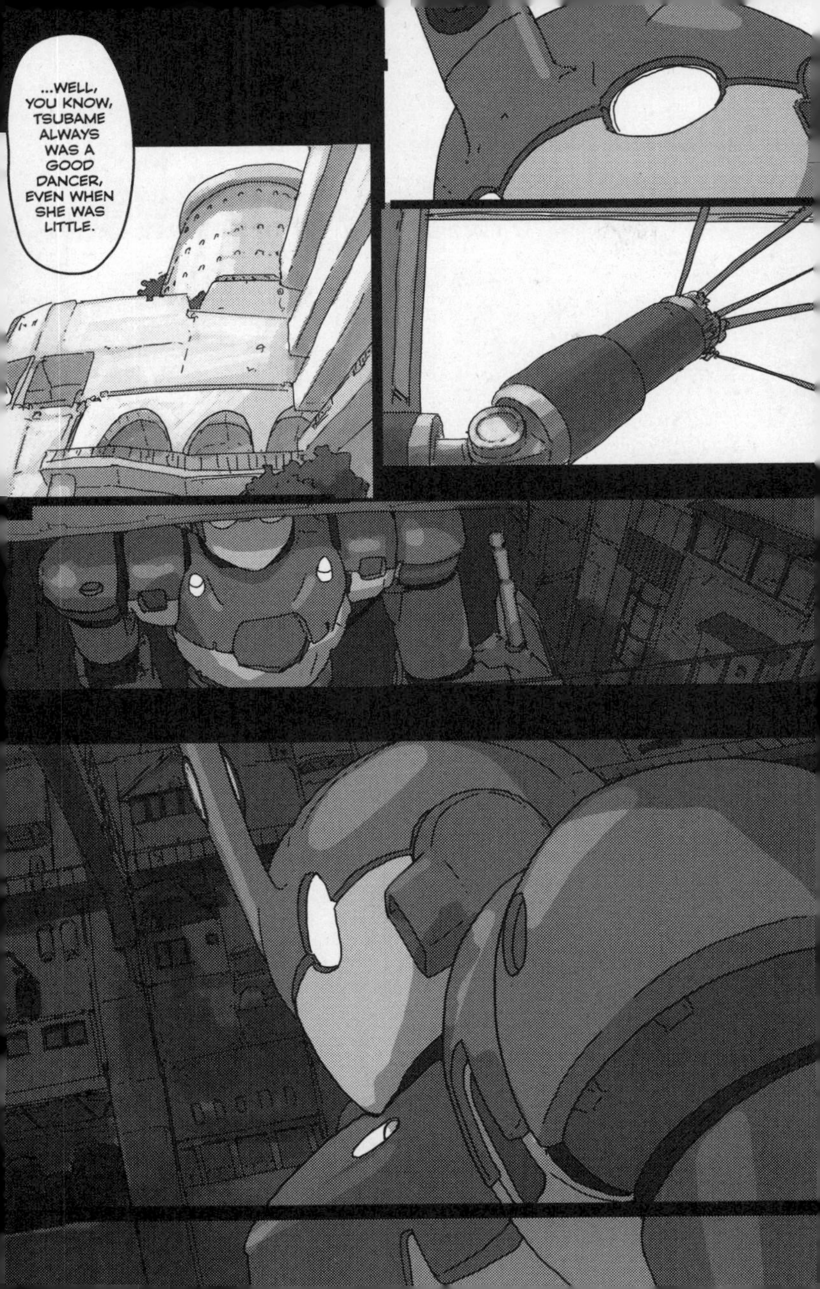
...WELL, YOU KNOW, TSUBAME ALWAYS WAS A GOOD DANCER, EVEN WHEN SHE WAS LITTLE.

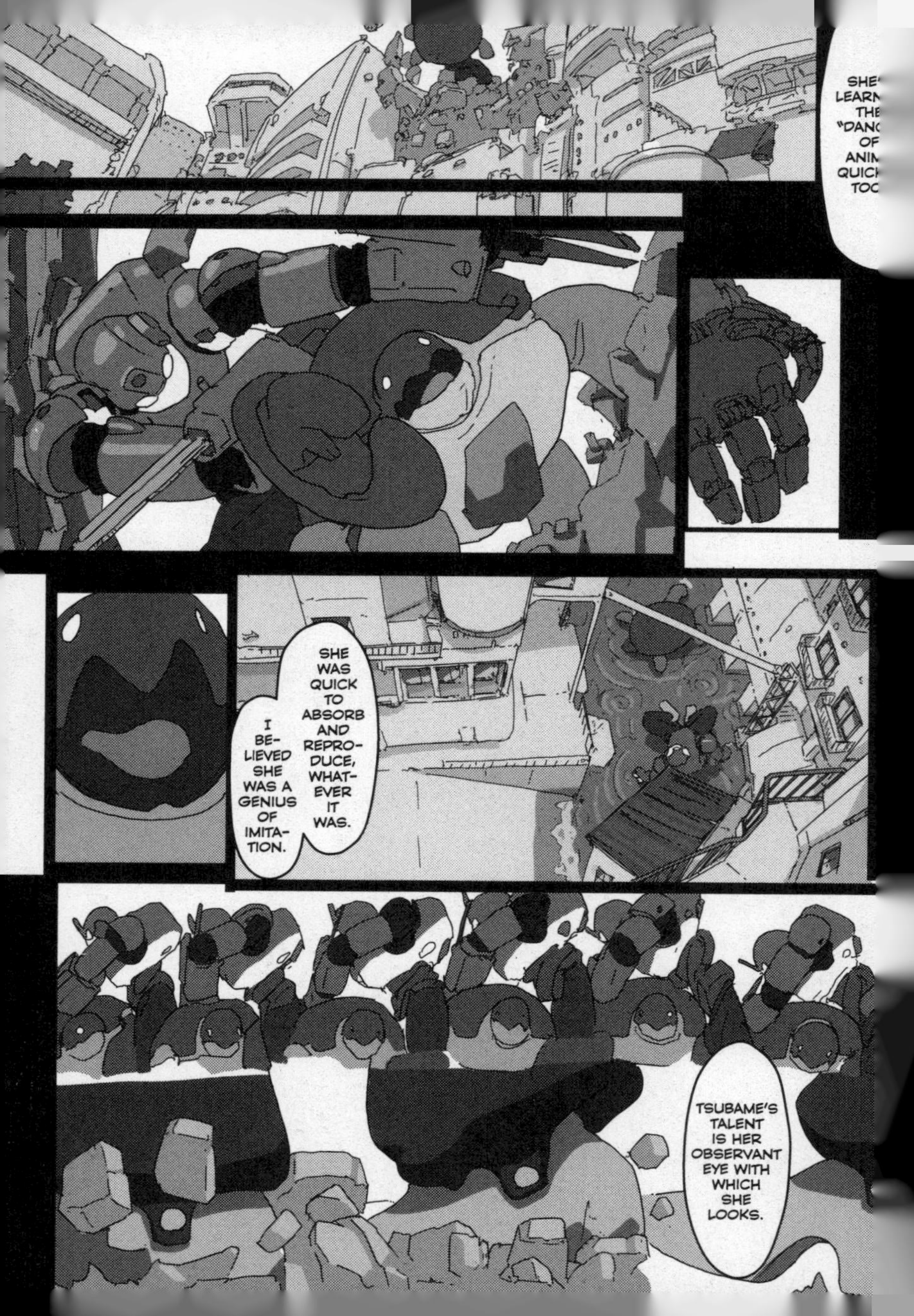
SHE' LEARN THE "DANC OF ANIM QUICK TOO
SHE WAS QUICK TO ABSORB AND REPRODUCE, WHATEVER IT WAS.
I BELIEVED SHE WAS A GENIUS OF IMITATION.
TSUBAME'S TALENT IS HER OBSERVANT EYE WITH WHICH SHE LOOKS.

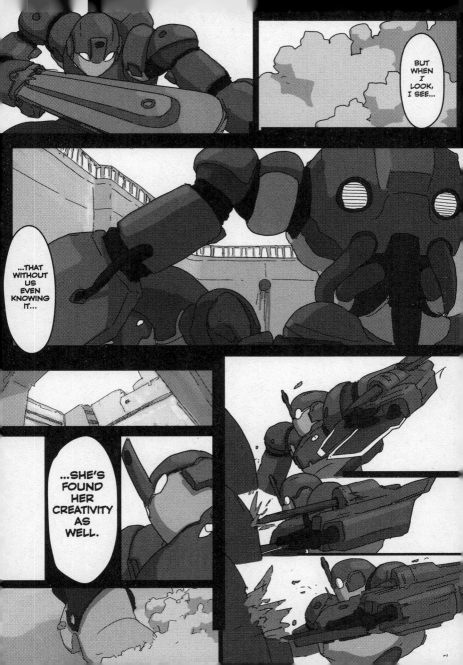

BUT WHEN I LOOK, I SEE...

...THAT WITHOUT US EVEN KNOWING IT...

...SHE'S FOUND HER CREATIVITY AS WELL.

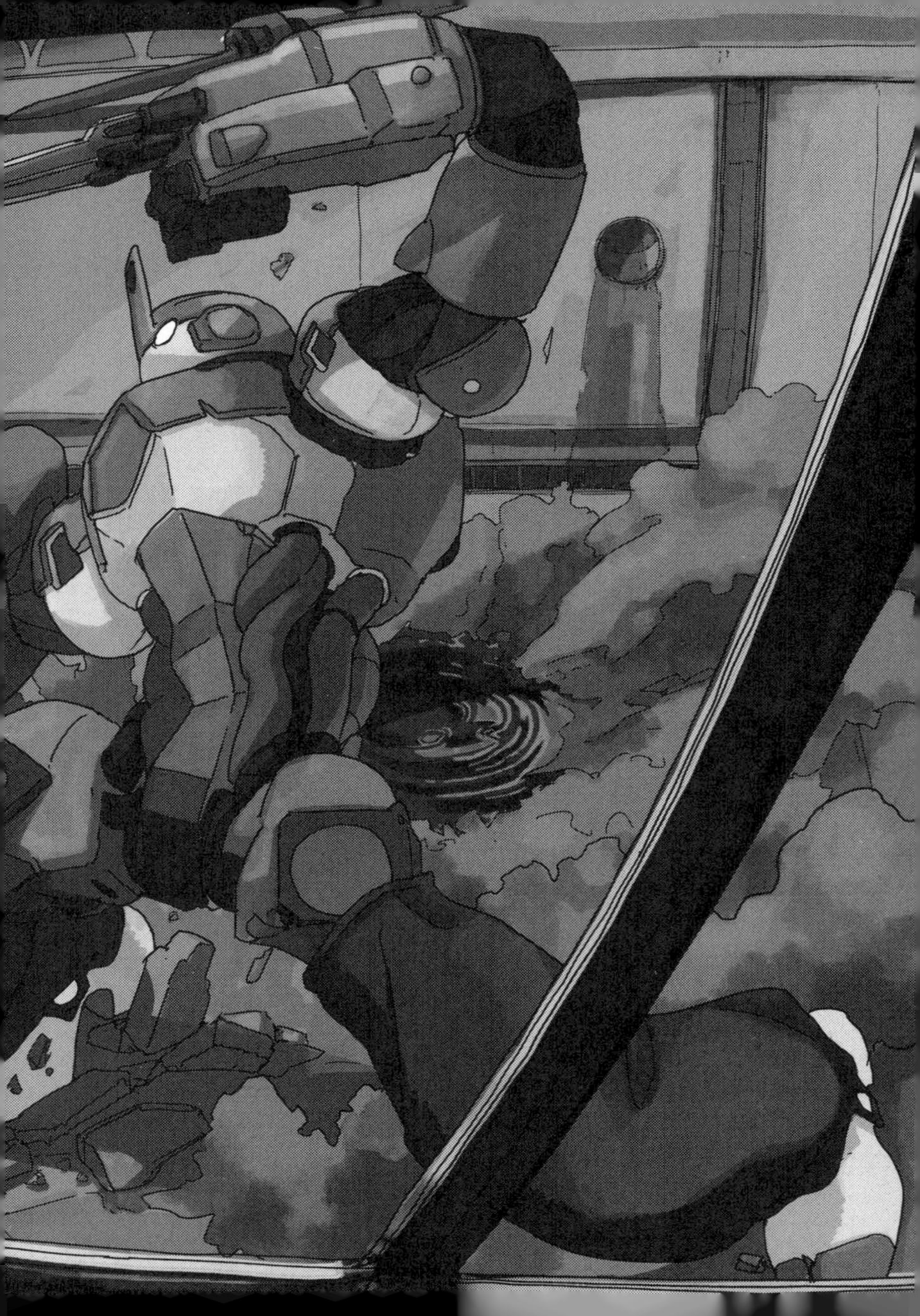

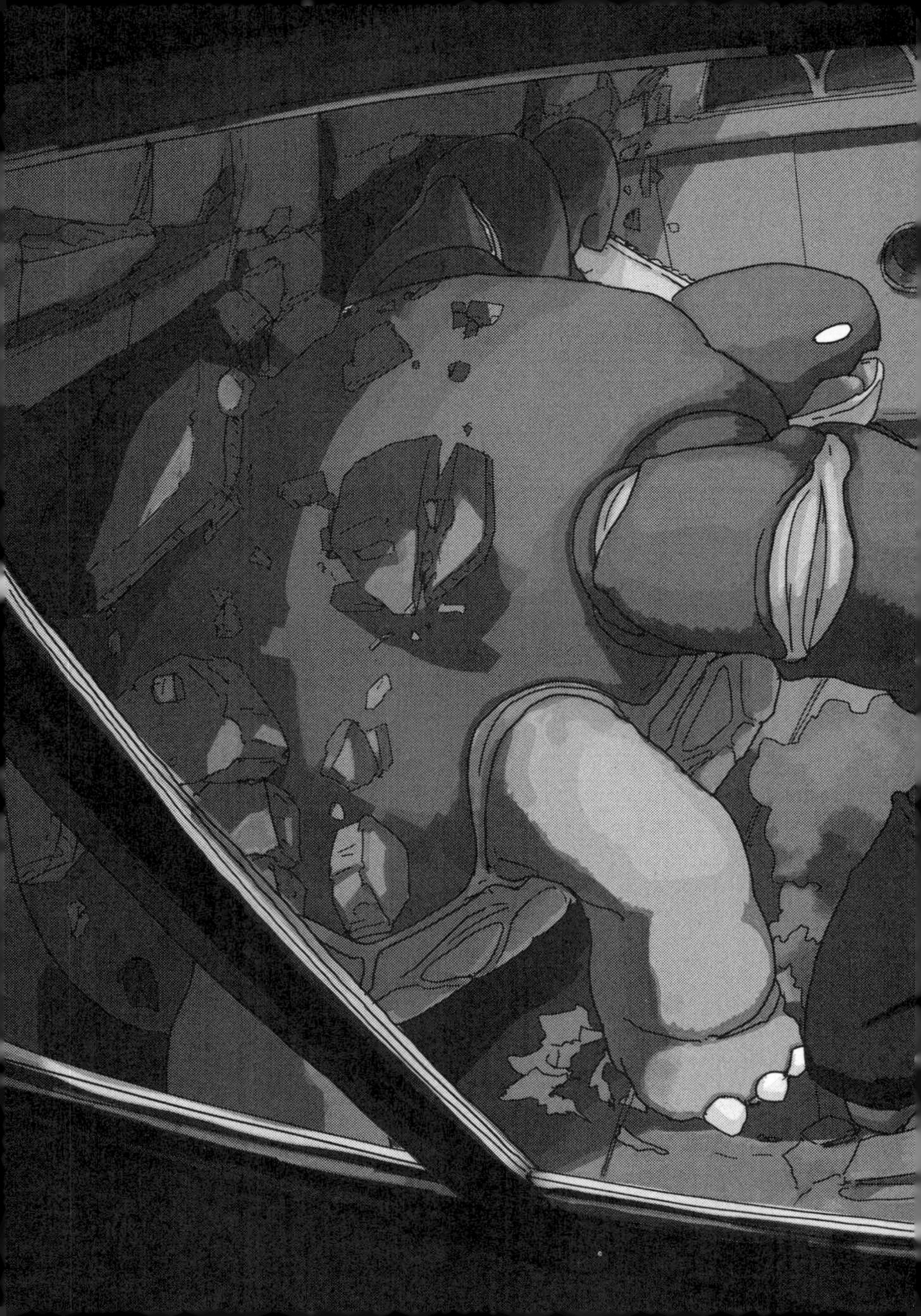

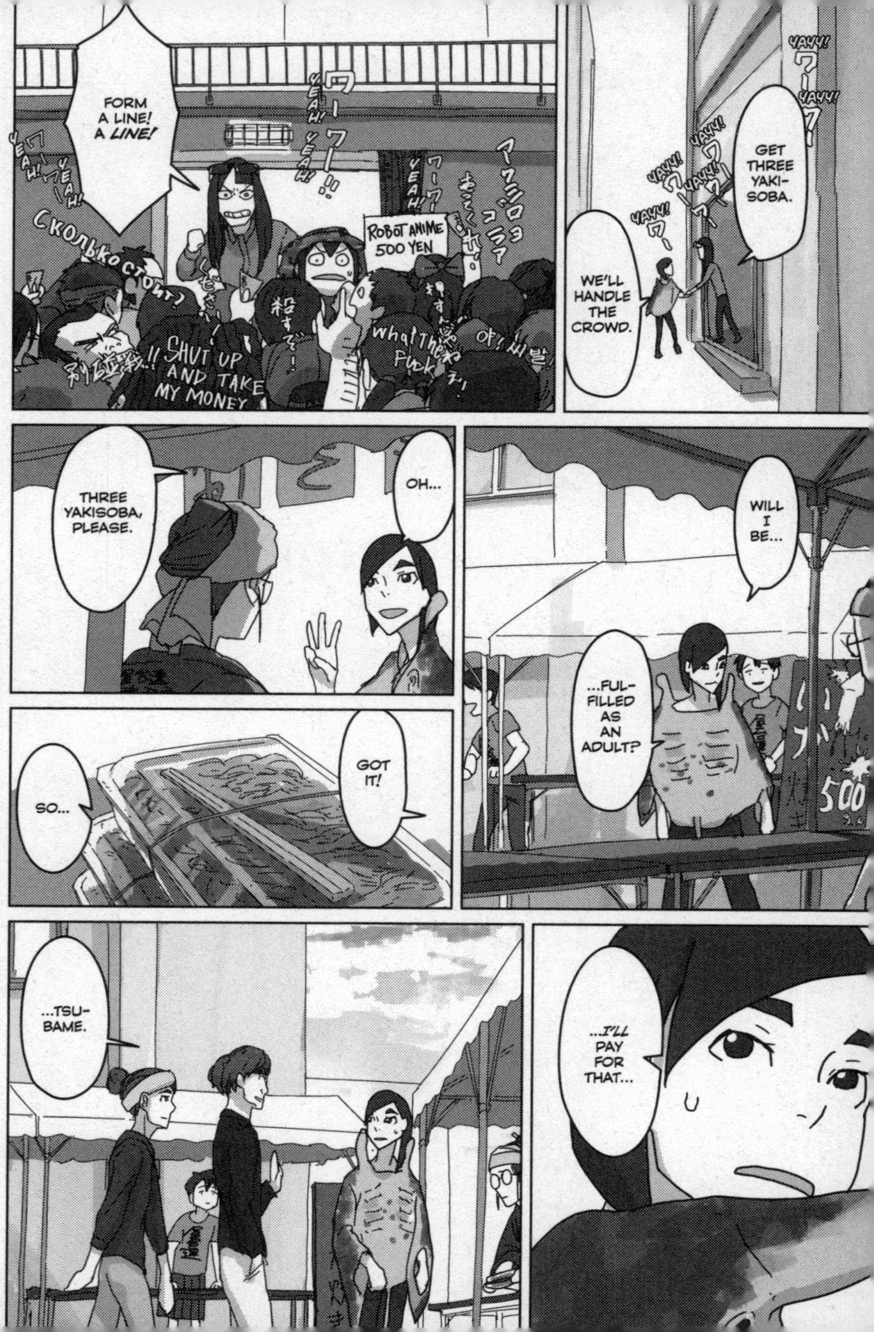
GET THREE YAKI-SOBA.
WE'LL HANDLE THE CROWD.
YAYY!
YAYY!
YAYY!
YAYY!
YAYY!
YAYY!
FORM A LINE! A LINE!
YEAH!
YEAH!
YEAH!
YEAH!
YEAH!
YEAH!
ROBOT ANIME 500 YEN
Сколько стоит?
SHUT UP AND TAKE MY MONEY
what the Fuck
WILL I BE...
...FUL-FILLED AS AN ADULT?
500
THREE YAKISOBA, PLEASE.
OH...
GOT IT!
SO...
...I'LL PAY FOR THAT...
...TSU-BAME.

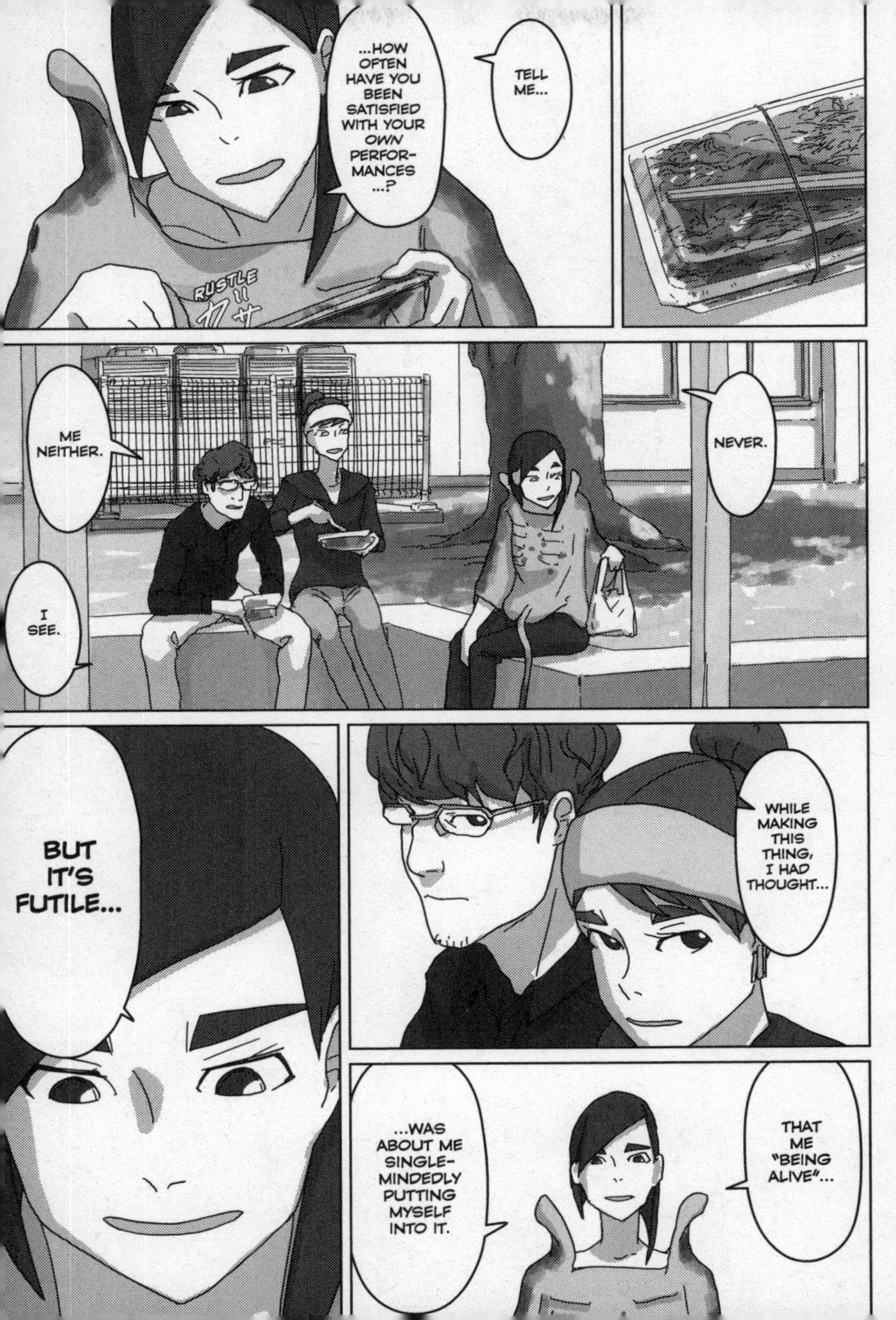
TELL ME...
...HOW OFTEN HAVE YOU BEEN SATISFIED WITH YOUR *OWN* PERFORMANCES...?
RUSTLE
NEVER.
ME NEITHER.
I SEE.
WHILE MAKING THIS THING, I HAD THOUGHT...
THAT ME "BEING ALIVE"...
...WAS ABOUT ME SINGLE-MINDEDLY PUTTING MYSELF INTO IT.
BUT IT'S FUTILE...

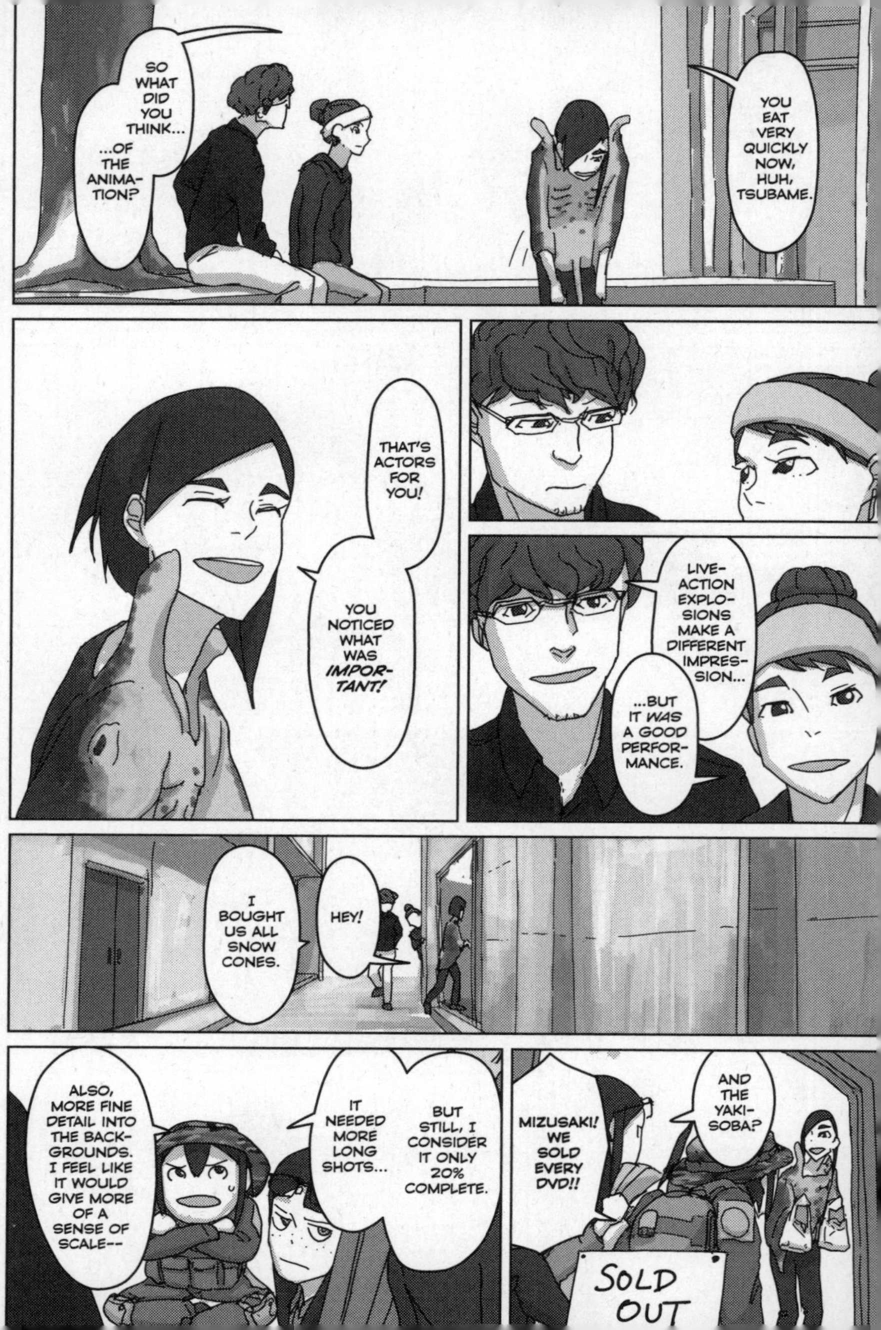
YOU EAT VERY QUICKLY NOW, HUH, TSUBAME.
SO WHAT DID YOU THINK...
...OF THE ANIMATION?
LIVE-ACTION EXPLOSIONS MAKE A DIFFERENT IMPRESSION...
...BUT IT *WAS* A GOOD PERFORMANCE.
THAT'S ACTORS FOR YOU!
YOU NOTICED WHAT WAS *IMPORTANT!*
HEY!
I BOUGHT US ALL SNOW CONES.
AND THE YAKISOBA?
MIZUSAKI! WE SOLD EVERY DVD!!
SOLD OUT
BUT STILL, I CONSIDER IT ONLY 20% COMPLETE.
IT NEEDED MORE LONG SHOTS...
ALSO, MORE FINE DETAIL INTO THE BACKGROUNDS. I FEEL LIKE IT WOULD GIVE MORE OF A SENSE OF SCALE--

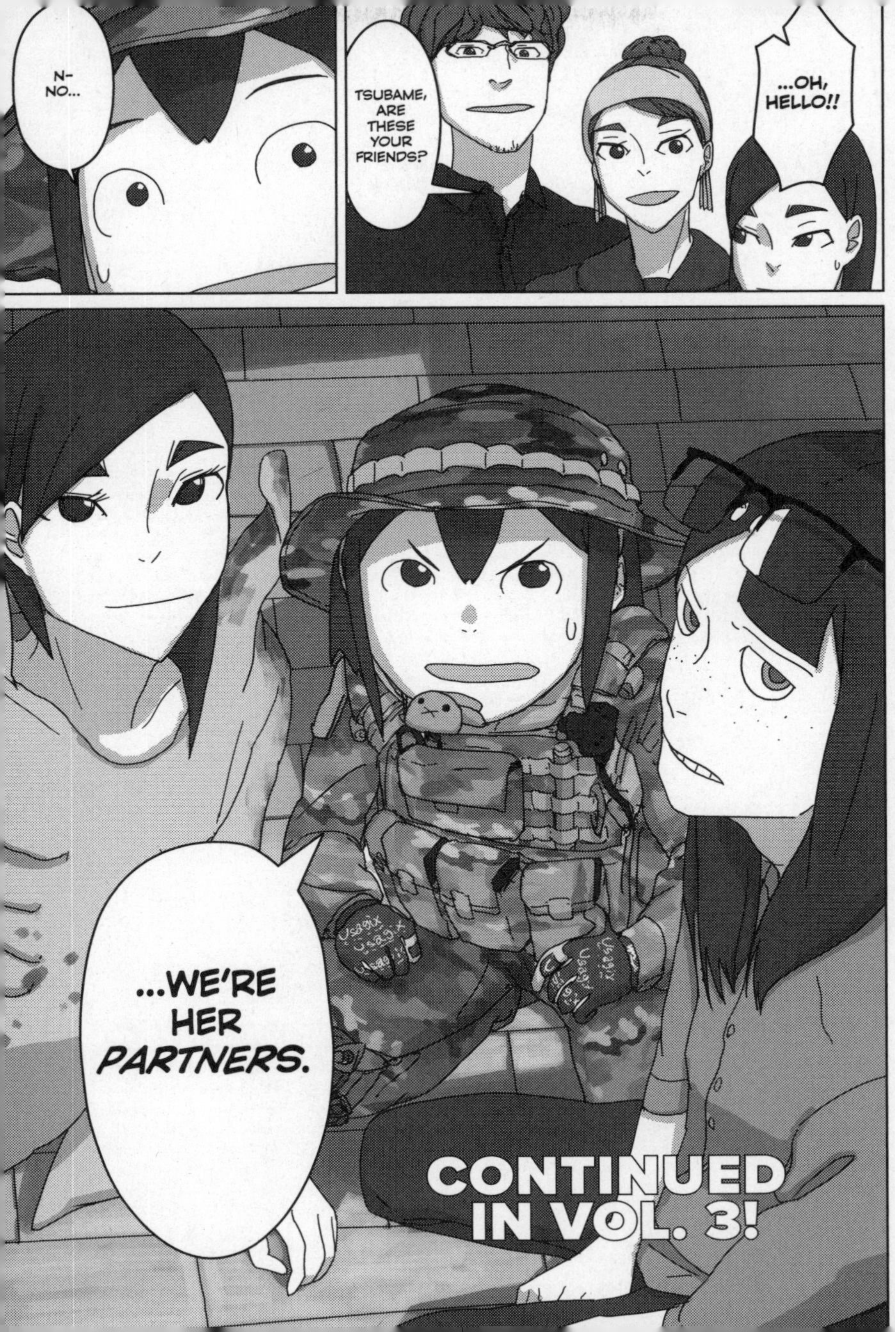
...OH, HELLO!!
TSUBAME, ARE THESE YOUR FRIENDS?
N- NO...
...WE'RE HER *PARTNERS.*
CONTINUED IN VOL. 3!

President and Publisher
MIKE RICHARDSON

Editor
CARL GUSTAV HORN

Designer
SKYLER WEISSENFLUH

Digital Art Technician
CHRIS HORN

English-language version produced by Dark Horse Comics

KEEP YOUR HANDS OFF EIZOUKEN!

EIZOKEN NIWA TE O DASUNA! Vol. 2 by Sumito OOWARA © 2017 Sumito OOWARA. All rights reserved. Original Japanese edition published by SHOGAKUKAN. English translation rights in the United States of America, Canada, the United Kingdom, Ireland, Australia and New Zealand arranged with SHOGAKUKAN through Tuttle-Mori Agency, Inc., Tokyo. This English-language edition © 2021 by Dark Horse Comics LLC. All other material © 2021 by Dark Horse Comics LLC. Dark Horse Manga™ is a trademark of Dark Horse Comics LLC. All rights reserved. No portion of this publication may be reproduced or transmitted, in any form or by any means, without the express written permission of Dark Horse Comics LLC. Names, characters, places, and incidents featured in this publication either are the product of the author's imagination or are used fictitiously. Any resemblance to actual persons (living or dead), events, institutions, or locales, without satiric intent, is coincidental.

Published by
Dark Horse Manga
A division of Dark Horse Comics LLC
10956 SE Main Street
Milwaukie, OR 97222

DarkHorse.com

To find a comics shop in your area, visit comicshoplocator.com.

First edition: June 2021
ISBN 978-1-50671-898-9

1 3 5 7 9 10 8 6 4 2

Printed in the United States of America

Neil Hankerson Executive Vice President • Tom Weddle Chief Financial Officer • Randy Stradley Vice President of Publishing • Nick McWhorter Chief Business Development Officer • Dale LaFountain Chief Information Officer Matt Parkinson Vice President of Marketing • Vanessa Todd-Holmes Vice President of Production and Scheduling Mark Bernardi Vice President of Book Trade and Digital Sales • Ken Lizzi General Counsel • Dave Marshall Editor in Chief • Davey Estrada Editorial Director • Chris Warner Senior Books Editor • Cary Grazzini Director of Specialty Projects • Lia Ribacchi Art Director • Matt Dryer Director of Digital Art and Prepress • Michael Gombos Senior Director of Licensed Publications • Kari Yadro Director of Custom Programs • Kari Torson Director of International Licensing • Sean Brice Director of Trade Sales

NOTES ON VOL. 2 BY THE TRANSLATOR AND EDITOR

Welcome back, and thank you for your patience! It seems like the English edition of vol. 1 of *Keep Your Hands Off Eizouken!* was well received, and that's something we also have to thank you for. Continuing from the notes section in vol. 1, the translator and editor would like to comment on some aspects of vol. 2 as well.

On page 10, panel 7, the phrase "Very interesting, but stupid" was, in the original Japanese, "Tamegoro!" So, this is a nonsense word originating from a 1969-71 variety show in Japan called *Kyosen x Maetake Gebageba Kyuujuppun* ("90 Minutes of Gebageba With Kyosen and Maetake). The show starred TV personalities Kyosen Ohashi and Takehiko Maeda (known as "Maetake"); *gebageba* is said to have been a play on *gebaruto*, the Japanese rendering of the German *gewalt*, "violence," a term associated with radical Japanese youth in the late 1960s; it may also be familiar from the famous Yiddish expression, "Oy gevalt!", as Yiddish is closely related to German. *Kyosen x Maetake Gebageba Kyuujuppun* was itself inspired by the 1968-73 US TV show *Rowan & Martin's Laugh-In*, with which it shared its format of rapid-fire comedy bits, often absurd or political. "Tamegoro!" was a trademark phrase uttered by one of *Kyosen x Maetake*'s habitual guest stars, actor Hajime Hana. The translator suggested that as the Japanese show was originally inspired by *Laugh-In*, to render it in English by using a trademark phrase associated with that show, "Very interesting, but stupid"—which, in *Laugh-In*, comedian Arte Johnson (dressed as a German soldier, so it sort of resonates with *gewalt*) would frequently utter in reaction to a previous sketch. Now, as editor, one of the things that astonishes me is that the creator of *Eizouken*, Sumito Oowara, was born in 1993; it's not like these shows were of his generation, either. However, you'll remember that in vol. 1 he dropped a reference to another TV show that aired in Japan in the early 1970s, as well as to the 1970s anime *Space Battleship Yamato* and *Future Boy Conan*. Asakusa is clearly a "roots" creator. ^_^

The way the dialogue is placed behind the bars on page 24, panel 1 is, as you might guess, another example (like the tilted and skewed dialogue) of Oowara-sensei's sometimes surrealistic treatment of balloon dialogue; it was that way in Japanese, so the letterer reproduced it that way in English, too. Actually, I don't think "surrealistic" is the precise word I'm looking for—I'm sure there's a technical term in comics studies that would be the *mot juste*. What I'm getting at, is that even though both the word balloon dialogue and the art share a common flat plane in a manga panel (i.e., both are 2D) we are usually supposed to pretend that the art is a depiction of something 3D (i.e., through perspective), yet the balloons are somehow 2D, existing without depth in a flat layer over the art. But a playful way to acknowledge this cognitive confidence trick is what Oowara does on occasion, by treating the dialogue as an object existing in the same "space" as the art.

On page 27, panel 1, the original joke involved a play in Japanese between the words *(dai)butai*, "(big) stage" and *(cha) budai*, "dinner table," so it was decided in English to contrast "the big stage" with the more modest world of "dinner theater." The title page of Chapter 10 (on page 39) is a play on the notion that in ancient Asian cosmology, the world is a disc supported on the backs of gigantic elephants, who in turn stand upon the shell of a giant turtle (the question of what the turtle is supposed to be standing on gave rise to the saying "turtles all the way down"—i.e., it stands on the shell of another turtle, which then stands upon the shell of still another turtle, repeated to infinity). Of course, Eizouken's world is instead supported by the robots and the Crurtle.

Thinking about page 89, it's something that other people have also remarked upon, but

part of the spirit of *Eizouken*—and you especially see it with Asakusa—is discovering the interesting, surprising, and even mysterious things in your everyday neighborhood that you may not have noticed before. Down the street from Dark Horse Comics is the local post office; across from that is an undeveloped lot at the bottom of an overgrown slope. Except there's an old, cracked, concrete staircase that descends the slope to the vacant lot; chained off, presumably for safety reasons. Who built it, I wonder? As Asakusa says, there must be a reason—but what happened to that reason, to make it abandoned now? The slope itself has a thicket that in spring can rise two meters high; look closer and you'll see edible berries there in season. Just how long have berries been growing wild there—and back when you had to gather much of your food, did this very same thicket, centuries ago, help to sustain peoples unknown to me (and, as humans have lived in the area not just for hundreds, but for many thousands of years, by peoples unknown to them, too)? And if you're looking for a cute creature to inspire a monster in your anime, raise up your eyes from the slope and look at the Willamette River behind it—and you might just on rare occasion spot a sea lion, even though to get there from the ocean they had to swim 160 kilometers first up the Columbia River, and then make a right turn for another 20 km up the Willamette! The point is, there's actually nothing special or exotic about Dark Horse's neighborhood—until you start looking more closely, that is. I'm sure the same would go for the neighborhoods where readers live and work, and hopefully that's something *Eizouken* can remind us of.

In 93.3, Asakusa is wearing the headband traditionally associated with ghosts in Japan. The way the dialogue is blurred in the foreground of page 102, panel 5, is another example of Oowara's treatment of 2D as 3D. People sometimes speak of "cinematic" effects in manga (and comics), but in this panel, Oowara depicts the art as though it really was being shot with a movie camera, using a kind of shallow focus effect where Mizusaki and Kanamori in the "background" are sharp, but Asakusa in the "foreground" is blurred. Except, as you see, he playfully reminds us again that word balloons aren't any less flat than the art by blurring Asakusa's dialogue balloons as well!

As with vol. 1, the editor recalls Kazuhiko Shimamoto's *Aoi Honoo* and the TV show based upon it, this time by pages 106-111; Shimamoto portrayed Hideaki Anno and Takami Akai having a similar bathhouse fight during the making of the *Daicon III Opening Anime*. As you might guess, page 119 shows various signs and banners the students are painting for the festival; in panel 1 is "Culture" (as in "Culture Festival"); in panel 3 is "Ice" as in "Ice Cream," and in panel 4 is "Maid" as in "Maid Café" (surely Asakusa has earned some maid work-study credits, with all the milk she's had to fetch for Kanamori).

On page 123, panel 4, you see the kind of bad language that a person raised by actors might fall prey to ^_^ Russian theatrical performer and director Konstantin Stanislavski (1863-1938) was a pioneer in developing the system of ideas behind what would later in the 20th century come to be known as "method acting;" Marlon Brando is often considered to have been the first American actor to establish themselves as a movie star through this approach. "M*C*B*TH" is a reference to the taboo among some theater actors against saying the name of the Shakespeare tragedy; instead, you're supposed to use a traditional euphemism, such as referring to it as "The Scottish Play." Which, in my opinion, makes Mizusaki's bold declaration on page 144, panel 1 even funnier.

Mizusaki's phrase, *sakuga otaku*, from panel 1 of page 127 was originally translated as "animation geeks"—"animation" in this context meaning not the medium of animation, but the technical skill, technique, and artistry of animation. In other words, it's the difference between a club that watches anime, and a club that makes anime. I decided however to leave in the original phrase, although I felt a bit guilty, as *sakuga otaku* isn't a translation, and after all, you paid to read one ^_^ But the term "otaku" has been in use in the international fan community for decades now, originally popularized by the early 1990s by Gainax's still-recommended *Otaku no Video* (available on DVD and Blu-ray from AnimEigo)—and heck, in 2021, you can buy *Otaku USA* magazine every month in Walmart. By contrast, *sakuga* is not yet in such common use as much among international anime fans, but it's a term that's been increasingly seen in recent years. Whereas fans often analyze anime in terms of its characters, story, or direction, *sakuga* is associated with looking more specifically at the animation of individual shots and sequences, and analyzing the method and style of the particular artists who animate scenes. Even among otaku, this is sometimes seen as a hardcore and granular way to look at anime, and like any fan look, politeness and consideration will come in handy (*"What do you mean, you've never heard of Yoshinori Kanada?!?"*). But at the same time, many people ready to list off the names of their adored husbandos and beloved waifus could not tell you the names of the anime artists who gave them their expressions, their gestures, their body language—all the distinct motions that portray the ways of the character. As Mizusaki said in vol. 1, "animators are themselves fine actors," and just as we know the names of the actors who portray the live-action characters we like, it can prove worthwhile to learn the names of the key animators who portray the anime characters we like. You may even find, for example, that things you liked from different anime shows turn out to have shared a common key animator who worked on both—again, like an actor playing different roles. I also apologize, by the way, if you've seen *Shirobako* and know all this stuff already :)

Page 132, panel 1 calls to mind how the innovative animator Noriko Takaya (the protagonist of *Aim for the Top! Gunbuster* was named after her) depicted the motion of the rocket nozzles at takeoff in Gainax's first anime, *Royal Space Force*, by using the "harmony" technique she originally developed for Hayao Miyazaki's film *Nausicaä of the Valley of the Wind*. This was the era when animation was still made by photographing a series of painted cels with a film camera, but Takaya came up with the idea of portraying the shifting carapace of the giant Ohmu in *Nausicaä* through constructing a single so-called "harmony" layer, made by cutting up an illustration of the creature into separate pieces, then mounting each piece individually onto an elastic band below. When the band was pulled, it made the pieces move with a unique sense of variable mass, giving a different impression from regular anime motion. I'm sure Asakusa and Mizusaki would appreciate this old-school technique; Kanamori might appreciate it because it sounds inexpensive. This is a real Japanese rocket, by the way, the H2-B, with its distinctive four solid fuel boosters wrapped around the bottom. Japan uses it to send fresh supplies and experiments to the International Space Station; it can lift 6000 kilos of cargo to the ISS (this mission will soon be taken over by a new rocket, the H3).

On page 144, panel 1—should you be inspired to emulate the passion of Mizusaki's performance—know that "eat a turd!" in the original Japanese is *kuso kurae da!* Now that's what I call street theater. Much tastier fare is promised by the lamp in panel 4, which is advertising *oden*, hot pot snacks such as daikon, boiled eggs, tofu, and fish cake, that are simmered in soy broth. It's one of the pleasures of a Japanese *konbini* (convenience store), although it's a traditional food cart item as well.

As you'll have noticed, Shibahama is a very cosmopolitan school (inspired by Sumito Oowara's own experience at a Japanese public elementary school where many of the students had diverse family backgrounds—as Oowara-sensei says, to him being Japanese is not a matter of color, religion, or name), so it's not surprising that the surging enrollment in panel 2 of page 156 speaks five languages. Ironically, because one of them is English, it would reduce the effect to actually translate the other four inside the manga panel itself, because then everyone would seem to be speaking English. So: to the right of the ROBOT ANIME 500 YEN sign is, in Japanese, a*kushiro yo, koraa, matte kure!* ("Hurry up, come on, wait!"); below the sign, in Japanese, is *osu nja nee* ("Don't push!"); in the lower right of the panel is, in Korean, *ya! shibal!* ("Whoa! The fuck?!"—i.e., a similar sentiment to the adjacent English); to the left of the hairy arm is, in Japanese, *korosu zo!* ("I'll kill you!"); below Kanamori is, in Japanese, *kudasai!* ("Please!"); in the lower left of the panel is, in Mandarin, *bie peng wo!!* ("Don't touch me!!"), and on the far left, in Russian, is *skol'ko stoit?* ("How much?"). This whole scene is making me very nostalgic for anime cons somehow ^_^ Well, hopefully we can meet at a manga panel before too long—and I'll definitely hope to meet you in vol. 3 of *Keep Your Hands off Eizouken!*

—CGH

REPENT, SINNERS! THEY'RE BACK!

Miss the anime?
Try the *Panty & Stocking with Garterbelt* manga! Nine ALL-NEW stories of your favorite filthy fallen angels, written and drawn by TAGRO, with a special afterword by *Kill La Kill* director Hiroyuki Imaishi!
978-1-61655-735-5 | $9.99

LOOK AT THIS
(the other way)

Sayaka Kanamori would like to thank you for your purchase of *Keep Your Hands off Eizouken!* and reminds all customers that this manga reads in the traditional Japanese style, right-to-left. To get your money's worth, please flip the book around and begin reading.

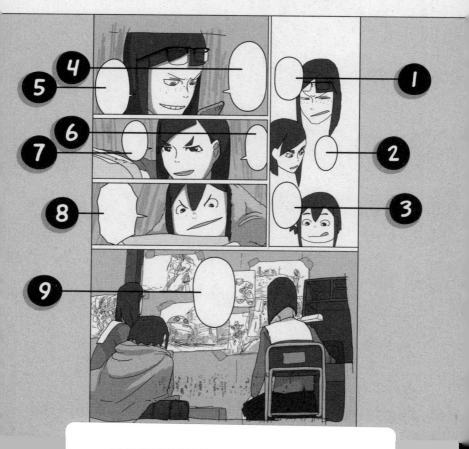